D0488121

TROUBLING THE WATERS

POLITICS AND SOCIETY IN TWENTIETH-CENTURY AMERICA

Series Editors

WILLIAM CHAFE, GARY GERSTLE, LINDA GORDON, AND JULIAN ZELIZER

A list of titles in this series appears at the back of the book.

305.896
G829

Troubling the Waters

Black-Jewish Relations
in the American Century

Cheryl Lynn Greenberg

PRINCETON UNIVERSITY PRESS

PRINCETON AND OXFORD

WITHDRAWN

LIBRARY ST. MARY'S COLLEGE

Copyright © 2006 by Princeton University Press
Published by Princeton University Press, 41 William Street,
Princeton, New Jersey 08540
In the United Kingdom: Princeton University Press, 3 Market Place,
Woodstock, Oxfordshire OX20 1SY

All Rights Reserved

Library of Congress Cataloging-in-Publication Data

Greenberg, Cheryl Lynn.
Troubling the waters : Black-Jewish relations in the American century /
Cheryl Lynn Greenberg.
p. cm. — (Politics and society in twentieth-century America)
Includes bibliographical reference and index.
ISBN-13: 978-0-691-05865-2 (cl : alk. paper)
ISBN-10: 0-691-05865-2 (cl : alk. paper)
1. African Americans—Relations with Jews. I. Title. II. Series.
E184.36.A34G44   2006
305.896′07300904—dc22   2005054622

British Library Cataloging-in-Publication Data is available

This book has been composed in Sabon

Printed on acid-free paper. ∞

pup.princeton.edu

Printed in the United States of America

1   3   5   7   9   10   8   6   4   2

For Michael, my brother
And for Dan, Rianna, and Morgan, rakkaimmilleni

Didn't my Lord deliver Daniel?
And why not every man?

—*Slave spiritual*

I thought trouble was something you were supposed to stay out of. . . . trouble was a negative word. I never knew you were supposed to go and get *in* trouble. But the truth of the matter is, if you take a song like

Wade in the water
Wade in the water, children
Wade in the water
God's gonna trouble the water.

. . . Well, you say what does it mean, telling you to wade in the water and promising you that it's going to be rough? And, of course, you go there because you don't want to be where you are before you go into the water. You have to really be ready to never again see the "you" that you are, standing before this trouble. And really the "you" that you are dies. You have to say goodbye to a part of yourself. You have to really be ready—oh, you don't have to be ready, you just have to push yourself. But trouble is the only way you achieve change in your life.

—*Bernice Johnson Reagon*

CONTENTS

ACKNOWLEDGMENTS

"Five nightingales are needed to make a melody." I apparently informed my friend Marja Nykanen of this in a dream she had (in Finnish, no less). Indeed, it has taken many more than five to make this particular melody, and I am grateful for the opportunity to thank them here.

The first part of any historical process is research, which many think is a lonely and dusty job. Dusty yes, but hardly lonely. In every archive and library I visited, I found willing helpers and kind advisors. I would particularly like to thank Cyma Horowitz and Michele Anish at the American Jewish Committee, Helen Schneider at the Anti-Defamation League, Julie Koven at the American Jewish Historical Society, the helpful archivists behind the desk at the National Archives, and the staffs of the Mary McLeod Bethune House and the FDR Library (except the woman who refused to let me use the more convenient staff bathroom even though I was pregnant). All the archives and libraries I used were public save those of the ADL and American Jewish Congress; I thank Alan Schwartz and Arnold Forster of the ADL and Marc Stern of the AJCongress for granting me permission to use and cite their materials.

At Trinity, Pat Bunker, my favorite research librarian, was remarkable at tracking down esoteric materials. I also thank my two student research assistants, Matt Geertsma and Jamie Katzman, although for them it was so long ago they have probably forgotten who I am. I appreciate the willingness of my interview subjects Arnold Forster and Will Maslow to give so generously of their time to someone they had never heard of. Arnold Forster was particularly kind, sending me his book, helping me research obscure questions, and enduring my every new query with good humor.

I love to teach, but I am particularly grateful for fellowships I received that provided me with that most desperately needed commodity, time off, and the unexpected but equally wonderful opportunity to form new and lasting friendships. At Harvard I spent a year at the Charles Warren Center, administered by the golden-throated Susan Hunt, and another at the W.E.B. Du Bois Institute, sustained by the irrepressible Richard Newman. His recent passing is a tremendous personal as well as professional loss for so many of us. Most recently, I was honored to serve as the Bicentennial Fulbright Chair in American Studies at the University of Helsinki, aided by three guardian angels, Terhi Mölsä, Mikko Saikku, and Markku Henriksson. Beyond the gift of time these programs gave me, I feel fortunate to be able to count all these people, and many of my colleagues and fellow Fellows, as my friends. Helping to make these leaves possible was Trinity's

Faculty Research Leave program, which twice provided me a paid semester off. A grant from the FDR Library supported my research trip to Hyde Park, New York.

Meanwhile, many friends, colleagues, and students kept my topic in mind during the book's long years of gestation, and sent me glorious and provocative snippets of black-Jewish history that I would not otherwise have found. I have enthusiastically incorporated them in the text and thereby taken full credit for them. Actually, the credit belongs to historical sleuths Bill Leuchtenburg, H. V. Nelson, Alex Lichtenstein, Tom Sugrue, Ben Keppel, Todd Vogel, Patrick Miller, Richard Newman, Ethan Felson, Greg Robinson, Marshall Stevenson, Andrew Newby, Bennett Muraskin, John Bracey, Erik Polakoff, Jim Miller, Richard King, Quintard Taylor, Erik Gellman, Bill Walker, Barbara Sicherman, Harry Stein, Tamar Kipper, Andrew Wertheimer, Mary Dudziak, Silvia Schultermandl, Derek Musgrove, Joe Ryan, Nancy Haggard-Gilson, and Bud Schultz.

The deepest pleasures of scholarship are conversations with thoughtful colleagues. Some I met briefly or know only through correspondence, others were or have become dear friends. Sharing their knowledge, thoughts (and disagreements) with me were Hasia Diner; Stephen Whitfield; Rob Weisbrot; Leonard Dinnerstein; Alan Snitow; Michael Galchinsky; David Biale; Carol Anderson; Norman Fainstein; Roger Daniels; Arnold Forster; Herbert Hill, tough fighter to the end; Ray Mohl; Marc Dollinger; Walter Jackson; Michael Rogin; Harvard Sitkoff; Susan Pennybacker; Lynn Dumenil; Mark Bauman; Larry Greene; Nancy Green; Clive Webb; Kenneth Janken; Jim Grossman; several OAH panel discussants and audience members; the Du Bois Institute's Working Group on Black-Jewish Relations, especially Lenny Zakim and Nancy Grant (both undoubtedly continuing their good works in another realm), David Theo Goldberg and Anna Deveare Smith; and my colleagues at the Warren Center and the Du Bois, especially my dear lost friend Betsy Clark, Jussi Hanhimäki, Jim Smethurst, Patricia Sullivan, Sarah Deutsch, and the incomparable Skip Gates and Cornel West. The fog of parenthood and the length of time this book has been in preparation (the two are related) have undoubtedly led me to forget to name several more people, to whom I apologize, and thank as well.

Whatever coherence and clarity this book has can largely be blamed on three faithful editors. Ron Spencer at Trinity read and critiqued early drafts and never even hinted at what a tedious task it was. Gary Gerstle is the series editor in charge of shepherding me through the process; his kindness and encouragement were matched by his thoughtful and insightful comments. My thanks also to the mysterious "Reader B" who offered many helpful suggestions and had such kind things to say.

Finding my publisher was what Yiddish speakers call *beshert*, or meant to be. I asked friends which presses they had most enjoyed working with. Princeton University Press received unanimously rave reviews, so I contacted history editor Brigitta van Rheinberg. Meanwhile, someone had suggested to her that she contact me. Our notes literally crossed in the mail, and I could not be happier with the result. Everyone I have encountered at the press and connected with the twentieth-century series has been lovely to work with, and Brigitta manages to be simultaneously an encouraging coach, a rigorous taskmaster, and a loving friend. I feel so fortunate.

In most acknowledgments, the mushy stuff comes at the end, and this one is no exception. I appreciate more than I can say the love and support I have gotten from my friends, my parents Irwin and Anita Greenberg, and my sister Madelyn, especially during some very difficult moments. Dan's family has embraced me as their own, and I feel lucky to be a part of their lives, even if I have never (yet) won a game of Pit.

This book was conceived just about the same time my older daughter was, which helps explain why it took so long to see the light of day (the book, not my daughter). I dedicate this book to my fabulous and loving girls, Rianna and Morgan, who never let the fact that I was trying to write a book get in the way of their spending time with me. I don't begrudge them a second. They are the light of my life. I dedicate the book also to Dan, my own true love, who has been beside me in every adventure and with me in all adversity. He is my secret miracle.

My brother-in-law, Michael Kelly, a journalist embedded with the Third Infantry in Iraq, was killed early in the war. Michael's was a passionate voice for decency and fairness, and if he and I didn't always agree in our politics, we shared a commitment to the integrity of the truth, the importance of every individual, and the conviction that arguments rooted in both justice and compassion would ultimately persuade everyone else we were right. The loss of his voice diminishes our civic dialogue. But the loss for those who loved him is far deeper and more anguished. His death as much as his life has changed me profoundly, and I dedicate this book to his memory, in the full knowledge that what really counts, more than words on a page, are the people we love.

Introduction

When Rabbi Abraham Joshua Heschel and the Rev. Martin Luther King Jr. marched side by side from Selma to Birmingham in 1965, the image symbolized for many the powerful "black-Jewish" alliance. Certainly, a shared commitment to equality and concerted joint action between blacks and Jews had helped produce substantial civil rights advances. By the late 1960s, however, this potent coalition seemed to unravel as the two groups split over both style and policy. The decline of cooperative action has led many to bemoan the passing of a "golden age" when Jewish Americans and African Americans not only worked together but shared a vision of the just society.

This book examines the reality behind the "golden age" by exploring its roots in the time before the heyday of cooperation and challenging facile explanations for its passing. Focusing on liberal political organizations as sites of interaction, I seek to temper the idealized vision of perfect mutuality by demonstrating that blacks and Jews had different but overlapping goals and interests which converged in a particular historical moment; that both communities recognized that convergence as well as an opportunity for cooperation, and came together in a structurally powerful way to achieve those goals more effectively; that fundamental differences of approach and priority remained, which manifested themselves in low-level tensions and occasional sharp disagreements; and that those divergent visions contributed to the later weakening of the alliance as external political realities changed. A blend of political, institutional, and social history, this is a case study of two important communities navigating among competing and sometimes contradictory demands. At the same time, the history of relations between African Americans and Jewish Americans also lies at the crossroads of many larger narratives about race, religion, ethnicity, class, politics, and identity in twentieth-century America. This book, then, also speaks to these broader subjects.

The topic of black-Jewish relations in the United States is not merely a subject for quiet intellectual study, however. It has a presence in American public culture that "black-Greek relations" or "Jewish-Presbyterian relations" generally do not. Stories about the subject enjoy wide circulation even in the nonblack, non-Jewish press. This fascination is evident too, if we consider other silences. Several years ago, during the fiftieth anniversary of Jackie Robinson's entry into major league baseball, reporters highlighted the role of Branch Rickey, the manager who signed him. That coverage never referred to "black-Methodist relations" although certainly if Rickey had been a Jew, the stories would have placed black-Jewish relations front and center. And as a nice Jewish girl devoted to teaching and researching African American history, the topic of black-Jewish relations is also quite personal. To understand myself, I had to make sense of all of this.

Even within the scholarly community, the study of black-Jewish relations has been a battlefield, filled with exploding polemics and shell-shocked casualties. Even excluding extremist rantings and anti-Semitic and racist diatribes, sharp and fundamental disagreements remain. While virtually all scholars and journalists acknowledge that blacks and Jews worked together for civil rights at mid-century, they differ over the nature and makeup of that relationship, whether or not it constituted an "alliance," the motives of the players, and the cause of their apparent ultimate estrangement.

One position, held by and large by the broader "lay" Jewish community and many Jewish academics, is that blacks and Jews have historically had an identity of interest and experience which brought them together in the twentieth century in what these nostalgists term a "natural alliance," or a "golden age," enhanced by Jews' enduring commitment to social justice. This cooperation was marked by a shared recognition of bigotry and discrimination, and a shared liberal vision of the post-civil-rights-struggle world. The alliance, which produced dramatic victories in court, in state legislatures, in Congress, and in public opinion, collapsed in the late 1960s, felled by militant black nationalist separatists who expelled white people, allied themselves with a third-world anti-Zionism, and spouted anti-Semitic rhetoric. Jewish activist-turned-academic Murray Friedman perhaps best embodies this view, summed up in the title of his book on the subject, *What Went Wrong? The Creation and Collapse of the Black-Jewish Alliance*.[1]

One opposing position, perhaps best represented by African American intellectual Harold Cruse,[2] questions not the fact of extensive Jewish involvement with black civil rights, but rather Jews' motives. It holds that Jews infiltrated and exploited the movement to promote their own interests, masking their true agenda (improvement of Jewish status) by claiming to be fighting for racial equality. Once discovered to be false friends, they were purged from an increasingly authentic nationalist struggle for self-determination.

Others question the extent of the alleged mutuality of interest. Many scholars from David Levering Lewis to Herbert Hill have argued that black-Jewish collaboration was, and is, primarily a story of elites, whose motivations were multiple and complex, neither wholly manipulative nor wholly altruistic.[3] The broader Jewish community, such scholars insist, was more often either uninterested in, or outright opposed to, the advancement of black people, especially when it threatened their hard-won turf. As for black folks, they argue, only African American elites viewed Jews as different from other whites. This interpretation that black-Jewish coalitions occurred solely among elites is disputed not only by historians such as Hasia Diner,[4] but also by many of the religious congregations to whom I speak, and by many activists, past and present, who have devoted themselves to the struggle for racial justice.

Meanwhile scholars who work on other arenas of black-Jewish interaction, like Jeffrey Melnick and Michael Rogin, remind us that Jewish involvement in civil rights was not the central story, but only one of a multitude of stories, all of which shaped what we call black-Jewish relations.[5] To these authors, the recently visible antagonism between the two communities is simply a public manifestation of longstanding differences.

When I was studying for my graduate-school qualifying exams, survivors advised that if I didn't know the answer to a question, I should respond, "Some of both." (In previous years, I understand, the answer was "the working class," an answer I also like.) I take my training seriously, and my current work on black-Jewish relations responds to each of the debates I've described with "some of both." The story is too nuanced to fit neatly into any of the either/or alternatives that have been constructed for it.

This complexity, after all, is part of the message of scholars like Melnick and Adolph Reed Jr.: there is no single black community, no single Jewish community. Both groups have polarizing internal differences based on class, region, gender, politics, generation, occupation, and a host of other less tangible factors. The resulting internecine disputes fractured unity, and community sentiment often collided with organizational priorities. There have also been many venues in which African Americans and Jewish Americans have interacted; there are multiple "black-Jewish relations." There is the relationship between the civil rights organizations in both communities that fought for many of the same goals, sometimes separately and sometimes in collaboration. There is also the relationship between black and Jewish activists within the same organizations, from the Communist Party to the Student Nonviolent Coordinating Committee. There is the relationship between blacks and Jews in the music and movie industries, in labor unions, and in the garment trades. There is the relationship between members of the two communities in their everyday interactions, affected as they necessarily were by the economic and power inequities that race and class differences produced and by recurring allegations of black anti-Semitism and Jewish racism.

These categories of relations overlap, surely, but they are not the same. Nevertheless, both scholars and polemicists often use idiosyncratic individuals to represent their communities: what I call the "Goodman and Schwerner Were Jewish" school. Neither the NAACP's Jack Greenberg nor the Federal Reserve's Alan Greenspan stands for all Jews; neither Dr. Martin Luther King Jr. nor Minister Louis Farrakhan reflects the beliefs of all African Americans. That Goodman and Schwerner were Jewish says nothing about the commitment of the Jewish community writ large to the problems facing African Americans. Nor is it valid to infer the end of political collaboration between black and Jewish organizations from violence in Crown Heights or anti-Semitic pronouncements by black rappers.

And yet there is something here. Individuals, community politics, economic realities, and intergroup relations within these different "black-Jewish relations" interact. In certain important ways, I would suggest that it is, in fact, no coincidence that Jewish-born Jack Greenberg served as the NAACP's chief counsel, Herbert Hill as its head of labor relations, Joel Spingarn as a founder, and Spingarn and Kivie Kaplan as its presidents. (Similarly I am not surprised by the interest of Alan Greenspan in the markets, given Jews' historical dependence on finance to keep them safe—and mobile—in anti-Semitic and periodically violent Europe.) It *is* significant that Goodman and Schwerner were Jewish (it may say something about what motivated these two to action), and that a disproportionate number of white civil rights activists were as well. Jewish agencies engaged with their African American counterparts in a more sustained and fundamental way than did other white groups largely because their constituents and their understanding of Jewish values and Jewish self-interest pushed them in that direction.[6]

This claim, of course, only raises the larger question of why that is so. And that can be answered only by recognizing that all these debates over the nature of black-Jewish relations I have described are rooted in larger questions about identity, race, class, and liberalism. And, like "black-Jewish relations," these terms are themselves contested.

First, what do we mean by Jews? Scholars have long debated the nature of Jewish identity. Are American Jews better understood as members of a religion or of an ethnic group?[7] To put the question in our framework, which model better explains Jews' disproportionate engagement with civil rights?

Many Jewish activists identified their religion as motivating their actions. "[I]t is our moral obligation as Jews not to desist from being a light unto the nation," one anti-segregationist Virginia rabbi preached in 1958.[8] But while faith clearly motivated many, Jewish engagement can not be attributed solely to religious impulses. Jewish activists' perceptions that Judaism demanded universalist equality is itself an interpretation shaped by historical forces. Both Christian and Jewish theologies proclaim that all human beings were created in God's image and describe the pursuit of justice as a moral imperative. Both also contain parochialism and bigotry. Judaism's theology is not ethically distinctive enough, nor have Jews throughout history routinely acted progressively enough, to account for the disproportionately high numbers of American Jews in civil rights efforts. Furthermore, we see this engagement operating even in those born-Jewish activists who did not consider themselves religious.[9]

Rather, the high level of Jewish civil rights engagement seems strongly related to Jewishness as a historical, ethnic identity, shaped by circumstances and forces peculiar to the Jewish people, and the attendant decision of much of twentieth-century American Jewry to stress social activism and cultural pluralism (and in some cases socialism or communism) as the highest expressions of that identity. Even in 2000, close to 90 percent of Jews interviewed reported their ethnic heritage to be "somewhat" or "very" important to them, a figure comparable to that for African Americans but substantially higher than those for other white ethnics questioned. But these Jews' attendance at religious services (more than half reported going only on "special occasions") is well below that of any other group. (Religion? Ethnicity? Some of both.)[10]

The concept of race requires similar examination. While "race" is a notoriously slippery concept to define, virtually no serious scholars any longer consider it a legitimate biological or genetic category. Not only has continuous intermixing of populations made race meaningless in this sense (there is no trait for which differences between putative racial groups are greater than those within the group), but as biologists remind us, every physical trait has a unique pattern of distribution, and any of these could plausibly have been called upon to define the boundaries of "races." A further difficulty in defining race lies in the assumption that individuals have only one race, when many people have ancestors from more than one racial group. The criteria for defining who is black, for example, have changed many times in this country.[11]

Nevertheless, it is no use pretending that race has had no lived historical reality. "Race" has meaning in the United States (and most of the rest of the world) based on the widely divergent historical experiences of populations whose ancestors came from different continents, and who enjoyed differential access to power based on that ancestry. In other words, "race" has historical meaning because people acted as if it had meaning. Much of our history is a tragic reflection of this fact. Scholars Michael Omi and Howard Winant have offered a useful definition of race in this context: "Race is a concept which signifies and symbolizes social conflicts and interests by referring to different types of human bodies." That is, "race" links certain physical phenotypical traits with certain abilities, behaviors, and desires; "racism" exploits those alleged links to justify unequal access to social goods based on those physical differences.[12] The social and historical reality of race does not imply that the meaning of race (or racism) is everywhere and always the same, but rather that in societies where access to power has been allocated on the basis of supposedly biological categories, the consequences have real and enduring legacies.

This ever-shifting terrain of racial negotiation helps explain why blond, blue-eyed Walter White, longtime executive secretary of the National Association for the Advancement of Colored People (NAACP), was considered (and considered himself) black, and how he successfully passed for white among a lynch mob. It is also central to any discussion of Jews, whose racial designation has certainly had its own ambiguities.

Particularly since the emergence of "whiteness studies" many scholars have advanced the thesis (and I am among them) that (European) Jews in the United States have benefited from having white skin, even when they rejected a white identity, and that their whiteness has informed their politics more than they recognize.[13] Others, particularly those who study Jewish history, and many leftist activists, flatly reject this claim, arguing that Jews have never been seen, nor have they ever seen themselves, as fully white. They would echo Birdie, the biracial protagonist of *Caucasia* who, posing as Jesse Goldman, remarks, "I wasn't really passing because Jews weren't really white, more like an off-white."[14]

But in the case of black-Jewish relations, the ambiguity of Jews' whiteness also played out in reverse. If Jews were not entirely white, they nonetheless often "stood in" for whites in black people's minds, and absorbed the full force of their racial resentment, promoted by both propinquity and the ubiquity of anti-Semitism. "[J]ust as a society must have a scapegoat," James Baldwin observed, "so hatred must have a symbol. Georgia has the Negro and Harlem has the Jew."[15] Unpacking race from ethnicity or religion is a challenge, especially when the players themselves were none too clear about the distinction.

Jews served this "stand-in" function because so many worked in black neighborhoods as landlords, shopkeepers, and middlemen. This attests both to Jews' greater willingness than other whites to serve black folk and to the differential black and Jewish economic potential in the United States. Rooted in the specifics of African American and Jewish American histories, rather than in any timeless truths, these facts remind us that black-Jewish engagement is historically contingent and ethnic rather than essential and theological. They also point us once again to a larger historical discussion that intersects this one, that of class. Even studies focused on political relationships between black and Jewish Americans must consider the role class position played: how did each community understand the class differences between them, how do those differences relate to the frequent allegations of racism and anti-Semitism, and how did they shape the reaction of both blacks and Jews to those allegations?

For a great many reasons related to these ambiguities of identity, race, and class, black and Jewish histories intersected in what publisher and nationalist ideologue Henry Luce famously termed the American Century. Blacks and Jews have been neighbors, competitors, allies, and antagonists, linked in the minds of bigots, mid-century progressives, and each other. Their relationship has had a particularly powerful resonance in the American imagination.

There are many ways to approach this complex story; I have chosen to focus on national black and Jewish civil rights agencies. I use such a lens because it seems to me that to determine the nature and extent of a black and Jewish civil rights collaboration, one must concentrate on relations between the political organs of the two communities. Certainly that cannot be the whole story; the American Jewish Committee does not speak for all Jews, nor does the NAACP speak for all African Americans. Nevertheless, these organizations are better bellwethers for identifying the broader community's convictions than are individuals.

In part, this is obvious; organizations represent more people than individuals do. But there is more to it. First, these organizations not only claim to represent their communities but also rely on a broad membership base to support themselves. They cannot safely go far beyond the range of views their constituents hold. The interactions of the American Jewish Congress Women's Division and National Council of Negro Women, say, were driven in large measure by the concerns and commitments of their constituent communities, whose attitudes were in turn generally shaped by their quotidian experiences and by their understanding of their place within the larger society. In other words, the many black communities affected choices made by black civil rights agencies; the many Jewish communities shaped Jewish communal responses to civil rights. At the same time (and this is my second reason for using this institutional approach), within both communities those who disagreed with these organizations also appear in agency records as gadflies; their letters, essays, and speeches allow us to at least consider these alternate perspectives. While no approach can adequately represent such complex communities, and no method can define precisely the extent of community agreement with any particular organizational view, considering both agencies and naysayers begins to fill out the picture of what we call black-Jewish relations. It helps us also to better understand the pressures those agencies faced and the decisions they made. And, finally, my study focuses on national liberal organizations, arguably among the most elite and typically managed from the top down, because by the second half of the century, when the civil rights movement hit its stride, they had become the most active and successful in promoting a politics of coalition between blacks and Jews.

Even when the topic is narrowed in this way, black-Jewish relations remain a chaos of contradictory perspectives. Black and Jewish political organizations and the communities they claimed to represent often held contrasting views. So did community members themselves. Organizations within the same community differed in approach, organizing principles, priorities, and focus. Defensive and ameliorative approaches coexisted in the same agencies. Local personalities, political dynamics, and population shifts created different patterns of interaction in every community. And even the same individual could hold conflicting and contradictory positions. But within the chaos was some consistency: as Kurt Lewin of the American Jewish Congress discovered to his surprise in a 1945 study he conducted, "many aspects of the inner structure are similar in different minority groups. For instance, not only the Jews seem to fight among themselves."[16]

Despite all these ever-changing variables, a fairly consistent pattern of challenge and conciliation between the two communities emerges. Differences in region, demographics, and local particularities affected the timing of this pattern, but not its overall shape or its structural tensions. Across the nation, African Americans and Jewish Americans, increasingly brought together as political allies, found themselves divided as racial, ethnic, religious, and class competitors. How they negotiated those contradictions defines black-Jewish relations.

If we look beyond these trees of black-Jewish relations for a moment, we also discover a forest: twentieth-century American liberalism, the larger political framework in which these organizations operated. Reshaped in the century's early decades, liberalism became for a brief span of time transcendent, only to lose much of its relevance and political credibility by the century's close. I suggest that the history of political relations between African Americans and American Jews reflects, in microcosm, the history of American liberalism. Not only have African Americans and Jewish Americans long been America's quintessential liberals, they have been so because of their deep commitment to what they understand to be its tenets: cultural pluralism, individual equality, and the obligation of the state to protect and extend both. The potency of postwar coalitions both resulted from and reflected the triumph of postwar liberalism; their subsequent decline can be traced to the fate of liberalism in the turbulent 1960s and beyond.

At the same time, the cold war helped insure that liberal, integrationist groups, as opposed to those farther to the left or right, would dominate the political landscape, and that their choices and their limitations would shape the civil rights agenda. The trajectory of black-Jewish relations, then, can tell us much about the fate and potential future of liberalism, at least as it relates to race. And to the extent that liberal values shaped the parameters of black and Jewish political collaboration, the trajectory of liberalism can tell us much about the fate and potential future of black-Jewish relations.

Both an intellectual construct and a political label, liberalism in the United States has had varied and often contradictory meanings over the life of the American republic, and I can do little more than trace its barest outlines here. Its origins lay in Enlightenment Europe, where it stood against despotism and religious control and extolled individual freedom. Yet most nineteenth-century liberals lived quite comfortably with racism, female disenfranchisement, and other positions we would today view as contradictions, understanding them as part of the natural order within which liberalism operated. Furthermore, given its origins in resistance to tyranny, traditional liberalism feared the state as potential usurper of rights and sought to minimize its power and reach. In the United States this distrust of government remained until the (often ignored) urgings of Progressives, the central planning of World War I, the New Deal, and finally World War II revealed to many liberals the power of the state to do good.

By the 1940s American liberalism had taken on a new character, chastened by Nazi racism, emboldened by new ideas of state power, heartened by the triumph of democracy, energized by anticolonialism but fearful of communism—or anything that looked like communism. This postwar liberalism has at its root four basic assumptions. First, rights accrue to individuals, not groups. Second, although achievement depends on the individual, the state has a role to play in guaranteeing equality of opportunity (but not equality of outcome). Third, in a capitalist democracy, liberalism stresses reform rather than revolution, compromise rather than confrontation. Finally, as its goal for civil society, liberalism enthrones pluralism, the championing of difference within a broadly agreed-upon framework of what constitutes socially acceptable behavior. The modern concept of liberalism is more complex than this, of course, but it is along these axes of individualism, moderation, limited state intervention, and pluralism that I suggest that the black-Jewish political relationship operated, and later, came apart.

Chapter 1 sets the stage for our inquiry. Despite their very different histories, by the early twentieth century both blacks and Jews in the United States faced discrimination and bigotry based on involuntary, inherited characteristics. While antiblack racism was always the more pervasive and deep-seated, both Jews and blacks endured exclusion from certain jobs, neighborhoods, schools, and social facilities. Racist and anti-Semitic references were prevalent in the media as well as in polite conversation, and while racism was certainly the more pernicious, both had been known to erupt into violence. All this impelled both communities to establish agencies to protect and promote their rights and opportunities; these ranged from mass to elite, nationalist to integrationist, local to national, conservative to radical.[17]

At the same time that each community was navigating its own way through the American system, the two groups came into increasing contact with each other. A black migration northward intersected with an eastern European Jewish immigration to American urban centers, North and South. This led to greater interaction, for better and for worse, and also to a greater awareness of each other's difficulties. Coupled with their commitment to safeguarding their own culture in the face of coercive assimilation, this awareness prompted a sense of identification between these apparently fellow victims, despite Jewish racism and black anti-Semitism.

The evidence we have suggests this affinity was more than the political calculation of elites. African Americans from all parts of the country reported that they considered the Jews a people apart, and a potential ally. Their newspapers bemoaned Jews' slaughter in European pogroms and praised their mutual aid societies and their commitment to union organizing. Black women in Harlem gathered baby supplies for refugees of Polish pogroms. The *Amsterdam News* explained such "tender feelings": "only these two [groups] knew what it meant to drink the bitter dregs of race prejudice."[18]

Most Jews, in turn, endorsed African American civil rights. Black workers trying to unionize in 1920 looked to the Workmen's Circle and other Jewish groups for help "because the Jews can sympathize and empathize more with them," the *Jewish Daily Forward* believed. "Many of us ourselves were oppressed in Old Russia as the Negroes are in free America. . . . We can understand them better and sound their appeal wide and quickly."[19] Liberal Jews, who interpreted their religion as a universalist call to arms, joined those from even more secularized, frequently socialist, backgrounds, whose stress on internationalism and on class had already led them to a concern for black civil rights.[20]

Where black and Jewish interests and concerns overlapped, individuals began, tentatively, to cooperate. Agencies followed, more slowly. Over time these contacts broadened into a more committed collaboration between civil rights organizations in the two communities. The economic and political struggles of the 1930s (subject of chapter 2) and World War II (chapter 3), served as the pivots for change. Both the burdens and the possibilities of the age affected African and Jewish Americans profoundly. Government now acknowledged its role in extending equality; liberal organizations could thus win meaningful advances. Each success brought increased strength and prestige to the groups that won it and encouraged the formation of even more potent political alliances. Meanwhile, developments in Europe underlined the dangers of fascism and the real—and horrific—implications of racism. And the incarceration of Japanese Americans in internment camps revealed that it could happen here. Thus the benefits of cooperation and the means to cooperate converged in the postwar years, and an active black and Jewish political partnership was born. This partnership was never seamless, and full unity was never achieved—nor sought. Nonetheless, the number of programs and goals shared by advocacy groups in the two communities had multiplied, and the positive initial experiences of cooperation encouraged the development of more expansive coalitions.

After the war, black and Jewish civil rights agencies spearheaded battles to establish fair employment, fair housing, and anti-Klan legislation; challenge restrictive housing covenants; and dismantle restrictions based on "race, religion, or national origin" in employment, private clubs, and colleges. They worked jointly on educational campaigns to challenge bigotry and promote pluralism. This partnership was concretized in the Leadership Conference on Civil Rights (1951), whose two leaders were an African American and a Jew. These organizations also collaborated in challenging restrictions leveled solely against one group or the other. They joined in the fight against segregated schools, transportation, and other public facilities; struggled to lift restrictions on the immigration of refugees; and formed coalitions with other ethnic, racial, religious, and labor groups to promote civil rights and civil liberties. All this is considered in chapter 4.

But this collaboration took place on the institutional level. Many Jews held racist views; few African Americans were immune to anti-Semitism. Although each group encountered discrimination, the experiences of most Jews diverged from those of most African Americans. Anti-Semitism in the United States was almost always less vicious than racism, and it certainly declined more quickly. Jews might be restricted from colleges, country clubs, and exclusive neighborhoods, but Jim Crow was an indignity and an economic barrier Jews never had to endure. Most significantly—and in part this explains the last two observations—almost all Jews were white people. Not only could many Jews therefore "pass," but social and economic opportunities were often based on skin color rather than on ethnicity or religion. Thus Jews' color and their job skills facilitated mobility into entrepreneurial positions, and into white-collar work generally by the 1940s and '50s, while most African Americans remained trapped at the bottom of any occupational field they were permitted to enter at all.

In spatial terms, by the 1930s and '40s upwardly mobile Jews in the North began moving out of neighborhoods—ghettos—that African

Americans had begun moving into, while keeping their jobs, stores, and other real-estate investments there. As their incomes rose, Jewish housewives began hiring African Americans as domestics, and Jewish businesses hired black employees. In the South, Jews opened or expanded businesses in an otherwise barely entrepreneurial region, serving the local black as well as white population. Thus, precisely at the time that Jewish and black civil rights organizations began to reach out to each other, Jews had also become landlords, rental agents, social workers, teachers, employers, and shopkeepers in black communities. For the masses of blacks and Jews, then, relations took place in interchanges where Jews generally held greater power.

By the early 1940s, these entrepreneurial and class tensions threatened to derail the fragile coalition, and black and Jewish agencies therefore set out explicitly to address them. African Americans demanded that Jewish groups intervene with Jewish businesses to stop exploitative and racist practices, while Jews lamented black anti-Semitism and defended the Jewish record regarding black civil rights. In this way community conflicts surfaced within organizational interactions. Meanwhile, elites in both communities led most of their civil rights organizations. The paternalism those elites could exhibit toward those they sought to help only inflamed feelings further.[21] The actions and responses of both sides reveal the deep fissures that class tensions created within an otherwise productive collaboration; these issues are explored alongside organizational developments in the book's first four chapters.[22]

Despite these tensions—or more accurately, helping to fuel them— both blacks and Jews shared the presumption that Jews would treat blacks more fairly than other whites would, because of the shared bond they both perceived in their historical experience of oppression. This enhanced mutual expectations that common cause might be made and was important for the forging of political ties. But while genuinely felt, the claim of black and Jewish kinship through suffering, made by both blacks and Jews, also obscured racial and class differences between the two communities and created unrealistically high expectations on both sides. When these expectations were disappointed, as in cases of economic strife, and when that mutual support weakened in later decades (the subject of chapter 6), the bitterness and recriminations proved particularly difficult to handle. Here, then, was the irony of the "golden age" of black-Jewish collaboration. That period of cooperation did indeed produce remarkable progress in civil rights. But at the same time it was wracked by tensions that constrained collaboration and prefigured the later collapse of mutual purpose.

Before proceeding with that story, however, chapter 5 pauses to explore liberal black and Jewish agencies' responses to anticommunism, crucial for understanding the relationship between American liberalism and black-Jewish relations. The postwar liberalism of pluralism, integration, and civil equality was always tempered by the cold war and the awareness that just beyond our borders, and even within them, lay direct threats to the American Way of Life. This was the era of the (second) Red Scare, colloquially known as McCarthyism after its most famous instigator.

Black and Jewish organizations found themselves enmeshed in a contradiction. On the one hand, most considered communism an ideology antithetical to the values of democracy, individual freedom, and entrepreneurial capitalism they embraced. On the other hand, many avid anticommunists were also racists and anti-Semites, painting civil rights organizations as subversive foreign agents bent on overthrowing American civilization. Both to protect their own programs and to defend the civil liberties necessary to a liberal democracy, black and Jewish organizations simultaneously proclaimed their own anticommunism and challenged the more draconian pieces of anticommunist legislation. They narrowed their conception of equality from *human* rights to *civic* rights while they campaigned on behalf of those rights even when accused of disloyalty. These contradictions shaped black-Jewish relations, liberalism, and the civil rights movement as surely as did economics and racial politics, and their implications are explored at some length before we return in chapter 6 to the chronological narrative.

The class tensions between most blacks and Jews that had long threatened their political collaboration intensified with the mass action of the 1960s. Jews' greater success in achieving middle-class status made them hesitant to employ confrontational tactics and aroused their suspicion of outspoken black leaders. And to some extent, blacks and Jews began to diverge in their goals. If the desire for liberal civil rights legislation promoted a "grand alliance," the struggle to define true equality and determine methods of enforcement spurred its unraveling.

This difference of views became public in the 1978 affirmative action case of *Regents of the University of California v. Bakke*, when black and Jewish agencies, disagreeing over the policy's approaches and mechanisms, took opposing sides. But the decline in cooperation predated *Bakke*, spurred by several failures of liberals in the previous decade to live up to their stated civil rights commitments. Those failures provoked an increasing nationalism and militancy within the black community, which increased fear and resentment among Jews. Both turned inward and away from coalition. Or at least it seemed that way, as the diatribes of black anti-Semites and the neoconservatism of many Jews dominated public discussion of black-Jewish relations by the 1980s.

But it is not that simple, chapter 6 suggests. Once again, the contradictions and ambiguities of the multiple black-Jewish stories make such generalizations impossible. I argue that neither black-Jewish relations nor black and Jewish liberalism are in as much decline as current wisdom has it. The book concludes with a look at the election of 2000, notable for (among other things) two striking black-Jewish moments.

Facile claims about the ending of a black-Jewish political partnership because of black extremism or Jewish self-serving manipulation miss the complexity and drama of the civil rights struggle. If there is a tragedy in the weakening of black-Jewish ties it is ultimately not about blacks or Jews, but rather about the loss of momentum in the struggle for justice. Perhaps a clearer understanding of both the real limits and noblest goals of the black-Jewish relationship can help forge a new, broader partnership. And perhaps understanding the limits of liberalism in a racialized state can help liberalism become truer to its own ideals.

CHAPTER ONE

Settling In

Writers discussing "black-Jewish relations" often treat the subject as time-less. Both those who argue for a "natural alliance" of African Americans and American Jews and those positing a more pernicious relationship imply almost by definition a longstanding and ongoing special connection felt by members of the two communities. Whatever the truth of such claims in the twentieth century, they are certainly false for the past, as a quick historical look will reveal. At the same time, many of the compo-nents that would shape the future relationship between black and Jewish Americans, for good and for ill, can already be seen in their distinct but overlapping histories. We begin, then, with the prehistory of black-Jewish relations in the American Century.

For most of the nation's history, demographics limited contact between the two communities. Jews were always a tiny minority of the American population. On the eve of the American Revolution, only approximately two thousand Jews lived in what would become the United States, primar-ily migrants from Spain and Portugal (Sephardic Jews). By the mid–nine-teenth century their ranks had been swelled by Jews from northern and central, primarily German-speaking, Europe (Ashkenazic Jews). At the start of the Civil War the Jewish population numbered between 150,000 and 200,000, less than one percent of the U.S. population.[1] Furthermore, most resided north of the Mason-Dixon line, while all but 200,000 of the 4.5 million African Americans lived in the South.

Not only were Jews few in number, they played almost no role in public debates over race during the period of slavery; in both the North and the South their activities were indistinguishable from those of other whites around them. Southern Jews feared that challenging racial hierar-chies so central to southern white identity would fan the flames of anti-Semitism. Virtually no Jewish leaders there, either religious or lay, pub-licly opposed slavery. David Einhorn of Baltimore, the one southern rabbi who did (in 1861), had immigrated from Germany as an adult. And as a result of his pronouncements he was forced to flee the city for his own safety, both justifying and reinforcing Jewish fears of speaking out against the South's "peculiar institution." Other Jews supported slavery not merely by their silence but by their actions as well, suggesting most did not see it as a particularly Jewish moral concern. Approximately a quarter of southern Jews held slaves, and since others worked as tradesmen or businessmen, their livelihood was deeply intertwined with the slave system.[2]

Northern Jews showed the same ambivalence toward abolition as did the non-Jewish white majority. While most northerners held racist views about the abilities of African Americans and the undesirability of mingling with them, it was far safer to express antislavery sentiment in the North by the 1850s than in the South, especially if couched in vague and antiexpansionist terms. Nevertheless, few northern Jews did so publicly, and fewer still joined the abolitionist cause, although more spoke out after the war began. No "special relationship" between blacks and Jews, no universalist ethic, led Jews, North or South, to challenge this violation of human rights. In most respects these Jewish immigrants considered themselves as much German as Jewish, and sought to blend into the larger white community with as little fuss as possible beyond establishing Jewish service institutions and defending their right to worship as they chose.

There is little evidence that African Americans, slave or free, felt any particular bond with contemporary Jews either. While slave spirituals such as "I Am Bound for the Land of Canaan" suggest a deeply rooted sense of identity with the children of Israel, this was by and large a connection felt with biblical, not actual, Jews, who, after all, had not given any reason for black people to establish a more current sense of commonality. And African American religion contained as much anti-Semitic sentiment as did the white Protestant churches from which black people had learned it. Those who longed for a present-day Moses also sang "De Jews done killed poor Jesus."

Such attitudes proved quite durable, lasting beyond emancipation and into the next century.[3] While more Jewish than white gentile businesses proved willing to serve black people after the Civil War, so few Jews lived in the South that most African Americans had no direct interactions with them that might counteract these stereotypes. Thus, few Jews or African Americans drew substantive connections between the experiences of their two peoples before the end of the nineteenth century. It was at this point that two massive migration streams intersected: African Americans and eastern European Jews both moving to northern and urban areas. In those earliest years, simultaneous cooperation and conflict characterized black-Jewish interactions, an unstable combination that remained at the heart of their relationship for the entire century to come. Both communities recognized reasons to cooperate, but also found themselves at odds given the asymmetries between them in class, historical experience, and racial identity.

Great Migrations I: "The standing of a man and a citizen"

The combination of what migration scholars have called push and pull factors propelled hundreds of thousands of African Americans from the southern countryside and towns toward what they hoped would be better lives in the North and in the city. Jim Crow, racism, and debt peonage or sharecropping kept black southerners from achieving economic stability in the South, while the ubiquitous threat of racial violence and lynching made living there dangerous for those who desired equal opportunity. For thousands, the North seemed a happier choice. The growing reliance on mechanization and a series of natural catastrophes, including floods in Mississippi and the spread of the boll weevil, pushed African Americans from the land as well.

At the same time, northern and urban opportunities beckoned. Industrialization increased the need for factory laborers, a process accelerated by World War I as war production expanded and one major source of labor recruits, European immigrants, was cut off. Immigration restrictions imposed in 1921 and tightened in 1924 maintained the labor shortage, and northern industrialists energetically wooed southern black workers to meet their labor needs.

But African Americans who came north acted as agents of change, not merely as pawns in a national economic process. This migration was a social movement, shaped by internal information networks and community ties. African Americans who had already come to northern centers wrote home of the comparative social freedom and economic opportunity they enjoyed, prompting thousands of friends and family members to join them. "Tell your husband work is plentiful here and he wont have to loaf if he want to work," wrote a woman newly arrived in Chicago. A new migrant to Philadelphia hadn't "heard a white man call a colored a nigger . . . since I been in the state of Pa. I can ride in the electric street . . . cars any where I get a seat. . . . I am not crazy about being with white folks, but if I have to pay the same fare I have learn to want the same acomidation." The black press also encouraged the migration, none with more enthusiasm than the Chicago-based *Defender*. "Our entrance into factories, workshops and every other industry open to man places us on an entirely different footing," it exulted in 1918. Many migrants recognized the price they paid for such advantages, but remained nonetheless. "I am doing well no trouble what ever except i can not raise my children here like they should be this is one of the worst places in principle you ever look on in your life but it is fine place to make money," one Cleveland resident observed.[4]

Although women as well as men moved north looking for better jobs and greater equality, the link between employment opportunities, full citizenship, and manhood was raised again and again. "I just begin to feel like a man," a Philadelphia migrant wrote. "I have registered—Will vote the next election and there isnt any 'yes sir' and 'no sir.' " "[W]ith the right to vote goes everything: Freedom, manhood, the honor of your wives, the chastity of your daughters, the right to work, and the chance to rise," promised W.E.B. Du Bois at the 1906 meeting of the Niagara Movement (out of which would spring the NAACP). The *Defender* opined, "Every black man for the sake of his wife and daughters especially should leave even at a financial sacrifice every spot in the south where his worth is not appreciated enough to give him the standing of a man and a citizen."[5]

Thousands took such advice. In each decade between 1890 and 1910, almost 170,000 African Americans left the South. Between 1910 and 1920, that figure jumped to 454,000; in the decade following it reached 749,000. This was the Great Migration. Between 1910 and 1920 Chicago's black population increased 148 percent and Detroit's 611 percent. Black New York, Pittsburgh, and Philadelphia expanded similarly. This was also an urban migration; even southern cities saw a rise in their black population while the southern countryside saw pronounced declines. Norfolk, Virginia's black population rose by 73.3 percent between 1910 and 1920; Atlanta experienced a 21 percent rise in the same decade and another 43.4 percent in the decade following. Similar increases in Baltimore, Birmingham, Houston, and Memphis suggest these cities' experiences were not idiosyncratic. Meanwhile, white farmers in parts of Texas, Mississippi, Georgia, Kentucky, and Louisiana complained of severe labor shortages.[6] And in some northern cities, especially New York, the southern migration joined with a substantial inflow of Caribbean immigrants.

Despite the relative security and prosperity the North offered, life for African Americans and West Indians remained insecure and far more constrained than it was for whites, including immigrants. Not only did rural agricultural workers lack needed urban and industrial skills, racism limited their opportunities to obtain them. Even for those with skills (and recent scholarship suggests that a substantial proportion of these migrants and immigrants were not "peasants" but laborers of varying skill levels), most occupations remained closed to them, and job and class mobility proved virtually impossible.[7] Generally they received only the lowest and least-skilled jobs. In cities with large immigrant populations, even some unskilled industrial jobs were closed to them, leaving many with access to employment only in the service sector. Whatever their jobs, black workers often received lower wages than those paid to similarly employed white workers. One New York employment agency posted two jobs: "An elevator boy wanted—Colored; hours 8 A.M. to 8 P.M. daily, $65 per month. Elevator boy wanted—white; hours 8 A.M. to 7 P.M. daily; $90 per month." Adam Clayton Powell Sr., pastor of the Abyssinian Baptist Church there, observed, "Even in New York it costs an elevator man 365 hours of extra labor and $300 a year to be colored."[8] Some few achieved professional degrees despite overwhelming racial and economic barriers but because they could generally practice only within their own, poorer, community, their income was similarly incommensurate with that of whites in the same occupations.

Residential patterns were also largely determined by race. Most landlords would rent to black people only if they could not find white tenants, making only the worst areas available for black settlement: the South Side in Chicago or the Black Bottom and the ironically named Paradise Valley in Detroit. These already substandard neighborhoods worsened with overcrowding and the poverty of their inhabitants, problems compounded by the unconcern of local politicians and service organizations who provided poorer services to black areas. Morbidity and mortality rates were far higher in black districts, and mobility out of these slums far harder to achieve.[9]

Because white landlords and neighboring communities only saw race, black people from all classes and occupations, the native-born and the foreign-born, long-term residents and new southern migrants, were forced to share physical, if rarely social, space. Differences of culture, politics, and behavior often led to misunderstanding and anger. Long-settled residents looked with suspicion on those unused to city life. Many blamed the newcomers for the worsening conditions and an increase in discrimination. Prewar black Chicagoans "were just about civilized and didn't make apes out of themselves like the ones who came here during 1917–18," complained a longtime black resident. "We all suffer for what one fool will do." Mary White Ovington, one of the NAACP's founders, warned of the "surplus women" among the migrants who "play havoc with their neighbors' sons, even with their neighbors' husbands." Most black residents understood the motives behind the newcomers' decision to migrate, but worried about the impact their number and their rural ways would have on race relations. The Detroit Urban League's director explained that migrants did not receive a particularly warm welcome "from the great majority of colored citizens of the better class. . . . They try to decide whether his coming is a benefit or an injury to them."[10]

Perhaps even sharper divisions were drawn between the native and foreign-born. African Americans resented what they saw as arrogance and political radicalism in the foreign-born, who in turn criticized the native-born as lazy and passive. Paule Marshall reported that the West Indian women she grew up among considered themselves "different and some-

how superior . . . more ambitious than black Americans, more hard working"; foreign-born Ray from Claude McKay's *Home to Harlem* felt "superior to ten millions of suppressed Yankee 'coons.' " They found in
African American worship services "over-emotionalism which danger-
ously borders on fanaticism." For their part, African Americans complained about West Indian "rabble rousers" and made derogatory comparisons between these entrepreneurial "monkey chasers" and Jews.
Certainly most understood that both suffered from white racism; that did
not prevent a certain amount of nativist suspicion or sense of competition
and resentment.[11]

Beyond divisions based on geographic origins were those of class. Social
relations rarely transcended class lines; the well-to-do traveled in exclusive circles, seeming disdainful or patronizing to the poor. Black New
York social workers taught immigrant girls "neatness, orderliness and
decorum, while they have learned to ply the busy needle" while the
wealthier resided in architect-designed brownstones in "Sugar Hill" or
"Strivers' Row."[12]

Nevertheless, African American urban residents were not merely victims of racism or intraracial strife. Their neighborhoods, constrained
though they were by poverty and discrimination, and divided though they
were by class, nativity and culture, nonetheless offered opportunities for
community building impossible in more rural settings. This was particularly true in the North. In the absence of legal bars to black voting or the
quasi-legal apparatus of violent intimidation, concentrated black communities became potent voting blocs when not gerrymandered into impo-
tence. Black newspapers and magazines like the *Chicago Defender, New
York Age, Baltimore Afro-American*, and *Pittsburgh Courier* enjoyed
wide circulation, supported by large populations facing similar obstacles
and sharing similar concerns. Black urban churches, so often crucibles
of community and politics, could attract huge congregations that would
become seedbeds for activism. New York's Abyssinian Baptist Church,
for example, served as the springboard for the political career of Adam
Clayton Powell Jr. Sociologist Aldon Morris identified scores of black
urban churches, North and South, that served as catalysts for civil rights.[13]
Artistic life flourished, obvious in the art and literature of the Harlem
Renaissance and the music scenes of Memphis, New Orleans, Kansas
City, and Chicago.

The racial segregation that forced families of all occupation and class
levels to share space also offered rich opportunities for political organizing. The National Association of Colored Women (NACW) was founded
in Washington, D.C., the product of efforts in Boston, New York, Washington, and Chicago. The National Association for the Advancement of
Colored People (NAACP) and National Urban League (NUL) located

their headquarters in New York, as did Marcus Garvey's Universal Negro Improvement Association (UNIA). The National Council of Negro Women (NCNW) was also founded there in 1935. Black Republican and Democratic clubs emerged in virtually every northern city with a substantial black population and Chicago elected the century's first black congressman (and first ever for the North), Oscar DePriest, in 1928, followed by Arthur Mitchell in 1934 and William Dawson in 1942. That same year Harlem provided the voting bloc needed to elect Adam Clayton Powell Jr. From nationalist to integrationist, from accommodationist to radical, from religious to secular, from local to national, from top down to bottom up, hundreds of self-help and defense agencies competed for the allegiance of the black community. The triumvirate of accommodationist Booker T. Washington, iconoclastic immediatist W.E.B. Du Bois, and nationalist Marcus Garvey are the best known, but thousands of others from socialist and trade unionist A. Philip Randolph and antilynching crusader Ida B. Wells to leaders of local political machines, women's clubs, religious bodies, and fraternal organizations, offered their own strategies for challenging prevailing racism.

Certain realities governed most black organizations of the period. Reliance on self-help made good sense in an era of segregation and racism. And because the larger society viewed assimilation as the ticket to success, most emphasized middle-class norms. Still, they grounded their arguments in race pride and the dignity of black people.

Politically, their range of strategies was limited, given the general poverty and political weakness of these emerging black neighborhoods. Whether nationalist or integrationist, few had the resources or the clout to take on broad social problems or influence politicians. Nevertheless, since laws and policies that shaped black lives were controlled by white people, even the smallest and most nationalist of organizations found themselves engaging with political issues from lynching to worker protection. Many black activists were liberals or leftists who sought to use the power of the state to protect individual rights, but they were also pragmatic "race men" and "race women" who recognized that in a nation so rooted in racism, such protection would not come easily or quickly. Virtually all African American organizations seeking to improve the race pursued both self-help and political action, and combined appeals to racial unity with pragmatic efforts to reach out beyond the black community.

Nevertheless, while sharing the goal of improving the lot of African Americans and overcoming political constraints imposed by poverty and discrimination, each of these groups had its own philosophy, strategy, and constituency. The UNIA, founded in 1914 and guided by the principles of its founder Marcus Garvey, advocated not only a return to Africa for all those of African descent, but black unity "to work for the general uplift of the Negro peoples of the world . . . [and] to conserve the rights of their noble race." Black people's potential was limited only by their failure to aspire to greatness. "Up, up you mighty race!" thundered Garvey. "You can accomplish what you will!" The UNIA promoted black pride so effectively that light-skinned Adam Clayton Powell Sr., described Garvey as "the only man that ever made Negroes who are not black ashamed of their color."[14]

Perhaps more unexpected, the UNIA also struggled for equal rights and opportunities for black people within American institutions. As Garvey insisted, "To fight for African redemption does not mean that we must give up our domestic fights for political justice and industrial rights. . . . We can be as loyal American citizens . . . as the . . . Jew, and yet fight for the redemption of Africa." Thus, for example, the UNIA worked to expand black access to New Deal programs while respecting existing rules and restrictions. In this the UNIA proved itself remarkably liberal. Unlike Father Divine, a black religious leader who forbade his many followers to accept government aid, or the Communist Party, which challenged the New Deal's capitalist premises, UNIA representatives helped those needing relief by documenting their eligibility and helping them fill the forms out correctly.[15]

Farther to the left, the African Blood Brotherhood of Cyril Briggs (1919) similarly combined nationalism and pragmatism. "The Negro Race is above all races the most favored," its "Race Catechism" taught. But Briggs also urged his followers, "Make the cause of other oppressed peoples your cause, that they may respond in kind and so make possible effective coordination in one big blow against tyranny."[16]

More middle-class in orientation, and wholly female in membership, the National Association of Colored Women similarly devoted itself to self-help as a matter of race pride. Black women's clubs had organized around the country to aid their communities by supporting women and families; in 1896 leaders came together to form a national body. These primarily middle- and upper-class black women conducted a host of uplift programs under the guiding principle of their motto, "Lifting as we climb." The NACW grew quickly, claiming 45,000 members by 1910 and over 100,000 by 1924. It was emphatically an all-female organization, "not because we wish to deny the rights and privileges to our brothers in imitation of the example they have set for us," its first president, Mary Church Terrell, chided, "but because the work which we hope to accomplish can be done better, we believe, by the mothers, wives, daughters, and sisters of our race than by the fathers, husbands, brothers and sons."[17]

Social work was becoming increasingly professionalized in these years, and clubs abandoned traditional models of "doing good" to employ new, more "scientific" methods on behalf of their poorer, uneducated, and rural black sisters. Certainly their class position came across in both tone and method. Terrell called upon members to "inculcate correct principles, and set good examples" for the "little strays of the alleys," who needed to "come in contact with intelligence and virtue, at least a few times a week."[18] Nevertheless, the NACW also provided crucial support systems for both those women who migrated to new locations and those who remained where they had been raised.

From its inception the NACW also engaged in political action. In its first five years NACW chapters in Louisiana, Tennessee, and Washington, D.C. petitioned to end segregation. The national body dedicated itself not only to "raising to the highest place the home, moral and civil life " but also to ending lynching, disenfranchisement, and segregation, and pursuing temperance, peace, health care, prison reform, and aid to the poor. It challenged the President and Congress on racial violence and employment discrimination and pledged support to the Niagara Movement that would become the NAACP. Its president, Mary Talbert, worked with Congressman L. C. Dyer on a federal antilynching bill.[19]

Despite its emphasis on racial self-help, the NACW recognized the unity of all struggles for equality, and the importance of interracial outreach. As black clubwoman and educator Anna Julia Cooper explained in 1893, "The colored woman feels that . . . not till the universal title of humanity of life, liberty and the pursuit of happiness is conceded to be inalienable to all . . . is . . . woman's cause won—not the white woman's, not the black woman's, not the red woman's, but the cause of every man and of every woman who has writhed silently under a mighty wrong."[20] By 1922 the NACW had established an "Interracial Cooperation" department that met and coordinated strategies with white women's groups, including Jewish ones, on mutual aims.

This era of migratory ferment produced many such national organizations. Fraternal and sororal orders and professional groups ranging from the Alpha Kappa Alpha sorority to the Negro Masons and the National Association of Colored Graduate Nurses endorsed self-help and political action to improve the lot of black people, often working in coalition to achieve their goals. One of the largest was the National Urban League (NUL), a 1911 merger of three social service agencies aiding black migrants. It blended its own form of paternalism with substantive employment, training, and antidiscrimination programs. Led by both African Americans and sympathetic whites, supported by large business and philanthropic donors as well as by members of more modest means, the League sought primarily to integrate black people into the mainstream of American life.

This required two steps: initiating rural migrants into urban and middle-class behaviors, then convincing employers to provide them with opportunities. "Do not loaf. Get a job at once," the Chicago Urban League advised. "Do not carry on loud conversations in . . . public places."[21] The League's philosophy presumed that black people were just like white people and therefore should not face discrimination. But fearing confrontation would alienate employers it generally operated behind the scenes, employing tactics of persuasion rather than protest or legal challenge.

From the start, Jews constituted a disproportionate number of white NUL leaders. They included those from elite German Jewish families such as banking scions Paul Sachs and Ella Sachs Plotz (who also served on Fisk University's board) and Edwin and George Seligman, as well as more radical eastern European Jews like Abraham Lefkowitz, a New York labor organizer. One Jewish donor, Julius Rosenwald, president of Sears, Roebuck, was recruited by Sachs and became the League's second-largest contributor in those early years, after John D. Rockefeller Jr. These were broadly philanthropic and activist Jews who committed themselves to a wide range of causes. Edwin Seligman, for example, also championed conservation, tenement house reform, and the settlement house movement. Individual Jews also played leading roles in establishing local Leagues and in funding their projects. According to Richard Maass, president of both the White Plains Urban League and the local American Jewish Committee, "There were a large number of Jews on the board of the Urban League. Our problem was to get WASPs, white non-Jews on."[22]

Challenging the racial status quo most directly was the NAACP. Founded in 1910 by leading black and white progressives including W.E.B. Du Bois, a harsh critic of both Booker T. Washington's accommodationism and Garvey's militant nationalism, the NAACP from its inception demanded (rather than requested) equality of black opportunity under law, and sought the immediate granting of full citizenship rights to all black people. Because of its focus on legal challenges and on the leadership obligation of educated blacks (the "Talented Tenth" Du Bois called them), much of the NAACP's membership and leadership was drawn from the white elite and the black professional class.

Like the NUL, its members and leadership were integrated from the start. Also like the NUL, a larger proportion of those whites were Jewish than was the white population as a whole. Of the sixty signers of the "Call" to the organizing conference, forty-six were white; at least four were Jewish. Jews made up fully one-seventh of its first general committee and board of directors. These were among the leading Jewish activists of their day, including Lillian Wald, founder of New York's Henry Street Settlement; banker and philanthropist Jacob Schiff; Rabbi Stephen Wise of New York's Free Synagogue; and Rabbi Emil Hirsch of Chicago's Temple Sinai. Joel Spingarn, professor-turned-activist, headed the NAACP's board of directors; his brother Arthur led its legal committee. Du Bois called Joel "one of those vivid, enthusiastic but clear-thinking idealists which from age to age the Jewish race has given the world." Prominent Jews figured also among the organization's earliest advisers and financial supporters, including jurists Louis Marshall, Morris Ernst, and Felix Frankfurter; banker and later New York governor Herbert Lehman; Jacob Schiff; Julius Rosenwald; and Franz Boas, the father of cultural anthropology.[23]

Not surprisingly, the NAACP held a strongly integrationist position, rooted in a liberal faith that enforcing the Constitution would, without resort to fundamental economic reform, go a long way toward remedying the burdens of racial discrimination. As Mark Tushnet, historian of the NAACP, notes, most members of the organization "accepted the premises and results of American democracy on every issue other than race and did not attempt to link the race issue in a systematic way to anything else." Longtime director Walter White's support of the New Deal and similar legislative and legal programs revealed his belief, in the words of New Deal scholar John Kirby, that "liberal reform . . . offered the surest guarantee for the ultimate creation of a racially just society." There were those, Du Bois among them, who argued for a greater emphasis on economic self-determination and insisted that challenges to economic and institutional structures were necessary to fully address the problems facing black people, but the narrower legal approach prevailed.[24]

This was no capitulation to the forces of accommodation, however. From the start the organization employed publicity and protest to educate white Americans about the violations of black people's constitutional rights, and pursued legal remedies for segregation and racial discrimination. Its earliest victories included *Guinn v. United States*, voiding grandfather clauses in state constitutions (1915); *Buchanan v. Warley*, overturning the right of cities to district neighborhoods by race (1917); and *Moore v. Dempsey*, upholding the right to a fair trial and due process (1923).

Nor did its liberalism preclude militancy. Following a season of racial violence against African Americans, including a particularly bloody riot in East St. Louis, the NAACP staged a "silent parade" up New York's Fifth Avenue in 1917 in which ten thousand supporters marched to muffled drums. Anger and frustration were heightened by the rhetoric of the world war, fought to make the world "safe for democracy." The Association held a conference on racial concerns just six weeks after the United States entered the war, attended by more than seven hundred activists. Their sweeping demands for reforms went unheeded. The irony of black soldiers fighting for rights abroad they did not enjoy at home was lost on no one. As Du Bois closed a 1919 *Crisis* editorial on that subject,

We return.
We return from fighting.
We return fighting.[25]

Meanwhile, Marxists and others on the left, concerned with the economic system and with workers, engaged with the emerging trade union movement. Because most AFL unions were racist or at least racially exclusionary, black socialists, communists, and unionists were forced to fight two battles simultaneously. While continuing their struggle to be admitted to white unions (some of the most accessible of which were the Jewish-led unions of the garment trades), they also sought to organize African Americans into their own unions. The most powerful and successful of these was the Brotherhood of Sleeping Car Porters and Maids, founded and led by charismatic and outspoken socialist A. Philip Randolph.[26]

Like the NUL and NAACP, these efforts were also integrationist, but for a different reason; leftists believed that the problems of working men and women centered on their domination by capital. Racial divisions only strengthened the hand of bosses by dividing workers who might otherwise recognize their shared oppression.[27] Thus men and women like Randolph remained committed to interracial organizing and coalition building throughout their political careers. Yet most of them, like Du Bois, never relinquished a sense of the importance of racial solidarity and race pride, the need to establish a power base from which to organize and demand justice. It was the staunchly interracial Randolph who insisted that the proposed 1943 March on Washington to demand equal opportunities in wartime be an all-black affair. The National Negro Congress, organized in 1939 as an umbrella organization for black civil rights organizations, was similarly both leftist and racialist in its outlook.

Also prominent in both self-help and political activity were black urban churches and their denominational bodies. These churches grew enormously with the influx of so many migrants. Established congregations grew, and new ones emerged both within traditional denominations and outside them. Urban African Methodist Episcopal (AME), AME Zion, and Baptist churches saw remarkable increases in their membership, while new groups such as that of Daddy Grace's United House of Prayer for All People, Black Hebrews, and Noble Drew Ali's Moorish Science Temple answered the need for others. These religious bodies ran the gamut from otherworldly to activist, from politically conservative to leftist. Some, like the Nation of Islam, were nationalist, but several, such as Father Divine's Peace Mission, eschewed racial designations along with racism. Virtually all black churches endorsed some form of self-help, establishing benefit societies and homes for the elderly, soup kitchens and community centers, industrial training schools, employment bureaus, and kindergartens.

Again, mutual aid was often supplemented by political action. Many religious leaders embraced the African American tradition of ministerial activism and immersed themselves in political struggles. Bishop Reverdy Ransom of the AME Church and Adam Clayton Powell Jr., who inherited his father's congregation in Harlem, are perhaps the best known, although hardly the only ones so active. From the earliest days of his pastorate before the turn of the century, Ransom publicly advocated full equality for African Americans and later held several political appointments. Powell, who entered adulthood in the Depression, routinely marched parishioners out of the church and into the streets for protests. In 1941 he moved from the church to the City Council and then to Congress where he represented Harlem for twenty-six years. The National Fraternal Council of Negro Churches, organized in 1933 to expand cooperation among black churches, was lobbying Congress ten years later on behalf of civil rights legislation.[28] The Great Migration had invigorated black political organizing. That organizing, in turn, whether focused on self-help or political challenge, provided the crucial scaffolding for the civil rights battles to come.

Great Migrations II: Experts in Estrangement

This early twentieth-century African American migration and consequent political organizing had its counterpart in an eastern and southern European immigration and the development of Jewish defense agencies. Among the millions of immigrants who came to the United States after 1880 were more than two million Jews from eastern Europe.[29] Like their African American counterparts, they were generally poor and often poorly educated, and most moved as family groups, intending to stay. Also like black migrants, their ways clashed with those more-established members of their community already living in American cities. But unlike African Americans, most came from urban centers in Europe, and therefore already possessed both the tangible and the intangible skills needed to succeed in the industrial city. By 1897 almost half of all Jews in Russia lived in cities, and another 30 percent in commercial towns.[30]

And these immigrants enjoyed another benefit African Americans lacked—they had white skin. Rarely perceiving their whiteness, seeing themselves (and often viewed by the mainstream) as different and other, they nonetheless were able to take advantage of the opportunities open to those whose skin color they shared. Americans of European origin quickly learned to identify as whites since most rewards and opportunities in America were apportioned not by ethnic origin or religion, but by race. Jews were no exception to this pattern, although for them the shift was more gradual. Contemporaries debated whether Jews were white, non-white, or constituted a separate race, leading scholars to describe them as "not-yet-white." Still, while Jews were initially unsure of their place in the American binary racial schema, their commitment to a white identity grew over time. Although anti-Semitism was real, race was the deeper cleavage in American society, and American Jews had a vested interest in remaining on the safe side of that divide.[31]

This was especially true in the South. The tiny Jewish communities there perceived themselves as exceedingly vulnerable. Although a bastion of fundamentalist Christianity and political conservatism, the South tended as a whole not to be as anti-Semitic as those beliefs might suggest. Most Jews assumed that was because race so shaped the southern mental landscape that they were included within the protective framework of whiteness. Nevertheless, a strong evangelical and fundamentalist tradition, the periodic resurgence of anti-Semitic organizations, and the widely held canard that all Jews were radicals ensured that anti-Semitism was never far from the surface. Jews had seen blood-curdling evidence of that with the lynching of Atlanta Jewish businessman Leo Frank.

In 1913 Frank was accused of molesting and murdering Mary Phagan, a young white employee in his pencil factory. Convicted largely on the testimony of an African American janitor, the only other suspect, Frank was sentenced to die. The overt anti-Semitism surrounding his trial convinced the governor to commute Frank's sentence to life imprisonment. This decision led an outraged mob to drag Frank from prison in 1915 and lynch him. That a Jew could be the victim of such vigilante violence reminded Jews that while racism might be the stronger sentiment, anti-Semitism did not lag far behind.[32] As Daniel Elazar put it, "In sum, the Jews were accepted but were not really at home." He argued that as a result of such vulnerability, "Southern Jews . . . remained far more conscious of being Jews despite conditions that otherwise would have promoted assimilation."[33] Harry Golden, writer and longtime southern resident, himself a racial liberal, analyzed that vulnerability differently. He pointed to the southern Jew's "relentless struggle to become *one* with the population mass which surrounds him. . . . The studied attempt to avoid all debate . . . [has made it] hard to find six Jews below the Mason-Dixon line who hold sufficiently strong convictions to be 'accused' of anything. . . . Primarily the Jews of the South reflect to a large extent the mores, the hopes, the politics, and even the prejudices of the society around them."[34]

On the other hand, the transformation of Jews, North or South, into white people was never complete. Most Jews never felt fully comfortable with a white identity because they rejected the ideology of racial superiority that usually accompanied an explicit self-definition of whiteness, because they resisted identifying with those who despised and persecuted them in Europe, and because many Jews continued to insist they were a people (even a race) apart. Jews' ambiguous status as white people was thus the basis both for their greater receptivity to racial equality than other whites, and for the limits on that receptivity that whiteness often set.

Not that anti-Semitism wasn't itself a significant cause of discrimination in the United States Anti-Semitic attitudes had long been broadly held; now they calcified. Racially based social tensions created by emancipation and a growing Asian presence in the West, the shifting patterns of immigration from northern and central to eastern and southern Europe, and the political transformation of Darwin's evolutionary theories into seemingly immutable social laws, spurred an increasing social conservatism. The impact on Jews was visible in the widespread appearance of exclusionary advertisements, the circulation of anti-Semitic slurs and canards in books, newspapers, and the new motion picture industry, and the anti-Jewish rhetoric by the resurgent Ku Klux Klan and other white supremacist groups. Some occupations remained virtually closed to Jews, especially those in top-tier fields like banking, as did numerous social and educational opportunities. Restrictive housing covenants bound homeowners of many neighborhoods together in a commitment not to sell to "Negroes or Jews."

Even elite Jews experienced such exclusion despite their financial success (achieved primarily by serving as middlemen and filling economic gaps). In 1877 the prominent banker Joseph Seligman was refused accommodations at the Grand Union Hotel in Saratoga Springs despite frequent previous stays. By the end of that decade Jews were excluded from urban social registers around the country. Private clubs, professional societies, and colleges limited the number of Jews they would accept, or excluded them entirely. In the 1920s, responding to the growing number of eastern European Jews interested in higher education, Harvard, Princeton, Columbia, Yale, Duke, Rutgers, Cornell, Johns Hopkins, Northwestern, Ohio State, and Washington and Lee, as well as the Universities of Cincinnati, Kansas, Minnesota, Virginia, and dozens more set quotas limiting Jewish enrollments.[35] Nor was this anti-Semitism merely socially or economically inconvenient. The Frank lynching demonstrated to Jews across the country that in the eyes of whites, Jews remained outsiders in fundamental and dangerous ways.

Despite these real threats to their security, the combination of their urban skills, help from the already established German Jewish community, and white skin allowed eastern European Jews to rise more quickly than African Americans and to overcome their perceived differences from the mainstream more quickly. Much hardship and struggle lay between the immigrants and success, but the road that led there held fewer obstacles.

Constrained as they were by anti-Semitism and anti-immigrant sentiment, Jewish immigrants, settling largely in northern urban areas, became industrial workers and small entrepreneurs in disproportionately large numbers. They quickly became a presence in trades they had engaged in back in Europe, and those that German Jews had taken up before them, such as garment manufacture and wholesale merchandising, and their peddler carts and small shops became ubiquitous in their own neighborhoods and in those of other poor immigrant and migrant groups.

Although the majority of Jews settled in large cities like New York, Chicago, Philadelphia, Baltimore, Cleveland, and Boston, almost a quarter settled in smaller communities in the North or joined the few Jews already settled in the South and West. In the smaller towns and in the South, they were heavily involved in small-scale shopkeeping and entrepreneurship, and their political and social behavior tended to be more conservative. "[C]ivic vulnerability and the precariousness of economic success . . . acted as reinforcements of the inwardness of the local Jewish community," observed Ewa Morawska in her study of the Jews of Johnstown, Pennsylvania. James Weldon Johnson described a (fictional) southern Jewish train passenger conversing with white southerners and northerners. When discussing "the race question," noted the narrator (himself black but passing for white), "the diplomacy of the Jew was something to be admired; he had the faculty of agreeing with everybody without losing his allegiance to any side." These Jews tried as best they could to remain inconspicuous.[36]

Immigrant Jews came from a variety of religious and political backgrounds. Most arrived as Orthodox, religiously devout Jews, although many—particularly those in the larger cities—fell away surprisingly quickly from the most stringent requirements of their faith, as American life and financial necessity challenged such practices as not working on their Saturday Sabbath. Eastern European Jews transformed American Orthodoxy with their different liturgical traditions and less formalized style of worship. By the turn of the century they controlled its central organizing body, the Union of Orthodox Jewish Congregations.

Other Jews arrived already less religious and some even secularized by eighteenth- and nineteenth-century European liberalizing movements. The "Jewish Enlightenment," or *Haskalah*, paralleled the broader European enlightenment, and stressed Jewish emancipation and citizenship, secularization, and the dismantling of intermediary institutions between Jews and the state. These Jews expressed their ongoing commitment to Judaism through a more acculturated style of observance that elevated those practices least at variance with their new lives, and jettisoned those most in conflict with it. They embraced modernity with its commitment to individual rights and understood the relationship between Jewish freedom and broader emancipatory programs.

The heady revolutions of 1848 and the rise of socialist, communist, and trade unionist ideologies invigorated other Jews. By 1900, for example, close to a third of all Russian university students tried for subversion were Jewish. Despite their universalist message, however, Jewish leftists identified strongly as Jews, especially after the pogroms of the 1880s. And their faith in universalist equality came directly from their political convictions.[37]

These secularizing and universalizing trends were evident within the new Reform movement. Emerging first in Germany, Reform Judaism established itself in the United States with the Union of American Hebrew Congregations (UAHC, 1873) and Central Conference of American Rabbis (1889). These Jews stressed their religion's moral and ethical precepts over its ritual demands, and emphasized the universalist message of their faith. "We accept as binding only its [Judaism's] moral laws and . . . reject all [rituals and laws] . . . as are not adapted to the views and habits of modern civilization," declared the "Pittsburgh Platform," adopted by the Reform rabbinate in 1885. "We deem it our duty to participate in the great task of modern times, to solve on the basis of justice and righteousness the problems presented by the contrasts and evils of the present organization of society." Much of secularized Jewish political life in America embraced the same ideals. As historian Deborah Dash Moore explained, by the 1920s American Jews had developed a "political ideology of American Jewish ethnicity" that embraced liberalism, civil rights, civil liberties, internationalism, and support for those in need.[38]

The American Jewish identification with liberalism (much less socialism) seems implausible on its face. Rarely do either individuals or collectivities embrace ideologies at odds with their self-interest. Jews, increasingly commercially successful and eager to integrate into American civic life, ought to have embraced racial and economic conservatism. Yet, as historian Stephen Whitfield and others have noted, most Jews did no such thing. "By the mid–twentieth century," he observed, "the Jews have become perhaps the most conspicuous players for political stakes that are apparently more high-minded than self-interest," evident, for example, in the number of Jews in black civil rights organizations.[39] Of course, high-mindedness does not contradict self-interest, but redefines it more broadly. Given their historical experience with persecution and the dangerous intolerance of parochial and authoritarian societies, and recognizing the security and freedom civil emancipation had brought them in Europe, Jews understood their self-interest as rooted in liberal values of tolerance and broad access to the opportunities of civil society.

Despite its identification with liberalism, Reform Judaism had vocifer-
ous critics. Anger over Reform's seeming wholesale abandonment of Jewish tradition came to a head when its 1883 rabbinical ordination banquet
served shrimp, a food forbidden by Jewish law. This provoked those Jews
less willing to forsake tradition to establish a more conservative rabbinical
school in 1887, the Jewish Theological Seminary, and ultimately Conservative Judaism itself through the founding in 1913 of the United Synagogue of America. Picking a careful and often not fully consistent path
between Orthodoxy's strict adherence to Mosaic law and Reform's re-
sponsiveness to modern realities, the Conservative movement, like Reform, highlighted Jews' divine mission as "healers of the world." By and
large, Orthodoxy remained dominant in the areas of earliest eastern European settlement, with Conservative and later Reform synagogues increasingly common in smaller towns and areas of subsequent Jewish resettlement. That is, as Jews increasingly prospered in America, they not only
moved out of their poor neighborhoods, they also moved away from ritual observance. Politically this meant over time an increasing number of
Jews in religious groups most likely to desire Jewish integration into mainstream society and to emphasize ethics over ritual.

Not all Jewish immigrants identified with Judaism as a religion. To most
socialist and communist Jews, community rather than religion defined Judaism. Some sought the creation of a Jewish homeland (although other
Zionists were deeply religious), others maintained their ethnic commitment
through the promotion of Yiddish culture or political organizing. All took
their identity as Jews seriously, although they defined that identity in radi-
cally different terms. These identities were also surprisingly fluid; an individual might be both an observant Jew and enjoy Yiddish theater; another
might be a Zionist, read a socialist paper, and buy kosher meat.

Like other immigrant and migrant communities, eastern European Jews
generally settled in poorer neighborhoods and established strong community institutions reflecting a wide range of interests and needs. The *Jewish
Daily Forward*, a Yiddish newspaper with a circulation of 147,000 in
the 1920s, reflected the socialist and unionist convictions of its founder,
Abraham Cahan, while the *Tageblatt* (circulation: 60,000) offered a religious perspective. Lending and mutual aid societies provided cultural and
social spaces in addition to financial support. Yiddish writers, poets, and
playwrights like Jacob Gordin and Sholom Asch enjoyed tremendous
popularity in the dozens of Yiddish theaters. Debating societies flourished
in a community so politically engaged. The relatively small number of
Zionists created their own institutions, and religious Jews established the
structures necessary to perpetuate their traditions, from ritual baths to
rabbinical courts.

This influx of poor, immigrant Jews, speaking a different language and with seemingly backward customs, embarrassed the already established German and Sephardic Jews. A German Jewish social club in New York City pressed for "more polish and less Polish." Some resorted to racial stereotypes in their despairing depictions. An article in the German Jewish press called the new immigrants "wild Asiatics." The *Hebrew Standard* referred to them as "miserable darkened Hebrews." In 1901 Rabbi Abram Isaacs described the German ("Western") Jews' view of the eastern Europeans: "ignorant, superstitious, bigoted, hypocritical, cunning, ungrateful, quarrelsome, unclean, and in may other ways abominable." The feeling was mutual, he reported; to eastern European Jews, "the Western Jew is a cad. His . . . philanthropy [is] ostentatious and insincere; his manners a cheap imitation of the Gentiles upon whom he fawns; . . . his assumption of superiority" evidence of his stupidity.[40]

For German Jews, the immigrants, with their anachronistic Yiddish, irrational Orthodoxy, and un-American socialism, threatened their own precarious acceptance in American society. "If there should grow up in our midst a class of people . . . who . . . adhere to customs and practices abnormal and objectionable to our fellow citizens," the 1891 UAHC convention concluded, "then all of us will suffer. . . . [T[he question is largely one of self-preservation." Convinced "[e]ducation, moral and religious, and instruction in manual labor," would "lift them from the slough of despair," German Jews, like elites in the black community, established programs to both aid and "elevate" their poorer coreligionists. The English-language Jewish press, like the *Chicago Defender*, helpfully published lists of dos and don'ts for immigrants including admonitions to obey the law and avoid radicalism.[41]

Both the need to defend Jews against expressions of anti-Semitism and the desire to assimilate the immigrants led to a great deal of Jewish organizing, first among the German Jews and then among the immigrants themselves. As with African American organizations, Jewish agencies varied substantially, but all combined self-help and political action to achieve their goals.

Reform German Jewish women of middle- and upper-class backgrounds formed the National Council of Jewish Women (NCJW) in 1893 to promote pride in Jewish identity while encouraging greater integration into the wider social world. Despite its relatively narrow class and ethnic membership, non-Jewish women's groups tended to view the NCJW as the voice of all *Jewish* women; male Jewish organizations generally considered it as speaking for of all Jewish *women*.[42]

During the Progressive Era the NCJW, like black women's clubs, focused on benevolence and uplift to aid new immigrants and the poor. One speaker at a 1903 New Orleans NCJW meeting advocated "lifting up and

educating and civilizing the Russian Jews. . . . [Y]our children, though
educated, cultured, refined, wealthy, will find themselves . . . judged by
the Russian Jews."[43] Despite their embrace of the new techniques of professional social work, their charitable efforts, like those of other German
Jews, were often perceived as condescending by resentful recipients of
their aid. Anzia Yezierska's fictional Hanneh Breineh offered a damning
portrait of the "kind rich ladies" who "should only have to feed their own
children on what they give me." When the "Social Betterment Society"
withdrew its meager aid because the family had received an unreported
gift of cake, Hanneh's boarder Sophie burst out, "You dare call yourselves
Jews? You bosses of the poor! . . . You are the greed—the shame of the
Jews!" Others criticized the NCJW by name. One *Forward* article lamented that NCJW members, "Rich Jewish Aristocratic Women from
Uptown" who "shower favors upon and seek remedies for downtown
Jews," offered pennies "with their bediamonded hands more to show
their delicate alabaster fingers with well-manicured nails than really to
save the unfortunates."[44]

But the NCJW provided far more than charity work. Like the NACW
it quickly became politically active, forging coalitions with black women's
groups and developing a broad network to lobby for social issues including education, health, peace, housing, and discrimination. Such expansive
concerns were motivated by two strong convictions: that Judaism demanded equal treatment for all, and that broadly defined protections were
Jews' best hope for their own security. Here, self-interest and universalism
came together. Yet historian Faith Rogow has argued that partly in order
to forestall gentile fears of a Jewish conspiracy, the NCJW never claimed
to speak for Jews, and defended its positions almost exclusively in terms
of "universal humanism."[45] If so, the NCJW was employing a strategy
other Jewish groups would also adopt: a sincere, if partial, claim of universalism that masked self-interest, which would later be challenged by
erstwhile black allies as devious or manipulative.

The NCJW kept motherhood at the center of its efforts, not simply
because it justified the organization's political activities, but because its
members genuinely considered it a motivating principle. And the NCJW
never abandoned its concern for traditionally female issues like religious
education, mothering skills, and housekeeping. Nevertheless, like black
women's clubs, NCJW chapters recognized that their goals—cleaner living spaces, better-quality food, good schools, decent working conditions—relied as much on governmental action as on self-improvement,
and could be achieved only if articulated as social goods. Nor did the
organization limit its vision to issues of immediate concern to families.
The NCJW supported most Progressive Era legislation, opposed the Espionage and Sedition Acts of World War I, and advocated U. S. membership

in the League of Nations. In doing so, it allied itself with other women's groups, including the NACW, the Women's Trade Union League and Women's International League for Peace and Freedom. Sometimes it did so over its own ethnic interest. During a strike against a Jewish business owner, for example, the owner's wife supported the strikers. As Hannah Solomon, one of its founders, pointed out, the NCJW had been radical from its inception. It was a "council," not a "society," and of "women," not "ladies."[46] Interestingly, the NCJW came to many of its programs and positions well before male-dominated Jewish groups did; it was years ahead in advocating open immigration, Progressive Era labor and social reforms, addressing universal rather than just Jewish needs, and in endorsing specific legislation.[47] As the leading Jewish women's organization, the NCJW grew rapidly, by the 1920s embracing the eastern European women it had earlier considered clients. By 1925 it claimed more than fifty thousand members.

The NCJW was not the only significant Jewish women's organization. B'nai B'rith, American Jewry's oldest and largest fraternal organization, created a women's auxiliary in 1897. The first YMHA women's auxiliary formed in 1888. Reform Temple Sisterhoods began in the 1890s and coalesced into the National Federation of Temple Sisterhoods in 1913, a year after the formation of the Zionist women's group Hadassah. There were so many women's groups that in 1923 they created their own umbrella organization, the Conference Group of National Jewish Women's Organizations. These organizations challenged traditional roles for Jewish women by becoming active in the public sphere, whether on behalf of women's issues, religious freedom, or the establishment of a Jewish homeland; indeed, many of these women joined secular, non-Jewish organizations as well.[48]

Male-dominated organizations also proliferated. (While women joined these groups, they rarely challenged men's leadership there until much later.) As elite as the early NCJW and as rooted in the German Jewish community, the American Jewish Committee (AJC) organized in 1906 to challenge discrimination against Jews in the United States and Europe. Responding to horrific Russian pogroms, the Guggenheims, Jacob Schiff, Louis Marshall, Cyrus Adler, and other prominent German Jews created the civil rights agency to press U.S. leaders to protect Jewish lives in Europe. While eastern European Jews were represented on the AJC's executive committee, it was directed by German Jews, many of whom had ambivalent feelings about the newcomers and their foreign attitudes. Some local chapters excluded eastern European Jews informally—and occasionally formally.

Like the NAACP and NUL, the AJC reflected integrationist convictions, reflected in its programs of immigrant acculturation. Jews, like all citizens, had to share equally in all opportunities afforded by American society, but their own heritage, suitably muted and privatized, was something to celebrate, not jettison. But such convictions dictated the AJC's opposition to Zionism. As that movement to provide safe haven for persecuted European and Russian Jews gained momentum, other activists (including eastern Europeans resentful of German Jews' domination of the AJC), organized a separate body to advocate for Jewish rights including the creation of a homeland. In 1916 almost four hundred representatives from diverse Jewish organizations met to form a new American Jewish Congress (AJCongress), which held its first official meeting in 1918. Yet its more militant character, promising "Not relief but redress . . . not charity but justice," ensured that it would never be the broadly representative body its founders had conceived.[49] The AJC saw the AJCongress not only as a challenge to its power but also as irresponsible and potentially dangerous despite the involvement of such prominent and respected Jews as Justice Louis Brandeis. Louis Marshall called Congress supporters "noisy, blatant demagogues," and the AJC agreed to work with it on peace and resettlement issues only if it made no ideological pronouncements.[50]

These differences resembled those between the moderate NUL and the more confrontational NAACP. Dominated by eastern European Jews frustrated by the AJC's German Jewish elitism, and led by Rabbi Stephen Wise, a Progressive Era liberal and a signer of the NAACP's *Call*, the Congress was less wedded to the upper-class status quo. Wise helped lead the Congress to a political stance no less integrationist but more progressive on racial and class issues and more given to public protest. Still, nothing in its initial aims, which employed the language of self-help and group pride, explicitly required it to make common cause with other minority peoples. The AJCongress sought "to secure and safeguard the civil, political, economic and religious rights of Jews" and to coordinate all Jewish efforts toward that end "in a spirit of self-help, self-expression and self-determination."[51]

Explicitly dedicated to a civil rights agenda broadly construed, the Anti-Defamation League (1913) organized in reaction to the Leo Frank case. Operating under the auspices of B'nai B'rith, the ADL's founding platform committed it "to secure justice and fair treatment to all citizens alike," although in practice in its early years the agency focused almost exclusively on fighting anti-Semitism. Like the NAACP, the ADL, AJC, and AJCongress had litigation departments to challenge discrimination through the courts, as well as departments to combat anti-Semitism through fact finding, political pressure, and individual interventions. To unify and amplify their voices, these groups and the political agencies of the fund-raising Jewish Federations called Community Relations Councils created an umbrella organization, the National Community Relations Advisory Council (NCRAC), in 1944.

Immigrants' socialist and communist commitments also found ample organizational expression. Not only did large numbers join non-Jewish leftist groups like the Communist and Socialist Parties, they also organized or brought from Europe leftist and trade-union organizations of Jews, like Workman's Circle (*Arbeiter Ring*), a mutual aid society devoted to working-class and leftist interests; and the General Jewish Workers' Union, or *Bund*. There were enough leftist Jewish newspapers to fight one another as well as more reactionary publications. And in 1934 the Nazi threat prompted Jewish unionists to establish the Jewish Labor Committee to rescue their European counterparts from the growing fascist threat. Later the JLC committed itself to challenging anti-Semitism and racism in, and on behalf of, the union movement.

Pluralism

These black and Jewish organizations, and other religious, racial, ethnic, and political ones like them, operated in an era when American identity was under deep scrutiny. The flood of immigrants and the trajectories of black migrants altered the racial and ethnic character of every region of the country. This unsettled many of the white Americans, primarily Protestants, who had for so long dominated the social and political life of the nation. Because they believed in the supremacy of their western European–based culture and values, they and the academicians who reflected their concerns urged the prompt and unconditional assimilation of immigrants and sought to bar those deemed least likely to do so. Neither subtlety nor compromise was among nativists' strengths. As one New York City teacher put it, newcomers "must be made to realize that in forsaking the land of their birth, they were also forsaking the customs and traditions of that land."[52] A small group of scholars, primarily from the very populations under suspicion, challenged this coercively assimilationist or monocultural model by positing in its place two alternative paradigms for American society: the melting pot and pluralism.

British Jewish playwright Israel Zangwill popularized the former term in his 1908 play of that title. The melodramatic tale of two immigrants—David Quixano, a Russian Jew, and Vera Revendal, a Russian Christian and revolutionary—played to immense acclaim across the country. Quixano falls in love with, and ultimately decides to marry, Vera, although he discovers in the course of the play that her father, a Russian army officer, had ordered the killing of Jews—including David's mother—in the Kishinev pogrom. In the play's triumphal ending, Vera's father confesses his guilt, Vera and David are united, and David's symphony in honor of the melting pot ideal, *The Crucible*, is performed.[53] This vision of the ideal American society, still a monocultural and assimilationist one, nonetheless challenged older assumptions by insisting on the value and uniqueness of an American culture shaped by contributions from many ethnic, national, and religious traditions.

Others argued for a more expansive, less assimilationist conception of culture, which they called pluralism. Formulated primarily by minority scholars like (Jewish) Franz Boaz and Horace Kallen and (African American) Alain Locke, pluralism called for the recognition of the unique cultures of different groups, which were to retain their distinctiveness in private while conforming in public to the monocultural norm. It presumed both the inherent worth and the fundamental similarity of different cultural values, behaviors, and practices. Pluralists, whose views would gain traction only after the Second World War, believed both that cultural diversity contributed to the richness of American life, and that each cultural community shared a commitment to the "American" ideals of tolerance, democracy, and human equality. The clearest illustrations of this ideal might be World War II movies like *Bataan*, whose all-American fighting force included Jake Feinberg, Felix Ramirez, F. X. Matowski, Bill Dane, Jesus Katigbay, Wesley Epps, and Yankee Salazar.[54] Thus pluralists could endorse both accommodation to putatively American behavioral norms and a degree of cultural relativism, seeing no contradiction between them. Furthermore, the insistence on the right of individuals to celebrate their cultural and religious practices implied as well the right to reject such practices if one chose. This focus on the individual fit in well with the longstanding American social ideal of "rugged individualism" and its political commitment (Jim Crow notwithstanding) to the rights of individuals rather than groups. In all this, pluralism dovetailed neatly with an emerging notion of modern political liberalism that would become preeminent by mid-century.

While pluralists sometimes vacillated about whether cultural characteristics were learned or inherited,[55] most considered culture volitional, thus linking pluralism with liberal notions of equality. Author and educator Horace Mann Bond argued in a 1925 *Crisis* essay that differences among the races were the result "not of the germ-plasm but of the social mechanism." Warning about the dangers of "too strong a race-consciousness," he urged "a realization of ourselves as simply and wholly human; not separable by any anatomical, or intellectual, or temperamental barriers from our fellows. . . . Than this there can be no diviner racial goal." Locke concurred. While "Negro life and experience should have and are having increased and increasingly effective expression," he wrote in 1949, "all we should be sanely concerned about is freer participation and fuller collaboration in the varied activities of the cultural life." Complete integration was "as right as it is inevitable."[56]

Pluralism's inclusion of racial groups in the pantheon of worthy cultures, something few melting pot enthusiasts did, was a step forward. But the tendency to subsume racial differences under the heading of ethnic and cultural ones underestimated the power and resilience of racism. Liberal pluralists' insistence that one's cultural values determined one's success and that African Americans (and other nonwhites) were in those crucial ways just like white ethnics, lessened the likelihood that these scholars would recognize the fundamental differences in the barriers facing racial groups and white ethnic communities that resulted from the racialized nature of the American opportunity structure.

In part because liberal pluralism preserved as well as lauded separate identities and validated the legitimacy of black and Jewish cultures, most African American and Jewish defense agencies came to embrace it, at least in theory. In the early years, however, their programs remained firmly assimilationist. The NCJW and NACW struggled to force their poorer sisters, and often their own middle-class constituency, to act more like the white Protestant mainstream; the ADL continued to do so through the middle 1940s.[57] Some took up Locke's refrain, arguing that ending racism and anti-Semitism would—and should—end all need for separate institutions of any sort. Sociologist E. Franklin Frazier claimed, "It is seldom that one finds Negroes who think of themselves as possessing a different culture from whites and that their peculiar culture should be preserved. . . . The Negro minority is striving for assimilation into American life."[58] Many Jewish leaders shared this outlook, scholar Seth Forman has argued. They urged "complete racial integration of Jewish neighborhoods, community centers and agencies without ever considering the need for autonomous Jewish institutions."[59]

Still, these groups' vision was broader and more accepting than a strict assimilationist one, and its very assumptions required the recognition of cultural diversity. In a 1915 speech, Brandeis identified a "new nationalism" that "proclaims that each race or people, like each individual, has the right and duty to develop, and only through such differentiated development will high civilization be attained." In the 1930s and '40s the AJC and ADL designed books for young people, radio programs, and *I Am an American* pamphlets, reminding audiences of the contributions of Jews, African Americans, Mexican Americans, and others to American life.[60]

Similarly, pluralism provided political grounds for challenging discrimination as a failure of democracy. If Jews and African Americans shared the same values and aspirations as other citizens, they deserved full equality. "American citizens of all races who are bound together by their common concern for their common community and by their respect for the rights

of their neighbors have an inescapable responsibility for working to remove social or economic handicaps from minorities within our population," the NUL's "Credo" read. "The problem faced by these minorities
in their everyday living and working situation is not a racial problem, but
a problem of American democracy."[61]

But because pluralism largely ignored the structural nature of racism, it
approached discrimination as a set of individual acts (in the case of segregation, codified by law). This had real consequences for the civil rights struggle, especially as liberalism, pluralism's champion, achieved political dominance after World War II. The concept of civil rights became fixed within
a framework that still set white Protestant norms as the standard and acknowledged the western European tradition as America's unifying cultural
heritage. By the late 1960s these two assumptions, along with the facile
equating of ethnic and racial experiences and the failure to challenge structural or institutional impediments to racial progress, led many black organizations, and some Jewish ones as well, to reject pluralism and turn instead
to nationalism, identity politics, and a multiculturalism that downplayed
the centrality of European traditions in American life.

Of course not all social thinkers of the early twentieth century embraced the notions of nativists, pluralists, assimilationists, or melting pot
advocates. Nationalists—Zionists, Garveyites, and others—objected to
the assimilative nature of all three of the prevailing ideologies, and insisted
more than did any integrationists on the intractability of the barriers to
full participation in American life. Nevertheless, even nationalists insisted
that their advocacy of an extranational homeland did not contradict their
commitment to American values. Du Bois, an NAACP founder, was also
a fervent Pan-Africanist; Brandeis worked tirelessly to both protect Jewish
rights in America and promote Zionism. While the substantial differences
among organizations should not be minimized, their shared faith in a
modernist, liberal vision is striking, as is the fluidity of these ideological
boundaries, at least for individuals.

Making Common Cause

Pluralist rhetoric implicitly recognized that many groups struggled against
marginalization or exclusion. Even in the early years of the twentieth century black and Jewish organizations and leaders called attention to each
other's plight. The NAACP, for example, took note of the Jewish experience in both Europe and America. Certainly its interest came in part from
the presence of Jews among its leadership, a fact also true of the NUL.
One could make a similar argument of self-interest for leftists like Paul
Robeson, who told the *Tageblatt*, "The Jewish sigh and tear are close to

me. I . . . feel that these people are closer to the traditions of my race."[62] But even those groups with completely African American leadership made more reference to Jews than to most other minority groups. Mary Church Terrell referred to European anti-Jewish pogroms in the midst of a tirade against lynching. To praise West Indians' success, Jamaican-born journalist W. A. Domingo likened them to New York's Jews: "they are both ambitious, eager for education, willing to engage in business, argumentative, aggressive and possessed of a great proselytizing zeal for any cause they espouse." Despite Garvey's diffuse anti-Semitism, even he frequently made admiring references to Jews, particularly their Zionist and community-building efforts, two praiseworthy activities from a nationalist standpoint.[63]

Jewish groups proved similarly sensitive to African American problems. The NCJW, horrified by the Frank lynching, used the opportunity to condemn similar atrocities committed against African Americans. Jewish individuals who embraced black causes drew parallels with their own experience. "Whether it is because I belong to a people who have known centuries of persecution, or whether it is because naturally I am inclined to sympathize with the oppressed, I have always felt keenly for the colored race," philanthropist Julius Rosenwald explained. As historian Cyrus Adler observed of Louis Marshall, "It may be, because he was a Jew and was aware of the oppression to which minorities are subject, that he took up the cause of the Negro."[64]

Jewish newspapers covered stories of lynchings and racial violence in the United States. The *Forward* called the 1917 race riot in East St. Louis, "A regular pogrom on people who had the misfortune to be born with black skin." The *Tageblatt* mused, "Who but a Jew knows so well what it means to be dealt out segregation laws and pogroms?" A lynching in 1921 provoked the *Forward* headline, "Hair Stands Up When You Read about the Slaughter of Negroes in Georgia." The Yiddish-language press reprinted the Tuskegee Institute's annual lynching reports. Unlike other white Chicago papers in the teens that blamed racial tensions on newly arrived black migrants, the *Jewish Daily Courier* criticized white racial attitudes and expressed concern that such views could lead to anti-black violence.[65]

Women's groups more than their male-dominated counterparts moved from words of concern to joint action in the early twentieth century. The NACW cosponsored conferences with the NCJW in the 1920s, a decade before male groups collaborated in such structured ways. During World War I at Camp Upton Hostess House on Long Island the YWCA's Colored Work Committee "registered and entertained the wives, mothers and friends of black and Jewish soldiers," since racism and anti-Semitism made neither group welcome at most social gatherings for men in uniform. Following the 1919 race riots in Chicago, the local NCJW chapter joined with black women's clubs there under Ida B. Wells's direction to help pass civil rights protections.[66] While individual Jewish men and women alike involved themselves with black causes, among liberal organizations women's groups were far more likely to concern themselves with the other. Unlike the NCJW, and despite its founding as a result of the Frank case, the ADL said almost nothing at the time about the lynching of black citizens. The NCJW passed a resolution condemning lynching in 1923, more than a decade before other Jewish groups would do so.[67]

But the organizations most committed to joint action in the early twentieth century were those of the left, which were more committed to racial justice than liberals. Both blacks and Jews participated in leftist groups in disproportionate numbers; this is hardly surprising as the Communist and Socialist Parties addressed the problem of racism in America earliest and most forthrightly. Not only was the left also sympathetic to the problem of Jews (one reason that African Americans fighting anti-Semitism so often came from the left), many eastern European Jews came to this country already committed to leftist politics and were thus among the earliest Jewish activists on behalf of black civil rights. Black communist leader James Ford praised "the Jewish people," who, "[t]o their eternal credit . . . have played a prominent role in every progressive movement, in every struggle for Negro rights." He claimed one hundred thousand Jewish CP members in 1939, one-fourth the number claimed by the AJCongress.[68] These men and women committed themselves to the cause of the poor and downtrodden, a political conviction that universalized their concern beyond any narrow or parochial commitment to their own group. They were among the first to go South and organize African American sharecroppers and tenant farmers, to unionize sweatshops in northern cities, to raise questions of racial justice. While distrusted by those in the political mainstream, including most liberal black and Jewish organizations, and hounded by the government as subversives, leftists, among them a significant number of blacks and Jews, played a crucial and underappreciated role in highlighting the problems of American minorities.

Only slightly more acceptable were socialist trade unionists. As World War I's labor demand drew black workers north, the Jewish-organized needle trade unions broke with American union tradition to aggressively recruit them. Not only did the socialist leanings of many Jewish unionists encourage their inclusive thinking, it made good sense for these early industrial unions to organize all potential members. While craftsmen hoped to protect job security by limiting access to training, these newer unions represented workers in unskilled and semiskilled jobs who could be easily replaced. Exclusion of any group would virtually guarantee strikebreaking. Still, the benefits of interracialism were rarely obvious to other industrial unions, which retained racial bars even when they ran counter to members' class interest.[69] The interracial solidarity of these Jewish unions that seems in hindsight like the obvious product of self-interest was in fact radical for the time.

Scholars Take Aim

Certainly the presence of so many blacks and Jews who did aid the other community needs some explanation. Why would A. Philip Randolph lend his name to fighting anti-Semitism and Julius Rosenwald donate millions for black education? Why were there so many Jews, proportionally speaking, in the leadership ranks of the NAACP and NUL? "The Jewish people have been fairer and squarer in their treatment of Negroes than any other people in the world," Randolph's *Messenger* wrote. The *Defender* agreed: "They have stood by us and have aided us when all other groups in America have turned their back on us."[70] Hasia Diner has suggested that fighting racism allowed Jews to prove themselves good Americans, upholders of the liberal American creed of equal opportunity. It allowed them also to fight anti-Semitism by indirection; if racism could be eradicated, discrimination of Jews would also cease. Jewish journalists who lamented black lynchings feared more mob attacks on Jews; to prevent additional Leo Franks, all such violence must end. Similarly, African Americans lamented Jewish troubles as a way to call attention to their own, similar plight.

David Levering Lewis attributes a more elitist political agenda to black and Jewish leaders. He argues both were similarly assimilationist and concerned about maintaining control in their communities during this period of high migration and social dislocation and suggests they made common cause to educate the black and Jewish urban newcomers in the ways of the American middle class. As he puts it, "theirs was a politically determined kinship, a defensive alliance cemented more from the outside than from the inside. . . . Both groups saw each other more as means to ends, rather than syncretic and equal partners in a struggle for citizenship without disabilities."[71] These political elites concluded that fighting for civil rights and advocating assimilation would further their goal of security, and working together would be mutually beneficial. Lewis, however, argues that while this collaborative strategy helped Jews achieve most of their goals, the record for African Americans was more mixed. A black-Jewish partnership helped win civil rights, but Jews' remarkable economic and political success invited invidious comparisons with African Americans. Many Americans view Jews as a "model minority," one that overcame hardship and discrimination to flourish in America. Because this paradigm does not take into account the whiteness and middle-class back-grounds of those Jews, it has led some conservatives to blame the failure of black people to rise as quickly on blacks' own shortcomings rather than on the society that constrained them. When judging the partnership, Lewis sees the perniciousness of the paradigm overshadowing the gains in rights. While I find a more widespread concern in both communities for the other than Lewis posits, and some might differ with his weighting of the collaboration's successes and problems, it is clear that assimilation-ist elites led the way in the early years of black-Jewish interaction, and that they sought to advance their own interests in doing so.

Numerous scholars have noted that those African Americans and Jews who became most committed to the other group's causes looked to that other community for political and financial support. Morris Hillquit, a Jewish socialist, requested and received the enthusiastic public support of Randolph and Chandler Owen when he ran, unsuccessfully, for mayor of New York in 1917. Walter White of the NAACP frequently used his well-placed Jewish advisors to raise money in their community, for instance sending a willing Spingarn a "draft of the letter to go to wealthy Jews" for editing. Yet such support sometimes came at a price. Rosenwald Fund contributions to the NUL were on occasion contingent on the League's making specified changes. When it resisted, those contributions lessened and finally stopped altogether.[72] While such pressure was rare, it was nonetheless real.

Still, the sense of connection ran deeper than financial interest. Some leaders recognized the potential power to be gained from making com-mon cause; others came to interracial concerns through ideology. For Jews, both their religious and their ethnic cultures emphasized a universal-ist ethic rooted in historical experience and in biblical injunction. "Noth-ing will so test the sincerity of our religion, our moral obligation . . . as will the exigencies of this [racial oppression], which is among the greatest of all our problems," Rosenwald declared. Milton Himmelfarb termed it "that Jewish particularism which likes to regard itself as universalism." Louis Marshall, who came to the NAACP first because its cases had posi-tive implications for Jews, stayed on as legal advisor because of this broader understanding.[73]

For African Americans the need for models for survival and allies in the struggle also prompted the turn toward Jews, a similarly oppressed population. Booker T. Washington observed that "[t]he Negro has much to learn from the Jew," and James Weldon Johnson argued that Jews were "the example which we should set before us for solving our own prob-lem."[74] For leftists, internationalism and a commitment to the unity of the working class led inevitably to struggles on behalf of all victims of oppression. If racism and anti-Semitism were tools the ruling class used to maintain its hegemony, challenging both would hasten the overthrow of capitalism. Finally, specific situations of shared discrimination, like the exclusion of black and Jewish servicemen from hospitality houses, lent themselves to short-term joint action. Thus history, pragmatism, idealism, and self-interest combined to lead many individuals to deep personal commitments on behalf of the other.

As Separate as the Fingers

Whatever the tangle of explanation, however, the fact remains that beyond this cadre of elites, and beyond the rhetorical and journalistic interest the larger black or Jewish population occasionally took in the experiences of the other, most blacks and Jews simply did not see themselves as making common cause in the first decades of the twentieth century, despite seeking many of the same goals. There are many reasons for this. First, the problems each community faced were dramatic and urgent. The barriers to full citizenship and equal opportunities were immense; most blacks and Jews were too preoccupied with their own difficulties to pay much attention to the plight of others. For the same reason, most black and Jewish civil rights organizations, which might have helped their constituencies make the link, did not collaborate even on mutually beneficial programs. Small, limited in resources, and politically weak, these agencies had their hands full addressing the immediate and pressing problems confronting their own group.[75] Second, the strategies most commonly employed in this era—moral suasion, court challenges, behind-the-scenes maneuvering—did not lend themselves to the large-scale and public collaborations more common in the later civil rights era.

Third, for groups seeking acceptance into mainstream society, linking one's fortunes with other out-groups seemed counterproductive. Leo Frank is a case in point. Scholars have often identified the railroading and lynching of Frank as one of the earliest spurs to Jewish recognition that their condition was bound up with that of African Americans. This was, in part, true. Jews now understood that racism threatened them as well as black people. This is why the ADL's founding mission included a commitment to universal civil rights. On the other hand, for many Jews the Frank case demonstrated the crucial importance of Jewish assimilation. The sooner Jews could blend in with other white people, the sooner such dangerous anti-Semitism would abate. Particularly among southern Jews, the Frank lynching may have actually lessened the likelihood that they would openly embrace the cause of black equality.

Fourth, the sense of a shared historical experience with oppression was a limited and often theoretical one, diluted by anti-Semitism on one side and racism on the other. Although every poll documented lower levels of anti-Semitism in the black community than in the white, and lower levels of racism among Jews than among white gentiles, bigotry still helped keep the two groups politically separate.[76]

Finally, most relationships between African Americans and Jews were in fact deeply unequal. Black and Jewish experience might appear parallel, but in fact most interactions between them were hierarchical. Increasing numbers of black migrants moved into Jewish neighborhoods and met Jews as employers, teachers, landlords, and shopkeepers, not as fellow oppressed people. Jewish impresarios and producers hired black musicians, actors, and entertainers; Jewish union leaders represented black workers.

Ironically, these black-Jewish tensions were the product of both the chasm between ordinary blacks and Jews, and the greater affinity each felt toward the other. The process had its own inexorable logic. Newly arrived Jews filled available entrepreneurial niches as shopkeepers, property managers, teachers, social workers, and the like. They competed by serving poor neighborhoods where they exhibited greater flexibility, catered to their clients' special needs, charged lower prices, and sold on credit. Because Jews did not fully accept their whiteness, this openness extended to race. They embraced American racism far less quickly and completely, and therefore proved less resistant to having black neighbors and clients than did most other working-class whites. This, combined with the fact that Jews were generally less prone to resort to violence to express grievances, meant Jewish districts all over the country turned slowly into black ones beginning in the teens. And as Jews earned their way out of these neighborhoods, they often kept their businesses and jobs there.[77]

For most Jews, their economic involvement in black communities affirmed their lack of bigotry. They saw themselves as fellow strugglers: hard working, near-poor, oppressed by discrimination, managing only by pressing family members into service. Jewish businesses provided affordable—if not high quality—goods and services, and if their prices were higher than downtown stores, so was the risk in a poor area.

For African Americans, Jewish store owners' general unwillingness to hire area residents, their high prices and poor-quality merchandise, the economic success that enabled them to move into more desirable neighborhoods, and their willingness in the South to practice segregation, all marked them as no better than other white people. Jewish housewives who hired black domestic workers treated them in the same exploitative ways as Christian white women did. Jewish employers were little more likely to hire or promote black workers than were their gentile counterparts and while Jewish-run unions more often accepted black members, their leadership remained firmly Jewish.

But black anger was often more intense toward Jews than toward other whites. Because so high a proportion of whites working in black areas were Jewish, black resentment of the pettiness of social workers, paternalism of teachers, and greed of landlords and their agents landed on Jews. And the anti-Semitism that African American Christians had imbibed, along with the disappointment many felt that Jews, fellow victims, failed to treat them more sympathetically than other whites, fueled anti-Jewish anger based in large measure on class privilege.[78]

The Jewish view of themselves as economically and socially vulnerable and the African American view of Jews as economic insiders both had validity. But because both sides consistently painted their differences as arising from racial or religious friction these tensions were never adequately addressed, and they remained to limit political collaboration even once it had begun. This is not to deny the role racism and anti-Semitism played in black-Jewish tensions. Rather, the refusal to consider class explicitly as an aggravating factor limited the reach of any resolution. Questions of race, religion, and class were intertwined, in ways usually invisible to those involved. Jews' race allowed them more mobility up the class ladder, but because they were blind to structural racism and often held racist attitudes of their own, many blamed blacks' failure to rise on black people themselves. Meanwhile Jews' economic power over blacks, however limited when compared to that of white Christians, fanned preexisting anti-Semitism in the black community. Jews, legitimately angry at such bigotry, could not see the class-based resentments that lay beneath.

Black-Jewish relations in the early twentieth century, then, were marked by contradictions that would continue through the century. On the one hand, both endured discrimination; to challenge it, both organized in a variety of agencies, most of which shared a basic commitment to liberal American values. And some individual elites recognized the similarities of black and Jewish experience and acted upon them. On the other hand, the two communities' racial, religious, and (ultimately) class differences prevented them from using shared grievances as the basis for political collaboration.

Such small steps toward cooperation would increase in both frequency and scope as the threat of Nazism in the 1930s brought racial issues to the fore. At the same time, the same constraints of bigotry, organizational weakness, and most agencies' quiet and nonpublic political style would delay the development of a potent black-Jewish coalition for at least another decade.

CHAPTER TWO

Of Our Economic Strivings

The economic catastrophe of the Great Depression encouraged greater political activity by both blacks and Jews at the same time as it heightened economic tensions between them. The contradictions between shared political concerns and competing economic interests that had emerged in the early years of the century intensified; relations worsened between the two communities at the same time that their civil rights agencies came into increased contact. The black-Jewish coalition was off to a rocky start.

For African Americans, the era brought gains as well as losses. Economically devastated, black communities organized politically and, as a result, benefited from government programs for the first time since Reconstruction. This experience offered valuable lessons about the usefulness of political mobilization and the efficacy of outspokenness. The spur to organizing and the increased political power of black civil rights agencies (including those with substantial numbers of white and Jewish members) encouraged more far-reaching political coalitions. However, the new outspokenness also brought more vocal criticism of Jewish business practices in African American neighborhoods.

Black political successes could not have occurred without, and indeed helped shape, a sea change in the federal government's attitude toward minority rights and its willingness to remedy inequality and ameliorate hardship. This transformation of the political landscape would in the next three decades alter public discourse on democracy, equality, and identity; reshape relations among activist organizations, and between them and governmental structures; and help catapult liberal organizations to the center of American political life.

Meanwhile, the rise of Nazism led Jewish organizations not only to seek allies wherever they could (the subject of the following chapter) but also to confront more openly those they considered anti-Semites, including African Americans. Yet while both blacks and Jews exhibited a greater willingness to protest, the traditional and often defensive style of their political organizations remained largely unchanged until the end of the 1930s, thereby minimizing the opportunity to address these tensions directly and forge a more mutually productive relationship. The increased hardship and the greater willingness of the two communities to challenge each other, without an increased recognition of common goals, meant a worsening of both formal and informal relations between them. Not until both groups recognized their common problems and saw in the emerging redefinition of liberalism the potential for greater success by working together would these problems be tackled. Until then, black-Jewish relations were developing on two intersecting but separate tracks simultaneously: the expansion of antidiscrimination efforts and increasing economic conflict.

"Can't stand these hard times long"

The crash of 1929 and ensuing Great Depression harmed every stratum of American society, but none were so hard hit as those already marginalized. By the end of the 1920s African Americans had made limited but real strides in employment, real estate, and business, particularly in the North. The Depression wiped out most of those gains. Black employment levels plummeted. At the height of the Depression almost 25 percent of the American labor force was unemployed; the black figure was double that. Those with jobs saw their incomes drop just as they were being called upon to support more unemployed family members. While African Americans made some gains in the Depression era, thanks to the New Deal programs that helped feed, clothe, educate, train, and employ the needy and that opened some new opportunities for black people, these could not compensate for such massive losses. Furthermore, federal antidiscrimination provisions were only as effective as local officials chose to make them; gross inequities marred the distribution of aid in this most desperate of times.[1]

Jews suffered during the Depression as well, and if the devastation did not extend as broadly within that community, it was certainly catastrophic for those who found themselves unemployed. Twelve percent of Jews lost their jobs, and Jewish agencies were overwhelmed with applications for aid. In 1931 alone they reported a jump of almost 50 percent in the number they helped. Many more Jews were underemployed, including doctors and lawyers forced to take other jobs or work without any assurance their clients or patients would be able to pay them. Yet the community's economic recovery occurred more quickly than that of most other groups.[2] Their concentration in areas hit hard by the economic collapse—the garment trade, the arts, and the luxury goods trade—was offset by their large representation in civil-service positions, the numbers of which increased with the New Deal, and their substantial presence in teaching, the professions, and the wholesale and discount business, none of which suffered as dramatic a collapse as other sectors. And younger Jews' relatively high levels of education allowed them to move into new and more stable jobs more rapidly than those with less schooling.

Nevertheless, the Depression had a strong psychic impact. Recent Jewish immigrants felt particularly vulnerable to any shift in fortune. And historically, hard times produced an increase in anti-Semitic behaviors; many feared violence or pogroms might come to their new land as it had to their old. The rise of Nazism and the growth of domestic anti-Semitic organizations reinforced such concerns.

"A force for constructive action"

Both the black and the Jewish communities thus saw pressing reasons to redouble their efforts to end discrimination and to respond publicly and politically to the emergency at hand. For African Americans, the Depression was an economic crisis of such magnitude that it required urgent action from every community organization. Although black churches; civic, social, and professional organizations; service agencies; and political groups provided aid to the desperate, they were quickly overwhelmed by the need. But the presence in the North of urban voting blocs offered new opportunities for political organizing, while the relative willingness of the Roosevelt administration to consider racial equity brought renewed energy to the task. Both helped shift African American tactics from self-help toward political action.[3]

In the Jewish community, synagogues, Federations, and service agencies offered aid from job placement to feeding and clothing the needy. In fact, the Depression spurred the development of Federations as consolidated support agencies. But by 1934 almost 90 percent of all needy Jewish families had been transferred to public relief and, like black groups, Federations turned to activism along with other forms of support. While Jewish agencies less often aired discrimination complaints publicly, they did track religious discrimination, filing complaints on behalf of those unfairly denied public or private jobs, housing, employment, or assistance.[4]

Such efforts succeeded; the number of black federal employees grew from fifty thousand in 1933 to almost two hundred thousand by the end of World War II. Thousands of Jewish teachers, lawyers, and others found positions in New Deal and other government agencies. Hundreds of thousands of needy black farmers, tenants, unemployed people, and laborers received government aid or job training, as of course did similarly poor Jews.

The New Deal also benefited black and Jewish elites, who became increasingly active in national politics. While anti-Semitic accusations of a "Jew Deal" were exaggerated (approximately 4 percent of New Deal appointees were Jews), numerous prominent Jews became well-placed government advisors, including Bernard Baruch, Louis Brandeis, Felix

Frankfurter, Benjamin Cohen, and Samuel Rosenman. Henry Morgenthau Jr. became Secretary of the Treasury. Other Jews worked in the Departments of Labor, Interior, and Agriculture, and the Securities and Exchange Commission. Nonetheless, as Henry Feingold has pointed out, most "were not Jewish men of influence, but rather men of influence who happened to be Jewish."[5]

More of a departure from the past was the number of highly placed African Americans. Explicitly concerned with racism, Roosevelt's "Black Cabinet" won appointments and discrimination prohibitions in dozens of agencies. Mary McLeod Bethune directed the Division of Negro Affairs of the National Youth Administration; Robert Weaver served as racial adviser in the Department of the Interior and went on to the Federal Housing Authority and War Manpower Commission. Lawrence Oxley headed the Division of Negro Labor in the Labor Department, and *Pittsburgh Courier* editor Robert Vann served as special assistant to the attorney general. In 1937 William Hastie became the first African American federal judge. Despite the stubborn resilience of racism in New Deal programs, these developments had tremendous psychological impact. As the NAACP's Roy Wilkins observed, the presence of African Americans at the highest levels made black people feel "that they were getting through to the man."[6]

African Americans' greater access to the political and economic system further invigorated black organizing. Existing groups like the NUL and NACW expanded, and were joined by new organizations like the Young Negroes' Cooperative League (1932), Negro Labor Committee (1933), and Southern Negro Youth Congress (1937). The National Council of Negro Women (NCNW), organized by Mary McLeod Bethune in 1935 to "harness the great power of nearly a million women into a force for constructive action," hoped to coordinate the efforts of the numerous black women's organizations and ensure black women's representation in national affairs. The National Negro Congress (1936) sought to become a coordinating agency for groups fighting for racial equality. Its objectives included "decent living wages," voting rights, opposition to union discrimination, equal access to relief, and "complete equality for Negro women."[7] As we will see, its leftist origins and leadership limited the number of mainstream organizations that would formally affiliate and brought its early demise. But during its brief life the NNC joined activists from the Communist and Socialist Parties together with church, fraternal, and cultural groups to challenge lynching, discrimination, and police brutality.

While African American and Jewish institutions continued to reflect the wide range of political attitudes in their communities, it was primarily liberal and leftist organizations that took the lead as the New Deal pressed liberalism toward greater social democracy and garnered widespread support. Roosevelt's programs had kept people from starving; liberals and progressives now argued that the state had both the power and the obligation to act in order to protect the well-being of its citizenry. In this way the New Deal completed the transformation of liberalism's attitude toward the state. No longer suspicious of government as a potential tyrant, liberals now embraced government as a potential savior.

The New Deal protected union organizing and extended relief to unemployed families, demonstrating that the state now concerned itself not simply with citizens per se, but with their specific condition as workers, parents, or farmers. It was a plausible step to grant protection on the basis of race or religion as well, as several programs explicitly did. Whether that protection should take the form of improved separate facilities or integrated ones remained a contested issue, and indeed, whatever the nature of the protections, local officials implementing those programs often ignored them altogether. Nevertheless, liberalism as an ideology had definitively moved from its earlier antistatist position to one of state activism on behalf of individual rights and guarantees, including those of racial and religious equality.

New Deal liberalism protected capitalism as well, albeit with new restrictions. Much as leftists desired it, there was little indication the majority of Americans were interested in any other economic system. While Jews remained overrepresented in the Communist and Socialist Parties, most rejected their anticapitalist ideologies despite the strong stands both took against anti-Semitism, and the CP's active Jewish recruitment. Native-born Jews had not had their politics forged in Russia, and by the end of the decade the Nazi-Soviet pact and Stalin's antagonism toward Jews had driven many Jewish communists from the Party into the progressive wing of the Democratic Party.[8]

Similarly, despite communist-led drives to organize black workers, fight evictions, and improve black living standards, black CP membership did not grow substantially. Rather, most progressive black activists worked alongside communists, and only so long as their goals were compatible. In the New Deal era the numbers attracted by Party efforts were virtually matched by those abandoning membership. As historian Carol Anderson has demonstrated, to many African Americans, communists seemed less concerned with race than with the promotion of communism. And for both the black and Jewish communities, growing anticommunist sentiment in the United States made alliance with the CP both unattractive and dangerous. As Roy Wilkins once remarked, "God knows it was hard enough being black; we certainly didn't need to be red too."[9]

Communists were active in virtually every struggle for black equality, North and South, from unionizing drives to antilynching campaigns. In many instances, they spearheaded the efforts. Yet even the CP seemed to move toward liberalism in this era, with what it called the Popular Front: engagement with liberal organizations to further mutual goals of equality, worker rights, and increased government aid. While this increased the left's political impact, it also tempered its radicalism. Even leftists seemed, for a brief time, liberals.

At the same time, the Democratic Party was coming to meet them. The New Deal drove northern Democrats left just as leftist Jews and African Americans (as well as disgruntled black Republicans who could see in that party no further sign of Lincoln) were looking for more congenial homes. By embracing the notion of an activist government committed to remedying inequity the Democratic Party appeared well on its way to becoming the embodiment of leftist as well as liberal ideals.[10] Meanwhile socialist trade unions could now find an organizational base in the new and activist Congress of Industrial Organizations. Many CIO unions accepted African American members (often despite strong local resistance), a triumph for liberal activism. In the Depression, then, the middle moved left, and the black and Jewish left moved a bit toward the middle. The New Deal reshaped liberalism and by doing so, provided Jews and African Americans with a lasting—albeit sometimes troubled—political home.

Nationalist organizations fared poorly in an era filled with newsreels of Fascists and Nazis marching in Europe. The triumph of liberalism over the alternatives of the left and right, and its general embrace by the public, strengthened the legitimacy and therefore the power of organizations like the ADL and AJCongress, the NAACP and NUL, over more nationalist, parochial, or radical ones. By the end of the war, the most visible civil rights programs came from liberal black and Jewish agencies.

Increasingly, those agencies' attention turned to European Nazism and to the resurgence of domestic organizations of like mind, such as the Klan, which made all gains vulnerable. In the Jewish communal field, a new Jewish Labor Committee (1934) took as its mandate the rescue of European Jewish trade unionists. Leftist in its politics and sensitive to the dangers of group hatred, the JLC embraced antiracism from the start.[11] Meanwhile established Jewish organizations focused increasingly on rising anti-Semitism, from domestic hate groups to anti-Jewish violence in Germany. This heightened American Jewish sensitivity to all forms of bigotry. But it also fed Jews' sense of danger.

Racial violence also spurred black organizing. The best known case is that of the "Scottsboro boys," nine young black men arrested in Scottsboro, Alabama, in 1932 for allegedly raping two white women on a freight train. Sentenced to death, their defense was taken up by the NAACP, the leftist International Labor Defense (ILD), and dozens of "defense" committees before their sentences were finally overturned. (This case had a Jewish aspect as well. The lead lawyer, Samuel Leibowitz, was Jewish. During his summation the prosecutor asked the jury if they would allow Alabama justice to be "bought and sold with Jew money from New York.")[12]

Then there were lynchings and race riots. In 1935 Harlem exploded, releasing years of tension and resentment in a rampage that did over two million dollars' worth of damage. Inevitably, Jewish stores were attacked; many merchants and several historians saw an explicitly anti-Semitic component to the rioting.[13] Elsewhere, white people attacked black workers trying to join unions, tenants wishing to move into previously white buildings or neighborhoods, or those unlucky enough to get in an angry white man's way. In 1934 Claude Neal, charged with the rape and murder of a white woman, was brutally tortured and killed by a white mob in Florida. Radio and newspapers publicized the events in advance and thousands came from eleven southern states to watch. Souvenir photos were sold.

The newly energized black civil rights organizations publicized details of each atrocity and mounted vocal protests against the violence, which in turn brought them greater recognition and membership. Following a 1932 Georgia lynching, the NAACP organized a letter-writing campaign by prominent citizens, called public meetings, and encouraged "specially aggressive students at Howard University to hold protest meeting on campus."[14] Black organizations had been active in antilynching efforts for decades, but this level of public protest was, in the words of historian W. Fitzhugh Brundage, "without precedent." In this decade, he found, "Activists did not adopt new tactics so much as apply familiar methods with a newfound urgency."[15] Lynching publicity also reinforced the power of the media to shape public opinion, and encouraged the black press to expand coverage of abuse and discrimination. A positive contribution to the advancement of civil rights, that practice also heightened tensions with Jews, whose business practices received more frequent, and public, scrutiny.

"Most diplomatically"

While liberal black agencies stepped up their efforts, however, their political styles remained basically unchanged through the middle 1930s; this limited the potential for coalition building. Newer groups might throw up picket lines in protest, and the black press might be aggressive in its coverage of discrimination, but the established organizations generally maintained their preference for quieter methods. The NAACP, focused on civic inequality, was increasingly challenged by younger, more radical thinkers who, with Du Bois's encouragement, pressed the Association to more directly confront economic inequality. The NAACP did become more public in confronting racism and it organized workers' councils, as did the NUL, to press for black workers' interests (as well as to counter communist attempts to do so). These councils accomplished little, however, and the NAACP did no more. Nor in most cases was it willing to endorse mass action, leading a frustrated (and increasingly separatist) Du Bois to resign in 1934 from the organization he had helped found. Anti-lynching campaigns were the exception, as anti-Nazi protests would be for Jews; such gruesome physical violence warranted an entirely different level of response. But for the most part, pragmatism dictated less militant tactics. Furthermore, for a variety of reasons, until 1936 the NAACP's legal work consisted primarily of reactions to specific cases. Only toward the end of the decade did the Association begin its broader, proactive challenge to discriminatory institutions and patterns. Without that broader vision it was unlikely the NAACP would actively seek coalitions in a common pursuit of justice.[16]

The NUL's style remained similarly circumspect. As it had from its inception, it believed behind-the-scenes action most likely to succeed. Its Depression-era efforts to improve employment opportunities consisted primarily of intervening forcefully but privately with each New Deal agency and local employer rather than, for example, pursuing antidiscriminatory legislation.

Jewish organizations proved even more reluctant to shed their cautious operating style and less likely to endorse public action. Arnold Forster, a passionate advocate within the ADL of such action (he would become the League's chief counsel in 1946), insisted in his autobiography, "The simple fact is that even entering the forties, Jewish defense agencies as we know them today were all but nonexistent."[17] As an architect of ADL's later, more aggressive style, Forster understandably exaggerated these organizations' earlier quiescence. Still, his observations have merit. In 1937 the AJCongress decided, in response to information about the growing strength of the Klan, to appoint a committee "to see whether the problem is one with which the Congress should deal," although it had been aware of the Klan's anti-Semitic (not to mention antiblack) activities since the Congress's founding.[18] If the Klan was not clearly a problem "with which the Congress should deal" it is hard to imagine what would qualify.

Like their black counterparts, Jewish organizations in this period conducted studies, and if the situation warranted intervention, proceeded with tact. If Jews challenged anti-Semitism openly, S. Andhil Fineberg of the AJC explained, they might make the situation worse. "So . . . getting all Jews to stop publicizing anti-Semites by writing about them in the newspapers, answering them and the like, was an important part of our program." Such discretion succeeded in winning new Jewish job placements and easing some religious employment restrictions. "Outstanding employers of labor have been conferred with to the end that they might see the unfairness of such discrimination," boasted the AJCongress in 1933.[19]

Nevertheless, the choice to avoid public confrontation also had its costs. When quiet methods failed, those agencies had to accept a still-anti-Semitic status quo. In 1941 the ADL met with the International Business Machines Company regarding allegations that it would not hire Jews. The IBM representative explained the problem lay not with the company but rather with its clients, who "usually stipulate the type [of machine operator] desired." Reassured, one ADL executive committee member proposed sending IBM "a letter of thanks." Fearing any further communication would "magnify the importance of the issue" and seeking to deflect the "not very tactful" approach to the same company made by the AJCongress, the League decided to take no further action on the matter.[20]

The NAACP's and ADL's reaction to published materials they deemed offensive nicely illustrates this decision to approach bigotry with restraint. Each routinely screened books and movies, then contacted publishers and producers whose works contained anti-Semitic or racist references. As Richard Gutstadt, the ADL's national director, wrote to the League's New York director Leonard Finder, the technique is "familiar to you." He suggested that Finder privately communicate "that we have had a great many complaints indicating that the book is creating ill will which they certainly do not desire."[21] The tone was as important as the message. Regarding an "undesirable" film called *The Wandering Jew*, Finder advised his staff, "Please be sure to have those boys who write to the management . . . do so very tactfully. While we wish to have the management made aware that we realize and resent the undesirable message of [such] pictures . . . we do not wish to make enemies."

Gutstadt linked this approach with the League's broader agenda. Not only would tact make media leaders more likely to acquiesce to ADL requests, it also laid the groundwork for developing strategic alliances that could be a powerful tool in furthering the organization's goals. "The approach might be that . . . we would appreciate it if upon occasion of any doubt as to the advisability of contracting a picture, he [the theater manager] would call your office. . . . The gradual building up of cooperating agents . . . may prove to be an essential and important part of the work which you do. . . . It is not, after all, the specific instance of the Wandering Jew that concerns us primarily. It is . . . the opportunity to evidence a tactful and friendly approach and thereby to establish a friendly relationship."[22]

The fears of backlash that motivated the choice of strategy had a basis in fact. During discussions of how most effectively to challenge the anti-Semitic content of the film *Golgotha*, Finder warned that anti-Semitic radio priest Father Coughlin had become involved in the controversy, and if the film's promoters found "any evidence of Jewish 'interference' . . . they probably would be willing to make capital of it. . . . Therefore any representations made by us should be done most diplomatically."[23]

Thus fear of backlash, faith in polite and rational discourse, and the desire to build strategically important relationships led Jewish groups to conclude, like the NUL, that quietly building good will would serve their interests better than a more confrontational approach. And indeed, these methods succeeded again and again. "We regret exceedingly to learn from your letter . . . that the illustration . . . is giving offense to anyone," wrote John Williams, chairman of the publishing company whose book, *Fun With Figures*, contained a puzzle titled "Out-Jewing the Jew (It Can't Be Done)." "We are sorry indeed that offense has now been taken; we can assure you none was intended." However implausible his claim, the point had registered. And ADL did use its new connections to distribute or promote positive materials. Nevertheless, as with challenges to employment discrimination, their polite approaches had their limitations. When *Time* referred to "TVA's hard-boiled Jewish director," Finder argued, "Since we cannot change their attitude, there is no sense in protesting needlessly and arousing animosity."[24]

The NAACP also scrutinized books and movies for racist content, and employed similar tactics in response. In 1932 Walter White explained to the publisher of *Ten Little Nigger Boys*, "The term 'Nigger' is one which is most objectionable to colored people and to a great many white people. We feel certain that so reputable a publishing firm . . . would not wish to give offense to any considerable group of American citizens. We feel also equally certain that use of this objectionable phrase was an unwitting one." ("Unwitting" was too kind; the publisher replied that while "We quite appreciate the fact that the term 'nigger' is objectionable to colored people. . . . [T]his little book is so amusing, and innocuous in every respect, that it never occurred to us that there would be any criticism.")[25]

Again, such strategies paid off. "We are extremely sorry that we used the word 'darkey,' " the publisher of an offending ad apologized. "We did not realize the implications that you say apply to the word and we will see that it is not used in the future." And again, the NAACP's positive contacts allowed the Association to pursue a more proactive strategy of promoting books it considered good on the subject of black history or race relations.[26]

Yet just as this approach sometimes led Jewish groups to accept anti-Semitism, on occasion gentle rebukes left a broader racism untouched. A 1939 advertisement for a memoir of a white woman who married a black man and was forced to flee the South describes her longing for the home of her youth: "The languorous, moonlight nights . . . the darkies toiling and singing in the cotton fields." Although the whole image of happy, singing black workers is an offensive racial stereotype (not to mention incongruous for a book purporting to be a "moving protest" and a "dramatic chronicle of a disturbing social problem"), an NAACP staffer simply circled the word "darkies." And indeed, after receiving a letter of protest, the publisher agreed to change the word to "Negroes" or "colored people" in subsequent advertisements.[27]

Looking back on the period, Harry Golden twitted African Americans and Jews for their nonconfrontational approach to such stereotyping. As a New York hotel clerk in the 1930s, he distributed tickets to struggling Broadway plays, including *Tobacco Road*. "It was nothing more than a surface caricature of a few stock characters out of vaudeville," he explained, including blacks, Jews, and Irishmen. "Of the groups thus stereotyped, only the Irish knew what to do. As soon as the Knights of Columbus acquired some strength, they . . . settled the entire matter one Saturday night simultaneously in New York and in Boston—with eggs and tomatoes. The stage-Irishman disappeared from vaudeville, and to this day no one accuses the Irishman of being oversensitive and few Irishmen have heard the label 'chauvinist.' "[28]

Even if they shunned mass action or militant confrontation, liberal black civil rights organizations did routinely and publicly protest racist incidents. In this they were different from Jewish groups, who were far more reluctant to publicize anti-Semitism. When they did protest, Jewish agencies sought to have non-Jews lead the charge in order to cloak their presence and thereby minimize any anti-Semitic response. As AJC's Fineberg explained, "if statements were to be made on behalf of Jews, . . . Christian names were better" because they "had no obvious self-interest."[29] On the one hand, it is not surprising that Jewish groups, who hesitated to go public with problems facing their own people, would resist doing so for others. On the other hand, this fear of direct attack also made organizing against racial discrimination more attractive to Jews, as an indirect way to fight anti-Semitism.

For the moment, this was not to be. Quiet diplomacy, legal briefs, press releases, political appointments—these had a significant impact on black life but were not tactics conducive to interracial outreach or making common cause with Jewish organizations. Those Jewish organizations, with their private contacts and the use of non-Jewish front groups, were reasonably effective in combating anti-Semitism. Yet their style made it less likely they would go public on civil rights issues or engage actively in coalition building. And the deep suspicion of anti-Semitism made cooperation with black people, many of whom were outspoken in their criticism of Jewish businesses, highly unlikely. Despite rhetoric about the universal rights of citizenship and equal opportunity, liberal black and Jewish groups persisted in defining those goals narrowly, even if individual Jews (and other whites) worked in black civil rights organizations, or a few black leaders emphasized the dangers of anti-Semitism. Equality meant securing it for one's own group; it did not yet mean getting there by securing it for all. In a few years this would begin to change, propelled by world events and new leadership. A second generation of Jews and northern-born African Americans was coming of age, more at home, and more willing to speak out on a wider range of issues. Yet they were not yet in positions within defense agencies powerful enough to overcome the parochial vision and quieter, cautious tactics of their parents.

Blacks and Jews Together

Economic interactions far outpaced political ones; because of proximity, black suffering in the Depression had a Jewish dimension. African Americans, who so often moved into previously Jewish neighborhoods, encountered Jewish merchants, landlords, and rental agents. In a 1941 meeting with the AJC regarding Harlem, Aubrey Mallach, research assistant at the (non-Jewish) Community Service Society, "admitted the possibility that if Negroes . . . did own . . . [a] high . . . proportion of Harlem real estate [before the Depression], much of it reverted to the original Jewish owners." An AJC report calculated that up to half of Harlem's buildings were Jewish-owned.[30]

Many stores serving economically devastated black communities remained in Jewish hands as well, and this proportion rose as beleaguered and poorly capitalized black-owned stores went under. A 1942–43 Wayne University study of three black and mixed neighborhoods in Detroit found Jews ran between 30 and 70 percent of its businesses, highest in those areas most recently inhabited by Jews. The ADL estimated that "95 percent of the businessmen in . . . [Chicago's South Side neighborhood] are Jewish." Jews owned so many of the pawn shops in black neighborhoods that Langston Hughes entitled the book of poetry in which a "Hard Luck" man was so desperate for money he had to pawn his clothing, *Fine Clothes to the Jew.* (As he reflected later, "But it was a bad title, because it was confusing and many Jewish people did not like it.")[31]

Black domestics seeking day work stood on street corners in the Bronx; many of the housewives who picked them up were Jews. Black musicians, whose pay scales and work opportunities both declined during the Depression, continued to rely on Jewish club owners, agents, and middlemen. In some cities Jews even took over black crime networks; in Harlem, for example, the Jewish "Dutch" Schultz took over the lucrative numbers game in 1931 by cutting out the largely black "runner" middlemen who had routinely taken a cut of all winnings.

Indeed, if Jews on the whole fared better economically in the Depression than other groups, they did so in large measure because they inhabited the economically crucial but vulnerable niche of wholesale and discount marketing. Those who remained afloat there did so only with tremendous struggle. If store owners or employers managed to keep their businesses, they saw their profits plummet as clients lost the ability to pay for the goods they offered. Customers more often requested credit, a far riskier proposition than cash transactions. Jewish merchants, desperate for business, took that risk more often than better-financed chain stores. But credit, while crucial, also produced tensions between struggling store owners desperate to collect and their poverty-ravaged patrons, regardless of race or religion.[32]

The labor Zionist *Jewish Frontier* concluded that Harlem's higher rents and poorer services came not from the ethnicity of the providers but from "the inevitable ruthlessness of the profit system, on those that fatten upon it." In such situations Jews were "in the unhappy position of being a scape-goat for a scape-goat." Most business owners saw their activities in a more positive light, but all faced the same pressures. To survive, many felt compelled to raise the price of credit or offer poorer quality goods, exacerbating tensions. Some even resorted to illegal measures like short weighting or false advertising.[33]

But honest or dishonest, merchants were responding to the exigencies of the situation, and all were caught in the fury and resentment cost-cutting behaviors produced. From the shopkeeper's point of view, there was little alternative. The risks were high, and most, near-poor themselves, could not make ends meet any other way. From the consumers' perspective, greedy merchants took advantage of the desperation and isolation of ghetto inhabitants to steal what they could from those who could least afford it.

To add insult to injury, white local businesses rarely hired black employees, and virtually never for positions beyond the most menial. In the South, the indignities of segregation and prohibitions against trying on or returning items added to poverty's burdens. Such resentments were felt by black people at all economic levels. The new willingness in urban black communities to go public with grievances heretofore limited to private grumbling meant vocal street protests in city after city. Often collectively labeled "Don't Buy Where You Can't Work" campaigns, these primarily northern and midwestern protests brought thousands into the streets. Marches and picket lines in front of stores demanded the hiring of black clerks and an end to unfair business practices.[34]

In neighborhoods in which blacks and Jews had had hierarchical and potentially tense business interactions for over a decade, resentments escalated on both sides. Issues between owners and clients, between whites and blacks, seemed to many in this decade to become black-Jewish fights. Given the substantial Jewish presence in black neighborhoods, many protests targeted stores that were owned or operated by Jews.

Fanned by preexisting anti-Semitic sentiment and the longstanding resentment of black residents, these protests occasionally turned overtly anti-Semitic, making negative references to Judaism, gratuitously identifying the offender as a Jew, or singling Jews out for behaviors common to all whites. The resulting conflicts were a conflation of legitimate indignation at unethical business practices and an anti-Semitic tendency to blame Judaism for those practices and therefore vilify all Jews. Jewish store owners, in turn, not only denied accusations of illegality and defended their practices as socially acceptable and economically necessary, but called attention to the anti-Semitic component of the protests at least in part to deflect the criticism.

Both the ADL and the AJC kept extensive files on black complaints of Jewish businesses because they considered them, whether legitimate or not, troubling examples of rising black anti-Semitism. By November 1939 the ADL believed that in New York at least, "the problem is assuming alarming proportions." The League filed the complaints in folders labeled "Negro Race Problems." Until 1941 this longstanding category contained information not about civil rights violations but rather about black criticism of Jews. Available executive meeting minutes for the major Jewish agencies reveal that in this period, discussion of antiblack racism was exceedingly rare. The NAACP's attempt in 1934 to garner Jewish organizational support for the Costigan-Wagner antilynching bill failed. While individual Jews contributed, the NAACP received moral support from the NCJW and the Rabbinical Assembly, $25 from the AJCongress, and $100 from the AJC, far below the $1000 it had requested.[35] For Jewish groups the problem of the Negro was primarily the problem of black anti-Semitism.

Black Anti-Semitism or Jewish Exploitation?

The experiences of Walter White, longtime head of the NAACP, illustrate the difficulty of characterizing these entrepreneurial interactions. Secretary of an organization devoted to the interests of black people and reliant on the help of Jewish donors, advisers, and attorneys, White both opposed anti-Semitism and criticized Jews in ways Jewish leaders considered anti-Semitic. Yet the methods he used were precisely those both blacks and Jews had employed against white Christian discriminators—polite references to shared values and careful selection of the particular arguments that would hit home in each case. Much organized black-Jewish interaction in the Depression era presented such contradictions and White frequently found himself at the center of the maelstrom.

November 14, 1938

HORNSTEIN BROTHERS STATIONERY STORE
Gentlemen:

I am the individual to whose son you sold a basketball, about which I called at your store recently. You made the statement that you guaranteed everything that went out of your store. [White recounts how the poorly made ball fell apart.] . . .

I neither expect nor ask any adjustment since your manner the other night showed the type of person you are. I want to say this to you, however, as members of a race which at this particular stage in the world's history should be busily engaged in making friends instead of more enemies, particularly in view of the news out of Germany during the last three days. I have been exceedingly fortunate in that I have had the opportunity of knowing honorable and decent Jews, like Governor Lehman. But I want to say to you quite candidly that your type of merchant, selling shoddy goods, are doing more to build up anti-Semitism . . . than some of you appear to realize. Having for many years opposed anti-Semitism in the U.S. and elsewhere, you can imagine what effect conduct like yours has upon persons like myself.

Ever sincerely,[36]

White maintained that complaints such as these addressed unfair business practices. As he had with publishers of racist materials, White simply highlighted arguments he believed most likely to persuade the recipient. His letter identified the Hornsteins' religion because he considered it both relevant and an effective strategy in the wake of Kristallnacht for convincing the owners to reconsider their actions. Jewish business owners and organizational leaders, on the other hand, insisted a store owner's religion was irrelevant to the exploitation, so identifying it was a dangerous form of anti-Semitism. Doing so held the group responsible for those few exploiters who happened to be Jewish, and sought to justify anti-Semitism by blaming it on the actions of Jews themselves. Because these were recurring debates and involved those who would seek to make common cause on other issues, they are worth a closer look.

Scores of black complaints about Jewish business behavior in the Depression drew explicit attention to religion. As White's letter reveals, the willingness to do so was not limited to the margins. Around the country the black press highlighted instances of discrimination practiced by Jewish store owners.[37] Attorney Irvin Mollison reported that in Chicago's black neighborhoods, "all of the intelligent educated classes of Negroes as well as the masses of uneducated Negroes believe that they are the victims of Jewish merchants and traders who come into the colored community and sell shoddy goods at high prices." The AJC reported "frequent complaints by Negroes against discrimination or exploitation by Jews" in numerous cities.[38]

Many such complaints proved valid. As the ADL reported in 1941, "Careful investigation does reveal considerable Jewish exploitation of Negroes in the field of merchandizing, and in the areas of property for lease and rent, this exploitation becomes most apparent. Discrimination against Negroes by Jewish employers, many of whom do substantial business with Negroes, is also marked."[39]

Yet other data suggest Jewish exploitation of ghetto customers was less common than the exploitation non-Jews practiced. Several studies reveal that contrary to the black community's beliefs, Jewish businesses generally charged prices no higher than those of black-owned stores, and many did hire African American workers. The Wayne University study of the Hastings area of Detroit found of twenty-nine Jewish stores there that employed help, twenty-eight employed African Americans (and only one employed a Jew), a ratio higher than both black and white Christian stores. The same pattern held true for a better-off black neighborhood.[40]

Nor did Jewish owners charge higher prices for shoddier goods. The study priced eleven basic grocery items in 176 Detroit stores. Black-owned stores charged the highest prices for eight, Jewish-owned stores for two, white-Christian-owned stores for one. While examiners did not test the quality of the goods, they did rank 60 percent of the Jewish stores and 48 percent of black stores in the poorest areas "good" or "very good" in appearance; 29 and 33 percent, respectively, were judged "poor."

Stereotypes about poor landlord-tenant relations, which also produced substantial tensions between blacks and Jews, seem also to be partly true and partly distorted. In the same Detroit neighborhood half of those residents surveyed reported having a Jewish landlord, certainly a high proportion, and a third of those believed they had been treated "unfairly." But comparing those results with white gentile landlords, investigators concluded, "The general impression that there is a great deal of conflict between Jewish landlords and Negro tenants appears to be a result of the fact that the *number* of Jewish landlords is a large one, not that antagonism is more intense."[41]

While anti-Semitism played a role in black anger, more significant in many cases was black disappointment. The Detroit study found that both African Americans and Jews had higher expectations of Jews, as fellow oppressed people. Yet both acknowledged those expectations were not always met. When asked whether they agreed with the statement that "Jews have an obligation to treat Negroes better than do non-Jewish whites because Jews know what it is to be persecuted," 71 percent of Jews and 63 percent of African American youths surveyed answered in the affirmative. But when asked whether, "in general, Jews treat Negroes better than do non-Jewish whites" only 52 percent of Jews and 50 percent of blacks agreed. As the study noted, "Obviously, some of the same people who thought they *should* treat Negroes 'better' admit that this belief is not carried out in practice."[42]

The first statistic suggests that ordinary blacks and Jews both recognized at least some shared experience of discrimination. More interesting are the results for the second question. The gap for both races between hope and reality reveals not only frustrated black expectations, but also a level of Jewish guilt suggestive of the widespread—albeit relatively superficial—Jewish commitment to black civil rights that more than a decade of Jewish press coverage has also indicated.

These higher expectations blacks had of Jews extended well beyond Detroit. Activist and NCNW treasurer Bessaye Bearden warned, "Minority groups—and I speak now with reference to Jews and Negroes—must understand one another and must work harder than ever before for that type of interracial cooperation that will give added strength and force to our efforts toward a wider human understanding." Instead, "far too often we find the Jewish employer who registers an objection to the hiring of Negro youth." Even street-corner orators made the same argument: "the way they [Jews] have been cursed and beaten and robbed in Europe, you'd think that they would be considerate of us [Negroes] over here, where we are on the bottom. Instead, they rob us just like everybody else does."[43] That both groups expected more from Jews based on a presumptive shared history of oppression, and believed that expectation was not being met, goes far toward explaining why Jewish businesses were singled out for special scrutiny and why relations between blacks and Jews have received such attention in analyses of racial and ethnic relations.

Higher expectations, however, can fully explain neither the tendency of African Americans to identify offending Jews by religion, nor the willingness of some Jewish business people to engage in exploitative practices. Jews focused on the first problem, African Americans on the second. In that sense Jews and blacks understood troubling business interactions in completely different ways. Where African Americans saw exploitation by Jews, Jews saw black anti-Semitism.

Certainly Jewish reaction was understandable. The rise of fascism and especially Nazism, with its overt anti-Semitism, made Jewish groups particularly sensitive to and concerned about the danger of any anti-Jewish expression. "JEWS! JEWS! JEWS EVERYWHERE!" warned a 1938 German American Vocational League broadside which alleged they were stealing white workers' jobs. "OUT WITH JEWS! . . . WAKE UP! WAKE UP! WAKE UP!"[44]

That same year, Frank McCallister, southern secretary of the Workers Defense League, an organization dedicated to workers rights and civil liberties, reported the "existence of numerous vigilante 'shirt' movements," the Klan's "phenomenal revival and growth" and its organization of "a systematic boycott campaign against Jewish business men and job discrimination against Jewish workers," growth of "anti-Semitic sentiment among workers employed by Jewish operators," and "distribution by the tens of thousands of anti-Semitic leaflets, pamphlets, stickers, and various publications." The NAACP contacted the AJC with similar concerns and proposed a conference to "determine the possibility of working out a program of cooperation.[45] All this informed Jewish response to black complaints about Jewish businesses.

African American groups, particularly those who enjoyed close contacts with Jews, shared their concern that black anti-Semitism was increasing. Walter White undertook an informal survey of black attitudes toward Jews across the country in 1935 to determine the depth and breadth of the antipathy. Three years later the Chicago Urban League conducted a similar local investigation, about which White commented, "the whole question of anti-Semitism, apart from its immediate connotations, seems to me of tremendous importance in that we must oppose bigotry and racial hatred no matter against whom it is directed."[46]

While most of the evidence gathered suggested black complaints were grounded in concrete situations, some did espouse overt anti-Semitism. According to the black Chicago paper *Dynamite* (which the ADL described as "small but noisy"), "Those JEWS . . . take advantage of the Black People. . . . Inferior merchandise, short changing and weights, . . . trick contracts . . . and various other schemes too numerous to mention are practiced by JEWS on COLORED people." In such situations, black organizations cooperated with Jews in addressing the problem. In this case, the ADL "work[ed] closely with Negro leaders, Jewish merchants, Negro clubs and business associations, and it is probable that the entire matter will be composed to the satisfaction of both groups in the next few months."[47]

More often, however, Jewish groups raised the specter of Nazism to avoid acknowledging that Jews engaged in unfair behaviors. A 1941 AJCongress article argued, well after specific exploitative situations had been documented, that a "well-organized fascist-inspired . . . campaign" explained African American complaints against Jewish business practices in Harlem. The *Forward* went further. Not only was this "anti-Semitic propaganda . . . the work of American Nazis and Fascists," but "The Negro intellectuals . . . admitted that all these legends [of Jewish exploitation] were without the slightest foundation." (The ADL staffer who collected and translated such articles put a question mark next to that last sentence.)[48]

Beyond the question of the role fascism played in fostering black anger against Jews lies a more complex question: whether such anger was actually anti-Semitic. The answer to that depended on one's interpretation. Jewish leaders saw anti-Semitism not only in instances of explicit bigotry, like the *Dynamite* article, but also in the routine identification of exploitative businessmen as Jews, insisting religion had nothing to do with the behavior. White's letter to the Hornstein store reveals the tendency within the African American community, by contrast, to see the owner's Judaism as directly relevant, and therefore not anti-Semitic. In the context of a world struggle against a vicious anti-Semite, White believed, being Jewish had—or ought to have—everything to do with it. The *Pittsburgh Courier* editorialized that the racial discrimination practiced by a local business "is more puzzling because it is operated by Jews. . . . Booted about in Palestine, Russia, Germany, Italy, England, they flee for asylum here and set up bars against a common sufferer."[49]

But Jewish agencies argued that while specific criticisms might have merit, it was inappropriate and dangerous to generalize about an entire people based on the case of a few individuals and thereby legitimize group hatred. White's Hornstein letter seemed to do just that. So did his 1940 comment that the "considerable" black anti-Semitism in Baltimore was not "caused by anything else except the discriminatory policy of department store owners like [Jewish] Mr. Hutzler." White was hardly alone in blaming black anti-Semitism on exploitative actions of particular Jews. Such generalizing occurred all the time. "Yes there is anti-Semitism among a large part of the Negro population, largely because of some covetous and greedy Jewish landlords and merchants," Charles Houston observed. "Anti-Semitism is regrettable," asserted a 1938 *Amsterdam News* editorial," but the Jew himself is its author, insofar as it concerns the American Negro."[50]

Jewish civil rights agencies themselves concurred with the analysis. The ADL and AJC concluded after their joint national investigation that not only were black complaints against Jews in large measure accurate, "It is these attitudes which are utilized in the promotion of anti-Semitic agitation among Negroes."[51] But for them, this linkage of exploitative acts by Jews and black anti-Semitism was precisely the problem. Absent pre-existing anti-Semitism, individual acts of exploitation or discrimination would not generalize to a wholesale criticism of a group. Virtually every individual interviewed by White, the ADL, or the AJC on the question of black anti-Semitism referred to specific Jews' unfair practices as creating or reinforcing anti-Semitic attitudes. Christian behavior obviously did not have the same effect.

In some black commentary Jews were made to stand in for the racist behaviors of all whites. The (North) *Carolina Times*, for example, ran a story headlined, "Jews in the South Must Stop Practices of Discriminating [against] Negroes in Stores," as if non-Jewish whites acted any differently. Jim Barber, a Harlem resident interviewed by Ralph Ellison in 1939, complained bitterly about white businessmen exploiting blacks. Midstream he altered course to blame Jews. "I have to get these white cats told. . . . They just the reason why I cain't get ahead now. They try to get all a man's money. . . . I ain't giving these Jews my money."[52]

The ADL's Abel Berland understood this pattern of using Jews to represent whites. "[W]hile the Jewish merchant conducts his business no differently than a non-Jew," he observed, given the virtual Jewish monopoly in Chicago's black areas, "the anti-white sentiment of many Negroes is translated into anti-Semitism, particularly in view of the reported abuses of the Negro public by the merchant."[53]

But understanding did not mean acceptance. Jewish leaders insisted singling Jews out for behaviors common to many whites was anti-Semitic. Rather, these businessmen were simply rational operators; neither religion nor race explained their practices. An AJC investigation of Jewish business practices in Harlem described "the entirely reasonable principle of economics as well as the course of New York City history applying to the present housing situation in Harlem. . . [;] this went far beyond any question of Jewish management or ownership, or abuses by any particular group of landlords" since even black landlords acted the same way. The report urged the AJC to "bring every grain of constructive truth to the attention of people like Clayton Powell, Roy Wilkins, and other leaders of the American Negro community."[54] While this analysis was neither incorrect nor unfair, from the perspective of many African Americans it begged the question of whether or not landlords and business owners, among them Jews, were indeed exploiting black people.

Jewish organizations responded similarly to most complaints about Jewish merchants. Jews should not be singled out for blame when acting as others did. When discrimination occurred in the South, agencies noted that Jim Crow was standard practice there. Several black papers published a 1941 story about discrimination at Kaplowitz's, a Jewish-owned department store in Washington, D.C. It had issued the following notice to its employees: "During busy periods and on sale days we wish to avoid waiting on COLORED TRADE. Of course, we have quite a few very valuable customers among colored people. . . . If you know these people it is good business to give them service . . . in such a manner that it will not look like a colored convention. . . . All others— . . . in some way, without offending them, get them out as quickly as possible."[55]

The ADL responded. "Actually, the Kaplowitz store was by no means the only offender, nor were the Jewish stores the only ones guilty," one memo noted. Another argued that Washington "practices the same discrimination as in the South, but it is definitely due to the pressure of non-Jews. . . . The fact that other people are guilty of similar things does not excuse the Jewish store, but it does throw a different light upon the assertions." Since all white southern businessmen acted in racist ways, if only Jews "individually alter their present policy, it would affect their business, and would be opposed by the majority of residents of the community."[56]

Indeed, this was precisely the argument Jewish merchants themselves often made. In 1938 White complained to Victor Ridder that in Baltimore, "[o]ut of nine large department stores . . . seven . . . are operated by Jews. . . . [A]ll nine of them bar Negroes no matter what their appearance, education or background may be." All seven "justify it on the ground that they might lose some white trade if they stopped discriminating against Negroes."[57] Ultimately, the ADL concluded, "if it [discrimination] be common practice . . . then, however regrettable the practice may be, it is hardly fair to pick only upon the Jewish organizations and effect thereby some justification for negro [sic] anti-Semitism." The AJC commented, defensively but accurately, "Objectively, there are Jewish[-]owned stores that accept Negro customers and Christian[-]owned stores that do not. However, there can be no doubt that most of the blame for the situation is placed on the Jews."[58]

In other words, Jews, who at opportune moments identified themselves as a disadvantaged minority, in these situations defended themselves on the grounds that they were simply white people. In this, Jewish agencies (as well as the offending Jewish businessmen) revealed the limitations of the egalitarian vision they claimed. The president of all-black Morgan State College in Baltimore commented, "To summarize, I would say that in the Baltimore community the Jews are white people with all the white people's psychology and prejudices when it comes to dealing with Negroes."[59]

On the other hand, Jews' whiteness (and therefore, by implication, their racism), cannot fully explain their ill-treatment of African American clients either. While black store owners did not treat their clients in racially discriminatory ways, they did charge similarly high prices for similarly poor-quality goods. Class as well as race determined business owners' behavior, as the AJC's discussion of economic forces suggested. Jews bore the brunt of such complaints, but they were not acting white so much as capitalist, two categories often conflated in segregated and discriminatory America. As George Murphy wrote, "I am persuaded that many of the middle class Jews do not like to consider this problem in its true light because they are members first of their class, and then of their race."[60]

Many other African American leaders also recognized the economic dimension. They believed Jews hid behind allegations of fascist influence and black anti-Semitism to avoid taking responsibility for the unfair business practices such exposés revealed. Again Walter White is a case in point. In 1938 Chicago ACLU lawyer Ovrum Tapper objected to an anti-Semitic comment made by a local NAACP member, A. C. MacNeal. White confided to Houston, "I, frankly, confess that I am getting a little sick of some Jews yelling anti-Semitism when Negroes make protest against discrimination by Jews against Negroes." In a second letter he expanded, "here is the A.C.L.U.'s Chicago attorney asking us to get rid of a member of our branch with whose point of view he does not agree. O, consistency, thou are a jewel!" But, "more important," was the source of MacNeal's "bitterly critical" remarks about Jewish southside businessmen. "Where, I should like to ask Mr. Tapper, is the dividing line between legitimate protests against exploitation whether it be by Jews, Gentiles, Catholics or Hottentots on the one hand, and anti-Semitism on the other?"[61]

That these conflicts were about class, not just racism or anti-Semitism, is highlighted by a letter from a Boston ADL representative describing tense postwar relations between African Americans and Jews in that city. As black residents moved into the previously Jewish neighborhood of Roxbury and bought multifamily houses, some sought to evict the building's remaining tenants. As the local ADL observed, "In many instances eviction notices from newly made Negro landlords to Jewish tenants led to trouble."[62]

Nevertheless, if black-Jewish entrepreneurial tensions were largely rooted in issues of class and race, the widespread black tendency to identify the religion of the owners, and the suspicion among a sizable minority to suspect worse treatment from Jews, indicates the persistence of black anti-Semitism. This layering of explanations meant that most Jews and African Americans would view the same conflicts very differently. Jewish leaders insisted criticism of Jewish merchants was anti-Semitic because it blamed all Jews for the actions of some, inappropriately targeted racists by religion, and ignored white Christian violators. Black groups maintained the criticism was legitimate because the Jews identified were indeed exploitive or discriminatory, and because Jews portrayed themselves as fellow oppressed and should therefore reflect that sensitivity in their treatment of black customers.

Countering Black Anti-Semitism

Nevertheless Jewish organizations recognized the seriousness of black-Jewish economic tensions, regardless of their origin. They required a response beyond deflecting blame. Two possibilities recommended themselves: stressing Jewish benevolence to the black community or confronting the behaviors of Jewish businessmen. Primarily, they chose the former.

If racist Jews reinforced black anti-Semitism, perhaps fair-minded Jews would reverse the damage. The AJC publicized "Jewish Contributions to Negro Welfare," and the ADL solicited articles from black clergy praising Jews. A 1939 *Forward* article on problems between blacks and Jews in Harlem reminded readers that, "We Jews, suppressed and persecuted for so many generations, must regard the faults and weaknesses of certain Negro elements with sympathy and understanding. By his very nature the Negro is friendly and genial. . . . It is our duty to extend a friendly hand. . . . [W]e must bring the Negro closer to us; we must enlighten him as to who are his true friends."[63]

But these rhetorical efforts were seen as paternalism, if not outright racism, to many in the black community. Louis Wright, a Harlem physician, explained to White in 1935 that "[c]olored people feel that Jews have exploited them and that many of these same Jews have adopted a patronizing attitude towards them, which they resent." Irvin Mollison elaborated regarding Chicago. "Negroes," he suggested, "have no faith in the profession of friendship announced by most Jewish people. They believe that Jewish people are . . . full of hypocrisy so far as the recognition of the equal rights of the Negro. . . . Particularly do they resent the activities of Jewish merchants . . . and 'philanthropic donors' who not only, in their opinion, exploit them, but follow up their exploitation by setting up in the colored community various agencies for the purpose of the control of Negro public opinion." He offered "the example of the Rosenwald Foundation attempt . . . to select the books which would occupy the shelves of the George Cleveland Hall public library" and to control the local UL. "In other words the notion that Negroes are not only exploited but that the exploiters seek to make them amenable to the exploitation is extremely annoying to many people in Chicago."[64]

The *Pittsburgh Courier* articulated that resentment in a 1938 editorial. "From the lips of almost every Jew who has protested last week's editorial [criticizing Jewish exploiters] has fallen the name of [Julius] Rosenwald. We are reminded of his contributions to the educational and spiritual welfare of the Negro race. . . . [W]e are not ungrateful." But his own practices, they noted, fell short; his Sears-Roebuck company refused to hire black workers. "Thus the graduates of Rosenwald schools can go without bread so far as the Rosenwald business institution is concerned," the editorial concluded. "We are grateful but we are hungry."[65]

Not all black leaders saw Jews' contributions in the same harsh light. Kelly Miller, essayist and Howard University dean, wrote in 1935 that "[t[he cultural development of the Negro centers around Harlem under sponsorship and encouragement of members of the Jewish race." Other centers of black urban life, like Philadelphia and Washington, on the other hand, have "developed no cultural leadership of the race. . . . This discrepancy may be accounted for by the fact that the cultural life of these communities . . . is under dominant Gentile control which has little interest in developing special Negro gifts and cultural capacities. But the Jew who controls the theaters, concerts, and amusements and largely the channels of literary publication . . . , has given the Negro his chance."[66] Miller was a conservative, suspicious of what he saw as a trend toward radicalism among African American leaders, and sympathetic to a more accommodationist politics. But his positive reports of Jewish aid would be echoed by other black leaders, especially those from organizations that relied on Jewish support, including the NAACP, NUL, the Negro Labor Committee, and the Brotherhood of Sleeping Car Porters and Maids. The NUL's Mr. Wood welcomed "that very liberal group to us, the Jew," at its 1939 annual meeting.[67] Nevertheless, a sense of Jewish condescension would continue to mar black-Jewish relations in the ensuing decades.

Most Jews remained oblivious to the ways in which their tone gave offense. Certainly, paternalism was a style of the time. Jewish organizations treated Jewish constituents in much the same way. Arnold Forster describes ADL efforts in this regard, reminiscent of the *Defender*'s campaign to uplift new northern migrants: "Incredibly, the League established a desk concerned with *Jewish* conduct, and it presented the Jewish community with a roster of dos and don'ts: *Dress conservatively; Don't be loud in public; In Miami Beach don't wear a mink coat over a bathing suit; Don't flash diamond rings on your fingers.* The ADL even produced a film teaching appropriately tasteful dress."[68]

Black leaders expressed a similar (and presumably similarly unconscious) paternalism toward their own people. Chandler Owen, preparing anti-Nazi material for the black press, advised "that information concerning the nature of Nazism and Fascism must be couched in relatively simple terms . . . for by and large the readers of colored newspapers have a limited education and must be shown by pictures, stories, parables and other devices in order to insure continued reader interest." White's criticism of Baltimore department stores barring African Americans rested in part on their doing so to all black people "no matter what their . . . background.[69] The observation that Jewish organizations sometimes viewed black people patronizingly must be understood within that context.

In a few cases, Jewish leaders responded to black economic criticism by intervening with Jewish businessmen, particularly in areas where positive black-Jewish relations already existed. While such actions were rare before the early 1940s when a political relationship had begun, they were nonetheless significant. (Later, more extensive interventions are discussed in the following chapter.) These early efforts occurred not necessarily because Jewish organizational leaders recognized the legitimacy of black grievances but rather because of their conviction that reforming Jewish behavior would minimize gentile antagonism.

The Cincinnati AJC sought to establish a "Business Ethics Committee. To foster maximal ethical standards in Jewish business . . . to help answer accusations in antisemitic [sic] literature." The Chicago ADL responded to the *Dynamite* articles not only by enlisting the support of black groups (which it was able to do because of previous good relations), but also by working to improve the behaviors of Jewish merchants. As the League explained, "This local situation is dangerous inasmuch as, should disorders break out, the Negro-Jewish question would appear in an intensified form in other cities which at the present are experiencing no trouble."[70] Still, despite their origins as tools to combat anti-Semitism, these were among the earliest efforts to redress legitimate and longstanding African American grievances against Jews.

The conflicting interpretations of black economic criticism of Jews do not explain the failure of the two communities to make common cause. The more fundamental barrier was the absence of a sense that racism and anti-Semitism were linked. By and large, neither black nor Jewish leaders had moved toward a broader, unified attack against bigotry. Despite the professed interest of Jews in black people, and despite the participation of individual Jews in black organizations, even when the problem of blacks and Jews overlapped, available evidence suggests that until the 1940s Jewish agencies concerned themselves almost exclusively with problems as they affected Jews. In 1938, for example, the Chicago ADL charged a Chicago realty firm with discriminating against blacks and Jews. The firm replied, "'It is true that the properties we are selling at this time are restricted against any person who is not a Caucasian, but there is no restriction whatsoever as to Jews.' " Presumably reassured, the matter ended there.[71]

In this period, most Jewish leaders did not see it in their self-interest to link their fortunes with those of African Americans or address their problems in any systematic way. T. Arnold Hill of the NUL observed that compared to the outreach of the Catholic church, "the Jew makes a poor comparison."[72] And despite a greater willingness to engage the Jewish community directly, black-centered organizations also saw little advantage in taking on Jews' problems. When tackling issues that affected both groups, such as restrictive housing covenants, biased juries, or the rise of white supremacist organizations, they focused exclusively on racial discrimination.

This failure to constructively engage the other community meant economic tensions would dominate black-Jewish relations. In those few localities where individual Jews or African Americans did embrace the struggles of the other, relations were generally positive. Mayme Osby Brown of New Orleans, editor of the *Louisiana Weekly*, reported, "we count the Jewish element as being among our best friends. The several Jewish rabbis are always allied with us in any progressive movement, and their aid is usually among the first to be sought by us in any undertaking. They speak for us and to us whenever requested, and their meetings are always open to us, with no segregation."[73] Such was most often the case in larger cities with a substantial Jewish population and relatively progressive politics, although the presence of a brave individual activist could strengthen black-Jewish ties even in small towns. But in most smaller and southern communities, where Jews felt more insecure or African American political activity was muted, economic relations constituted the primary point of black-Jewish interaction and class trumped any common ground. There, tensions between owners and clients exacerbated preexisting black anti-Semitism and Jewish racism and set the tone for relations between the two communities. The executive director of the Indianapolis YMCA believed "there is some feeling of antagonism against the Jews, not as a group, but directed at a class who conduct business in a Negro community . . . but turn nothing back to the group in the matter of employment of Negroes."[74]

Absorption in the problems of one's own community, the failure to recognize linkages between oppressions, is hardly surprising. It is the change in both communities in later years, the new willingness to engage in the other's issues or see common cause where others saw none, that requires further explanation. Anti-Nazi protests provided the impetus for that change. There, self-interest coincided with joint action. Black groups embraced the Jewish cause, equating anti-Semitism abroad with its racial counterpart at home, and Jews sought allies to help bolster the war effort and combat domestic anti-Semitism. Nazism helped Jewish leaders to appreciate the similarities between black and Jewish problems. Pragmatically, Jewish organizations would come to recognize the difficulty of winning black allies while economic tensions persisted. African American agencies, in turn, would prove more willing to challenge black anti-Semitism after their antifascist involvement with the Jewish community at the end of the decade. As the next chapter details, this departure from the attitudes of previous decades would spur the development of a substantive black-Jewish political collaboration and begin to challenge the contradictions between economic conflict and anti-discrimination programs.

CHAPTER THREE

Wars and Rumors of Wars

The rise of Nazism proved pivotal for the development of a political relationship between blacks and Jews. The need to organize against the rising tide of hatred in Europe and to some extent at home, challenged the two communities to transcend entrepreneurial tensions and compelled their civil rights groups to reconsider their behind-the-scenes strategies. Earlier approaches were slow to change, but by the early 1940s a wide range of liberal black and Jewish agencies had become more public and more political. In addition, their desire to bolster strength through coalitions with like-minded groups moved them for the first time beyond idiosyncratic contact toward a more constructive and enduring relationship. A number of jointly pursued and mutually beneficial political initiatives helped counteract the frictions between African Americans and Jews, and open the possibility of a stronger and more extensive political collaboration after the war. Such an outcome was by no means inevitable, however. An emerging sense of common cause, tempered by continued economic tensions and political hesitations, defined black-Jewish relations in this period.

New collaborations were the result of several separate but overlapping factors. The growing strength of Nazism in Europe made it clear to American Jews that their determination to go it alone was insufficient to the task of saving their European coreligonists or stemming the rise of domestic anti-Semitism. AJC's A. N. Franzblau advised, "[W]e must use liberal Christian aid to support us in our fight against our enemies and we ourselves must be in the first ranks, aiding liberal Christians in the fight for Democracy."[1] As part of their new outreach effort, in the late 1930s Jewish civil rights agencies formally requested that black groups join them in aiding Jewish refugees and disseminating antifascist propaganda. But Jews also challenged every community that expressed anti-Semitic or antidemocratic sentiments, including those of putative allies like African Americans.

Making the case against Nazism also led Jews to more public condemnations of bigotry. This they discovered to be a more effective tactic than quiet maneuvering. Jewish leaders organized mass rallies against fascism and invited prominent liberal non-Jews, including African Americans, to speak.[2] These pleas for tolerance were broad-based. Universalism strengthened their argument, and provided an ideal strategy for Jewish leaders still reluctant to attack anti-Semitism head on. In any case, Nazism taught them that independent action was not enough, and that only by eradicating all forms of bigotry could any group live in safety.[3] At the same time, increased attention to the plight of the Nazis' victims gave Jews greater visibility and legitimacy as a political voice for oppressed people. Thus the political crisis began to expand both Jews' clout and their commitment to broad-gauge antidiscrimination protections.

Both increased concern and the improving social and economic position of American Jews following the Depression also brought Jewish organizations increased numerical and financial support, and therefore increased power. By the end of World War II, the ADL, AJC, AJCongress, and NCJW had seen dramatic increases in both their memberships and their budgets. Not only did this provide them the luxury of greater resources to devote to coalition-building efforts, but it meant they were becoming players on the local and national stages.[4]

The threat abroad also affected the strategies of African American organizations. The emerging European holocaust, which stirred the conscience of many Americans, could be profitably compared to the oppressive state of American race relations. The *Pittsburgh Courier*'s "Double V" campaign linked victory against bigotry at home with victory abroad; such antiracist rhetoric won liberal black groups new adherents and brought greater visibility to their cause. Their strategic willingness to challenge all forms of bigotry made them more likely allies. Meanwhile, two decades of accumulated legislative and legal victories had also brought greater membership and power to the civil rights organizations that won them. The NAACP, for example, by 1946 had grown to more than one thousand chapters, with close to four hundred fifty thousand members. Like Jewish groups, then, black groups now had both the resources necessary for coalition building and the political visibility to make such coalitions more desirable.[5] And for them, Jews were a particularly attractive ally: not only powerful and well-organized, but also now particularly sensitive to the dangers of bigotry.

The timing, too, was propitious for these efforts. Across America, news of the genocidal violence in Europe reinforced the commitment to a pluralist and open society. Not only blacks and Jews but many other ethnic, religious, and racial groups, as well as social scientists, liberals, radicals, and trade unionists now recognized that divisions of race, religion, and ethnic background could no longer be considered secondary social problems. Bigotry had to be challenged directly. Such heightened engagement was evident everywhere, from the writings of Reinhold Niebuhr and Ruth Benedict to the activity of union locals and newly organized human rights commissions. Black-Jewish political collaboration expanded within that larger framework of commitment.

A generation of younger African Americans and Jewish Americans was coming of age at this moment of potential coalition. Outspoken leftists like Abram Harris pressed the NAACP to adopt more activist, mass strategies, and they organized a more militant National Negro Congress (NNC). Similarly, younger Jews in the ADL and AJCongress pressed their organizations toward greater public action. Arnold Forster reports, for example, that in the late 1930s when gangs of Irish teens were attacking and beating young Jews on the streets of New York, ADL's leaders counseled quiet diplomacy through the Catholic churches. Meanwhile, its younger members, himself included, organized vigilante groups to protect Jewish victims and give back what they had received.[6] These young turks decried what they called the "sha sha" tactics of their elders. Thus at the helm, or at least in young leadership positions, were individuals in both communities who sought more aggressive and public approaches to long-standing problems.

What changed in this period, then, was not the commitment to challenge racial or religious discrimination, but rather the decision to work against it together and with other allies. This was not a shift in attitude so much as a shift in political calculus. At such a time, strategies based on broad appeals to antidiscrimination seemed the most potent; these early mutual civil rights efforts were the product of overlapping self-interest. In this period, discussions of civil rights almost always referred either implicitly or explicitly to both racial and religious discrimination; to fight against one was to fight against the other. The coincidence of self-interest provided the real momentum for collaboration. Still, this was a far broader sense of self-interest than the narrower vision of earlier years, one that recognized a shared agenda and embraced joint action as an effective strategy.

"Over his dead body": Community Divisions

Although broad patterns of emerging black-Jewish political cooperation can be identified, it would be an error to conclude that liberal civil rights organizations had come to agreement on methods, political styles, or agendas. Neither every black nor every Jewish group worked in the same way, made the same assumptions, or shared all of the same goals. Intra-community competition and disagreement remained intense. The black community remained deeply divided by debates over nationalism versus integration, radical politics versus liberalism, and by accusations that elite, middle- and upper-class institutions like the NUL and NAACP ignored the real needs of the masses of black people.

These were not simply theoretical debates; the NAACP, NNC, NUL, Civil Rights Congress, and others often came into conflict over specific policy decisions. When New York's twenty-first congressional district election pitted a black man, Reverend Lorenzo King, against the white progressive incumbent Joseph Gavagan in 1938, the NAACP urged a vote for Gavagan, a hardworking advocate of antilynching, antidiscrimination, and other legislation beneficial to African Americans. "We Negroes must take more than a narrow and immediate view," the Association argued. "To jeopardize legislation for the benefit of the great masses of people simply to have one more Negro member of Congress, desirable as this is, would reveal, in our opinion, a failure to see the picture as a whole." In the resulting flap, several black ministers espousing a more nationalist line lambasted the NAACP. Reverend Adam Clayton Powell Jr., "told his congregation that if any member of his church joined the N.A.A.C.P. it would be over his dead body."[7]

Even among integration-oriented organizations, differences could outweigh similarities. The NUL warned in 1943 that other black-focused agencies, including the NAACP, did not recognize "the dangers of separatist political action by Negroes" (an accusation the NAACP denied) and complained of "unwillingness on the part of the Association to cooperate." Despite the NAACP's insistence that "the responsibilities of organizations like ours at a time like this are too numerous and important to spend time on needless misunderstandings," friction between the two groups continued.[8]

The NAACP advocated collaboration only on a case-by-case basis, and refused to relinquish any autonomy. In 1942 the NAACP Board of Directors agreed to "cooperate as fully as possible with other organizations in efforts to integrate the Negro . . . [on condition] that it be understood that the NAACP shall take the lead in every instance where it is practical." In 1943 the Association agreed to "combine on a minimum program with . . . [other] enlightened groups," noting not only the imperative to "seek allies" but also the institutional advantage in doing so. "Of course we as an organization get the credit for being the spearhead organization," it noted parenthetically, "so that this procedure is sound from the point of view of our organization as well as from the point of view of our aims."[9]

Gender continued to play a role in the selection of political partners. Black women's groups often sought out women's groups in other communities for joint action. "Recognizing that discrimination, lack of opportunity and injustice based upon race, creed or country of origin constitutes the greatest danger to national unity on the home front," the NCNW explained in its 1944 report, the Council had "invited the cooperation of other national women's groups to meet and discuss the possibilities of joint social action at a well attended National Planning Conference on

Building Better Race Relations." Such efforts proved substantial and abiding. The group "maintains regular contacts with women throughout the country," the report continued. As further evidence of the close ties among black and white women's organizations, this report found its way into NCJW files.[10]

The Jewish community proved no less divided, nor did their agencies work together more harmoniously. Class and politics separated the more radical Jewish Labor Committee (JLC), made up of working-class unionists and active (or former) socialists, from the middle-class Jewish organizations, which in turn still divided between the "old money" German Jewish elites of the AJC and the more liberal eastern European Jewish organizations such as the AJCongress. The resulting political styles of these organizations clashed as well. The AJC continued to insist on quiet diplomacy even after the ADL and AJCongress moved toward a more public approach. "Anyone who was opposed to tangling with the anti-Semites in public was said to be guilty of *sha sha*," explained Fineberg. "The AJC was accused of being *sha sha*. Of course, against that I would talk about the *oi vey* group, those who would be crying '*oi vey*' . . . too loudly."[11]

Nathan Perlmutter, who held leadership positions in both the AJC and the ADL, theorized what might be at the root of their differences. "[T]he ADL was more militant in fighting anti-Semitism," he concluded in his reminiscences, in part because "a young lawyer class, a middle class had less to lose in pursuing truth through militancy than the more conservative, wealthier, more integrated . . . German Jewish community. For them to be militant might complicate relationships with Gentiles. . . . I think professionally the ADL was somewhat contemptuous of Brotherhood Weeks [for example] while the Committee was more kindly disposed."

He attributed these differences not only to class but also to structure. The AJC "studied things thoroughly." Its decisions usually "come out . . . through the same door ADL came out. But it takes them so much longer. I suppose it's because the AJC is the long shadow of social workers" and because the Committee considered its primary obligation to be the education of its membership. The ADL, by contrast, "was more the long shadow of the lawyer mentality" and considered its central mission to be combating bigotry. Thus the League "is more result oriented." Also, and because it welcomed as supporters those who already shared its agenda, the ADL was "more timely in gut responses to what it is that is happening."[12]

Yet the ADL also came in for criticism for being too quiet, from those favoring the still more public approach of the AJCongress. These critics made the same complaints about the League that the ADL had against the AJC. "The Difference between the Congress and the A.D.L." the *Jewish Post* editorialized in 1946, was the former's willingness to pursue public, mass action against bigots. When a coalition sought to haul profascist agitator Gerald L. K. Smith into court, the ADL refused to participate, arguing it gave him another platform to spread his views. The AJCongress, by contrast, "a prominent member" of the coalition, "believes . . . that to allow Mr. Smith to continue his attacks on democracy unmolested by laws already on the statute books is to repeat the same error made by the Jews of Germany." Furthermore, the *Post* argued, such timid policies demoralized the Jewish community. The AJCongress's approach, by contrast, "has the merit of giving democracy a chance to work, use [sic] the checks and safeguards guaranteed to all minorities, and has faith in the people who make up the nation."[13] The AJC did not share the *Post*'s enthusiasm, but agreed with its characterization of the AJCongress, noting in its *American Jewish Yearbook* that the Congress "differs fundamentally from the American Jewish Committee in sponsoring mass activities." It also observed, rather more snippily, that "[A]lthough its leaders claim that it is a 'democratic organization,' there is no record of a popular or democratic election since its organization."

Zionism remained another point of difference among community agencies. Support for Zionism had grown since the early years of the century, but pockets of resistance remained, and different organizations pursued the dream of a Jewish homeland with varying levels of energy and varied conceptions of what that state would look like. The AJC characterized itself as "anti-nationalistic, [but] . . . definitely pro-Palestine," and counted among its leaders "leading non-Zionist members of the Jewish Agency for Palestine" while the AJCongress was "nationalistically motivated," with prominent Zionists among its leaders. As historian Henry Feingold observed, "Rather than bringing unity to the divided Jewish community, the Zionist thrust tended to stiffen the lines of confrontation."[14]

Even questions of race divided Jewish agencies. Despite the skepticism of much of the Jewish community about making common cause with black people, the NCJW (and to a lesser extent the AJCongress and the Union of American Hebrew Congregations) had begun calling for closer ties by the 1920s, based primarily on Jewish concerns with social justice. Other Jewish groups came to this position only later. And disagreements over strategies to improve race relations and strengthen black civil rights would continue to create Jewish interagency friction in the coming decades.

The greater racial activism of the NCJW reveals that gender differences in both outreach and priorities also remained. With several important exceptions, Jewish men and women continued to operate in different spheres even when the agendas of those spheres almost completely overlapped. (The *American Jewish Yearbook*, for example, did not include the NCJW under civic protection organizations, listing ADL, AJC, AJCongress, and JLC as the "four organizations in the United States concerned with the problem of protection of Jewish rights.")[15] In some cases, women expressed resentment at having been excluded from deliberations. More often, Jewish women's groups themselves elected to operate within a female sphere, coordinating efforts with other non-Jewish women's groups. Such gender separatism operated to a greater extent than in the black community, where both men and women recognized that while tactics and alliances might differ, all were pursuing the advancement of the race.

And like male groups, women's groups competed among themselves as well. "I had not been notified [by cosponsor NCJW] of the conference which the National Council of Negro Women held in Washington," sniffed Beth Levin Siegel, chairman of the Interfaith Affairs Committee of the AJCongress's Women's Division, in a letter to the NCNW. The IAC "has dealt almost exclusively with the problem of the Negro this year and we have been informed by many Negro leaders that we are the first Jewish women's organization that has had an active program dealing with the problems of the Negro. . . . It was therefore quite a shock" to discover that the NCJW did not see fit to invite them. Both Jewish groups were busy scoring points, the NCJW by not inviting the AJCongress Women's Division, and the latter by asserting that only it was active in civil rights causes.[16]

As historian Gerald Sorin summarized, "The community was rent by various strategies and ideologies and degrees and kinds of religious persuasion, as well as by duplication and competition." The AJC put a more democratic spin on the situation. The AJC, AJCongress, ADL, and JLC, "though having practically the same purpose, are responsible to different sections in the community. . . . It is safe to say, therefore, that . . . the four organizations together probably constitute a cross-section of the entire Jewish population in the United States." Yet, even excluding women and leftists as it did, the AJC reported that "[t]he differences in orientation and the methods of work which characterize these organizations gives rise to frequent conflicts."[17]

Despite these real differences, on questions of intercommunity collaboration liberal Jewish and black groups proved remarkably consistent. Although their styles and their constituencies differed, they shared a vision of a fully equal, democratic and nondiscriminatory America. Different organizations might move more or less quickly to that realization, or use different tactics to achieve their goals, but they ultimately reached the same conclusions on most policy issues. This process of convergence had begun by the late 1930s, as the pressures of anti-Nazi organizing compelled Jewish civil rights organizations to begin to resolving their differences with black groups. This was not a simple task.

"A dangerous policy"

The factors militating against closer relations remained. If in some areas mutual support now seemed advisable, in others self-interest continued to dictate caution. Well into the war years Jewish groups struggled internally over whether forging closer ties with black organizations would be in their interest.[18] What would, in hindsight, seem a great and almost inevitable coming together of two oppressed groups actually occurred quite haltingly, especially on the Jewish side.

Part of Jewish hesitation to take on questions of black civil rights directly came from fear that Jews' already tenuous position in America might be further jeopardized by any perceived alliance with an even more reviled group. As the ADL's Philip Frankel put it in 1943, "The difficulties facing the Jews, as a minority group, are sad enough without tying ourselves up with another minority group of less influence, and by so doing, probably taking on some of their troubles—a group whose difficulties, in my estimation, are even more deplorable than our own." Such suspicions were probably accurate. While a 1944 poll suggested that 12 percent of non-Jews "appear to be definitely anti-Semitic" and 42 percent "susceptible" to anti-Semitic propaganda, a 1943 poll revealed that "90 percent of the American people stated that they would rather loose [sic] the war than give full equality to the American Negroes."[19]

Through the early 1940s, most Jewish organizations tempered pro–civil rights pronouncements with warnings against linking their concerns too closely with those of African Americans. A 1943 internal study doubted it was "wise for Jews as a recognized group to emphasize their concern for the removal of prejudices and discrimination against Negroes."[20] There was no unanimity within the Jewish community that racism was a Jewish problem.

Some feared that making common cause with African Americans could threaten the achievement of larger democratic goals. The AJC reported its "strong feeling that it would be unwise to bracket Jews and Negroes in the general promotion of tolerance. It has felt that such a bracketing would be harmful to both Jews and Negroes as separate groups." Too much public emphasis on racism, or an explicit black-Jewish partnership, could prevent the formation of a more effective and broad-based progressive coalition or even create a backlash. This embodied the liberal commitment to building consensus by avoiding seemingly irreconcilable differences over race.[21]

Furthermore, for many Jewish organizations, working for black equality meant more than promoting antidiscrimination measures. Just as the

NCJW, AJC, and ADL had sought to reform Jewish behavior to minimize anti-Semitism, so too did they see work within the black community as central to advancing civil rights. Perhaps the most dramatic example comes from a 1943 letter from Finder to an ADL colleague: "While it is true that we do not want it to appear generally that we are assisting [Negroes in their struggle for equality], because southern whites particularly would view this as proof of the 'Jewish-Negro' relationship, nevertheless we should do what we can both to abate anti-Semitism among the Negroes, and to create a better understanding of democracy among them." As the current political expression goes, he just doesn't "get it." Attacking racism is not synonymous with countering supposed antidemocratic or anti-Semitic tendencies of African Americans, important though those activities might be. And his evident concern that some might see a "'Jewish-Negro' relationship" reveals just how dangerous most Jews, even those committed to black equality, perceived such a coalition to be. "Do not let the K.K.K. ever get hold of the picture showing me in deep discussion with Dr. Holmes of Howard University!" his letter jokingly concluded.[22]

Indeed, not all Jewish leaders were yet convinced that racism and anti-Semitism should be attacked as twin facets of a single problem. AJC's Alfred Bernheim commented in 1942: "We have had no faith that a general attack on . . . all prejudice in the abstract can be very effective in combating anti-Semitism specifically. . . . If the eliminating of anti-Semitism must wait for the elimination of all prejudices which men and groups possess, there is not much hope of accomplishment." As George Murphy Jr. of the NAACP observed, many in the AJCongress, NCJW, and B'nai B'rith "refuse to accept the premise that Negro and Jewish problems stem from the same cause." When the Association considered approaching whites who "also suffer . . . from being underprivileged" to build civil rights support, it did not think of Jews. Rather, "our natural allies are the working class and their organizations."[23] So much for the "natural alliance" of similarly oppressed blacks and Jews.

Jewish agencies were only reflecting the views of their constituents. Jewish leftist Louis Harap, writing in *Negro Quarterly* in 1942, observed; "[T]he full and active realization on the part of Jews of their common destiny with Negroes has come very slowly. And because this realization is incomplete there is as yet no unity of organized Jewish and Negro action toward those common objectives." This was particularly true of southern Jews. In 1945 Alexander Miller, director of the ADL's Southern regional office, noted "the growing clamor of some Negro leaders for active participation by Jews in helping them. They feel that the Jews, as fellow objects of persecution, should be the first to rush to the aid of the Negroes and at the same time should be the last themselves to act in a prejudiced manner." While he agreed, such a hope was, he concluded, "completely in variance with the behavior pattern of the Southern Jewish community, which has clothed itself quite completely in the mores of this area."[24]

If anything, Jewish agencies were ahead of their community on these questions. As Rabbi Lou Silberman of the Reform movement's Hebrew Union College lamented in 1943, African Americans "resent our indifference to their problem. They feel that minorities ought to stick together. . . . That there has been little . . . done in this direction is an indication that the status of being a minority does not always carry with it sympathy for other minority groups. Though the pulpit declaim it and the Social Justice Commission affirm it, . . . the sympathy of the Jew for the Negro is often more homiletical than practical."[25]

Loose Lips Sink Ships

Their commitment to the war effort also made Jewish organizations hesitate. Black organizations occasionally embraced confrontational tactics to further their goals, which most Jews considered ill-advised, especially during wartime. Recognizing the potency of mass action that local African American communities had employed to good effect in the Depression, the NAACP and other liberal black organizations sponsored public demonstrations and picket lines against discrimination during the war, and challenged local officials over segregation. Although when it came to anti-Nazi rallies, groups like the AJCongress enthusiastically signed on, in most cases Jewish groups avoided any action that might be seen as a challenge to those in power. They did not want to alienate those they hoped to convince to intervene in the European conflict. It was not that Jewish groups refused to work with black organizations, but they expressed caution about choosing appropriate situations. "Anything that we can do with right-minded, temperate individuals and agencies should be done," urged Gutstadt in a clear articulation of 1940s white liberalism.[26]

Most black groups, on the other hand, recognized that the conciliatory tactics they tried during World War I had produced no benefits for them. So when A. Philip Randolph proposed his mass protest march on Washington in 1941 most black organizations signed on, whereas many Jewish groups, even those who had enjoyed good working relations with Randolph in the past, read it as a sign of potential subversion.

Responding to a 1942 query about working with Randolph, Paul Richman of the ADL warned Finder, now the League's director, "I wonder if you are aware that the Department of Justice is watching him closely for subversive activities. . . . He has been causing the President . . . a great deal of anxiety with statements involving threat, bordering on sedition." Gutstadt elaborated. "The violence of his recommendations . . . might conceivably affect our relations with some government bureaus because Randolph does not hesitate to whip the Negroes up to the adoption of methods calculated seriously to embarrass Washington."[27]

The equation of protest and subversion was made easier by Jewish concerns about black loyalty. In 1942 Stanley Jacobs warned, "The A.D.L. is reliably informed that 85 percent of the responsible Negro leaders secretly applaud Japanese victories over the forces of the United Nations and this sentiment is evidenced increasingly in the Negro press." Meanwhile, another report warned of "the dangers attendant on the current demands of the Negro leaders for an immediate solution of the social aspects of the Negro problems." It would be "courting disaster for Jewish organizations and interests to be tied in intimately with Negro causes and leadership" because "[i]t is certain that the demands of the Negro leadership will lead to violent resistance in the southern and border states." Furthermore, "The disloyal attitudes of the Negro leadership and a large percentage of their followers might break into a national scandal at any moment."[28]

Wartime had heightened Jewish concerns about the impact of Nazi propaganda in black communities. Many Jews in fact considered subversion and anti-Semitism as one and the same. Certainly white anti-Semites were busy associating Jew-hatred with opposition to the war. "NO WAR FOR ME To Save the British (or Yiddish?) Empire!" one handbill read. "Christians Unite You Have Nothing To Lose But The Jews."[29] Jews feared African American communities, given their economic resentments, might fall prey to the same views. They saw evidence in the continued criticism the black press leveled toward Jewish business owners. A black Memphis paper published "The Indigestible Jew"; a 1942 *Crusader* editorial urged a "solid front" against the Axis powers, then complained about the exploitation of Harlem's Jewish merchants. "It is an accepted fact that the Jew is a shrewd trader, but this is no time for shrewd tricks. . . . We know that the jews [sic] employ more Negroes than any other group, and we appreciate it, but we also know that he gets it all back with interest, through high rent, shotty [sic] merchandise and short weight." Such concerns led the JLC, AJCongress, ADL, and AJC to monitor "the street scene"—local newspapers, political orators, handbills, and the like—carefully in black as well as white neighborhoods around the country.[30]

Worries that black communities could be Nazi breeding grounds were hardly unique to Jews. Black organizations, including the Brotherhood of Sleeping Car Porters, the UL, Harlem's Negro Labor Committee, and the NAACP, launched their own investigations.[31] Most agreed with the ADL's assessment that "pro-Axis propaganda in Harlem emanates from pro-Axis sources." While a few argued that many of these agitators were simply nationalists trying to advance their own cause (in Harlem, for example, nationalists pressed for a boycott of Italian ice vendors following the Italian invasion of Ethiopia), there was no disagreement that such propaganda could be found in numerous black communities and that black communities were vulnerable to Axis sympathies.[32]

These fears prompted the ADL to cooperate directly with the authorities investigating suspicious behavior. It sent undercover agents to meetings and organizations suspected of pro-Nazi sympathies and cooperated with law enforcement to shut them down. Its files were "better than those of the F.B.I.," boasted a member of its national advisory council.[33] A 1942 ADL memorandum described an FBI-sponsored raid on Chicago's Temple of Islam (a "Jap-Negro organization" according to the ADL). The raid relied on the infiltration of the organization by "a Negro employed by us and who was . . . quite instrumental in assisting in the arrests of these [68?] individuals." The memo's author, Miles Goldberg, concluded, "I believe this is a very good example of concrete cooperation and services rendered to one of the important government agencies by the A.D.L." If some believed such activities skirted the edges of legality or blurred the line between undesirable and illegal organizations, the ADL did not. The potential danger and the lack of adequate government oversight warranted such action.[34]

Such suspicion was not motivated by racism; Jews acted similarly when they suspected white disloyalty. Some situations even prompted Jewish organizations to override their oft-stated commitment to free speech. ADL counsel Arnold Forster contacted Post Office chief inspector Aldrich in 1941 regarding the book *The Octopus*. "Under no construction whatever can it be said that the book is legitimate in its purpose. . . . We are convinced that wise discretion would rule that the book is an unmailable piece of literature under the postal laws and regulations." In a letter to Max Kroloff, Forster acknowledged, "Nothing in the book . . . comes within the prohibition of any of the statutes. However, a reading of the statutes leaves the reader with the impression that books of a certain 'odor' cannot go through the mails. In view of the fact that Aldrich is supposed to be an understanding person and because he probably realizes the real need for unity at this time, I can see where he might stretch a point and rule as I have requested." While neither this effort nor a previous one to block the mailing of *War, War, War* succeeded, the urgency of the ADL's concerns (or at least, Forster's) about subversion is evident. These concerns seemed reasonable to those in authority as well. While Aldrich denied Forster's request, he did suggest, "In view of the possible subversive nature of the book, you may desire to bring it to the attention of the Director, Federal Bureau of Investigation."[35]

The Jewish community was not unified in the conviction that black anti-Semitism constituted such a danger. As late as 1943 the AJC believed that "Anti-Semitism among Negroes . . . has not been sufficiently exten-

sive or menacing to require a sustained and concentrated program."[36] Nor
did most respond to the fear of subversion by collaborating with the FBI
as the ADL did. It was the ADL too, who raised the strongest concerns
regarding Randolph. Nevertheless, every Jewish group monitored the political scene. Although most African Americans (and most whites) remained loyal to the war effort, no Jewish organization could risk ignoring
any potential danger signs.

Jewish fears intensified almost to the point of paranoia. In 1939 an
ADL staffer contacted Finder with his concerns about a new film, *Mr.
Smith Goes to Washington.* "In the course of the two hours' unreeling,"
he complained, "the United States Senate is pretty completely besmirched;
and the press is shown to be easily controlled by one or two politicians
who presumably can take such a man, let us say, as Representative Torkel-
son, and by their control of propaganda agencies show him to be a de-
mented screwball, when actually he is a young American idealist fighting
for the 'right.' "[37] The news from Europe was enough to make anyone
paranoid, of course. But understandable though such oversensitivity may
have been, it made it more difficult for Jews to trust any other group
enough to embrace coalition, much less one that seemed to hold anti-
Semitic or disloyal attitudes.

Wartime Blinders

Despite Jewish concerns that black organizations were not properly committed to the war effort, the urgency to win the war limited insurgency
and sensitivity to discrimination among virtually all civil rights groups.
Although African American organizations did protest antiblack discrimination, they, like Jewish groups, labor, and even civil liberties watchdogs,
muted criticism regarding other drastic violations of minority rights.

When the order came down from President Roosevelt to incarcerate
those of Japanese descent on the West Coast, including American citizens, virtually no organization made protest. Although Italian and German Americans were not similarly jailed en masse, and although no evidence of espionage was ever produced to justify the roundup, neither
Jewish nor African American organizations seemed to recognize the racism of the internment order until much later. Neither, in all fairness, did
the ACLU, the CP, or even the Japanese American Citizens' League. The
two agencies that did initially raise questions, the NCJW and the
NAACP, quickly capitulated to pressures to support the war effort. Indeed the NAACP's objection was based in part on the difficulty of har-
vesting needed crops in the West without reliable Japanese American

workers. The NCJW only asked that as they were individually cleared, prisoners should be quickly returned home.[38]

The need to demonstrate loyalty in an era where both blacks and Jews were looked on as suspect peoples; the need to cultivate the good will of Washington, in Jews' case to aid fleeing European refugees, and in African Americans' case to secure equal rights; and a still poorly developed commitment to challenging (or even recognizing) the human rights abuses of groups other than their own all help explain both the silence over the internment and the slowness of black and Jewish organizations to act publicly and jointly on broader civil rights issues.

Thus the war, which would provide new opportunities for black and Jewish organizations to work together on mutually beneficial goals, also hindered the full development of those opportunities. Jews' understandably fierce devotion to the Allied cause drove them to court the good will of Washington and to equate any expression of protest during the war with subversion. This, coupled with Jewish suspicion of black loyalty and sensitivity to any hint of anti-Semitism, limited the scope and depth of any potential coalition building. That, in turn, limited the advance of a civil rights agenda. The unwillingness of either African Americans or Jews to see the plight of other minority groups as necessarily linked with their own ensured that the collaborative efforts they did engage in had a relatively limited vision.

Common Interest, Self-Interest

Nevertheless, despite chilly exchanges over black-Jewish business tensions, and despite these real hesitations about making common cause, by the late 1930s the urgency of the European situation led Jewish organizations to contact black civil rights groups for support. Black organizations willingly embraced the anti-Nazi crusade and saw the opportunity to also generate support for their own goal of black equality. The first steps toward black-Jewish cooperation rested on clear and mutual self-interest.

In 1938 the Joint Boycott Council of the AJCongress and JLC sought the NAACP's endorsement for their boycott of Nazi products. "As an organization which has fought valiantly for the rights of the colored population in our democracy and as members of a people who have suffered all sorts of indignities at the hands of Hitler's hordes, you too must be vitally interested in doing your share," the Council wrote.[39]

Certainly most African Americans sincerely opposed anti-Jewish violence and fascism generally. "As a race of people whose souls have been made sensitive through many years of persecution and suffering," wrote the members of Bethesda Baptist Church in New Rochelle, New York, "we extend our profoundest sympathies to the Jewish people in their present plight, particularly in Germany. . . . We further pledge ourselves that unsolicited by any individual or organization we will . . . assemble for a benefit entertainment . . . to aid the cause of the Jewish refugees." Following a 1936 visit to Germany, W.E.B. Du Bois wrote in the *Pittsburgh Courier*, "There is a campaign of race prejudice carried on, openly, continuously and determinedly . . . against the Jews, which surpasses in vindictive cruelty and public insult anything I have ever seen; and I have seen much." The black Crusader News Agency covered European atrocities against Jews along with news of African Americans.[40]

Anti-Nazi sympathy also corresponded with direct black self-interest. Chester Ames telegraphed the NAACP, "Why not present attitude of US toward Negroes in comparison to Germanys [*sic*] attitude toward Jews?" Many recognized that the present crisis presented an opportunity to bring their own issues more dramatically to public attention. In a 1934 radio address William Pickens compared Nazism with "ku kluxism in Georgia . . . vigilantism in California, and . . . lynching in Mississippi." A 1938 NAACP press release announced: "NAACP SECRETARY DENOUNCES NAZI POGROMS; Says All Must Unite to Protect Minority Rights Here and Save Democracy."[41]

African American leaders made the same point over and over again. Judge Ira Jayne of Michigan's third circuit court wrote to White in 1938, "[E]very time I go South it makes me madder. No . . . schools, no legal protection, no hope, a dollar a day—we get all excited and froth at the mouth at the Germans and the Jews. Why doesn't our great President look out the window in Georgia this morning and 'scarcely believe that such things can be'?" White replied, "Your letter is filled with such superb indignation and points out so effectively the hypocrisy of the American attitude of howling about conditions four thousand miles away while they ignore longer lived things right under their noses that I wish you would grant us permission to quote from it." With a sensitivity that demonstrated that real sympathy for Jews' plight had not taken a back seat to self-interest, Jayne hesitated. "I'm afraid that the interpretation might be put on it [my letter] that I do not think the plight of the Jews serious and I do not want to say anything at this particular time to add to the burden of my Jewish friends."[42]

In March 1938 the U.S. State Department urged twenty-nine nations to provide safe haven for German refugees. Roy Wilkins of the NAACP urged "most strongly that the Association take note publicly in some fashion that will attract attention. . . . I feel that this opening is a made-to-order one for us." That day, White cabled Secretary of State Cordell Hull:

AMERICAN NEGROES APPLAUD ACTION OF UNITED STATES GOVERN-
MENT. . . . WE SHARE . . . INDIGNATION AT THE OUTRAGES BEING
PERPETRATED UPON MINORITIES BY THE NAZI GOVERNMENT. BUT
WE WOULD BE EVEN MORE ENTHUSIASTIC IF OUR GOVERNMENT
COULD BE EQUALLY INDIGNANT AT THE LYNCHING, BURNING ALIVE
AND TORTURE . . . OF AMERICAN CITIZENS BY AMERICAN MOBS ON
AMERICAN SOIL WHICH HAVE SHAMED AMERICA BEFORE THE
WORLD FOR A MUCH LONGER TIME THAN PERSECUTION UNDER
ADOLPH HITLER.

Even more baldly, George Schuyler commented, "While we are all in a state of incandescent indignation over the treatment of members of the Jewish faith in Germany I trust that some of this anger will be directed toward similar treatment of colored citizens in the United States. . . . More than 5,000 Negroes have been lynched, and not a half-dozen lynchers have been convicted or even arrested. I doubt that so large a number of German Jews has been murdered by Hitler's gorillas."[43]

Black organizations pressed their case whenever American politicians pronounced sympathy with European Jewry. "SEN. KING, SORRY FOR JEWS, URGED TO SUPPORT FEDERAL ANTI-LYNCH BILL" read one NAACP press release. In the NUL's journal *Opportunity*, Kelly Miller linked the ideas of Hitler with those of Senators Vardaman and Tillman, and observed that America had lynched its black citizens while Germany hadn't yet "reached such depths of depravity." As James Ford observed, "Naturally, the Negro people in condemnation of Nazi persecution, also called attention to their own struggle against the lynch terror and persecution at home. This was natural."[44]

Black leaders also exploited hostility to domestic anti-Semitism. White wrote President Roosevelt that he was "very much disturbed, as I know you are, at the spread of anti-Semitism in certain quarters in Washington." As he explained, "My reason for writing you about this is that this ties in with an attempt by certain persons . . . to tie in anti-Semitism with prejudice against [African American] Dr. Robert C. Weaver" of the U.S. Housing Authority, in hopes of blocking appropriations for public housing serving African Americans. "Frankly, I don't know what the complete answer is to this tendency to express anti-Semitism and anti-Negro feeling with housing the victim except that I would urge that more Administration support of housing instead of less would be the best answer."[45]

Black leaders played the loyalty card as well. African Americans would be far more enthusiastic participants in the struggle against fascism if the United States had "given us our just share of American democracy," Wilkins observed in a 1937 column. Three years later an NUL fund-raising letter warned: "The Negro has always remained, despite the disadvantages under which he lives, loyal to American institutions and ideals but we cannot assume that he will not be influenced by a force of disunity unless a counter effort is made by those whom he respects."[46]

The American entry into the war provided further opportunities for black groups to press for domestic reforms. The Double V campaign, spearheaded by the *Pittsburgh Courier* and advanced by the NAACP, demanded antisegregation, antidiscrimination, and antilynching measures as both morally compelling and crucial for victory. "Our program of equal treatment, without discrimination or segregation for Negroes in all aspects of the war effort [is crucial] not only because that alone is compatible with the total war effort which the international situation calls for, but even more because that alone is compatible with the ideals which we have proclaimed for the war," a 1943 NAACP memorandum argued. The Association for Tolerance in America, with some of the nation's most prominent African Americans on its board, placed transit ads depicting black men in uniform. Their captions read: "500,000 of these lads are fighting for you. Let them and theirs share in our democracy."[47]

"How can we secure the confidence of the brown peoples in the South Pacific, or retain the confidence of our yellow allies in Asia, or win the friendship and cooperation of our swarthy-skinned Latin-American neighbors to the South," asked Lester Granger of the NUL, "when we cannot establish a decent working relationship between white and Negro Americans at home, even in the midst of a life-and-death War?"[48] The impetus behind Randolph's proposed March on Washington was to capitalize on concerns that if not granted equality, African Americans might not fully support the war.

Slouching toward Coalition

Despite hesitations and limitations of vision, the war years also brought ample opportunity for black and Jewish agencies to move beyond mutual protest of Nazism and build coalitions around shared concerns. The selection of those issues remained dictated by self-interest, but the momentum and the rhetoric generated by them would ultimately propel both communities into a new relationship. Shaken by the virulence of racial and religious hatred, these organizations, and those in other communities as well, began to appreciate how support of others' causes was in fact in their own interest.

African American groups recognized the potential for effective interracial collaborations. A 1943 NAACP memorandum instructed the Association's branches to call together black organizations and "those white leaders known to be friendly" to "insist . . . sturdily on further advances for Negroes . . . [while] making such advances acceptable to whites." In some southern communities however, "it may be wiser to urge that inter-racial conferences . . . should be called by progressive white organizations." Here the Association proved as cautious as Jewish organizations, recognizing that in some cases its visible leadership would lessen the chances for success. Certainly, though, no one had lost sight of the promotional possibilities. If the NAACP could "show substantial unity among Negroes behind our program," this "should get for our branches the prestige that will come from taking the initiative."[49]

Meanwhile, Jews hoped coalitions with black partners could help combat anti-Semitism. In 1940 an ADL speaker proposed to students at City College of New York that they create a committee "consisting of members of . . . Negro and Jewish societies" to promote black-Jewish cooperation. Jewish members were further instructed "to use this committee as a . . . possible spearhead for cooperation with Harlem Negroes on the Jewish question in Harlem."[50]

A few recognized the imperative to combat Jewish racism if they were to ask African Americans to challenge anti-Semitism. Finder applauded the words of Julius Thomas, NUL director of public relations, at a 1943 Goodwill convention. "I noted particularly your comments about the need for internal education among Negroes. . . . [W]e [similarly] . . . devote part of our work to the education of the Jewish community in terms of teaching its members their responsibility to their fellow citizens and to our democratic structure." Finder proposed the two groups work together on this issue. This was direct self-interest. Yet already it was being redefined to include the interests of others. "Do not construe any of this as indicating that we have been oblivious to the interracial problem before," Finder assured Thomas. "It is intended only to state that we are desirous of doing even more if we can."[51]

The desire to win black support for Jewish issues also helped motivate liberal Jewish groups to participate directly in black civil rights struggles. As Richard Bluestein of the New England ADL office argued, "If we are to secure the confidence of the negro [sic] leaders throughout the country [in] the good will and good intentions of the Jewish leaders, we should take some concrete steps to aid them in the alleviation of some of their many problems."[52] In other words, like black groups, Jewish ones weighed action on behalf of African Americans in light of their institutional self-interest. ADL's Richard Gutstadt believed the Bronx employment agency his office was promoting would not only be useful in ameliorating exploitation of black domestic workers but also "be of considerable value to our efforts at establishing the League's prestige."[53]

But the very understanding of institutional self-interest had shifted from earlier years. Every organization concerns itself with expanding its reach and prestige; what is interesting is the sorts of actions a group considers positive in achieving those ends. Ten years earlier, such an effort on behalf of black women would not have been viewed by most ADL members (or by most white Americans) as an enhancement of the group's status. It might improve the ADL's status among African Americans, but desiring to do so was also new for the ADL. On the other hand, the question remains, prestige as what? A fighter for universal civil rights, or a protector of Jewish interests? In previous years, Jews had sought only the latter. In this era, many Jewish leaders began to understand the link between the two, and promote their support of civil rights as serving both ends at once. When asked to advise a Jewish law firm on whether to represent black teachers faced with discrimination in Evanston, Illinois, Gutstadt offered to investigate the details of the situation "before a Jewish firm sticks its neck out. I told him, however, in addition, that there were times when the defense of right and in defense of the democracy for which we are so articulate, that it might be necessary to take a chance."[54] For both Jews and blacks, the collaboration of wartime emerged out of clear and explicit self-interest, but a self-interest that corresponded with a broader moral vision.

Coming Together

Generally black and Jewish political cooperation emerged first on local issues, particularly on efforts to improve race relations within specific cities or neighborhoods. Later, this cooperation would extend into the more visible forum of national politics. Especially during 1943, which saw a spate of race riots across the country, many cities and states responded to the violence or threat of violence by establishing "unity committees" and similar ad hoc structures to examine the state of race relations and ameliorate the worst of the problems. Jewish groups, while concerned with racial violence, also viewed these committees as an opportunity to promote a broader message of tolerance and antibigotry that would challenge anti-Semitism as well as racism. Thus they willingly participated in these committees all across the country along with African Americans and others newly committed to improving race relations and helping Americans to accept rather than resist difference.[55]

Participants in these local coalitions, whether appointed by officials or organized independently, reveal the extent of this new commitment to challenging discrimination and prejudice. The lists read like a liberal who's who. According to the organization's by-laws, the Chicago Council

Against Racial and Religious Discrimination's executive committee consisted of local representatives of the AJCongress, American Friends Service Committee, ADL, NUL, NAACP, March on Washington Committee, Chicago Civil Liberties Committee, Commission on Race Relations of the Chicago Church Federation, CORE, Catholic Youth Organization, Immigrants' Protective League, Inter-Denominational Council of Negro Churches, and a few others. The New York–based Council Against Intolerance in America included Walter White, Rabbi Stephen Wise, A. Philip Randolph, Robert Wagner, Rexford Tugwell, Dorothy Thompson, Alfred E. Smith, Thomas E. Dewey, Harold Ickes, Herbert Lehman, and Reinhold Niebuhr. The City-wide Citizens Committee on Harlem (which had organized before the war), chaired by Algernon Black and Rev. Powell Sr., included Granger, White, Wilkins, City Councilman Stanley Isaacs, Randolph, Channing Tobias (YMCA), Anna Arnold Hedgeman, Frank Crosswaith, Rabbis David De Sola Pool and William Rosenblum, Reverends Powell Jr. and John Johnson, and Judges Anna Kross, Hubert Delany, Myles Paige, and Justine Wise Polier (daughter of Stephen Wise).[56]

The religious, racial, and ethnic breadth of these committees was desirable for all concerned. For officials it provided the best hope for promoting broad unity and racial peace. African Americans recognized the great potential for forging new and far-reaching alliances in the fight for civil rights. Jews hoped to keep anti-Semitism on the agenda and to resolve black-Jewish tensions. And they pressed for other white groups' participation. As Arnold Wallack of the ADL explained, "[I]t is undesirable to give the impression that it is the Jews only who are concerned with Negro welfare so that the Negro-Jewish relationship is one which becomes closely identified within the general public mind." And for all who looked to these groups for real rather than simply rhetorical advances, breadth offered the best hope. The wider the net, the more likely "that representations on the committees be truly popular" observed Gutstadt.[57]

Some committees were pure window dressing, limiting themselves—or limited by their charters—to purely rhetorical efforts, but others had considerable power and made substantive recommendations. In Chicago the committee helped subdue white tensions over integrated housing, and called for state fair employment laws to prevent a repetition of the race riots that followed World War I. Others won passage of antidiscrimination laws or regulations, conducted educational programs, challenged racist advertisements and textbooks, and supported efforts to integrate facilities or workplaces. In Indianapolis the Citizens' Council publicly debunked racist rumors that elsewhere had prompted riots. The City-wide Citizens' Committee on Harlem, cooperating with the ADL, AJCongress, and other liberal groups, successfully lobbied to strengthen the State War Council's Committee on Discrimination in Employment. As Charles

Collier Jr., the City-wide's executive secretary, wrote to Finder, "These results of our joint effort have been gratifying. We wish to express our sincere appreciation for your helpful cooperation."[58]

In each case, these groups explicitly addressed both racial and religious bigotry and discrimination. Dr. Homer Jack, Unitarian minister and executive secretary of the Chicago Council Against Racial and Religious Discrimination (the title alone illustrates the point), testified in 1945 before an Illinois Senate Committee that "[w]hile the Negro faces the greatest discriminations, it is often felt by Jews and Catholics and by Americans of Mexican and Japanese descent." (Note the sensitivity to Japanese Americans. Blindness to the discriminatory nature of the wholesale incarceration cleared up immediately after the war, a point discussed further in the next chapter.) The ADL's Jack Baker noted that within the Council Against Intolerance in America, discussions of Jewish as well as black problems with discrimination "shows that at least this group was fully aware of the complexity of the minority problem."[59]

Here was the core of the civil rights movement that would burst onto the public scene with such energy in less than a decade. Yet despite the breadth of participation in such programs, in these early years among the white organizations it was the Jewish ones that generally proved the quickest to recognize the imperative of black civil rights and the necessity for strong coalitions, in part because they more quickly appreciated the danger of racism that Nazism raised. "When Hitler and the Nazis . . . started a racial persecution against the Jews, I have acquired the knowledge that I have to fight . . . every racial prejudice wherever it is existing," a German Jewish refugee explained to Walter White.[60] Although they spent most of their efforts on the immediate dangers of Nazism, and despite their hesitation about joining too closely with black leaders or organizations, by the late 1930s Jewish organizations were attentive to the problems facing African Americans. Meanwhile black groups moved quickly to translate such interest into long-term coalitions on behalf of civil rights.

Apart from broader unity committees, local chapters of the NAACP, NUL, AJC, ADL, NCJW, NCNW, NACW, JLC, and AJCongress labored jointly, and often with other allies, in numerous states and cities to improve race relations and pass civil rights laws, attesting to the broad-based appeal among both blacks and Jews for such efforts. While the laws they won varied from place to place, by the late 1940s dozens of cities and states had some provisions against discrimination "based on race, religion, or national origin." Other activities ranged from political to social programs to combat discrimination. The Jewish Anti-Defamation Council of Minnesota urged the governor to acquiesce to the request of the state's Negro Defense Committee to permit black citizens to serve in the

Home Guard. Granting this "as a matter of right [allows] . . . our State . . . [to] lead the way to the implementing of the democratic principles that the country is now pledging and preparing itself so earnestly to defend," it argued.[61]

Intergroup efforts occurred from coast to coast. In 1942 several Jewish agencies in Oakland supported a petition drive protesting "discrimination against Negroes." The following year the Brooklyn "colored YWCA" (as the ADL called it), organized a borough-wide committee "to foster a program of inter-racial, inter-religious, and inter-cultural good-will" with support from local black and white churches, the ADL, NAACP, Brooklyn UL, and state War Council Committee on Discrimination. In Brooklyn the local B'nai B'rith lodge opened a "recreation and . . . day room" for the six hundred men of a black infantry unit based there. At the dedication party, the wives of lodge members served as hostesses. "I believe this example of friendly cooperation between the Jews and Negroes is newsworthy," the lodge representative wrote to the city editor of the liberal newspaper *PM*. "In the interest of inter-racial goodwill my lodge would appreciate it if *PM* would be able to devote some space to this event."[62]

Slowly black and Jewish groups moved toward cooperation on national issues. Jewish women were first; the NCJW added an antilynching plank to its national platform in 1935, well after chapters had begun lobbying on its behalf. Most male-dominated Jewish agencies took longer to join national efforts; while there was ample involvement in local issues in the early 1940s, there was little discussion in AJC or ADL files of participation in antilynching, anti–poll tax, or other federal legislative efforts. As their 1943 joint study put it, "Few Jewish organizations have developed policies and activities for combating general prejudice and discrimination against Negroes. This is in line with the general under-development of programs for social action which attempt to deal directly with problems which aggravate relationships between various segments of the American population."[63]

But such efforts had begun. By that year the ADL had joined the effort to integrate the armed forces, at least on a voluntary basis, and began challenging racism along with anti-Semitism in American social and economic practice. The interfaith affairs committee of the AJCongress Women's Division announced as its 1943 program "a study of Negro problems and a concerted effort to bring about social action which will help to solve them." Its chair called on the NAACP and other "national Negro organizations (women's organizations especially)" for suggestions and planned an "inter-racial Conference of national women's organizations." As she wrote to Roy Wilkins, "It is not difficult to get discouraged in this effort to arouse some interest and subsequent social action . . . but we just *won't* give up, will we?"[64]

Black groups, long willing to support anti-Nazi and prorefugee efforts, also embraced other issues dear to Jews. Walter White, for example, explored with the AJC ways to reprint and distribute a 1941 *Atlantic Monthly* article critical of anti-Semitism. The author's words, wrote White, are "an inoculation against racial or religious prejudice. . . . Even an anti-Semite could learn how his liberties are in danger through indulgence of prejudice."[65]

Ironically, given initial Jewish opposition, one of the more significant coalition-building experiences was the product of Randolph's threatened March on Washington. Executive Order 8802 mandated that companies with military contracts could not discriminate in employment on the basis of race, religion, or national origin. The order also created a Committee on Fair Employment Practice (FEPC) to hear complaints. The black community convinced President Roosevelt to issue the order, but in areas with large Jewish populations such as New York City, Jews actually constituted the majority of complainants. As a result, the struggle to enforce the executive order and expand it to all industries brought Jewish and black groups into frequent and productive contact.[66]

The wartime FEPC had offered the strongest civil rights employment protection yet provided by government, in part because the NUL and NAACP, soon joined by all the major Jewish organizations, Federal Council of Churches of Christ in America, National Catholic Welfare Conference, Catholic Interracial Council (CIC), CIO, AFL, and National Lawyers' Guild, pressed Roosevelt to expand its original powers and scope. Perhaps more important, these liberals insisted that the government bore responsibility to eradicate discrimination. In the words of Nathan Perlman, equal opportunity in all areas of employment "should be the privilege of American citizenship." So when the FEPC lapsed after the war, the coalition, now the National Council for a Permanent FEPC, lobbied and testified before House and Senate committees on behalf of permanent legislation. Rabbi Cohen emphasized at a 1944 NAACP meeting "how firmly the Jewish community stands with you." That first effort failed, killed by a Senate filibuster, but the Council persevered for another decade, an energetic and early (if unsuccessful) example of a liberal, black, and Jewish partnership.[67]

Beyond specific advances won, each instance of collaboration gave black and Jewish (and other liberal) leaders, both local and national, the opportunity to meet one another and work together. They identified shared problems to be fought in tandem, and came to appreciate somewhat better each group's separate burdens. When mutual action proved effective, it encouraged further cooperation.

Additionally, antibias work compelled a universalist language that extended the commitment of coalition partners. "Let us pull off our gloves today and be perfectly at home, forgetting whether we are white, Negro, Indian or Chinese, but remembering that we are just fine women here together who have come to give the best that God has given to us to help to create a new and beautiful world," Mary McCleod Bethune urged as she opened the 1944 National Planning Conference on Building Better Race Relations.[68]

Looking Inward

In part to sustain support for these fruitful programs, black and Jewish organizations turned inward to challenge the prejudices of their own community and move their constituents toward the greater mutual commitment they had themselves only recently made. The tactics they employed—hesitant, limited, and focused on the direct benefits received—remind us of the deep suspicion many members of each community felt toward the other, and that these early instances of black-Jewish collaboration were driven by, and limited to, perceptions of overlapping self-interest. Yet at the same time, the act of defining that self-interest required that it be embedded in a more universal context, a crucial step toward building a more sustained coalition. Internal reeducation efforts, limited though they may have been in this period, also enhanced the growing mutual trust by deepening the commitment of the broader black and Jewish communities to universal rights.

Jewish organizations defended their efforts on behalf of black civil rights to their constituents as directly promoting Jewish security. A 1941 ADL memo about the recent rise in racist activities by the Klan in Miami reminded readers that they must fight hate groups regardless of the target: "Though some leaders declare the Klan, in its resurrected form, will not be anti-Semitic, the inescapable fact is that the nightshirt organization represents an extra-legal movement to take the law into its own hands so far as Negroes and Catholics are concerned. And when any minority race or faith is attacked, other minorities inevitably become the targets of hate." Rabbi Berman put the same sentiment more bluntly in 1949: "I think the [AJ] Congress has made a great gain in Chicago in that we are helping the Jews there to understand that this is a common struggle and not something we are doing out of the graciousness of our hearts for Negroes."[69]

Jewish leaders also argued to fellow Jews that furthering black civil rights was crucial to advance the war effort. "One of the sorest spots of America's life as a nation, which was cited by every enemy as an example of hypocrisy and double-dealing, is the Negro problem," the AJCongress warned in 1942. It must be addressed in order to "rebuild its [the nation's] morale." "Is This a White Man's War?" wondered Rabbi J. X. Cohen, listing the ways in which racism both materially and psychologically depleted American war-making capabilities.[70]

Yet such arguments from self-interest inevitably universalized the struggle. As Rabbi Silberman observed, "There can be no doubt that the juxtaposing of . . . the Negro and Jewish question will offer offense to some, perhaps to many, Jews who do not like to think of themselves in such a category. Yet the patterns of discrimination in both cases have much in common and the sources of prejudice . . . have close connections." At least some had finally come to see Jews' interest as tied to that of universal equality. "Human freedom is indivisible," proclaimed the ADL in 1943, in explaining its "Philosophy with Reference to the Negro." "[I]t must apply to Negroes if it is to be effective for whites. It must be the birthright of Jews if Christians are to be truly free. Discrimination against any minority group is an attack against the foundations of democracy. . . . [T]here is no security for one unless there is security for all."[71]

When black groups addressed their constituents they similarly linked the struggle against anti-Semitism explicitly with advancement of their own agenda. Randolph, long reliant on Jewish trade union support, insisted black anti-Semitism was "dangerous and downright stupid" because "[i]n our various battles . . . against Jim Crow, . . . Jews . . . rallied to our support. And not just with words." Furthermore, "[o]ur appeal to Jews and the others on Rankin's blacklist will come with ill grace if we keep on nourishing our own pet prejudices."[72]

Black leaders explained to black audiences that a fight against anti-Semitism was actually a fight against racism. "If we do not make this effort . . . to join hands with the Jews in a common cause . . . we are bound to suffer needless ills," Arthur Huff Fauset wrote in 1944. "For . . . surely . . . if Fascism makes any headway in America, it will strike out at Jew and Negro alike." In a revealing hint of the patron-client style that would continue throughout the partnership he continued, "What the Jew lacks in numbers the Negro can help to make up; what the Negro lacks in experience, political wisdom and in economic opportunity, the Jew can help add to." Similar arguments came from other black editors and journalists, from William Pickens's "'Wolfing It' on Our Friends," to the *Chicago Defender*'s warning about "The Danger of Anti-Semitism." It is "The Way of Madness," opined *Opportunity*. And linking the cause with a broader value, the *Louisville Defender* chastised its readers that "Jew Baiting Tactics Are Undemocratic."[73]

Like those of Jews, such appeals to self-interest rested on liberal, universalist appeals for justice, evoking a theme that would come to define the civil rights struggle. As White told the *Amsterdam News* in 1938 following news of Kristallnacht, "We Negroes know what this means since it has happened to us. . . . We must join with all those condemning Nazi terror because what happens to one minority can happen to others—a lesson which Jews, Negroes and all other minorities must learn." In fact anti-Nazism proved a potent opportunity to call for making common cause. Claude McKay editorialized: "My reaction, as a Negro, to the Nazi persecutions of the Jewish people is that every minority group should join hands with the Jews as well as all progressive people who want to see democracy live." According to Mordecai Johnson, Howard University's president, "Negroes instinctively belong on the side of all decent-thinking people who are revolted by Nazi terror. . . . No minority can protect itself from the fate which has befallen the Jewish minority in Germany today, by attempting to achieve self-protection alone."[74]

This, then, was mutual collaboration, recognition that advancing the cause of the other could advance one's own cause. Out of this came a recognition of common ground and thus the possibility for cooperative action on issues with less direct joint impact. Indeed, a sudden flurry of writing on black-Jewish relations by progressive integrationist leaders in both communities suggests a shift toward more sustained mutual concern was already becoming visible. In the January 1941 issue of the *Jewish Forum*, Harold Debrest urged the ADL to "become an American society for the defense of all nationalities," especially "efforts of the Negro." The year following, the Reform movement's Central Conference of American Rabbis inaugurated annual sermons for "Race Relations Sabbath." In a call to action, the Conference proclaimed, "Negroes are victims of harsh discrimination and flagrant injustices, which cry aloud to God and to man for remedy and redress. . . . We Jews, who ourselves have been victims of injustice should be especially sensitive to this." White, Everard Hughes of Wilberforce University, and Rabbis Walter Plaut and Lou Silberman contributed articles on the subject of black-Jewish relations to *HUC Monthly* in April 1943. That same year Ben Richardson, associate pastor of Harlem's Abyssinian Baptist Church, penned a series on Jews for *People's Voice* with the collective heading, "This Is Our Common Destiny." Even the UNIA suddenly felt obliged to publicly rebut accusations of anti-Semitism. These were calls for making common cause—"We must realize that Negroes and Jews have a common destiny here," Hughes argued— but not necessarily for more. "I do not advocate here a Jewish-Negro coalition," White insisted, echoing earlier Jewish sentiments.[75]

Leftist groups moved more quickly than liberal ones to embrace coalition. And because their universalist message was embedded in their politics, they called not simply for mutual concern but for unity. Jacob Weinstein, writing in the labor-Zionist *Jewish Frontier* in 1935, insisted that the two groups "must understand each other and combine with other minorities to break the vicious hold of that arch-predatory minority—the capitalists and their flunkies." As James Ford saw it, "The Negro masses in active struggle against anti-Semitism, the Jewish masses in active struggle for Negro rights—Only this will deprive reaction of its Ace Trump!" As if in response, the Bronx Council of the Jewish Peoples Committee voted in 1940 to forward to the NAACP "its sympathy for your struggle. . . . Our membership is well aware that . . . the struggle of the negroes [sic] for their rights as Americans is the selfsame struggle as that of the Jews for their rights." And in 1942, Jewish author and editor Louis Harap and L. D. Reddick, African American curator of the Schomburg library collection and lecturer at New York's City College, argued forcefully for alliance in the Negro Quarterly. The articles were reprinted the next year in a pamphlet provocatively entitled Should Negroes and Jews Unite? with a passionate introduction by Randolph.[76] This recognition of the shared and pressing concerns of oppressed groups, emerging naturally from communist and socialist ideologies, was also spurred by tactical decisions such as the 1935 declaration of a Popular Front, the International's mandate to work with liberal institutions for progressive change.

All these calls for a more active working relationship between blacks and Jews emerged out of their historical moment—the plea for unity against fascism, the mutual need for allies. They came, too, from the sickening realization in 1943 that lack of progress in race relations had brought Nazi-like mob violence to American shores in the shape of race riots. Liberal and progressive organizations, and Jewish groups in particular, reexamined their commitments in that light. Following the Detroit riot, ADL's A. Ralph Steinberg raged, "I know damn well what should be done, and I just want to make it a matter of record that I believe . . . our policy . . . on the whole Negro question [is] something that needs a little focusing. Some day the handling of the Negro question is going to blow up right in our faces." Not just ineffective, he declared, the policy "stinks!"[77]

From Rhetoric to Action

Reddick argued that if coalition efforts were to move forward, merely speaking against bigotry within one's community was inadequate; internal practices must also change. Jewish leaders must use community pressure against unfair Jewish businessmen, and black leaders must remind their communities that an exploiter "who happens to be a Jew. . . . should be fought not as a 'dirty Jew' but as a callous landlord or dishonest merchant." The same "two-flank approach to anti-Negroism will go far toward stamping it out among the Jews."[78]

In the best of cases, progressive-minded black and Jewish activists acknowledged Reddick's argument. The editor of the Negro World Digest contacted the ADL in 1940 to help him publish information combating black anti-Semitism. In its 1944 national "Wartime Conference" the NAACP passed a resolution condemning anti-Semitism and promising to "adopt a program of action among all branches for the purpose of eliminating anti-Semitism among Negroes." The same year, Charles Johnson of Fisk University, editor of *Monthly Summary of Events and Trends in Race Relations*, began including anti-Semitism in those reports.[79]

Some Jewish leaders viewed these efforts as too little and too late. In language reminiscent of White's laments about Jews, Abel Berland of ADL's Chicago office complained in a 1943 internal memorandum: "While every right-thinking Jew wants to see a lessening of the discrimination against the Negro and a general improvement in his condition, it is unfortunate that in our contacts with the Negro leadership" they focus on "how we can be of assistance," and too rarely "what the Negro community itself can do to cooperate in eliminating anti-Semitism among its constituents. I do not mean that we should withhold cooperation unless the Negro community reciprocates, but I do believe that we ought to emphasize . . . with Negro community leaders that there be a quid pro quo."[80]

A few black leaders admitted their neglect of the issue. In 1946 Robert Carter, the NAACP's associate general counsel, acknowledged that for many years "we haven't done any particular thing" regarding anti-Semitism "except to apprise our membership of the fact that we have to work with other minorities."[81] And black organizations did reveal ambivalence about their fight against anti-Semitism. Unwilling to separate black and Jewish political relations from the more problematic economic ones, the Chicago UL declared that it "has stated publicly its opposition to any campaign that is . . . an attack against a whole race of people, but at the same time has expressed its recognition of the fact that there might be certain unfair and over-reaching practices carried on by Jewish merchants . . . which give rise to criticism and indignation." The 1944 NAACP resolution against anti-Semitism also resolved to work with Jewish groups to end "anti-Negro . . . practices . . . which foster anti-Semitism among Negroes."[82]

But African Americans also had their own complaints about lack of balance. As White lamented to Victor Ridder regarding Baltimore, "Some of us are doing everything we can to combat anti-Semitism among Negroes, but we are not going to get any help from some of those in the Jewish group who should be working to stop prejudice among Jews themselves while they are asking others to join in protesting Nazi outrages against Jews. It is a complex and difficult situation."[83] Much skepticism remained in the black community about the reliability of these new friends. Frank Crosswaith of the Negro Labor Committee called a 1942 conference regarding the "high degree of racial tension" and anti-Semitism in Harlem. The NLC, JLC, Sleeping Car Porters, Council for Democracy, Friends of Democracy, and Union for Democratic Action jointly invited representatives from selected organizations to a closed meeting "so that all delegates may speak their minds as openly as possible." Despite the fact that "[o]nly those organizations have been called to participate which have an honorable record in trying to bring about genuine interracial justice in employment opportunities and in other respects," the meeting made little headway. Black participants made it clear that they "considered the method and the extent to which the various committees were willing to deal with their problems as wholly insufficient," while an ADL representative there complained that the speakers "did by no means go to the roots of the problem."[84] The commitment to common cause had not yet proven itself durable.

Jewish leaders also accepted the need for internal action and began to explore ways to confront black-Jewish tensions head on. As a start, the ADL sought permission to reprint up to 10,000 copies of Reddick's article (although not Harap's "Anti-Negroism Among Jews").[85] And for the first time, Jewish agencies moved beyond defensiveness regarding economic tensions. When the *Forward* complained in 1939 that the black press's discussion of the slave markets had been conducted "with the obvious intention to incite riots," an ADL staffer drew an x across the organization's copy of the article and across the top scrawled "tripe."[86]

The ADL, at least, now acknowledged the claims of black critics. In 1942 Gutstadt confessed, "There are definite areas of irritation for some of which we are responsible" and so, must help resolve. "Since the violations of decency which mark some of these Negro-Jewish relations are thoroughly reprehensible, there is reason to believe that we can appeal to the decency and good sense of our own people." Rejecting the League's previous strategy, he argued, "It will not suffice for us to point out that people other than Jews similarly violate decency in their exploitation of the Negroes. . . . I believe that we ought to explore the possibilities of stimulating the greater ethical consciousness within our own group."[87]

Earlier approaches did not disappear entirely. Maurice Rosenblatt called for Jewish leaders to "become interested in Negro problems, if this involves merely the paying of lip service." In 1941 the ADL commissioned black journalist Chandler Owen to help decrease tensions between blacks and Jews. His first article, "Should the Negro Hate the Jew?" "through concrete examples showed his colored readers that there always had been a strong bond of sympathy between Negro and Jew, and that Jewish impresarios, businessmen, industrialists and union leaders had been in the forefront of those desiring to give the Negro an even break." Like the AJC's "Jewish Contributions to Negro Welfare," which highlighted the activities of individual Jews active in black causes, the "Anti-Defamation

League Vitally Interested in Welfare of the Negro Community" reminded readers that Jews "have a natural sympathy and understanding for the plight of the Negro" and listed concrete activities the ADL had undertaken to promote black equality.[88]

Jewish groups still did not see themselves as patronizing. And compared to their contemporaries, perhaps they were correct. When a Mrs. Scott reported to her Philadelphia meeting of the National Legion of Mothers and Women of America that "colored people. . . . are harmless. I for one would rather have the friendship of a colored person rather than a communist" (and received applause), the AJC's Sidney Wallach copied the meeting minutes to Walter White with the cover note, "I don't know how you feel about condescending statements like the attached from people who are known to be chock-full of bigoted feelings, but I thought you might be interested." (To which White replied, "I am glad to see the statement anyhow, though it does make me slightly ill.")[89]

Nor did black leaders necessarily hear these examples of Jewish good will as paternalistic. White suggested to the ADL that to lessen black anti-Semitism, it should work with the black press for "[s]ome means of perpetuation of name of Jew like JES [Joel Spingarn] who took uncompromising stand."[90] While modern readers recognize the paternalistic tone, it was certainly unconscious. Perhaps a better characterization is tokenist. But that type of sentiment dovetailed with the contemporary approach to civil rights. For example, in 1944 the AJC reprinted articles about (Jewish) Samuel Klein of the St. Louis Urban League who had hired a black secretary. The pamphlet, with its cover depicting Ruth Seals taking dictation from Klein, bears the title *He Practices Racial Tolerance*. In it Klein boasted that "Miss Seals, understanding the instinctive prejudices some of her co-workers might feel, . . . always managed to be in the locker room when the other girls were not there. She had no thought of joining them when they had lunch together. . . . Miss Seals, keenly aware that she had not only to prove her own ability but able to stand as a credit to her race, responded to friendliness with friendliness, but never with even a hint of aggressiveness."[91] When Lester Granger discussed African Americans' experience with radio in 1946, he celebrated three Jews who hired black performers for nonstock characters: Danny Kaye (Butterfly McQueen), Eddie Cantor (Thelma Carpenter) and the director of *The Eternal Light* (Juan Hernandez, cast as a rabbi).[92]

Both black and Jewish leaders, then, used examples of moral individuals to counter stereotypes about entire groups. There is a certain irony in this, given both communities' insistence that the actions of immoral or criminal individuals ought not to be used to create or reinforce generalizations about their group. And they unreflectively accepted the widespread liberal tokenist understanding of racial progress. But more im-

HE PRACTICES RACIAL TOLERANCE

SAMUEL KLEIN, *Pioneer in Good Will*

He Practices Racial Tolerance, pamphlet, reproduced courtesy of the American Jewish Committee.

portant, such efforts did represent the first real attempts by Jews to address the economic barriers limiting African Americans and to resolve intergroup tensions.

"Oh for the life of Community Service!"

More so than in the previous decade, Jewish organizations in areas with developing black-Jewish political collaborations also addressed business tensions directly by confronting Jewish discriminators. The ADL met with Jewish department store owners in Washington, D.C., to urge "greater discretion" in the treatment of black customers. In Cleveland the Jewish Community Council intervened with unfair Jewish landlords and credit merchants. In Detroit the Council set up an investigative body regarding complaints. In Baltimore the AJC tried (unsuccessfully) to change the policies of Jewish department store owners, and in St. Louis to encourage Jewish employers to hire more African Americans. Still, these were baby steps. The AJC's 1943 report noted, "Jewish communities have only recently become aware of the problem, and if they have recognized the problem, few have taken the trouble to do anything about it."[93]

A closer look at the situation in two cities suggests the challenges involved in taking action and highlights the gulf between Jewish community professionals and the population they claimed to represent. It also details the ways that challenging black anti-Semitism brought Jewish agencies increasingly into the business of confronting Jewish racism and building closer political ties with black organizations. Jewish organizations were still pursuing the same political goal: the protection of Jews. But wartime threats convinced them they had to address public expressions of black anti-Semitism head on, not only by pointing out the fallacy of equating group character with individual behavior, but also by confronting the problematic behaviors themselves.

In Chicago, the shift from defensiveness to intervention occurred quite suddenly. In 1942, after meeting with black leaders regarding anti-Semitic tensions in that city's black neighborhoods, the ADL's Stanley Jacobs "emphatically made . . . clear to the Negro representatives" that "I am of the opinion that some of the Negro leaders are primarily resentful of Jewish business successes."[94] Yet soon thereafter the ADL was mediating between Jewish merchants and aggrieved black patrons. Following the race riots in 1943, it took a more structural approach, organizing "Jewish and non-Jewish businessmen in the Negro community into a chamber of commerce, whose purpose it will be to raise the business standards of the community. . . . develop positive public relations with the Negro community, and spearhead drives for the improvement of the condition of the Negroes."

The proposed "chamber of commerce" proved so complex and contentious that, Abel Berland complained, "In spite of nearly twenty meetings . . . we have not yet reached a stage of development that would permit a full picture of what is being planned."[95] He described the difficulties in a memo to ADL director Richard Gutstadt, suggesting the vast differences in perception between his organization and the merchants, and among the merchants themselves. After one meeting with Jewish business owners, he admitted, "Dick, of all the groups with which I have ever worked, this was the most difficult, and the most divided. (I was ready for the dry cleaners when we concluded.)" Opinions ranged from advocating "long-

range program[s] for alleviation of Negro conditions . . . to an unwillingness to take any steps . . . , as the Negroes were too demanding, that this
was not a Jewish problem, etc. . . . The meeting finally adjourned with
the survivors ragged but undaunted and giving bright promise of bigger
and more acrimonious meetings in the future. Oh for the life of Community Service!"[96]

The group finally agreed to move forward with a large community-wide
meeting, and the South Central Association (SCA) was launched in July
1944. The Association announced as its mandate: "To improve the living
conditions of the Negro. . . . To . . . appeal . . . to all employers to elimi-
nat[e] policies of racial discrimination. . . . To improve the standard of business ethics in the Community." This last the Association promised to do,
with unintentional ominousness, either through education "—or, if necessary, through . . . elimination of the violators." SCA challenged explanations given by employers who refused to hire African Americans and initiated "a program to encourage the efficiency, punctuality, competency and
regularity of Negro workers on the job." In an evaluation of black-Jewish
tensions in Chicago in 1947, Berland reported "the pressure has been somewhat relaxed. Of course, there is room for much improvement."[97]

A letter a year later suggested the magnitude of the improvement that
had occurred. Harry Englestein, a founder of the SCA and owner of
South Central Department Store, 99 percent of whose clerical staff and
several of whose store executives were black, received an award from
the Mayor's Commission on Human Relations for improving intergroup
relations. "It has not always been so," noted Berland. "In total candor
it must be said that in the past the gentleman's practices and views are
alleged to have been responsible for engendering a certain amount of
friction and misunderstanding." [98]

Certainly neither Jewish racism nor black willingness to identify Jewish
business owners' religion ended in Chicago. A 1949 ADL memo warned
that "The major activity of the [South Central] Association seemed to be
a cover-up for some of the unethical practices of some of the merchant
members."[99] The *Chicago Defender* published a letter to the editor in July
1952 criticizing the ADL and its parent organization, B'nai B'rith, "the
members of which talk about civil rights and yet sell run-down buildings
to Negroes." When the ADL objected, Mr. Browning, executive assistant
to the publisher, made it clear "that he was suppressing many complaints
he received regarding the practice of Jewish merchants on the South side."
Nevertheless, while such complaints continued to surface periodically,
they did so with far lower frequency following the organization of the
SCA and similar efforts. These programs had improved black attitudes
toward Jews.[100]

In New York, at the NAACP's suggestion, the AJC organized a series of autumn 1939 meetings between black and Jewish editors, publishers, and political leaders. The first formal meeting on September 26 called for "Negro and Jewish editors" to discuss how African American agencies could help challenge negative views of Jews. Carl Murphy of the Baltimore *Afro-American*, Robert Vann of the *Courier*, Earl Brown of the *Amsterdam News*, Ted Poston of the *New York Post*, L. Fogelman of the *Forward*, Hy Wishengrad and L. Schuster of the Jewish Telegraphic Agency, and S. Dingol and A. Glantz of the *Day*, along with Walter Mendelsohn, Newman Levy, Sidney Wallach, and Norman Belth of the AJC; Hubert Delany; Lester Granger; Thurgood Marshall; White; George Murphy; Elmer Carter; and Judge Myles Paige, attended.[101]

George Murphy advised White in advance of the meeting that "unless people who attend this conference are going to get down to the root of the problem, which is economic, the results of the conference are going to be nil." They did; the meeting quickly turned into a discussion about exploitative business practices, and several proposals emerged. "Educate Jewish agents and owners to deal fairly with tenant groups," Murphy suggested. "Jewish housewives will have to learn that if they cannot afford to employ Negro help except at exploitation wages, then they will have to do their own work." He also urged the Jewish press to "do special features on the Negro in American life . . . [and] write articles on the cooperative leadership of Jewish and Negro people in helping to develop the early history of our country. Develop the idea that all minorities have a common fighting ground." Thurgood Marshall suggested that "it would be wise to include an article on the stores owned by Jews in Harlem and the practice of short-changing Negroes and other practices whereby Negroes get the attitude that Jewish merchants are not to be trusted." The *Forward* and the *Day* agreed to do a series of articles, according to an NAACP press release, "with a view to making the Jewish population as a whole understand that Anti-Semitism is not native with the Negro, but an outgrowth of bitterly revolting economic conditions. . . . Jewish People must see the similarity of their plight to that of the Negro and treat the Negro citizen with the understanding that a similarly persecuted minority can well afford to display."[102] Here is explicit expression of African Americans' higher expectations of Jews, and their conviction that the roots of black anti-Semitism lay in Jewish practices and in Jews' unwillingness to see African American issues as identical to their own.

The *Day* obliged. Its article on the Bronx "Slave Market" described "a picture which will bring you right back to the horrible days of 'Uncle Tom's Cabin.'" After describing the black women who stand on street corners waiting for domestic work, scrutinized and poked by would-be employers, the article concluded: "And to our shame, be it said, that Jewish women too come to buy the labor of dark slaves. . . . Daughters of a people who were the first to raise their voice against slavery because they more than others knew what slavery meant, help this trade in slave-labor." Meanwhile, the Jewish press ran stories stressing common bonds. A 1939 article in the *Forward* argued, "The Jews, more than any other group, sympathize with the suppressed black race because the Jews themselves are feeling the bitter taste of racial persecution. . . . Therefore, we should . . . treat them [Negroes] with particular consideration."[103]

The AJC proposed a further solution to the problem of Jewish business exploitation: a survey of all Harlem stores, preferably under the leadership of the NAACP. Those stores with quality merchandise, good customer relations, and black employees would receive a "seal of approval." Customers would be then urged to buy only in those stores. Meanwhile a black and Jewish "committee on employment" would put "pressure on Harlem merchants to give additional employment to negroes [*sic*]" and another "will bring pressure on real estate owners to improve conditions." But nothing came of this suggestion, or similar proposals made by the ADL. The latter's Committee on Inter-Racial Relations (CIRR) concluded in 1943 that "quite a few interfaith groups have formed, had meetings and passed resolutions and recommendations, but as yet none have had a tangible concrete program."[104]

There was, however, real movement on the problem of the Bronx slave market. Acknowledging in 1940 that "there is this exploitation and . . . much of it is done by Jewish women," the ADL supported a local improvement committee organized by Rabbi Jerome Rosenbloom of Tremont Temple, to "remove a condition which is certainly no credit to our people," and announced "a program of education among our Jewish women in order to attack the evil from that angle." Rabbi Simon Kramer, for example, wrote to his congregants that while "We cannot conceive of any Jewish housewife being guilty of such practices," nevertheless, "I am asking you to be very careful in your treatment of these part time colored houseworkers. . . . [B]e . . . considerate of the reputation of the Jewish community and the rights of human beings to fair and honorable treatment."[105]

Both the ADL and AJC also proposed replacing street-corner hiring with job centers that would ensure fair wages. Leonard Finder thought the center should operate "under Jewish auspices so that the colored people would . . . understand that a Jewish group is trying to be friendly" but others at the planning meeting feared a public Jewish presence and preferred an interfaith group. Two offices, advertising themselves in both English and Yiddish, opened in 1941 under the auspices of a Committee on Street Corner Markets. Officially, they were supported by the NAACP,

Domestic Workers' Union, the New York and Brooklyn ULs, Harlem's YWCA, and the Women's Trade Union League.[106]

This again highlights the complexity of assessing Jewish responses to black complaints. Organized Jewry may have reacted because they heard criticism of individual Jews as anti-Semitism, but the fact remains that they did respond, and they based their response largely on that shared sense of being a "similarly persecuted minority" that the NAACP had described. At the same time, the sharp differences between the views of Jewish leaders and at least one portion of their constituency are also laid bare.

On August 1, 1943, Harlem erupted into riot, the second in less than a decade. The ADL conducted a study to evaluate its causes. It found "no anti-semitic [sic] angle" but did insist, "There is no doubt, whatsoever, that there is a definitive feeling amongst the negroes [sic] of Harlem, and this is true of the negroes in other parts of new York, as well as in other cities of the United States, that they are oppressed by the whites." The survey concluded: "*Absence of acute race hatred* was indicated by the fact that there was no continuance of rioting after the first wave of excitement." Still, "*Underlying conditions* . . . must also be primarily blamed" including poor employment opportunities and living standards.[107]

Following the riot the ADL's CIRR met more frequently and decided on several approaches: seek the "cooperation of Negro leaders" and organizations, provide speakers and articles sympathetic to Jews for black audiences and newspapers, establish a "nonsectarian" committee to hear consumer complaints, and confront Jewish merchants directly regarding their behavior. The League had added an action component to its traditional rhetorical and defensive strategies.[108]

Eugene Holmes and Mordecai Johnson of Howard University, both public critics of black anti-Semitism, agreed to help provide speakers and editorials. Again concerned that a Jewish group not be the visible sponsor, the CIRR agreed to route all articles designated for the black press through the Institute for American Democracy, a non-Jewish group under ADL auspices that produced tolerance and prodemocracy materials.[109]

The Committee also held several meetings with the (Jewish) Harlem Merchants Association (HMA). As in Chicago, the Jewish merchants did not see eye to eye with the ADL, and progress was torturously slow. Interviewed by the ADL just before and after the riots, Harlem Jewish businessmen offered a wide range of views about the situation. Some acknowledged the legitimacy of black complaints. Others took refuge in arguing that "abuses of white merchants are not confined to persons of the Jewish faith." A few denied any basis for the complaints at all. Mr. Hamburger, a thirty-eight-year resident of Harlem and owner of an Army-Navy store there, complained that "the Negroes are a bad lot up here, stealing right and left. They have all the privileges they want—in fact too many" and had more money than he did.[110]

But the best example of the range of feelings comes from an unguarded moment captured in the transcript of a meeting with the HMA called by the CIRR in December 1943. With abundant generalizing, participants expressed views from racism to nationalism to enlightened self-interest.[111]

Store owner Eli Lazar began the meeting by acknowledging, "There's plenty of room for improvement among the merchants of Harlem," but Harry Schwartz demurred: "Most of the faults were forced upon us. . . . Negroes wouldn't go into a business if they couldn't steal from us." Lazar conceded, "There is shoplifting from some elements. But why is it so difficult for a person in many stores in Harlem to return an article for a refund?" Joseph Greif, another owner, answered, "Stuff not bought in my store is returned and they raise hell if I won't accept it. They steal it in the next store and return it in my store." All denied the accusation that they provided inferior merchandise, although Joseph Eschelbacher admitted, "Inferior goods have to be moved." He gave up his Harlem business for that reason: "[I] couldn't compete in a legitimate way. . . . People [in Harlem] came in with five cents, seven or ten cents. In order to give them something you had to have cheaper merchandise."

This was not about race but class. "You don't only have it in Harlem," he explained. "People feel that because they are poor people they are more mistreated." Harry Schwartz agreed. "It's not our fault but the people themselves. The moment you give them a good job they move out of Harlem—don't stick with their own kind." Greif demanded an investigation of both black and white merchants. "Colored merchants are up in Harlem too, but nothing is said about them."

When asked if Jews could do anything about these problems, Lazar acknowledged, "we must . . . give them a square deal every time," but Schwartz insisted, "The solution is education of the Negro. . . . A landlord in Harlem has to charge more rent because he can't get responsible tenants. They break the walls, etc." Greif took a different tack. "If they want to buy something, they can buy it or not. . . . If I overcharge they don't have to pay it." Admitting the long history of such practices, he observed, "I always did this. Lately, though, it was, [']you Jew.[']" Eschelbacher interrupted the speakers several times to insist, as several black nationalists already had, that the only solution was to "get the hell out of Harlem. Leave Harlem to Harlem."

William Sachs explained the CIRR's idea of a code of business ethics to be endorsed and posted by store owners. He asked, "Will it be worthwhile for us as Jews to do this?" Schwartz scoffed, "[I]t can't be done. . . . The stories that you hear are not authentic." They did agree to a policing system of some sort for all merchants, so long as it did not come from the HMA. "They know us too well," explained Eschelbacher. The group instead suggested the Uptown Chamber of Commerce, which included non-Jewish merchants as well. Sachs replied, "Uptown Chamber of Commerce is not interested in these problems. We have our own problem because we are Jews." While any business might conduct itself unethically, generally only Jews would be criticized for it, and therefore only the Jews felt concerned enough to mobilize against it. Ultimately, all present agreed to some form of "self-policing." After a similar meeting, the (Jewish) Associated Grocers of Harlem, Inc. agreed to abide by wartime price ceilings and to support a "non-sectarian interfaith program" (i.e., not just black-Jewish) to reduce tensions and promote interracial understanding.

Meanwhile, the CIRR began to pursue the establishment of a "non-sectarian complaint office" in Harlem to adjudicate disputes and a "non-sectarian committee on inter-racial relations." ADL's earlier objections had rested not on the importance of such offices, but on their being a solely black and Jewish endeavor. Until the riot, however, no non-Jewish groups had agreed to participate. That fall finally saw a series of planning meetings, and in November an interfaith group gathered to create a complaint bureau. Among the black participants were Judge Hubert Delany, the Reverends John Johnson and Shelton Hale Bishop, and Dr. Channing Tobias of the YMCA. White Christians included Protestant and Catholic clergy.[112]

At the December 2 meeting of the CIRR, however, Martin Frank raised an objection to the proposed bureau. As the minutes related, he feared it "might be very harmful to us. He said that the Jews are being accused of sharp practices ... in Harlem. ... [I]f this complaint bureau received many complaints against Jews, we would be substantiating the case against the Jew and bringing this factual information to an interfaith and interracial committee, and if it wanted to, it could make capital of the facts that the Jew is guilty of all these practices." This proved so persuasive that "it was decided to discontinue our efforts to establish such a complaint bureau." Instead, the Committee asked the Better Business Bureau to develop a plan to "raise the business standards of [all] the merchants in Harlem." William Sachs approached the Bureau's Mr. Kenner but, still concerned that this might provide fuel for anti-Semites, the Committee directed Sachs not to tell Kenner that the proposal came from the ADL. Receiving a positive answer, the CIRR set up a meeting between the Bureau and several Jewish businessmen.[113]

At that meeting Sachs explained that Harlem merchants "are losing the confidence of the residents." He "stated that the merchants ... were not without fault because ... they have overcharged their customers, sold them shoddy merchandise, taken advantage of them on credit transactions and have treated them unfairly in other respects." Kenner proposed establishing a local office on an experimental basis, reminding everyone that "it would have to function through the use of moral suasion and appeals to the common sense and sound business instincts of the merchant. . . . [A]ny effort at coercion would undoubtedly result in failure." While "he did not believe it practicable to have a colored person as head of the branch . . . he believed it should be practicable to employ colored persons in clerical capacities." Even within these limits the group was skeptical, although it agreed to explore the feasibility of opening a Harlem office. Either the office never materialized or it proved ineffective, since the ADL considered later proposals by the Uptown Chamber of Commerce to try something similar.[114]

The CIRR and AJC continued working on the "Harlem situation" for several more years, on their own and through the Mayor's Committee on Unity. In 1946 the ADL added business ethics to its "Internal Jewish Education Program." Finally, in June 1948 the ADL reported that "the Harlem situation has become academic" when the Mayor's Committee on Unity, local merchants, and several black groups agreed to establish a complaints office in the YMCA. Since there was no further discussion of these issues in agency files, black-Jewish tensions seem to have abated, perhaps in part because many Jewish businessmen whose fortunes had improved left Harlem after the war. And like Englestein in Chicago, New York had its own figure of transformation: Jack Blumstein, owner of Blumstein's Department Store on 125th Street. Target of the first "Don't Buy Where You Can't Work" picket line demanding jobs for black residents, he later served as ADL's representative in negotiations with other businessmen, and in 1949 was the only white person featured in an *Amsterdam News* editorial praising ten Harlem leaders. "THEY'RE TOPS" read the photo caption.[115]

Despite the broad sweep of the problems made apparent by the 1943 riot, it was primarily Jewish groups who responded with action in Harlem. While the ADL had held meetings with non-Jewish as well as Jewish business organizations, only those with Jewish merchants made any progress. However limited were Jewish steps to improve conditions, they were more substantial than anything attempted by white Christian groups there. And the willingness of prominent African Americans to work on this intractable problem demonstrates their commitment not only to improving conditions for black people, but also to strengthening the political ties between the two communities.[116]

These early black-Jewish efforts are significant also for their personal dimension. Jewish leaders often held interracial meetings at their homes, and entertained black leaders and occasionally their spouses at cocktail parties, meals, and similar affairs. The AJC's initial planning meeting for the 1939 gathering of black and Jewish editors, attended by Walter Mendelsohn of the AJC, White, William Hastie, and others, was held in New-man Levy's home. Mendelsohn hosted the December meeting at his apart-ment. Beth Siegel of the AJCongress Women's Division enclosed her home address and telephone number in a 1941 letter to Mary McLeod Bethune, adding, "If you expect to be in New York, it would be splendid to have you at our home for dinner." Lawrence Goldsmith hosted a cocktail party for the ADL's interracial "interfaith group" on Harlem at his home.[117] These personal relationships between black and Jewish leaders extended beyond formal political structures, and helped cement previously purely professional relations. It also suggests how far Jewish leaders had come from their reluctance to create strong black-Jewish connections.

As a result of these wartime programs, based on self-interest on both sides, an institutional dialogue began between the two communities that later broadened into a substantial collaboration on a broad range of civil rights issues. This period of approach and avoidance, suspicion and sym-pathy, tension and resolution, reflected the ambivalence of both blacks and Jews about each other and about making common cause. Jewish rac-ism and black anti-Semitism, combined with relatively weak power bases, pressing external concerns, and doubts about the efficacy of alliances, limited black-Jewish coalition building. But a new sense of the imperative to develop allies, and the growing visibility of black and Jewish civil rights organizations in an era of sympathy for pluralism and distaste for overt and violent bigotry, created the possibility for mutual action and mutual aid. The civic landscape was shifting around them, as progressive Chris-tian, labor, ethnic, and civic groups came to recognize the necessity of achieving civil equality. New conditions brought new approaches to old questions, and both blacks and Jews, while still prioritizing protection of their own, began to understand the importance of both challenging their own prejudices and strengthening the hand of other disenfranchised mi-norities. This would blossom into a partnership so compelling and effec-tive that it has been dubbed "the golden age" of black-Jewish relations. It is to that moment we now turn.

CHAPTER FOUR

And Why Not Every Man?

In 1945 the American Jewish Congress established its Commission on Law and Social Action (CLSA) to "combat anti-Semitic violence, defamation and discrimination" and to "fight every manifestation of racism and ... promote the civil and political equality of all minorities in America." The two commitments were linked because, in the words of its chairman, Shad Polier, "we view the fight for equality as indivisible and as part of the general struggle to protect democracy." The CLSA's methods promised make those ideals concrete. It intended to mobilize "the Jewish community as a whole" against all forms of legal and economic discrimination through legislation, court action, and public advocacy "in order that promises made, whether in constitution, statutes, judicial, administrative or executive decision, shall not become empty words." Not that older methods of community education were jettisoned—although CLSA generally disdained them—rather they were supplemented by this more activist, more structural, more public approach.[1] In all this, CLSA stands for the whole; the principles of community involvement, the indivisibility of equal rights, and the necessity for legal and political action to advance the promise of American democracy underlay the postwar civil rights efforts of liberal black and Jewish agencies alike and encouraged the creation of coalitions as a potent means of achieving their goals.

The postwar civil rights movement, sometimes referred to as the "golden age" of black-Jewish relations, was a product of its time. This was a cold war liberal attempt to end discrimination based on race or religion using the institutions of civil society: courts, legislatures, media, public schools, and voluntary organizations. These activists were convinced that a democracy could rectify inequality without jeopardizing basic social structures and assumptions, and that building broad-based coalitions offered the best hope for success. This chapter begins by examining the liberal political context of these civil rights efforts. It then explores how black and Jewish agencies, nationally and locally, separately and in coalition, maneuvered in legislative, legal, and educational arenas to pursue their wide-ranging concerns about the political process, employment, education, housing, racial violence, and social discrimination. But the trust thus built could not always overcome the disruptions produced by longstanding tensions and increasingly divergent perspectives. Many studies have examined sites of black-Jewish engagement in fascinating detail;[2] the hope of this more episodic exploration is to illuminate the often messy complexity of black-Jewish political relationships in this era of burgeoning civil rights activity.

Coalition Building in Political Context

Both the recent past and the realities of the postwar world shaped this civil rights movement. The New Deal and World War II strengthened a liberal vision of individual equality of opportunity as the proper goal for a democracy, with full integration as its civic expression. Both Nazism and Stalinism generated widespread suspicion of radicalism on the one hand and parochial nationalism on the other; only liberal organizations could gain any meaningful traction in such a climate.[3]

Among African Americans, liberalism exerted a particularly strong pull. The nationalism of Garvey had lost much of its luster. The inroads leftists and liberals had already made against segregation and racial inequality, however small, alongside a cold war skepticism about communism, led many to conclude that liberal integrationism was the most fruitful approach to the achievement of civil rights, a view expressed again and again in the pages of the NAACP's *Crisis* magazine. NUL director Lester Granger suggested to Howard University graduates that their special task was to "strengthen and broaden a spirit of goodwill between the races." While "complete disregard of . . . special group interests . . . would be too much to hope for at this stage," he urged unstinting cooperation on all issues of mutual benefit. This interconnectedness of minority concerns was not only an effective political strategy, it was an ethical imperative. "Learn to think as Americans and as Negroes secondarily," Granger urged, "but primarily as alert, humane and broadly intelligent members of the human race."[4]

Sometimes African American calls for integration sounded very much like assimilation. Sociologist E. Franklin Frazier found it "not strange that the Negro minority belongs among the assimilationist . . . minorities. It is seldom that one finds Negroes who think of themselves as possessing a different culture from whites." Nevertheless, most black leaders recognized that, at least for the foreseeable future, blacks constituted a distinct community worthy of respect.[5]

For Jews, appreciation of their security in the United States, and Stalin's increasingly open and violent anti-Semitism, kept communism from winning substantial support. At the same time, while Zionism remained a rallying cry, recognition of their minority status pressed most Jews toward liberalism and coalition rather than a more insular nationalism. As Polier put it, "With good cause, the maxim, *Juif, donc libéral*—a Jew, therefore, of course, a liberal—has been at once an accurate description and the motto of the most enlightened circles of world Jewry."[6]

Generational change in Jewish community leadership strengthened these perspectives; the older, German elite were yielding to a younger group whose roots in eastern European Jewry, poverty, and leftist politics made them both more activist and more universalist. What had not changed was their commitment to assimilationist pluralism, even as they understood that substantial barriers remained to Jewish advancement. A 1944 internal ADL debate, for example, pitted those who insisted that the "Jew . . . is not a member of any ethnic group" against those who considered that view a goal but not yet a reality. Both sides agreed that the "ultimate solution" was full assimilation.[7]

Liberal black and Jewish groups were not only in the ascendancy politically; after the war they were also in a strong position to pursue their goals. Increased attention to the plight of the Nazis' victims, wartime antiracist rhetoric, accumulated legislative and legal victories, and the improving social and economic position of Jews and blacks in the United States won their liberal organizations more adherents, greater financial support, and more prestige. This in turn enabled them to expand their agendas. Meanwhile the issues raised by the war encouraged an expansion of sites for liberal action. ADL national director Benjamin Epstein explained. "As an outgrowth of its extensive war program, ADL horizons were broadened . . . [to embrace] legal action and concern for the protection of the rights of all minorities. This program has generally been acclaimed."[8]

The war had also brought a renewed sense of urgency to the struggle for minority rights, and the need to move beyond rhetoric to action. A 1944 Urban League pamphlet directed at black and white clergy insisted that they must "do more than urge Negroes, Jews, and other racial minorities to be patient. They must urge that all of us . . . [act] for justice, democracy, and brotherhood. The time is ripe now to equalize educational and work opportunities; to administer justice in the courts; to give the ballot equally to all citizens."[9] The AJC committed itself to the "*Defense of Constitutionally Guaranteed Rights*" including security against lynching, protection of voting, and dismantling of segregation laws, and "*Equalization of Citizenship*"; that is, social and economic justice issues such as fair employment practices and equal access to public accommodations and education. Its monthly *Commentary* magazine became a central forum for liberal discussions of civil rights.[10]

Issues of race and racism had also become more public. The European holocaust reinforced the (at least rhetorical) commitment to a heterogeneous, pluralist society. The substantial wartime black migration north and into labor unions, particularly the CIO, advanced black interests as well. So did President Truman's engagement, especially the 1947 landmark report of his Committee on Civil Rights, "To Secure These Rights," which identified lynching; segregation; the poll tax; debt peonage; and inadequate education, health, and housing as failures of American democracy. Its scathing exposé of discrimination's effects and its powerful recommendations for sweeping reform galvanized liberal activists of all races and religions.

All this brought postwar legislative and political victories, including a strong civil rights plank in the 1948 Democratic Party platform, the desegregation of the armed forces in 1950, and several pivotal Supreme Court cases (thanks to a more liberal Court) including the most famous, *Brown v. Board of Education*, which in 1954 definitively overturned the "separate but equal" doctrine upon which segregation laws rested. Increasing public action by local black communities, such as the Baton Rouge bus boycott in 1953 and the Montgomery bus boycott in 1955–56, not only emerged from this new attention paid to race, but helped move those issues still closer to the center of national attention.

The process of building a liberal political partnership was further aided, ironically, by the cold war. Many communists had already quit the Party in the late 1930s after learning of Stalin's purges; more followed with each new example of Soviet repression. Anticommunist witch hunts further depleted the CP's ranks. Some, disillusioned, withdrew from political activity. But many joined more mainstream groups like the AJCongress and the NAACP and pushed them leftward. The impact of the cold war cut both ways. Liberal agencies limited their activities and strategies so as not to be branded communists themselves and generally shunned all leftist groups (subjects explored in the next chapter). Nevertheless, both the activism of disillusioned communists who embraced liberal organizations and the government's desire to lessen the contradiction between the cold war rhetoric about American democracy and the reality of racial discrimination provided civil rights with an opportunity and an energy that might not otherwise have been present.[11]

For liberal and progressive black and Jewish leaders, previous positive experiences of cooperation that created greater familiarity and sympathy fostered coalition as well. They helped convince both communities that civil rights issues were interconnected and that safeguarding the rights of others strengthened one's own security. This encouraged both black and Jewish groups to expand their collaboration to embrace issues of only indirect interest to themselves.

It was in the postwar period, then, that a black-Jewish political relationship solidified within the broader context of an activist liberalism, and its contours reflect its time. While hardly the "natural" or seamless "alliance" posited by nostalgists who describe a golden age of black-Jewish relations, it was nevertheless a relationship remarkable for its scope, its successes, its reciprocity, and (perhaps) its optimistic naivete. The number of issues black and Jewish organizations tackled together; the distance beyond direct self-interest many traveled to make such commitments; their willingness to take the battle into the courts, the press, the legislatures, and the private sector; their conviction that democratic institutions and people's hearts could be moved to do right; and the widespread support in both communities for their shared goals were both notable and unprecedented. No other ethnic or racial groups formed such a wide-ranging and successful collaborative working relationship. That it did not last and that it was threatened repeatedly by ongoing religious, racial, and class tensions only suggest the power of the coalition and the commitment of participants to endure despite daunting obstacles. If the war years marked the start of a sense of common cause among black and Jewish leaders, the next two decades saw not only a deepening of that feeling but also an expansion of it from elites to their communities more broadly. And central to these developments were black and Jewish liberal and non-communist leftist intellectuals like Hannah Arendt, James Baldwin, Daniel Bell, Rayford Logan, Sidney Hook, Irving Howe, and Lionel Trilling, whose public musings over both ideology and tactics profoundly shaped the contours of the postwar civil rights movement.[12]

Nevertheless, the limitations of black-Jewish collaboration were real, and mutual commitment not as universal as nostalgists suppose. This is in part because racial and class differences continued to keep most Jews and blacks separated even as they made common cause politically. On the one hand, Jews as a group committed themselves to the cause of black equality more fully and for a longer time than any other white community. On the other hand, most Jews were white people and held white people's attitudes to a greater or lesser extent. That meant not only a certain amount of Jewish racism, but also an unwillingness to dismantle existing social structures that conferred special benefits on those with white skin, whether they recognized those benefits or not. This problem was compounded by differences in class status, determined in large measure by race.

The other factor limiting black-Jewish cooperation was the nature of postwar liberalism itself, something largely beyond these actors' control. The Depression and war had recast liberalism. Still focused on the rights and obligations of individuals, not groups, liberalism now acknowledged the state's role in guaranteeing equal opportunity for those individuals. Yet given the communist threat from the left and conservative antistatism on the right, the majority of liberals sought "the vital center," moderating their calls for government to provide full opportunity and immediate equality. This limited both their strategic options and their success in challenging the structures perpetuating inequality.

Additionally, because democratic liberalism depends on majority support, most liberals tried to sidestep divisive and controversial issues for fear of alienating any crucial bloc within the Democratic coalition. In the United States, race is one such divisive issue, and the unwillingness of liberalism (or, more properly, of liberals) to confront it directly ultimately weakened the black commitment to coalitions with liberal whites or Jews. As George Johnson, dean of the Howard Law School, observed in 1949, "It takes an overwhelming majority to change the status quo." The failure to pass civil rights legislation resulted largely from "the failure on the part of those interested in [it] to . . . realize that legislators are only going to do those things that they think their failure to do will result in political suicide." Civil rights activists, he contended, have offered "no sustained demonstration of interest" that would compel such a conclusion.[13]

This unwillingness to press beyond consensus severely constrained liberals' conception of civil rights. Integration in such a context meant integrating nonwhites into social, economic, and political structures whose rules had already been established by whites. Further, whites retained the power to control those structures. As for the postwar liberal conception of the pluralist ideal, historian Kenneth Stampp articulated it in his paradigm-shifting book on slavery, *The Peculiar Institution*: "Negroes *are*, after all, only white men with black skins, nothing more, nothing less."[14] Such assumptions were noble, and crucial for the advancement of black equality in an era of open racism. But they limited black expression and narrowed the channels of legitimate black aspiration. In time, many black activists would chafe under such constraints.

Pragmatic Universalism

Liberals, in their turn, recognized that even their moderate goals enjoyed only limited purchase. They sought to strengthen their case by linking it to the politically popular rhetoric of democracy. "The power of one man to deprive another of a livelihood because of his race, religion or national origin is indeed a profound injustice," insisted the NCJW in 1942. "But . . . more than that, it is a blatant denial of the most basic principles of American democracy." Such necessarily universalist appeals proved a potent mobilizing tool, and virtually all calls for antidiscrimination legislation employed it.[15]

Certainly, these appeals were grounded in deeply moral language. "Respect for the civil rights of all men is each man's duty to God," proclaimed the Central Conference of American Rabbis' Commission on Justice and

Peace (CJP) at the conclusion of a 1948 conference on Judaism and Race Equality. "Either the Church must be actually and potentially a Church for all the people, irrespective of race and color, or it should cease to proclaim the doctrine of fatherhood of God and the brotherhood of man," the NUL insisted.[16]

Still, every religion contains such calls to ethical action. Black and Jewish groups heeded them because they corresponded with their interpretation of self-interest. This was a pragmatic universalism based on the moral lessons of the holocaust and the successes of domestic wartime coalitions. As Louis Ruchames, director of the Hillel Foundations of Western Massachusetts explained, "the lesson that . . . the rights of all men are interrelated, that no minority group is safe while others are the victims of persecution, has been seared into our minds and hearts through the burning flesh of six million of our brethren."[17]

In other words, concern for others *was* self-interest. One by one, black and Jewish agencies came to the same conclusion. "The Negro has to be ever mindful that as much as the Jew may be hated in America, . . . when it comes to real oppression, the Negro is going to be in the forefront of the Jews, . . . and he knows it," Hubert Delany reflected. "We know that we are going into the Harlem River one step ahead of you."[18]

Perhaps the most comprehensive argument for universalism, stressing both its moral and its practical dimensions, came from Isaac Toubin, associate director of the AJCongress. "The harsh truth is that left to ourselves, we can accomplish nothing; joined with others we can and have achieved significant results," he observed. "We must be concerned with safeguarding the democratic process as the best way to preserve our integrity and our identity as Jews. But democracy frequently ceases . . . at the boundaries of race, color and creed. It is not always the same race, color or creed that is subjected to abuse, but this abuse, no matter what its target, always poses the identical threat to the achievement of a peaceful and just communal life." So protecting Jewish interests required "fighting on dozens of fronts to establish and safeguard the rights of all groups in America wherever those rights are curtailed." [19]

Jewish groups pointed to strong ties between anti-Semites and racists. A 1954 ADL report on white supremacist groups noted the *American Nationalist* headline, "South Indignant as Jew-Led NAACP Wins School Segregation Case." Jews also recognized the centrality of civil rights for liberalism. As Alex Miller, director of the ADL's Southeastern Regional Office, presciently argued in 1945, moral questions aside, "What I am concerned with, if I am correct in analyzing the forthcoming struggle in the south, is that if the Jewish community . . . adopts a reactionary and prejudiced attitude toward the Negro, they may lose their liberal allies while not gaining any help from the other group."[20]

African American groups also understood universalism to be in their self-interest. While most who study black-Jewish coalitions focus on Jewish contributions to black civil rights, groups like the NAACP also made substantial contributions to Jewish and other causes not directly relevant to African Americans. As they had during the war, black leaders from Randolph and White to Adam Clayton Powell Jr. and Paul Robeson advocated for Jewish interests and for a Jewish state. African American soldiers like Leon Bass and Timuel Black who had seen the death camps firsthand spoke out about the importance of equal treatment and the dangers of bigotry. "The day that I walked through the . . . gates of Buchenwald and I saw what I saw . . . made me know that human life is sacred," Bass reflected. "Segregation, racism, can lead to the ultimate, to what I saw."[21]

The NAACP lobbied Haitian, Liberian, and Filipino UN delegates in 1947 to give "thoughtful consideration of implications affecting minorities everywhere" and support the creation of a Jewish state. Following the positive UN vote, CLSA director Will Maslow wrote Walter White a letter of thanks, convinced that "Haiti's shift was the direct result of your efforts." In January 1948 the NAACP's *Crisis* hailed the appointment of African American scholar and diplomat Ralph Bunche to head the UN Commission charged with setting up the fledgling Jewish state. "The salutations and good wishes of his fellow Americans go with him to the Near East," the editors commented. Yet so vehement was W.E.B. Du Bois on the necessity of a secure Jewish homeland that only one year later he lambasted Bunche as insufficiently concerned with Jewish interests. Jews continued to hail Bunche as a hero, and he received a Nobel Prize for his skillful negotiating. But the point here is the conviction of both liberals and radicals in the black community that Jews, like other vulnerable minorities, needed protection and support.[22]

Black groups also supported bills aiding Jewish refugees. In 1952 the NAACP's Youth Secretary helped organize a coalition of "youth and youth serving organizations" to fight the McCarran-Walter immigration bill, which "is biased against Jewish and Negro migrants." Its initial participants included no Jewish groups.[23]

Black organizations that supported these primarily Jewish causes did so for the same mix of altruistic and self-interested reasons that brought Jews to black civil rights. The NAACP supported minority freedom movements; both refugee policy and Israel fell clearly into that category. From the UN's founding, African Americans, along with colleagues from around the world, struggled to put issues of race, colonialism, and self-determination at the forefront of its agenda. As White wrote in reply to Maslow's letter of thanks, "If what I did was effective, it was not for Jews alone but for all human beings."[24]

This sense of the universality of civil rights and of coalitions' potential for success led many black and Jewish leaders to seek out as many partners as possible. "Up to now we haven't sought and organized sufficient support from people who fundamentally share our aims," lamented A. Philip Randolph. That included "all the people who are tagged with hoary stereotypes and plagued with discrimination." The CCAR urged in the pursuit of civil rights "a broadening of vision, which will include Mexican-Americans and Orientals along with Negroes as human beings created in the image of God and therefore entitled to full equality."[25]

Outreach efforts were not only idealistic but practical. David Robinson of ADL's Western Regional office was a member of a "little group of Catholic white men which has been meeting with Negro men and women" in Portland, Oregon, organized during the war by Reverend Thomas Tobin. When a black member observed that his community had been the primary beneficiary of the committee's efforts, Tobin demurred. As Robinson paraphrased it, Tobin replied, "'Don't be too sure that the sole benefits will come to you colored folks. It happens that every person present here this evening is either a Catholic, a Negro or a Jew. After this war we expect lots of trouble. A scapegoat will be sought. Whenever they start looking for scapegoats invariably they pick on Catholics, Negroes and Jews." As Robinson mused, "There are some 25 million Catholics . . . and about 13 million colored people and we constitute 5 or 6 million. Well integrated such a group can do something."[26]

The recognition of such connections led these organizations to suddenly, if belatedly, discover the link between the wartime incarceration of Japanese Americans and more general racism. Roy Wilkins of the NAACP, George Schuyler of the *Courier*, Fred Hoshiyama of the JACL, Sam Bloch, and Norman Thomas spoke at a 1944 mass meeting in New York City protesting Mayor LaGuardia's objection to settling relocated Japanese Americans there. In their strongly worded telegram they noted, "IT IS NOW KNOWN . . . THAT THE SOLE BASIS FOR THE CONCENTRATION CAMPS WAS THE COLOR OF THESE AMERICANS." Since Italian and German nationals were not barred, "SURELY THE MAYOR . . . [DOES NOT] ADVOCATE DIFFERENTIAL TREATMENT FOR LOYAL AMERICAN CITIZENS WHO HAPPEN NOT TO BE WHITE." At a 1945 conference in San Francisco to plan for the return of the evacuees, black, Filipino, and Korean organizations agreed that "any attempt to make capital for their own racial groups at the expense of the Japanese would be sawing off limbs on which they themselves sat." The NAACP helped California evacuees upon their return and supported legal efforts on their behalf. After the war black and Jewish agencies engaged in cooperative efforts with the JACL on various civil rights and civil liberties issues.[27]

Most postwar civil rights coalitions, both local and national, included some combination of liberal religious, women's, political, and labor organizations alongside those of blacks and Jews. Less well-organized and generally poorly funded, Mexican American, Japanese American, and other groups participated occasionally as well. "We must . . . recognize that the Jewish, the Negro, the Chinese, and all other racial problems are part of a whole, and as that whole is affected, so are we," argued Larry Tajiri, editor of the JACL's *Pacific Citizen*. In fact contemporary Jewish leaders rarely spoke of "black-Jewish relations." Rather, the reverse: they stressed the multifaith, multiethnic, broadly democratic nature of the coalitions they joined. This, of course, legitimated the cause and increased its likelihood of success. It also lessened the possibility, much feared by Jewish leaders, that a singularly black-Jewish partnership would, in the words of Alex Miller, "burden . . . the Jewish community with some of the same handicaps which the Negroes face" without advancing black interests substantially.[28]

Still, given their special interest and historical experience, it was African Americans and Jewish Americans who dedicated their efforts most energetically and persistently to such activities. Arnold Aronson of NCRAC and Walter White of the NAACP jointly headed the Leadership Conference on Civil Rights, the most significant civil rights coalition of the era. The NAACP and AJCongress jointly produced *Civil Rights in the United States: A Balance Sheet on Race Relations*, annual volumes on the progress of civil rights. And it was these two communities that forged a conception of equality and liberty that went beyond particularist claims toward a more universal vision of justice. "From our faith, our knowledge, our experience, we bring a deep conviction and a full determination to strengthen . . . the democratic ideal," promised Justine Wise Polier, head of the AJCongress Women's Division. "In this struggle we shall join with those who are dedicated to breaking down all barriers of discrimination and prejudice, so that the frontiers of our American democracy shall be enlarged to encompass all our citizens."[29]

The Contours of Postwar Liberalism

This was a deeply liberal political vision. Its proponents believed the state had a responsibility to protect and advance individual rights. As Shad Polier explained in 1949, "our problem is to strike down the barriers that already exist in law . . . where the Government . . . is imposing, sanctioning, aiding, abetting, encouraging" discrimination. "The need is equally great," he added, "for positive action by the Government; that is, not only for it to stop doing certain things, but for it to begin to do certain things . . . to intervene" to safeguard individual rights.[30]

But it could do so, cold war liberals believed, within existing legal and economic structures. As the AJCongress put it after the *Brown* decision, the Court's "inspiring reaffirmation of the basic principles of America's democratic creed" will "reinforce the faith of free men everywhere in the capacity of democracy constantly to improve itself through the orderly processes of law." Black and Jewish agencies filed cases and amicus curiae briefs arguing constitutional protections for minority rights. The AJCongress had more civil rights attorneys on staff than did the Justice Department.[31] Civil rights coalitions also worked on federal, state, and local legislation protecting individual rights and outlawing practices which identified and excluded people on the basis of racial or religious categories.

A new combativeness and the new prominence of legislative and legal action marked liberal civil rights efforts in these years. Liberals shared a faith that laws and court decisions could reshape community values. The *Brown* decision, the AJCongress believed, was "much more than a judicial decree. . . . It is a great moral pronouncement challenging all Americans . . . to weave not only the letter but the spirit of the decision into the fabric of our daily lives." NCRAC concluded that "reduction in prejudice is more likely to be brought about in this way than through . . . efforts to modify attitudes. It is this observation, well supported by the evidence, that has warranted increased reliance on law as an instrument of social change."[32] Still, laws and court rulings could not do the job alone. Because liberals believed discrimination operated through individual attitudes and behaviors (in this case codified by law), they also called on professional and social organizations to voluntarily end racial restrictions, and launched educational campaigns to promote equality, pluralism, and democracy.[33]

In this phase of the civil rights movement, then, black and Jewish agencies and their allies, using a combination of legal, political, and educational approaches, collaborated on desegregating hospitals, schools, housing projects, and beaches. They proposed civil rights planks for the Democratic and Republican platforms, coordinated lobbying efforts, and testified before congressional committees on civil rights, civil liberties, and social welfare. Black and Jewish leaders conferred on legislative and legal strategies. They monitored political races for both tone and policy proposals, and worked with officials to enforce existing laws. They struggled to open housing and broaden economic opportunity. The range of issues local and national coalitions took up was truly remarkable. A look at a few illustrative examples will help map the terrain.

Fair Employment Practices

As chapter 3 suggested, the postwar struggle to make the temporary FEPC permanent was one of the first to bring Jewish and African American organizations together. Both communities had benefited substantially from federal fair employment protections, and the FEPC embodied their shared goals. The narrative of this national coalition illuminates the contours of the emerging postwar civil rights movement, its strategy debates reverberated in later coalitions, and its failures revealed the stubborn barriers to full civil equality. The National Council for a Permanent FEPC (NCPF), while ultimately unsuccessful on the federal level, labored for over a decade, convincing numerous states and municipalities to establish local FEPCs and similar structures. Black and Jewish political leaders occasionally disagreed over approaches, but agreed that the FEPC was their highest priority. As Shad Polier explained in 1949, "It is basic to a social and economic security, without which even the right to vote does not mean too much."[34] NCPF constituent agencies lobbied, mobilized their communities, and reached out to new coalition partners. The cooperation and collegiality the collaborations fostered spilled into other efforts.

The NCPF served as a powerful mechanism for coalition building. By 1947 the coalition included the ACLU, National Catholic Welfare Conference, CIO, Workers Defense League, NCJW, Rosenwald Fund, NUL, AME Church, AFL, Federal Council of Churches, Council of Jewish Federation and Welfare Funds, CIC, NCRAC, JLC, B'nai B'rith, AJC, Jewish War Veterans (JWV), United Council of Church Women, ADL, NAACP, IBPOEW, and AJCongress—the core of the future Leadership Conference on Civil Rights. As NCRAC's Isaiah Minkoff observed, "after a period of time, we were able to eliminate suspicion and weld together a common action group which was able to determine priorities in the civil rights field, to develop joint programs and, where necessary, to act jointly."[35]

The issue itself compelled inclusivity, reinforcing the overlap between universal and particular concerns that made these liberal programs so compelling. The problem of discrimination was neither exclusively southern nor exclusively black, warned Felix Cohen in AJC's *Commentary* magazine. "Discrimination against Negroes in the North, . . . Spanish-Americans and Indians in the Southwest, . . . Orientals on the Pacific Coast, . . . [and] Jews, Catholics and foreign-born throughout the land, is morally as vicious as the worst anti-Negro discrimination of the South."[36] United, no group accepted self-serving compromises. When told that Congressman Roger Slaughter supported FEPC legislation only if it removed the word "creed," the NAACP secretary telegraphed, "I am certain all supporters of this legislation would share [our] preference . . . that the legislation go down to honorable defeat rather than accept a shameful compromise of this character."[37]

In part federal FEPC legislation failed because postwar politics shifted rightward. The 1945 full employment bill did not pass; later versions abandoned both its generous jobs funding and its centralized planning mechanisms. Congress rejected much of Truman's "Fair Deal" to expand health, education, and housing programs and civil rights protections. Perhaps the death knell for progressives was the 1948 walkout by the Dixiecrats from the National Democratic Party Convention in protest over its strong civil rights plank, and the dramatic electoral loss of Henry Wallace and his Progressive Party. The nation had moved to the right and the political centers of power moved with it.[38]

Contemplating the future of the Democratic Party, James and Nancy Wechsler observed in *Commentary* that "one great clash between the antiquated Democrats and a rising progressive bloc focused on the civil rights issue." In the inevitable battle, the authors concluded, there was only one hope: "the emergence of a unified, purposeful liberal political structure." That emergence was by no means certain, the writers warned. "Real and impressive differences exist among liberals in and out of Congress" over tactics, timing, and questions of constitutionality, and could, especially given an economic slowdown, make civil rights "a first casualty."[39]

"Impressive differences"

The differences the Wechslers pointed to were real, and emerged between coalition members and even within organizations. In 1948 Henry Epstein outlined several cases within NCRAC in which member agencies, despite agreement on an issue, fought so bitterly over both strategy and the allocation of credit that no action resulted. Despite extensive cooperation between AJC and ADL, members of the former complained about their "incessant bickering."[40]

Such bickering flared between the closest of allies. In a 1950 speech at Fisk University, Will Maslow, who had come from the FEPC to direct the CLSA, spoke openly of the failures of northern state FEPC laws. Roy Wilkins complained that Maslow's words had given aid and comfort to FEPC opponents. By being too candid, Wilkins lamented, Maslow did not give "too much thought to the overall battle of propaganda and public relations which must go forward constantly." Maslow fired back that "it is necessary to take the risks (which we believe to be small) of jeopardizing FEPC campaigns" in order "to air our dissatisfaction with the enforcement of Northern civil rights laws." As he concluded, "I am sure that we are and ought to be resourceful enough in any FEPC campaign to make a distinction between the Northern law which we praise and its enforcement which we disparage. Lawmakers too should be conscious of the fact that unless adequate provision is made for good enforcement, these laws will become a mockery."[41]

But the more significant divisions—within as well as between liberal organizations—emerged over mass-action strategies in this period of increasing political conservatism. A 1949 AJCongress convention debate over the use of such tactics in FEPC campaigns made explicit the issues that seemed to be at stake. Henry Berlin, who helped lead a successful campaign in Massachusetts to pass educational antidiscrimination measures, was "persuaded, not only from my own conviction, but conviction of my many friends in the legislature, that mass demonstration, to a certain extent, serves as an irritant" and so was counterproductive. Polier and Maslow disagreed. They both argued, much as George Johnson of Howard University had, that lawmakers would not vote for a bill without a strong demonstration of public support. Yes, agreed Berlin, but such demonstration does not require "picketing and hip-hooray." Mr. Goldberg of St. Louis objected. "I say protest, demand, and you get what you want." Polier offered a more nuanced assessment. "The march on Washington, which was threatened, and which was effective, was a very, very daring move. Whether or not they could have carried it through, we leave aside for the moment. But . . . it may not work again." The nation had been in crisis, and the protest "involved the most basic demand of 13 or 14 million people who had to be won over so that they could be put to work." But such conditions arose infrequently. This "was a daring thing." (Maslow interjected, "It was a bluff, too.")[42]

Polier then turned to the question on the floor. "But to . . . say that you are going to picket . . . [about] FEPC is to become ludicrous and silly. Who is going to picket?" African Americans, who faced the most discrimination, "would not entertain that idea for a moment. I know it. . . . I worked with them for many years." Then there was the moral question. Picketing "is a brutal statement of coercive effort." Certainly, all the panel members agreed, mass action was crucial in legislative battles. But they meant mass action as building organizational coalitions "to work out a common . . . strategy in the open." It might "involve talking with legislators," or leading delegations to confront political leaders. "It may mean the holding of educational conferences . . . so that you get it into the newspapers." But beyond that even this progressive organization would not go. "There isn't a place in the United States . . . where . . . if you handle these things in a mass, and you make a mess of it, you [don't] make enemies of everybody." Polier warned. "To say that if you demand and demand and demand, you will get, is not true and never will be true." Several delegates somewhat testily raised the counterexample of organized wartime Jewish boycotts against German products. Polier responded that "that represented a crisis in Jewish life, that matched exactly the crisis which produced the march on Washington, and it would be just as sensible for any Negro organization to say any time they were not satisfied with something, 'We are going to march on Congress,' as it would be for the American Jewish Congress to say that, 'We are going to boycott, because we once had one.' "[43]

That debate typified contemporary liberal opinion as groups struggled to balance their hesitation regarding mass action with their desire to promote civil rights. When CORE, a member of the Council for Job Equality on State Street in Chicago, proposed pickets and boycotts to compel Goldblatt Brothers Department Store to hire African American clerks, fellow Council member ADL demurred. Instead it "sought, in cooperation with other community groups, to develop [an] educational program" for the stores. Learning that CORE and a socialist group "still favor 'militant action' instead of negotiation," the ADL withdrew from the Council. The ADL's Civil Rights committee warned in 1949 that it "looks with disfavor upon picketing . . . as an expression of disapproval except [in] . . . special circumstances." Jews in particular feared mass demonstrations, so reminiscent of the demagogic rabble-rousing that had proven ruinous to European Jewry, but most liberals, white and black, shared their commitment to moderation.[44] Such commitments must not be confused with cowardice, however. When events required it, both black and Jewish liberal groups came around even to civil disobedience. Even the cautious NUL acknowledged at the end of the war that "there is not a prominent Negro in the United States today who has the support of other Negroes, who does not . . . [hold a] militant attitude opposed to all forms of discrimination.[45]

As a case in point, the Supreme Court declared segregated interstate transportation unconstitutional in 1946. To test that decision, CORE and the Fellowship of Reconciliation, whose commitment to mass action came from its organizing principles, called for a "Journey of Reconciliation" in which black and white passengers would ride trains together through the South. At first both black and Jewish liberals were skeptical. The NAACP's Thurgood Marshall warned that any "disobedience movement . . . would result in wholesale slaughter with no good achieved." Dr. Trigg, African American member of the Southern Regional Council, an interracial organization dedicated to advancing black rights and opportunities within the existing southern racial system, believed "that this 'planned' direct action only tends to antagonize people." Jewish leaders meeting in Chapel Hill "questioned whether anything new could be gained by such a trip." But most progressive liberals like Randolph and

Mary McLeod Bethune endorsed the action. Alex Miller cheered any "group willing to act instead of just talking."[46]

In the end, they all rallied. The NAACP provided legal defense for those charged with violating segregation laws; ADL's Sol Rabkin wrote to congratulate Journey organizers. Their report was "one of the most exciting social documents we have ever come across," he gushed, and volunteered to file amicus briefs for any cases that ended up in court. Inspired to apply the technique to matters of direct Jewish interest, his colleague William Sachs mused, "if teams of Jews and Christians could take similar bold action in their approach to resorts and hotels, we might ultimately be able to break down the discriminatory barrier" there.[47]

Liberal African American groups proved more willing than Jewish ones to move beyond caution. While distinctions between groups like the NAACP and those like CORE engaged in grassroots mobilization were real, they were less sharp than historians have suggested. The NAACP, NUL, and MOWM, briefed in 1945 regarding CORE's nonviolent civil disobedience training, all agreed "the project held great possibilities. None indicated opposition." Those present suggested that "participants may be able to gear in with projects already being carried on by the NAACP or other organizations with which help is needed." While the NAACP opposed Randolph's 1948 campaign to refuse conscription until the president desegregated the armed forces, it endorsed the picket line Randolph simultaneously launched, and held its own protest in Washington, D.C.[48]

In a 1951 internal discussion, both whites and blacks in the NAACP self-consciously chose greater militance. The issue was Truman's appointment of Millard Caldwell Jr., a Klan supporter and open advocate of segregation, to head the nation's Civil Defense program, over the objections of civil rights groups. The NAACP resolved that "so long as Caldwell is head of civil defense we will not accept any [defense] post. . . . Those who have already accepted such posts should resign." It further urged finding additional "ways and means of implementing action . . . including . . . plans to mobilize the people of the United States to go to Washington, issuance of pamphlets, newspaper statements, use of radio and every other device that imaginative and creative minds can bring to the fore." "It may be," observed board member Dr. Cahn, "that President Truman feels he has the Negro vote in his hip pocket. We must get out of his hip pocket. This situation calls for militancy and we shall be open to grave charges of political chicanery if we do not take a stand."[49]

A problem arose immediately. Several NAACP members were, by virtue of their employment as judges, health care workers, police, and the like, compelled legally or morally to serve in civil defense. This became the subject of several heated debates during which the question of the

NAACP's role in the civil rights movement arose repeatedly. Spingarn argued that while he strongly supported other tactics, it would not be in African Americans' interest to withdraw from civil defense. Cahn responded that "the NAACP is supposed to be a militant organization." Truman had granted the NAACP secretary fifteen minutes to present the group's objections. "Fifteen minutes for fifteen million people," Cahn complained. The board action "catches the imagination of the people." Some members argued that remaining in civil defense and fighting from the inside offered a more promising strategy. Others countered that "we cannot permit surrender to the Dixiecrats and be supine in the face of it." Dr. Wiggins feared the call for resignations would fail because it was "unpopular. The branches won't want it and the rank and file won't comply." He preferred a march on Washington to make their displeasure known. As the minutes report, Delany retorted "that everything that the NAACP has done in the past which put it on the map has been unpopular. . . . The question is whether we hate segregation enough to fight against it . . . whether [or not] we could take our members with us." In any case, be believed, "Negroes would follow militant leadership in any direction the NAACP leads."[50]

These disputes, like those of the AJCongress, revealed internal fault lines, certainly, but they also revealed universal agreement on militance. Even those who urged the removal of the resignation clause from the resolution (a position which ultimately triumphed) endorsed dramatic, public action to challenge Caldwell. Suggestion that resignations be replaced with a march on Washington hardly bespoke moderation. Views of specific tactics might differ but the conviction that militant, public action was necessary, and that the NAACP ought to be in the forefront of it, was unanimous. The Dayton, Ohio, NAACP threatened a "bus-riding holiday" in 1952 if the local bus line continued in its refusal to hire black drivers. If the policy did not change, warned Charles Francis, a local NAACP official, "We do not know what an aroused citizenry might do."[51]

"How we might unite our efforts"

Both black and Jewish liberal groups, then, shared what might be called a moderate militance as well as agreement on liberal civil rights goals. Recognizing that, in Lester Granger's words, "our interests are identical," these organizations began to explore the possibility of creating a broad coordinating body "to secure full civil rights for all Americans," not only as "a domestic necessity but an urgent factor in the world struggle between the free institutions of the west and the totalitarianism of the east." The NAACP's coalition lobbying effort, the Civil Rights Mobilizations, demonstrated the potential of such collaboration, but although "[r]elationships among the major organizations are cordial, [and] they . . . have a mutually high regard," a 1951 memorandum acknowledged, "cooperation among them is limited, rarely extending beyond exchange of publications, occasional conferences, and infrequent collaboration on specific issues."[52]

Participants at a December 1951 planning meeting called by Jewish organizations agreed. Shad Polier lamented, "[I]t is astonishing how infrequently the top lay and professional leadership get together, not for joint action, but for joint thinking." Racial violence does not "just happen. There was a history to such occurrences which could be anticipated, yet time and again we find ourselves working under pressure and emergency situations." Four months later, the discussion of housing discrimination they organized included a broad array of liberal groups, including the National Council of Churches in Christ, NCRAC, JCRC, National Conference of Christians and Jews (NCCJ), AFL, American Friends Service Committee, CIC, NUL, AJC, ACLU, AJCongress, Philadelphia Fellowship Commission, CIO, ADL, and JLC.[53]

These leaders, apparently, had not thought to include women's organizations. "Sometimes," complained Gertrude Weisman, president of B'nai B'rith Women's Supreme Council, "it appears that too little thought is given to the fact that one-half of the public are women, one-half of the members of the community whose . . . conditions . . . we wish to improve, are women, one-half of those in whom we desire to develop a greater appreciation of democracy are women." But women too, usually preferred coalitions of their own sex, "for women can best present our program to other women."[54]

The 1944 National Planning Conference on Building Better Race Relations had already brought together leaders of thirty Jewish, African American, Mexican American, and Catholic women's organizations, along with academic and political leaders to discuss the problems posed by discrimination, racism, and anti-Semitism. Panelists and delegates discussed "intercultural education" and social work, but emphasized political action. Organizations shared legislative and lobbying experiences regarding labor, immigration, education, FEPC, housing, voting rights, the poll tax, and segregation. In the words of Mary McLeod Bethune, "We have been doing the individual work. . . . Our thought [in organizing this conference] was how we might unite our efforts, to give strength, momentum to those important things in this important time." Pledging themselves to "joint social action in the areas of education, economic security, health, housing and citizenship," member groups continued to share ideas and organize mutual action in the years to come on a wide range of issues from lynching to the welfare of itinerant farm laborers. As Katherine Engel of

the NCJW reflected in 1952, her coalition experiences had taught her that
"[w]e must learn to 'cross lines of race, creed, color and railroad tracks.' "
The identification of class as a central and independent factor of analysis
put women's groups ahead of most men's, whose recognition of class
issues in this period rarely moved beyond support of labor unions.[55]

The most durable civil rights coalition, the Leadership Conference on
Civil Rights, emerged from the same stew of participants. Convinced that
the moment for fruitful coalition work had come, and presumably ignorant of Jewish attempts to organize a civil rights umbrella group, Randolph invited Walter White to "an informal conference of a small number
of Negro leaders" to do the same. Instructed by the NAACP's Committee
on Administration, White responded "that in view of the fact that numerous white or interracial organizations and a great many white individuals
have fought so valiantly during recent years for civil rights for Negroes
and other minorities, it would be a mistake for the Negro at this particular
juncture to isolate himself by acting unilaterally as a racial group." The
NAACP board approved White's participation in the all-black group, but
also invited the "nation's leading church, labor, fraternal and civic organizations" to another conference to be held in Washington, D.C., in May
1951 to discuss "the apparent trend toward appeasement of the Dixiecrats and other reactionaries" evidenced by recent civil rights setbacks.[56]
This became the LCCR, whose fifty-one cooperating agencies agreed that
congressional failure to enact civil rights legislation was not only an abro-
gation of America's highest democratic ideals, but also led to unaccept-
able mob violence. "We can no longer afford to pay the price in blood
and money and lose respect abroad which intolerance exacts from all of
us," the conference warned. "We will consent to no 'cease fire' in the
fight for full civil rights. We will not be intimidated by terror, nor will we
succumb to defeatism."[57]

White (later Wilkins) of the NAACP served as chairman and NCRAC's
Arnold Aronson as secretary of this broad coalition. Here at last women's
groups participated as well as men's, along with union, religious, political,
fraternal, and sororal organizations. Its executive committee included the
leaders of the NAACP, ADA, AJC, NCNW, AJCongress, JLC, CIC,
ACLU, BSCP, National Baptist Convention, IBPOE, American Council on
Human Rights, ADL, AFL, CIO, and several unions.[58]

One of the first issues the conference tackled was structural: Senate
rules governing debate made FEPC, and indeed, all civil rights legislation,
virtually impossible to pass. Any senator could prevent a bill from coming
up for a vote by filibustering. This could only be overruled by a vote of
sixty-four senators ("cloture"), a number difficult to achieve on behalf of
civil rights legislation in a body dominated by Southerners. The nine hundred delegates attending the 1952 LCCR orchestrated an elaborate lob-

bying campaign in the Senate to revise the cloture rule.[59] It failed, and filibusters remained the scourge of civil rights efforts through the decade, although a 1957 bill did manage to pass in the wake of the debacle at Little Rock's Central High School. Throughout the 1950s the LCCR continued its work against filibusters and for fair employment legislation. Its leadership also worked with members of the executive branch to secure greater compliance with existing antidiscrimination rules.[60]

Each year the LCCR set its legislative priorities. Its nine-point agenda in 1952, for example, called for an FEPC with enforcement power; revision of cloture; antisegregation, antilynching, and anti–poll tax legislation; the strengthening of the Justice Department's civil rights section; the establishment of a permanent Civil Rights Commission; statehood for Hawaii and Alaska; and home rule for the District of Columbia.[61]

Despite LCCR's efforts, Congress failed to enact any meaningful legislation of this sort. In 1955 the Conference called for a reassessment of its strategy. The ensuing debate over both goals and tactics played on now-familiar themes of militance versus moderation. One memorandum proposed the Conference work for more modest legislation such as an FEPC without enforcement power, to "break the stalemate on civil rights that has obtained in Congress for 90 years." Not unexpectedly, the suggestion provoked sharp opposition. Such a strategy implied that failure to pass civil rights legislation was the fault of inflexible civil rights groups, not Congress, dissenters argued. In fact, "intensified pressure on the entire civil rights front" would be more likely to produce legislation than abandoning the moral high ground. The executive committee agreed to press forward aggressively.[62]

LCCR was issuing a real challenge. The limitations of "vital center" liberalism—the desire to maintain consensus, avoid confrontation, and pursue moderation—were already evident to conference members. All present at a July 1955 executive committee meeting understood that because both Republicans and liberal Democrats vied for southern Democratic support, the *Brown* decision "was being used both by supporters as well as opponents of civil rights in the Congress as a justification for legislative inaction." Meanwhile, "the public at large was becoming complacent as a result of the gains achieved through the courts . . . and increasingly . . . cynical about the prospects for federal legislation." It recommended "stimulating greater publicity and grass roots pressure." Still, this militant-sounding rhetoric remained comfortably within elite liberal confines. Despite the mass actions beginning to emerge across the nation from bus boycotts to CORE demonstrations, the executive committee did not envision marches or protests. Rather, it intended greater citizen lobbying to ensure "the actual *passage* of overdue and needed civil rights legislation *in the 84th Congress*."[63]

Legislative Struggles

These coalitions took their energy and direction from their constituent organizations, and through the 1950s liberal black and Jewish groups placed civil rights legislation, equality of opportunity, and monitoring of racism and anti-Semitism at the top of their agendas. Again in the forefront was the NAACP, which had for years tracked every civil rights, labor, social welfare, and immigration bill introduced, and lobbied at every opportunity. It was active in a broad range of minority causes well beyond those of direct self-interest to black people, from resettling interned Japanese Americans to easing restrictions on the immigration of refugees. While the NUL, as a tax-exempt organization, could not lobby, its staff testified at congressional hearings in support of legislation regarding housing, employment, social security, FEPC, and the like. It also issued statements "alone or in conjunction with other organized groups, designed to mould public opinion."[64]

The major Jewish groups likewise engaged in lobbying, testifying before congressional committees, and similar legislative activity on behalf of a wide range of issues. The NCJW had thrown itself energetically into such work at least a decade earlier than male-dominated Jewish organizations. Before the war's end the NCJW was filing statements with congressional committees regarding civil rights and issuing public statements against the poll tax.[65] Its 1943 national convention took positions on lynching, child welfare, civil service, consumer protection, discrimination, voting rights, public health (including reproductive information), labor, divorce, education, home rule for Washington, D.C., and Social Security, and called upon its sections to lobby and mobilize on their behalf. Its 1950 election agenda looked outward, with support for the Marshall Plan, aid to underdeveloped nations, reciprocal trade agreements, and international control of atomic energy, alongside its domestic advocacy of national health insurance, federal aid to public schools, revision of Taft-Hartley, liberalization of immigration, FEPC, antilynch and anti–poll tax laws, and public housing. It issued voting records for all congressmen before elections, and, like the LCCR, proposed planks for the Democratic and Republican Party platforms.[66] The era of a separate women's sphere of interest, if it ever existed, was gone forever.

Jewish women may have arrived there first, but no Jewish organization stood apart from these battles. NCRAC's 1949 "Summary of Decisions by NCRAC Bodies" listed positions on discrimination in employment, education, housing, and social organizations, civil rights, defamation, loyalty oaths, cloture, and immigration taken by Jewish organizations.[67] While few of these federal efforts succeeded, a civil rights bill finally passed in 1957, strengthening the Justice Department's enforcement powers. Despite its limitations, the act was the first such federal legislation since Reconstruction.

Not unexpectedly, African American and Jewish groups monitored electoral politics closely, providing their members with information on candidates' views "from the admittedly narrow—but important—standpoint of what Negro voters may expect of them," as a 1948 *Crisis* editorial put it. The editors, good liberals, stressed the relationship of narrower racial self-interest and broader democratic values. "We do not suggest that Negro voters make their choices on strictly Negro issues, but it must be apparent to nearly everyone that the treatment of minorities ties in with the big overshadowing issue of democracy versus totalitarianism." All the major black and Jewish agencies reported both local and national political debates, described pending legislation, and offered suggestions for advocacy.[68]

Blacks and Jews understood they were linked not only in positive political collaboration but also in more poisonous ways. As Epstein noted in 1957, "Almost without exception, violence in the South over school desegregation has been accompanied by anti-Semitic tirades of the rankest type. . . . [T]he White Citizens' Councils . . . use anti-Semitism as a stock in trade, claiming that the Negroes were docile enough until whipped up by Jewish agitators as part of a devious Jewish conspiracy for world domination."[69]

"We now have the tools": Dismantling Legal Segregation

Jewish groups also filed amicus briefs in support of antisegregation cases. In Washington, D.C., for example, Mary Church Terrell and the Coordinating Committee for the Enforcement of D.C. Anti-Discrimination Laws brought suit against a segregated restaurant on the basis of one such law from 1873. Briefs arguing for the law's continued validity came from the ADL and Greater Washington Jewish Community Council.[70]

The legal involvement of Jewish groups was substantial. The NAACP and CLSA cooperated so extensively that in 1947 they agreed to exchange "not only our briefs but copies of our confidential project inventories, monthly reports, etc." As Thurgood Marshall noted, "The Legal Staff of the N.A.A.C.P. is more than anxious to work in complete harmony with the American Jewish Congress and to cooperate in every manner possible." A month later, Maslow and Marshall had agreed to joint staff luncheons "so that we may have an interchange of ideas and projects." Given the NAACP's cramped quarters, they agreed to meet at CLSA. "We can have sandwiches and cake brought in and serve coffee," offered Maslow.[71]

The ADL even advised the UAW concerning a segregation problem in Memphis. The union hall there had segregated toilets and the codirector of the UAW's Fair Practices and Anti-Discrimination Department contacted Sol Rabkin. Rabkin suggested possible legal challenges to the local segregation ordinance. Litigation based on private use, he noted, "might well succeed. On the other hand, if you lose in the lower courts you may be denied the use of the hall for a substantial period of time. Those are the dangers to be balanced. . . . I know what choice I would make, and I hope that you and your people make the same choice."[72]

Jewish organizations cooperated actively in the fight to integrate southern public schools, and filed supporting briefs in every significant case. Rabkin concluded after positive court decisions in 1950 that "segregation in public . . . schools is on the way out, and . . . we now have the tools with which to destroy all governmentally-imposed racial segregation. . . . [I]t will take time as well as courage and determination, but . . . it will be done." The AJC and the Rosenwald Fund underwrote Kenneth Clark's pivotal doll study that helped undergird *Brown v. Board of Education.* The Jewish student group Hillel led desegregation struggles at the University of Oklahoma and George Washington University.[73]

Jewish groups also proffered legal arguments for school desegregation. "If there are not sufficient Negroes in a particular area to make it feasible to have a separate Negro school, are not the Negroes disadvantaged by being compelled to travel longer distances to school or by being forced to be satisfied with the poorer facilities that their smaller number necessarily entails?" wondered Rabkin. This argument that allocations based on group membership threatened equal opportunity also suggests why these liberals, who saw rights embedded in the individual, would resist group-based remedies sought later in the civil rights struggle.[74]

Local Heroes

Activists were not blind to the fact that while legal segregation occurred only in the South, lack of racial equality was everywhere a problem. "Vast differences exist between the opportunities afforded whites and Negroes in every section of our land," noted the CJP in 1951. The absence of segregation laws in the North and West did not prevent its occurrence. Antidiscrimination laws, and their adequate enforcement, were crucial. Lacking federal legislation, these battles had to be waged on the state and local level; there coalitions mirrored national ones, sharing data and coordinating efforts.[75]

Although the fight for fair employment protections had stalled federally, local coalitions won them in northern and western states and cities.

Between 1945 and 1949 eight states enacted such laws. First was New York, whose State Committee Against Discrimination helped pass the Ives-Quinn Fair Employment bill. Still, SCAD relied primarily on "concilation and persuasion with business leaders." Its chair, Charles Garside, claimed in 1949 that "[w]herever it has been tried it met with success," but black and Jewish groups were unimpressed. "As a result of constant needling from AJC[ongress], NAACP and the Urban League, they are now abandoning that policy" and moving more aggressively to prosecute discriminators, noted Maslow.[76]

In Brooklyn, the AJCongress Women's Division, Urban League, and NAACP took discrimination complaints and provided investigators to test the law's application. The Bronx Council of CLSA asked its members to "scrutinize the help-wanted columns . . . for requests specifying race, religion or creed." More intrepid volunteers could "[v]isit employment agencies and firms advertising for help and make application to ascertain if you will be accepted or refused because of race, religion or creed." Maslow reported in 1949 that "considerable advances have been made. We . . . no longer see in New York any Help Wanted advertisements with the discriminatory legends. . . . We know, too, that employers no longer will openly inquire of an employee whether he is Jewish or not, because that is illegal." Turning to race, he added, "Negroes are now working in many plants, in large numbers where they did not work before." In fact, "[t]he advances for Jews have been at a much slower rate." The data suggests, however, that this was the case because Jews had less far to go. The "vast majority" of postwar discrimination complaints, Garside reported, involved "Negroes rather than Jews."[77]

San Francisco's Bay Area Council for Civic Unity won passage of several pieces of antidiscrimination legislation including fair employment. "Jews played the leading roles [in it], and Catholics occupied secondary roles in the 1940s and 1950s," historian William Issel has concluded. The coalition, which included members of local ADL, AJC, Hadassah, CRC, and AJCongress chapters, enjoyed "a more than twenty-year period of work with local and state African American, Asian American, and Mexican American organizations on behalf of racial equality in education, employment, and housing." With the NAACP, NUL, Chinese American Citizens Alliance, JLC, several Catholic priests, and others, the group sued the city housing authority over its segregation policies, and won passage of a state FEPC law and antidiscrimination provisions in urban redevelopment plans. C. L. Dellums, vice president of the Brotherhood of Sleeping Car Porters, Pacific Coast, added that the JLC, which worked "together hand in glove" with the NAACP and "Negro Trade Union Leadership," did more to pass FEPC there "than any other single agency."[78]

In Pennsylvania the NAACP, AJC, ADL, and CIC each loaned a staff member to work on the state's FEPC campaign. Meanwhile Philadelphia passed its own ordinance as a result of the effort led by the AJCongress Women's Division. The coalition the women built lobbied every candidate for city council, and publicized candidates' views on the measure. After the election, the group picketed at the public hearings and debates. The ordinance passed. By the early 1960s, twenty states and forty cities had some sort of fair employment laws.[79]

Local coalitions also battled educational restrictions. While southern public schools segregated pupils by race but not religion, both blacks and Jews encountered barriers to their attendance in private colleges and universities across the country. Many such institutions barred African Americans outright, while Jews were more often subject to sharply limited quotas. The NAACP intervened to assure the admission of a qualified Jewish student to a medical school whose "Jewish quota" had been filled. A joint effort by the NAACP, AJC, AJCongress, NUL, and ADL convinced the New York State legislature to create a state university system in 1948 to compensate for racial and religious discrimination at private institutions.[80]

Yet such partnerships often proved difficult to sustain on the local level. In 1955 the Portland, Oregon, NAACP chapter looked to build a local civil rights coalition. A memorandum listing LCCR member organizations for possible partnerships revealed that most had no local chapters there. Of those who did, virtually none would cooperate with the NAACP. The ACLU was organizing a chapter, but it was "[n]ot promising from left-wing standpoint." The AFL had a few local members sympathetic to the NAACP but was "certainly not to be relied on in a cooperative effort." The JACL has been "[m]uch more inactive since war." As for Jewish groups, the AJC representative "is on the ultra conservative side!" and AJCongress had no local chapter. The ADL cooperated occasionally, but would not do so "at this time." The NCJW will "[w]ork with UL but not with NAACP. We too radical?" While African American groups were more supportive, they were generally small and weak. The Colored AME Church, for example, had been helpful in the past but "the churches will have to be further educated here to be interested in political action." Or, like the BSCP, they "act pretty much to themselves locally."[81]

Even when local groups established connections, the nationals had some difficulty sustaining their momentum. In 1955 the LCCR called on local organizations to conduct rallies and other programs for Bill of Rights Day. In Denver, thirty groups cosponsored the rally attended by six hundred people. As the local LCCR representative reported, not only did they educate many citizens, and show local congressmen the large constituency for civil rights legislation, but also developed "a working relationship with the 30 organizations involved; this can serve as a basis for future cooperative activity." Yet the national LCCR had not yet decided "whether these local rallies should be one-shot affairs or a continuing program. If the latter, some carefully developed program should be developed." National leaders had not yet figured out how best to utilize the power of the grassroots.[82]

And, like their national counterparts, local coalitions fought among themselves. In 1954, the NAACP's Seattle branch attorney negotiated with the state of Washington on behalf of the ADL, NAACP, NUL, and the State Board Against Discrimination in Employment to replace "race" with "complexion" as a category on licenses. While the four groups preferred no reference to color at all, they agreed that physical descriptions could prove useful to police, and accepted the compromise. The Seattle UL, however, then rejected the deal, insisting that "complexion" still served as a racial designation. The NAACP lawyer reported back to the Attorney General's office that although he had expected resistance, "quite frankly I was astonished" at its extent and intensity. He concluded that "the situation has deteriorated to the point where no argument that I can make" could convince a majority, and withdrew the compromise.[83] That the NUL proved more militant and hard-line than the others reminds us of the extent of local variation and the dangers of overgeneralization.

Other limitations to local coalitions were structural. A 1949 NCRAC report about Illinois described the tremendous number of tasks facing local Jewish leaders, who, despite "a relatively high degree of interest" in intergroup relations, had "little time to devote to this admittedly important work." Even in larger communities, with greater staff support and "actual enthusiasm . . . for carrying on" such programs, there was a frustrating "absence of rationale and lack of 'know-how.' " While there was "some activity" in virtually every community, therefore, most of it was both occasional and limited.[84] Despite such difficulties, most civil rights battles, in the end, were fought on the local level. A look at some of these struggles over housing and vigilantism provides more detail about how these liberal coalitions worked, and suggests the enormity of the challenge civil rights advocates faced on the ground.

Raisins in the Sun

Both Jews and blacks had been contractually excluded from buying or renting property in many neighborhoods; these restrictive housing covenants helped ghettoize both populations. In 1947 the NAACP publicized the case of a "restricted" Washington, D.C., suburb whose residents filed suit to compel a non-Jewish woman to evict her Jewish spouse because the presence of Jews was causing " 'irreparable damage' " to the neighborhood. This and similar cases "illustrate the psychopathic lengths to which racial and religious prejudice have brought some sections of our population," *Crisis* observed. When the NAACP finally argued successfully before the Supreme Court in 1948 that restrictive housing covenants could not be legally enforced (*Shelley v. Kraemer*), it had come armed with advice and supporting briefs from the AJC, Jewish War Veterans, AJCongress, JLC, and ADL, all of whom had fought such covenants against Jews. The ADL's brief revealed the liberal assumptions undergirding its position: "Implicit in such a covenant is the anti-democratic and false racist doctrine that undesirable social traits are an attribute not of the individual but of a racial or religious group."[85]

Civil rights organizations also worked to expand other housing opportunities. New Deal rules had mandated that public housing be available to both races, but projects were usually segregated, in the North as well as the South. Racial discrimination also permeated other housing-related programs, even the provision of home insurance. And public resistance, which affected virtually all minority groups, was especially devastating for African Americans, who faced greater hatred and had fewer choices. Existing black neighborhoods, limited by deliberate policies to overcrowded areas with substandard housing, swelled further with urban newcomers who could find no other place to live.[86] Poorer social and educational services, and the resulting higher morbidity and mortality rates, were not housing segregation's sole consequences. Such crowding placed pressure on surrounding white enclaves, often poor themselves, which often responded with violence. Chicago alone had six disturbances between 1940 and 1952; a closer examination of three of them reveals the active engagement of both black and Jewish organizations, the complexity of coalition work, and the interconnections between racism and anti-Semitism.

Black Chicago, crowded and segregated, faced substantial housing pressure. Anxious whites living adjacent to black neighborhoods organized protective associations, especially given the Chicago Housing Authority's nondiscriminatory policies. Although careful planning brought peaceful integration in a few housing projects, others proved more resistant. In the summer of 1947 the Housing Authority admitted several black families to Fernwood Park, a veterans' housing project, and the largely white Protestant community protested through its civic association, newspaper, and alderman. A white woman who supported integration arranged with the ADL to show prodemocracy films in the local theaters. Because the local ADL had relationships with these theaters, they all agreed to show the ADL's *Americans All, Don't Be a Sucker,* and *The House I Live In*. Delighted, J. Harold Saks urged ADL regional offices to "establish cordial relations with your local exhibitors so that you may facilitate the use of this technique where it is warranted by the local situation."[87]

Unfortunately, the films and community meetings failed to calm protestors. The families moved in on August 12, and for the next several days angry neighbors gathered. Despite a police presence, the ADL reported, "Mobs totaling several thousand in the aggregate, armed with lead pipe, rocks and bricks, roamed the area, stormed the project, disrupted traffic, stoned houses, smashed scores of Negro-occupied cars, and attacked Negro passers-by." A group of "responsible Negro leaders" conducted daily meetings and, in the opinion of the local CLSA representative, was the only force "which has served to restrain the Negro community from taking vigorous reprisal action." The leaders of thirty-five civic groups, including black and Jewish leaders, called for more vigorous police action to quell the rioters, and finally on August 15, more than a thousand police officers encircled the demonstrators and arrested at least one hundred. At the arraignment, however, the judge commented that he opposed integration, and that while the protesters' actions were unlawful, the flawed integration policy would be corrected. Irate, civic leaders and the Mayor's Commission held an emergency meeting, where they learned the mayor was conferring with housing officials to find a "solution which would avoid violence." Fearing a revocation of the integration policy, the entire commission threatened to resign. Black leaders, they warned, had successfully kept the peace only because officials supported integration. If they withdrew their support, retaliatory violence was all but certain. Faced with this, the mayor and housing authority agreed to stand fast, and the police maintained tight control of the neighborhood.[88]

Although the violence eased, it did not end. Protesters stoned the houses of "those dirty Jews": three white supporters of integration, two of whom were actually Lutheran. The situation, the CLSA reported on August 18, "still threatens to boil over into a first class race riot with all the trimmings." Ultimately, the prointegration coalition argued, "the basic causes of prejudice and tension" must be addressed by ending "discrimination against Negroes and any other groups in the fields of employment, housing, health, education, recreation, and the enjoyment of civil rights." But even educating their own members proved challenging; the CLSA representative observed that the local Jewish community and rabbi might not help. "Certainly they are at present . . . frightened by the whole affair and I don't blame them."[89]

Tensions erupted again that same month on South Peoria Street, where two Jewish CIO activists had entertained black and white union members at their home. Rumors spread that the black guests were purchasing the house, and over the course of the next few nights, increasingly large and menacing crowds gathered; shouted racist, anticommunist, and anti-Semitic remarks; threw stones; and attacked Progressive Party counterdemonstrators. As Rabbi Berman narrated, "For reasons best known to themselves," the police "stood by and jeered; they turned their backs when stones were thrown or when people were beaten up." The AJCongress pleaded with the mayor to issue a statement "to the effect that every individual in Chicago had the right to live, to travel unmolested and to entertain whomever he chose." He instead issued a statement more critical of "the subversive elements" challenging the attackers.[90] In the ensuing court cases, the judge denied the violence was a race riot. That characterization, he wrote in his decision, "is a gross and unwarranted insult to the residents of this peaceful neighborhood." The violence itself "was the result of a miserable conspiracy, hatched . . . by a small but highly organized . . . band of subversive agents, professional agitators and saboteurs bent upon creating and furthering racial and religious incidents . . . for the purpose of discrediting the City government, the Police Department and the Court and the people who reside in this district." After stirring up the residents, he concluded, some "agitators were the victims of their own conspiracy, and . . . they were roughed up about it." He discharged the defendants. Appalled, the ADL, NAACP, and others protested the decision. Their coalition, the Chicago Council Against Racial and Religious Discrimination [CCARRD], whose members also included the local JLC and AJCongress, could not agree on further steps, however. Frustrated, the ADL's Nissen Gross concluded he had "gone overboard in letting all our activity on this situation be channeled through . . . [CCARRD] and the Commission on Human Relations."[91]

The largest outbreak, in July 1951, changed Gross's mind about the benefits of coalition. A black family had rented an apartment in the west Chicago suburb of Cicero, unaware they were the first African Americans in this community of 67,000. Angry whites warned the building owner not to rent to black families, and Cicero police discouraged the tenant, Harvey Clark Jr., from moving in. They may also have physically threatened him. Nevertheless, the twenty-nine-year-old bus driver and World War II veteran insisted on his right to live where he chose, and brought a van of furniture on July 8. The police prevented him from entering the apartment and threatened him again. Clark went to court, and a judge issued a restraining order against the police.

Thus protected, the family tried again on July 10. Almost one hundred people were on hand to greet them, shouting threats and insults. The police allowed the family to move in but did not disperse the crowd, which grew by that evening. Although the family then left the apartment, and the sheriff pleaded for calm, the crowd began smashing windows. The police made no arrests. The next day the crowd swelled again, and the NAACP pressed the sheriff to request mobilization of the National Guard.

He refused. By that evening, more than five thousand had gathered. All reports suggested the police sympathized with the protesters, although they roped off the building to protect it. But firecrackers, rocks, and stones knocked out all the building's windows, and finally the crowd stormed the building, vandalizing apartments, smashing the Clarks' furniture, and turning on the water and gas.

On Thursday the sheriff finally requested the National Guard. Meanwhile the crowd, now numbering close to ten thousand, had turned even uglier, threatening to burn and bomb the building. The police had cordoned off the street but the crowd pushed through. Arriving guardsmen marched shoulder to shoulder to push the crowd back. At this point rioters threw kerosene-filled bottles; fires broke out on the roof and inside the apartment. By the end of the evening, four policemen, four guardsmen, and nine civilians had been injured, four police cars overturned, and seventy rioters arrested. The police had finally been motivated to act in part at the sight of guardsmen knocked unconscious and bleeding from bricks hurled by the mob.[92]

An uneasy calm followed. The Guard was withdrawn on August 2, the building boarded up, and insurance coverage on it was canceled. The Clarks had lost everything. The grand jury investigation refused to indict most of the arrested rioters, but did return indictments against six people involved in renting the apartment, three of them African American, for "conspiracy to injure property by causing depreciation in the market price of the building by renting to Negroes" and causing the riot. The liberal community expressed shock and outrage. As the National Committee Against Discrimination in Housing observed, "This threat . . . affects every American citizen and every organization concerned with extending democratic rights to all Americans." Finally, after pressure from CCARRD, the U.S. Attorney General appointed a federal grand jury, which indicted four local officials and three police for "conspiring to deprive Clark of his constitutional rights." As a joint ADL-AJC memorandum observed, "It is hoped that the use of the federal civil rights statutes in this instance will serve to give added vigor to these laws which, in the past, have been in large measure ignored."[93]

Throughout the violence, the NAACP, ADL, AJC, CCARRD, and the Illinois Interracial Commission had sent observers to monitor the mob and the police. They held mass meetings, urged religious and civic organizations to call for calm, and met with officials to demand greater police and later National Guard action against the mob. Once calm had been restored, they filed suit against the city for failure to protect its citizens, pressed for both local indictments and federal intervention, raised money for the Clarks, and launched a long-term citizen education and action program to, in the words of CCARRD, "ensure that the Cicero violence would end in victory for democratic principles and not a defeat." As Nissen Gross reminded Arnold Forster, "I don't want you to get the impression . . . that this was in the main an ADL operation." The AJC, AJCongress, JLC, and "other civic, labor and religious groups were working together. This incident impresses upon my mind the need for the existence of an organization" like CCARRD. As a poignant postscript, CCARRD reported that Clark, who had two brothers serving in Korea, had not written them about the situation "because he didn't want to destroy their morale."[94]

Housing discrimination was hardly unique to Chicago. For many years segregation was an official policy of the Federal Housing Administration. Real estate boards, insurance companies, and lenders followed the same principles. All this occurred during a significant building and migration boom, which greatly heightened racial tensions and reinforced segregation patterns within cities and between cities and suburbs.

Even after the FHA changed its policy manual, discriminatory practices persisted. Yet the federal government "sidestep[ped] the issue," attorney and housing expert Charles Abrams told leaders of black, Jewish, and other liberal groups at a 1952 conference, leaving it to local governments to enforce civil rights laws. For the most part, they did not. Meanwhile, "demagogues and professional bigots . . . have become a troublesome factor." Exclusionary civic associations, press racism, threats of violence, and the collusion of state and local officials who exploited zoning laws, condemnation powers, and urban renewal plans to enforce existing segregation patterns, suggested the situation "is likely to get worse." Although covenants were now unenforceable, "Other devices are being used for excluding Negroes," Abrams observed, such as the refusal by mortgage companies to grant loans to black purchasers in white neighborhoods. As Maurice Fagan of the Philadelphia JCRC lamented, "Even liberals are not willing to engage in so-called 'block-busting.' It seems that organizations are willing to take up the cudgels for a Ralph Bunche and people of his stature, but the more difficult and larger problem is that of the ordinary middle-income Negroes." That group pledged legal, political, and educational challenges to local discrimination patterns.[95]

Given the absence of federal housing law, such efforts had to be local. The AJCongress, ADL, NAACP, NCJW, NUL, JACL, NCCJ, and Fellowship of Reconciliation met in New Jersey in 1944 in response to "violently anti-Japanese, anti-Nisei" pamphlets distributed by the American Legion protesting Japanese American resettlement there. As an ADL staffer commented, "This problem affects all groups interested in the question of minority rights." The Bayside, Queens, Jewish Center organized community meetings in 1945 to educate residents about interracial housing, while the ADL contributed "properly slanted books" to the local libraries. When a black family tried to move into Levittown in 1957, a "Levittown

Betterment Committee" protested, using fliers, newspaper advertisements, and pleas to municipal agencies. Many supporters joined them. The only local voice defending "Equality of Opportunity in Housing" was the AJCongress, through its local Women's Division and county chapter.[96]

In Detroit's Twelfth Street area the situation cut closer to home. Tensions arose in a Jewish neighborhood in 1948 as black residents moved in. "The first reaction was one of antagonism, panic, and rumor-mongering," the Jewish Community Council reported. "There was also a movement which began to resemble a mass flight." Desiring neither a segregated neighborhood nor "deterioration of relationships between Negroes and Jews," the JCC formed an interracial and interfaith Midtown Neighborhood Council. It took as its agenda plans to physically improve the area, and did not address race. "The experiment seems to be working out well," the JCC reported. "Panic conditions seem to have greatly abated and relationships between Jews and Negroes are much improved. There seems to be an increasing acceptance of the idea that Jews and Negroes can live in harmony in the same neighborhood."[97]

In other cases black and Jewish groups tried lawsuits, such as the decade-long litigation by the AJCongress, NAACP, and ACLU against New York's Stuyvesant Town apartment complex for its policy of excluding African American tenants. As Will Maslow observed, "No Jew was turned down there," but the AJCongress launched the case for both "a selfish and altruistic motive." While the altruism was obvious, selfishly, "[o]nce the law allows one group to be discriminated against, Jews can be discriminated against as well." This was a difficult legal case to win, as private developments were not subject to public housing laws. Still, Stuyvesant Town received government aid in the form of tax exemptions and use of eminent domain. As Maslow noted, that aid also made the case pressing. "Unless we can establish now that these urban redevelopment projects . . . cannot be operated on a discriminatory basis, we are going to freeze solid the patterns of discrimination and segregation and root them so solidly into the ground that it will be 50 years before we can knock them out." Finally, in March 1951, New York's mayor signed a bill prohibiting racial and religious discrimination in housing owned or funded by the city.[98]

In Sacramento, California, the liberal arsenal of coalition building, legal challenge, lobbying, and public education proved similarly successful. The NAACP's efforts to end segregation in public housing began to make headway only when it built a broad coalition with "the various minority groups, religious groups, labor unions, social worker groups and liberal groups." Publicity and lobbying failed, but when the coalition filed a lawsuit, the Housing Authority finally "bound itself to end racial segregation." The group then worked with housing officials to prepare tenants for the change. "Integration was instituted smoothly and is continuing with no adverse reaction whatever," reported ADL's Sol Rabkin and AJC's Frances Levenson. The lessons were clear to them: "the need for and the strength of broadly constituted citizen groups in securing re-form." Once the policy is changed, "Experience then shows that integra-tion can almost invariably be accomplished peacefully." While laws and ordinances barring public housing segregation were desirable, "the Sacra-mento story is an example of what can be accomplished even without a statute so long as there is an alert and organized citizenry." This may have been wishful thinking, but many local black-Jewish coalitions employed such strategies.[99]

Yet although such coalitions operated in many cities, and several states and cities did ban housing discrimination by the late 1950s, discrimina-tory practices persisted. At its 1959 meeting the LCCR called for an execu-tive order "forbidding segregation or other forms of discrimination based on race, religion or national origin in all federal housing programs includ-ing slum clearance, urban renewal, relocation, public housing, and insur-ing or lending functions related to housing."[100]

Mob Rule

As these housing disturbances demonstrate, civil rights efforts were often met by white violence. Employing time-honored methods of vigilante ter-ror and intimidation, reactionary whites menaced or killed hundreds of individuals they perceived as a threat to the racial order. These mob at-tacks were not confined to African Americans, although they were the most common victims. Southern synagogues and Jewish community cen-ters were bombed, as were black churches and homes, for being alleged centers of civil rights agitation. Nor was such violence limited to the South. In the early 1950s, roving gangs of young white men repeatedly attacked Jewish youths on the streets of Chicago's South Shore, for exam-ple. Still, although that situation was "rather serious" in the eyes of the ADL, there were stark differences from violence against African Ameri-cans. Most notably, the local police, once apprised of the situation, pro-vided "the fullest cooperation."[101] For black victims, geography and cir-cumstance determined the speed and adequacy of the police response. On a few occasions, police even cooperated with the mobs and had to be restrained by federal or state forces. Black and Jewish agencies separately or in coalition called for investigations of racial and anti-Semitic violence, North and South, and of excessive use of force by police.[102]

Both blacks and Jews faced northern mob violence and unsympathetic police in two notorious 1949 riots in Peekskill, New York. The Civil

Rights Congress invited actor, singer, and outspoken leftist Paul Robeson to perform there on August 27. A mob of close to five thousand people, mostly veterans, prevented the concert by blockading the entrance, shouting anticommunist, racist, and anti-Semitic epithets, and attacking concertgoers. Unbowed, the CRC rescheduled the concert for September 4. While the police had been unprepared for the first concert, they assembled for the second and, over protesters' jeers and taunts, the concert proceeded. Then, as a joint ADL/AJC report described it, "Clashes of riotous proportions broke out when . . . [those] in attendance ran into groups armed with bricks, stones and other missiles upon leaving the grounds. The inflammatory tone of the local newspaper . . . and the activities of professional anti-Semitic rabble-rousers heightened the situation." An NAACP report added more detail: "Nine hundred officers of the law permitted mobs to take over public highways, stone vehicles, overturn and damage private automobiles, and injure more than 100 citizens some of them so seriously as to require . . . treatment."[103]

Liberal black and Jewish organizations considered Robeson a provocateur and communist sympathizer, as did Governor Dewey, and Jewish groups advised their locals elsewhere to "quarantine" him by refusing him a platform to speak or perform. Nonetheless, they recognized the danger mob violence posed, and demanded an official investigation of the Peekskill riot. The NAACP likewise stressed its commitment to "the right of freedom of speech regardless of the political view of those involved." Praising indictments against several rioters, leaders called also for the prosecution of those who instigated the violence and the disciplining of police who failed to protect concertgoers. The mob's concurrent expressions of anti-Semitism and racism solidified the black-Jewish link. To a New York CRC member, "the feeling that prevailed in Peekskill was much like the lynch spirit which he had observed from time to time in the South."[104]

Police support of violence was a far greater problem in the South. Racist police brutality and Klan activity in Birmingham in the late 1940s, Alex Miller lamented, had produced "a fear-stricken community resembling one in a totalitarian state rather than in a democratic, freedom-loving country."[105] Local officials rarely brought perpetrators of racial violence to justice, so black and Jewish groups pressed for state and federal investigation and action. Because the Klan traveled masked, making it difficult to identify lawbreakers, the ADL's Southeastern office helped formulate legislation prohibiting the wearing of masks and the burning of crosses without permission; five states and fifty-five cities passed such laws. And the major Jewish groups finally joined the NCJW and their black colleagues in the fight for antilynching legislation.[106]

After a quadruple lynching in Monroe, Georgia, in 1946, the NAACP called a strategy meeting with the ADL, AJC, AJCongress, and a few others. The ADL, which had already publicly condemned the violence, involved itself in the ensuing local internal struggle between liberal and conservative Jews over whether the Atlanta Jewish Community Council ought to speak out as well. The interventionists finally won the day, resolving, "We believe the time has come for all good citizens of Georgia to recognize any violation of the sacredness of human life by mob action as a real threat and danger to rights and privileges of every citizen." Miller noted that this "was the first time that an important Jewish community of the South took positive action of this type" and exulted that "we have been able to educate to some extent our own people so that we are no longer as far in advance of them as we used to be."[107]

When two black prisoners were killed by a sheriff in Florida in 1951, the NAACP asked the ADL to press the governor for a response. As Arnold Forster explained by return mail, "The ADL has already taken action by sending a wire, together with other major Jewish organizations [AJC, AJCongress, JLC, JWV, NCRAC, Union of American Hebrew Congregations (UAHC)], to [the] Attorney General. . . . If there is anything further . . . we can do, please let us know." That telegram expressed shock at the "shameful occurrence" which "lead[s] us strongly to suspect a perversion of the American tradition of justice and equal treatment before the law." It urged that an "investigation be conducted as vigorously and speedily a possible and that every action warranted by the facts be undertaken with firmness."[108]

These liberal organizations used cold war rhetoric to their advantage. After the 1955 lynching of Emmett Till, a Chicago teen visiting relatives in Mississippi, the AJC insisted that the damage done to "American prestige abroad" compelled federal action. "Racial injustice in America . . . impairs national security," the NAACP's Roy Wilkins warned. "We can no longer permit any segment of our country to besmirch and endanger all of us."[109]

Yet despite calls to action and denunciations of the violence, many Jewish groups were also mindful of the vulnerability local Jews felt. After the 1951–52 spree of dynamiting and bombing in the Miami area that killed the state NAACP head Henry Moore and his wife and damaged Jewish synagogues, a Catholic church, and a black housing project, every major Jewish and black civil rights organization demanded immediate measures to apprehend the criminals and to prevent further violence. The ADL, AJC, and NAACP launched their own investigations. Nevertheless, the AJC report reflected reluctance to jeopardize what it perceived as the precarious acceptance of Jews by white gentiles there by too public a cooperation with civil rights groups. Because the "apprehension of vandals and criminals is basic to an orderly society" and crucial for Jewish security, it noted, vigorous investigation of antiblack vigilantism was required. "At the same time," it added, "there is a relationship of Jews to white Christians that needs to be maintained on friendly terms.[110] Such hesitations, most pronounced in the AJC, but present in all the Jewish groups, put limits on black-Jewish cooperation in the South, as we shall see. Nonetheless, national Jewish agencies were unambiguous in their insistence that police brutality and vigilante violence were unconscionable in a democracy.

"Say, fellow"

Far less controversial were educational campaigns. Ending racist practices ultimately decreased prejudice as it extended equality, all agreed. This could best be accomplished through law and legislation. But in the end, changing behavior, as well as enforcement of any new laws, was up to individuals. So, to bolster legislative efforts, or when legal recourse was unavailable, black and Jewish groups harnessed the powers of advertising and civic education to change hearts as well as laws. This dovetailed with liberals' focus on individuals rather than groups. As the CJP argued, "The major resistance to necessary changes lies in the moral weakness, in the prejudices and bigotries of many of our citizens" and so "the remedies must be largely in the hands of our homes, our schools, and our churches."[111]

While some agencies put more faith in educational programs than others, all agreed public sentiment in favor of civil rights was crucial for political advances. "Brotherhood in America will never be achieved by an annual Brotherhood Week," scoffed AJCongress's David Petegorsky, Still, educational programs challenged the "process of rationalization [that] constitutes the major source of . . . racial prejudice," and "can serve as powerful instruments . . . when they are integrated into the broader framework of a struggle essentially political in its nature."[112]

Mass meetings and public events advocated and modeled interracial harmony. Typical was the "Interracial and Interreligious Caravan: The World Tomorrow and Me" organized by the New York chapters of NCNW, AJCongress Women's Division, and Council of Church Women in 1945.[113] Emerging from wartime efforts to combat anti-Semitism and reinforce democratic values, such "intergroup relations" programs, including antibigotry literature, films, billboards, and radio spots, as well as discussion guidelines for schools, churches, and civic groups, promoted a liberal patriotism that celebrated freedom and the contributions of America's diverse peoples. In the words of the NAACP's Henry Lee Moon, these materials shared the "basic theme" of "the indivisibility of democracy" and sought "to overcome apathy, to create an awareness that the denial of basic rights to a minority threatens the majority, and to arouse to positive action against racial discrimination on moral, legal and practical grounds. Both informative and hortatory types of messages are used."[114]

To take a single year and organization as illustration, the ADL's Education Department program for 1955–56 included a national conference on "Human Relations Education" and plans for five regional conferences the following year; a source book on the subject for educators; elementary and secondary school books on pluralism and respect, including the *Rabbit Brothers*, *Little Plays on Big Subjects*, and *Junior Freedom* pamphlets on prejudice, the FEPC, immigration, and similar topics; teacher workshops; a national "Rumor Clinic"; a *Your Neighbor* comic book series (*Your Neighbor Celebrates the Jewish Holidays* proved the most popular, with half a million distributed to date); human-relations training for the staffs of civic organizations; short television films and radio, spots on changing neighborhoods and prejudice; television, radio, and dramatic scripts; and several handbooks, including a human-relations manual for student governments produced in conjunction with the National Students Association. The department had a staff of two.[115]

Liberal assumptions were manifest in all these programs. Once differences between groups were demonstrated to be simply variations on the same moral and patriotic themes, all vestiges of formal discrimination would cease. As Isadore Chein, a social scientist working for the AJCongress, explained, one must challenge "the artificial perceptual segregation of minority groups beyond the pale of democratic ideals." What if a passenger on a crowded bus overhears someone complain about "pushy" minority groups? He or she was advised to respond, "Say, fellow, that's not very democratic of you." One radio spot, whose "potent message wrapped up as a jive tune" was provided free to stations by an ADL affiliate, reminded listeners:

> You can get good milk from a brown skinned cow;
> The color of the skin doesn't matter nohow.
> Ho, ho, ho—haw, haw, haw,
> You can learn common sense at the groc'ry store.[116]

Ultimately, however, the battle could not be won by discussing populations. Rather, in the words of an AJC "Discussion Guide" on how to respond to bigots, "[E]stablish the 'decent' 'American' principles, and speak of individuals—preferably people known to the audience—rather than of entire groups, e.g. Jews, Negroes etc." An ADL campaign featured Jackie Robinson, Joe DiMaggio, Hank Greenberg, and others with the caption, "It doesn't matter what nationality he is; he can pitch." (Actually, none of them pitched.)[117]

Calling attention to race or religion emphasized differences among people who were, at heart, the same. "I wonder why you had to identify

[fighter Ezzard] Charles with the words—'a slender, coal-black Negro,' "
ADL's Hyman Haves queried a United Press reporter. Journalists must
avoid such racialized descriptions "[i]f we are to overcome prejudice in
this country and insure full democracy for all Americans." This was part
of a greater effort to curb stereotyping. The NUL pleaded with white
ministers, "The use of terms which discount minority groups should be
discouraged. . . . Stories disparaging Negroes, Jews, Irish and other minorities ought to be stopped. . . . Every such simple act may become a
victory for democracy" and can eventually alter "the social pattern." In
California a black-Jewish coalition challenged racial stereotyping in Hollywood "in which various members of minority groups are usually depicted in an unfavorable light, e.g. the Negro, the Mexican-Americans,
the Japanese, the Chinese, and sometimes, the Jew."[118]

Discrimination, by such reasoning, resulted from personal bigotry
rather than protection of socioeconomic advantage. The AJC, committed
to "scientific research to determine the nature of prejudice," pioneered
the way, commissioning German Jewish refugee scholars to produce a
"Study in Prejudice" series. *The Authoritarian Personality*, its pathbreak-
ing first volume, suggested that rigid conformity helped socialize bigots.
These studies helped reshape American socialization practices. Even the
popular musical *South Pacific* asserted, "You've got to be taught to hate
and fear."[119]

Such programs did have an impact. Following a successful meeting with
a realtor whose white clients had feared selling their home to a black
family, David Robinson observed in a postscript, "The real estate agent
advised us that he had read GENTLEMAN'S AGREEMENT [Laura Hobson's
1947 book about anti-Semitism] and that it had profoundly affected
his thinking. . . . I would like to believe there is some measure of truth
in it."[120]

Education proved most effective when linked to specific initiatives. In
Baltimore, the NCJW, NAACP, and B'nai B'rith Women used public education based on their power as consumers to challenge discrimination
policies. Mrs. Rogers, president of the Maryland State Council of BBW,
explained, "I went through the community and got signatures of [white]
women that our big department stores should allow Negroes to come in
and try clothes on. We fought for this until it came through." Although
"many Christian women shunned us, what are you Jews fighting for Negroes for? . . . [W]e stood up and fought like people, and thank God that
is not a question."[121]

Similarly, in May 1947 Minneapolis women's groups brought together
forty-four organizations to form the Joint Committee for Employment
Opportunity to combat local employment discrimination against African,
Jewish, and Japanese Americans. Having already won fair employment

ordinances, the committee argued that full compliance could only come when attitudes also changed. Thus it spearheaded a petition drive. "Democracy calls for equal opportunity for equal ability," more than ten thousand Minneapolis citizens agreed, "I shall be glad to be served by qualified sales persons or other employees of any race, creed or color without discrimination." By 1949, nine black women had for the first time obtained employment as salespeople in targeted downtown stores.[122]

CORE also combined public education and consumer pressure to good effect. In Chicago, it polled customers to demonstrate there was little resistance to the hiring of black clerks. Even more dramatic was its use of sit-ins, in which black and white CORE volunteers entered places of business that would not serve African Americans, and occupied seats until served. Beyond economic pressure, CORE's strategies sought to educate the broader public. In one St. Louis sit-in CORE members dropped leaflets from an airplane, although it proved "not very satisfactory because most of the leaflets landed on the tops of buildings." Others painted slogans on their shirts, like "Let's Make Democracy Work" and "All We Ask Is Justice," which CORE found "very successful in attracting attention to our cause." Even when such actions were pursued by individual organizations rather than coalitions, as in this case, groups shared information, tactics, and support. A 1949 CORE newsletter reminded readers, "[D]on't forget to send in news of whatever your group is doing. Others want to hear about it." Others did indeed: Maslow praised the *CORE-lator* as "filled with significant news items that could not be found anywhere else." Jewish leaders routinely contributed invited pieces in black journals and were quoted in the black press; black leaders appeared regularly in Jewish ones. And as is clear from their files, black and Jewish groups followed each other's activities closely and held on to their materials.[123]

The South, of course, proved a central battleground for public education campaigns, both because there was no hope of passing civil rights legislation without a substantial attitudinal change among white southerners, and because in the absence of such laws, only voluntary change was possible. Jewish groups seeking to rally the southern white community behind integration produced and distributed pamphlets and films, conducted discussion groups with local civic and religious bodies, and publicized peacefully integrated events as evidence that desegregation harmed no one.

In 1947 the Miami ADL office sponsored (and carefully orchestrated) several integrated events that occurred without incident. These included a local memorial service for President Roosevelt, banquets for the American Veterans Committee (AVC) and Negro Service Council, a train trip to an AVC convention in Milwaukee, and a meeting of the Dade County Fair Rent Council with the City Council. "[S]o far as it is known, for the first time at this meeting Negroes and whites sat together on a unsegregated basis at the Miami Beach City Hall," crowed Burnett Roth. As Gilbert Balkin noted, "This . . . gives the lie to the oft-contended positions . . . that Negroes cannot be invited to participate in Brotherhood Week and similar celebrations in this area 'because of the local situation.' " Miami's experience prompted Alex Miller to offer a "tip" for interracial meetings: hold them in "the most expensive and finest places in town. This will give the meeting such an aura of respectability that the authorities or even the local hoodlum elements would hesitate to do anything about it." In a letter to the national office Balkin concluded, "There is really nothing particularly remarkable in the above cases. They simply illustrate that 'it can be done,' given the will to put into action the democratic principles easily agreed upon in theory. . . . Each successfully completed program . . . constitutes an advancing step forward in the march of democratic progress in the South."[124]

Such challenges to prejudice were directed inward as well as outward. "Our lodge is planning on a Minstrel Show," a B'nai B'rith lodge wrote to the ADL in 1948. "Some members think this is derogatory to a minority group—most do not." "It is our feeling that a lodge of B'nai B'rith, which is dedicated to the bettering of inter-group understanding and relationship, would do well to avoid any form of entertainment which wittingly or unwittingly tends to offend any minority," Monroe Sheinberg replied. "We feel that the Negroes have a perfect right to object to the stereotyping of their words and actions which are found in the usual blackface minstrel show. We ourselves have frequently objected to the stereotyping of the Jew in alleged humorous skits." The NUL made similar interventions in the black community. "It is true that anti-semitism [sic] among Negroes is less prevalent than among almost any other group. . . . But the slightest tendency in this direction constitutes a racial disgrace which the Urban League consistently endeavors to wipe out."[125]

Social Discrimination

Perhaps nowhere was the link between civic education and liberal politics clearer than in fighting social discrimination. The exclusion of any group from places of public accommodation, quasi-private organizations and social clubs was antithetical to the liberal vision of civic equality. As an ADL manual on the subject explained, not only do such practices "give credence and support to the theory that differences of race, religion, or national origin justify unequal treatment of individuals" and make individuals in those organizations complicit in discrimination, but "[t]he exclusion of groups on irrational bases" creates a "climate ripe for segregation, ... discrimination, ... and second class citizenship. Social discrimination is part of a pattern, interrelated with and supporting all other areas of discrimination; and the problem must be treated on all levels at the same time." This was not just a southern issue; as Maslow pointed out in 1949 regarding FEPC, "There is a great deal of opposition even in the North."[126]

Yet few places mandated integration of such venues, and most of the South explicitly prohibited it. Without federal civil rights laws, legal recourse could be had only in those few northern states with such protections. Some liberals were not even sure such discrimination should be grounds for legal action, arguing that these institutions were private, and individuals had a right to free association. Given these constraints, even in the North civil rights organizations relied on careful monitoring and appeals to shared values of democracy and tolerance.[127]

Each case had to be approached individually, based on the reliability of local contacts, careful fact finding, and the potential for mobilizing mass support. Sometimes groups mounted public campaigns or legal challenges; in other situations behind-the-scenes negotiation offered more promise. Usually they tried several strategies simultaneously, placing pressure at every vulnerable spot. Progress was slow, and there were times when nothing could be done. But in all these efforts the liberal agenda was fully visible: legal equality, government action, personal rather than structural transformation, appeal to a democratic vision, and protection of individual rather than group rights.

In some cases, existing legislation made legal action the appropriate strategy. In New Jersey, a coalition of the UPWA-CIO, NAACP, AJCongress, and Civil Rights Congress brought suit against Atlantic City restaurants that refused to admit African Americans attending the UPWA's 1946 convention. In Minneapolis the ADL and AJCongress provided legal memoranda and briefs to the Minnesota Jewish Council in its ultimately successful fight to integrate a beach, a pattern repeated in many cities and towns across the country. It took three years of struggle by CORE, the ADL, NAACP, and the Workers Defense League to integrate the swimming pool at (Jewish-owned) Palisades Amusement Park in New Jersey.[128]

Still, even in the North, the law did not always prove a reliable ally. In Ohio, a public golf course converted to a private one in 1948 so that it could exclude nonwhite players. A group of African Americans took the club to court. They won on appeal, but only because the court found the course had not actually become private in any meaningful respect. The decision, ADL's Sol Rabkin and AJC's Alex Brooks pointed out, "exposes as a subterfuge a scheme frequently employed for the purpose of evading the provisions of state civil rights laws." While the ruling was therefore welcome, it left intact the right of truly private clubs to discriminate. Furthermore, violations of the law required trials by "juries, which, as experience shows, are often reluctant to find against the operator of a place of public accommodation."[129]

In State College, Pennsylvania, local barbershops refused to serve African American clients. In 1947 the local CORE, Hillel, and B'nai B'rith lodge collected more than eighteen hundred signatures on a protest petition, and each barber was contacted individually. Next, CORE took out advertisements to urge the barbers "on moral grounds" to change their practices. When this failed, CORE proposed launching a boycott and opening a nondiscriminatory barbershop. The Hillel director, concerned the latter might be "an admission of failure," sought Arnold Forster's advice. Forster agreed that it "would reflect an acquiescence to the situation" and feared a boycott would have little effect because most who objected to segregation presumably already refused to patronize discriminatory shops. Instead, he advised B'nai B'rith and CORE to remind the barbers of the state law barring discrimination in public accommodations and detailed the mechanisms for testing the law and proceeding against barbers who violated it. Select testers who were "popular locally," he recommended. "Care should be taken to obtain the best and most reliable citizens, persons who are very much respected in the community." These tests must receive press coverage, and the group should seek legal help from "sympathetic local lawyers" and national groups. Precisely the strategy employed in Montgomery in preparation for its bus boycott of 1955, Forster's advice reminds us of how completely civil rights groups agreed on both goals and approaches, strategized together, and refined techniques based on shared experience.[130]

Galvanized by the report, "To Secure These Rights," the Committee on Civil Rights in East Manhattan (CCREM) met in March 1949 to address local discrimination problems using similar techniques. The siting of the United Nations headquarters on the east side of Manhattan offered a marvelous public relations opportunity for enforcing desegregation laws, and the first project the group undertook was to survey discrimination in local restaurants. Gathering twenty-three sponsoring organizations, including the AJCongress, AJC, NAACP, ADL, ADA, Community Church, NCNW, Ethical Culture Society, JACL, JWV, National Council on Civil Rights, American Association of University Women, NCCJ, NLC, ACLU, CORE, NUL, Spanish American Youth Bureau, and several civic groups, CCREM surveyed every drugstore and eating place in the vicinity. Randomly selecting a quarter of them, it tested for discrimination in treatment. After careful training, testers were paired by race. Two black testers entered each restaurant, followed soon by two white testers. Acting like any other patrons, they ate and immediately afterwards reported their treatment to test supervisors. As the CCREM report explained, "although no Negro team was refused admission, in 42% of restaurants tested, the treatment of Negro teams compared with the white teams was so clearly inferior as to leave no doubt that it was discriminatory." CCREM reported its findings to the restaurant unions and owners' associations, and both groups pledged to "provide all patrons with full and equal accommodations equally and courteously given." The committee later publicized its findings to spur similar actions elsewhere in the community. It took two years to move even this far, in a state and city with a long history of antidiscrimination laws, and an unusually high level of racial diversity.[131]

Jewish and black groups also combined political mobilization, legal challenge, and public education to fight discrimination in one of the most popular American pastimes. The American Bowling Congress, incorporated in 1895, promoted the sport and organized tournaments of local teams. Early in the twentieth century it amended its bylaws to require that teams include only "individuals of the white male sex." The UAW, ADL, and NAACP spearheaded a campaign to convince the ABC to change its policy, creating a National Committee for Fair Play in Bowling in 1947 chaired by Hubert Humphrey. White, Randolph, David Dubinsky, and Steinbrink sat on its board. The big names at the top suggest not the elite nature of the movement but its concern with extending change into every aspect of people's lives. This was civil rights on the ground. The committee publicized the issue, lobbied ABC delegates to eliminate the restrictions, and asked teams and alley owners to press for change. Coalitions emerged in cities as disparate as Chicago, Philadelphia, Indianapolis, Cleveland, Santa Barbara, New York, Boston, Buffalo, Syracuse, Milwaukee, Minneapolis, Detroit, and Columbus. B'nai B'rith, UAW, AJC, Catholic Youth Organization, JLC, CORE, veterans' groups, ADL, AJCongress, NAACP, NCRAC, and even the American Legion coordinated local efforts. The NAACP, ADL, and JLC appeared before the ABC's Board of Directors. New Jersey activists picketed its 1949 convention. When all this failed, the NAACP, with the aid of the AJCongress, CIO, and ADL, filed complaints with the New York, Ohio, Illinois, and Wisconsin attorneys general that the ABC violated state antidiscrimination laws. Facing mounting pressure from all sides, not to mention "more than $40,000 in legal fees," delegates at ABC's 1950 convention voted overwhelmingly to end its whites-only rules. Its similarly besieged affiliate, the Women's International Bowling Congress, which had limited membership to white women, did the same.[132] Again the absence of federal civil rights laws hampered and complicated options to compel change.

The South posed even greater challenges. There, Jim Crow laws criminalized most integrated activities even if undertaken voluntarily. The National Duckpin Bowling Congress, which also restricted membership to "members of the Caucasian race," served a primarily southern sport. The ADL could only urge that "the discriminatory clause should be removed from the constitution . . . and also an educational job should be done in the states where the laws do not permit racial intermingling."[133] With such limited tools, challenging social discrimination proved extremely slow and difficult.

Still, whether failures or successes, these coalitions had another profound effect. Working together with those of different religious and racial backgrounds promoted the very change of heart these groups sought. As David Petegorsky argued, "Utilizing the forces of social control to combat racism and to improve group relations is important not only for its end results but because of the processes it involves." Because the problems of prejudice are shared by many groups, working together in "an equal status relationship" on issues of mutual concern is a far more effective challenge to bigotry than "a flow of 'canned' materials into the press of such groups." Regarding black anti-Semitism, for example, Maslow pointed out that when the CLSA supported a black Chicagoan's challenge to restrictive housing covenants in 1946, the *Chicago Defender* "carried the story in a headline, 'Jews Attack Restrictive Covenants.' That will do a hundred times as much good as a million leaflets that you distribute to Negroes, telling them that Jews are not exploiters."[134]

As CORE's Houser observed, education meant not merely disseminating pamphlets, but "creating the conditions of equality" both within the group taking action and in the larger society. Through its activities, CORE volunteers "of the Christian and Jewish faith, and of various races . . . learn by doing. . . . [I]nterracial and interfaith fellowship is part of the whole program." Similarly, Granger praised the "inter-faith, inter-race solidity" created by the NUL's "boards and committees. . . . This kind of teamwork between Negroes and whites, Jews and Gentiles, is a standing affirmation of faith in the democratic system."[135] Joint action itself reinforced pluralist values and challenged bigotry.

All this invites us to revisit the claim that black-Jewish collaborations were merely partnerships among elites. Most of these efforts were launched by local, middle-class, community leaders. If the CORE picketers, the CCREM testers, or the bowling clubs that fought the ABC are elites, then that concept has become too elastic to be useful. Indeed, even more than in earlier years, black-Jewish political cooperation received broad community support, confirmed by increased giving to civil rights agencies and staunchly liberal voting patterns.[136] Beyond the sense of shared oppression carried from earlier years, blacks and Jews in the 1950s (broadly speaking) endorsed liberalism's undergirding vision of individual freedom: the freedom to choose and celebrate one's identity and at the same time, freedom to enjoy equal access to the opportunities of employment, housing, voting, and civic life without reference to background or group membership. Certainly not every African American and every Jew embraced one another. Nor did the commitment to each other always extend beyond the rhetorical. Still, the evidence suggests that the devotion to liberal values and to civil rights for racial and religious minorities was broadly felt in this heyday of black-Jewish political cooperation. Such extensive political collaboration undergirds the arguments of those who consider this an era of black-Jewish "alliance." But if the two communities increasingly shared a commitment to liberal social justice, ongoing tensions threatened both their coalitions and that commitment.

"Constant 'needling' "

Longstanding biases held. Among Jews, racism persisted, although studies continued to suggest it was significantly less widespread and less virulent than views held by other whites. "I can quite understand your distress about anti-Negro statements by religious Jews, and I share your feeling completely," an ADL staffer wrote a Brooklyn woman, adding optimistically, "I suppose you realize that the people who disturbed you represent a definite minority among Jewish people, and that by and large the people who are most actively in support of pro-Negro and pro-democratic groups are the Jews."[137]

While tokenism did not raise black community hackles, other forms of Jewish paternalism still did. Walter White warned Jewish leaders of the "very dangerous attitude" of those pressuring him during the 1947 UN vote on Palestine. He saw "obvious condescension bordering on contempt for Haitians and Liberians because they are black and poor. . . . The language used . . . seemed clearly to indicate that the speakers felt that Haitians, Liberians and Indians should obey orders without question."[138]

In a private letter to Maslow, White complained again. "I would not have been surprised had these statements been made by semi-illiterate persons. But I was dumbfounded at the bluntness of the statements made by persons who ought to have known better." Similar incidents suggested to him that such attitudes were widespread. He described efforts to persuade a Jewish theater owner not to show the racist film *Birth of a Nation*. The owner refused, and added resentfully, " 'I have been a friend of *your* people but I don't expect any gratitude.' " White seethed. "I loathe the condescension implied in talking about 'your people' and was tempted to tell Mr. Brandt what I was trying to do at that very moment for *his* people" in refugee camps. Acknowledging these were "specific instances of prejudiced individuals" and that "you could cite examples of prejudice against Jews by Negroes who ought to know better," he concluded, "But don't you agree that it is your job and mine to fight as vigorously to eradicate anti-Semitism among Negroes and anti-Negroism among Jews as it is to fight our common enemy?"[139]

Other black leaders shared that resentment. In 1957 Kenneth Clark warned that "Jews who help Negroes in the struggle for equality do so from a position of unquestioned economic and political superiority. It may require a restructuring of the total pattern of this relationship . . . when and if the Negro attains the position where he no longer requires or desires the help of benefactors." Looking back, several Jewish leaders agreed. Albert Vorspan saw Jewish involvement in civil rights as "kind and benevolent . . . but it was also colonial." Jews had thought to do things "*for* Negroes rather than *with* them," acknowledged AJC's Harry Fleischman.[140]

Some Jews recognized the problem at the time. During its 1943 convention, the NCJW agreed to revise the wording of a resolution urging greater civil rights protections for African Americans. One delegate opposed the "part where it says that we should educate them [Negroes] to the point of self-respecting citizens. I think it would be an insult." Shad Polier warned in 1946 that "relatively speaking, we are a much more privileged group, and like all privileged groups . . . we tend, consciously or unconsciously, to slip into an attitude of superiority and of wanting to hold to ourselves the advantages." A 1948 ADL antibias guide advised that "the major responsibility for correcting any situation rests largely with those in a position of advantage. In our own country that is obviously the white man."[141] Such statements reveal an early appreciation of what scholars now call white privilege, the invisible benefits accruing to white people in the United States, and a recognition that racism and racial discrimination were, in the end, white people's problems and their responsibility. They offer a powerful, if partial, counterforce to Jewish paternalism. Jewish groups, in other words, may have acted paternalistically, but they did recognize their obligation not only as discrimination's victims but also its beneficiaries, to act rather than leave it to others.

African American anti-Semitism posed its own challenges to political collaboration.[142] As before, this manifested itself primarily in economic rather than theological terms. Jabs at the ostensible wealth and control of the Jewish community came from even prominent black newspapers and leaders. The *Chicago Defender*, for example, uncritically repeated an anti-Semitic slur made by Joe Louis's wife Marva in 1948 about British Jews wearing fur coats while others starved, which made even veterans of black-Jewish cooperation furious. "I am getting 'fed up' with this constant 'needling,' " complained Stella Counselbaum of the Chicago ADL office. "When a Negro newspaper of the standing of the 'Chicago Defender' prints anything as vicious as this they are making themselves a

party to the creation of the tension which they claim they would eliminate." Counselbaum was hardly a defensive Jewish advocate; she received
the NCNW's 1948 Honor Award "for work in human relations."[143]

Most common were invectives against Jewish business involvement in
black neighborhoods; many implied conspiratorial Jewish control. In
1956 the *Crusader* ran the headline "Grossman's Fights Negro Grocer;
Jews, Realtor, Conspire to Oust Businessman." The belief in Jewish exploitation persisted. An AJC study of Baltimore in 1949 revealed that 71
percent of African Americans there, compared with 51 percent of white
Christians (a frighteningly high number in itself), agreed with the statement that "in general Jews are dishonest in their business dealings."[144]

This delicate matter of Jewish exploiters continued to complicate the
interactions of black and white leaders; Jewish and black perspectives
remained divergent. In "Hating Jews," a 1947 *Pittsburgh Courier* editorial, Joseph Bibb called African Americans who endorsed anti-Semitism
"contemptible and idiotic." He argued that "'just plain white folks'"
were worse since Jews did business with African Americans—"at lofty
interest"—while most other whites "will have no part of you at any
price." Second, "Jewish people are . . . functioning with more interracial
organizations and giving the lifting hands to more colored people than
any other hyphenated American racial group." While "[w]e are fully
aware that many scheming, grasping Jewish people are drawing the life
blood out of our communities," he concluded, "we are compelled to conclude that the Jews are the best friends that the colored man in America
has." Most Jews were appalled. ADL's Abel Berland considered Bibb's
alleged anti-Semitism "confirmed by his article." But the former executive
director of the Chicago Urban League praised the article's stand against
black anti-Semitism, and White wrote Maslow that he "was puzzled by
your statement that . . . [the article] 'was in the worst tradition of [race
baiter] Gerald L. K. Smith.'"[145]

Both positions have merit. By using Jewish stereotypes as blanket indictments, Bibb was indulging in anti-Semitic practice. Yet his claims were
not incorrect, even if they were not representative acts of Jews in general,
and he raised precisely the points the ADL and AJC routinely made: Jews
were no worse than, and indeed were often better than, other white people; Jews had a special concern for African Americans; and the actions of
some Jews should not erase the contributions of others.

But black discussions of Jewish exploitation now routinely also included reminders of the two peoples' common agenda. A 1951 editorial
in the *Kansas City Call* noted with alarm that locally, "anti-Semitism is
growing among Negroes." After rehearsing the usual accusations, the editorial chided, "Negroes as one minority group should be the last ones to
exhibit a prejudice of any kind against another minority. The problems

of the two groups are so similar that it is hard to conceive how one could work contrary to the best interests of the other." Pointing out that "Jewish people all over the country are lending their support to our fight against injustice and bigotry wherever it exists," it concluded, "Disagree or quarrel with an individual Jewish citizen if you wish, but do not accuse the whole group of being like him."[146]

Even more dramatic was the change in Jewish leaders' responses. Increasingly, they acknowledged the legitimacy of specific criticism and turned to the activist precedents of New York and Chicago to address them. Charles Sherman's 1946 memorandum to the ADL Committee on Labor Relations minced no words. "It must be stated bluntly that with respect to them [African Americans] Jews are vulnerable. . . . The only Jew a Negro meets in the city is a pawn broker, grocer, insurance agent or landlord. The only Jew a sharecropper meets is a storekeeper or tradesman. As far as the Negro is concerned, Jews represent exploitation."[147]

Baltimore illustrates the changes in both Jewish and African American leaders. The AJC complained that the local NAACP chapter head, Mrs. Jackson, had consistently singled out Hutzler's, the Jewish-owned department store, for discrimination more widely practiced. But Sidney Hollander, Jewish leader and new president of the Baltimore Urban League, told Walter White in 1947 that while he believed Mrs. Jackson had an "anti-Jewish bias" that was hurting black-Jewish relations in that city, "I can't blame her too much for feeling as she does. As you know, I have something of the same feeling myself."[148] White, insisting that "we cannot permit any of our branches to be guilty of spreading prejudice against another minority whatever basis there may be"—a remarkable shift from his own earlier remarks on the subject—suggested a meeting with Mrs. Jackson but Gloster Current and Roy Wilkins counseled against it. "Organized Jewry in Baltimore, with such a champion as Mr. Hollander, ought to see that as long as Albert Hutzler continues his discrimination that just so long will the cleavage remain between the Negro and the Jew in Baltimore," wrote Current. "What is wrong in Baltimore is not the result of bias on Mrs. Jackson's part but is due to inability of the 'friends of the race' to make concrete headway within their own group." In any case, he concluded, "The militant program of the NAACP in Baltimore would not lend itself to close cooperation with the Urban League in that city anyway, and personally I do not blame Mrs. Jackson for taking the position that she has in this regard."[149]

White, shocked, wrote back. "It would be most regrettable for anyone connected with the NAACP to be guilty of prejudice or approval of prejudice against any minority. The Baltimore Branch most certainly should oppose discrimination by department stores but it is absolutely against the Association's principles to single out Jewish department stores for

attack as such when the gentile department stores are equally guilty."
White also gave a glimpse of intervention's private costs. Hollander "has
been fighting the discrimination in department stores there even though
it cost him the friendship of Mr. Hutzler who is not only a relative but . . .
one of Mr. Hollander's closest friends." In fact, he concluded, Hollander's
efforts have "resulted in a considerable change of policy by a majority of
the Jewish stores, while the two gentile stores are as adamant in their
prejudice as they have ever been."[150]

In 1947 the Essex County, New Jersey, JCRC, NAACP, UL, and others
drafted a letter to Nathan Orbach asking that he reverse his store's
whites-only hiring policy. The ADL suggested that Orbach first be approached informally by representatives of the Jewish groups. At that
meeting Orbach agreed to change his policy, and the group then sent the
letter to other stores, urging them to follow his lead.[151] That same year
the Detroit Jewish Community Council held a well-attended meeting
with East Side Jewish merchants and pressed for an end to exploitative
business practices. The JCC explained "that the Jewish merchants had
borne the brunt of the damage during the past riot, that that damage
had been wrecked [sic] upon Jewish stores because of the feeling in the
community that the Jewish merchants had been dealing unfairly and
took no interest in the Negro people."[152] Parochial and universal self-
interest came together neatly.

Meanwhile in Washington, D.C., NCRAC, AJC, AJCongress, ADL,
JWV, UAHC, and twenty-four Jewish Community Councils publicly
urged the National Theater to open its doors to black patrons, despite
the opposition of local Jews, including the theater owner. As ADL's Paul
Richman put it, "The conflict . . . seems to center primarily between Jews
who wish to prevent negroes [sic] from entering the theater and Jews
who are trying to get them in." The AJCongress launched a petition drive
among actors pledging not to perform there or in any other segregated
theater. Democratic symbolism proved particularly potent in this case.
"That democracy should be made a mockery of in the national capital of
this the world's greatest democracy, that the equal rights of men should
be flouted within the very shadow of this nation's governmental buildings,
seems to us monstrous and intolerable," NCRAC insisted.[153] Jewish leaders' more positive engagement in these issues occurred for several interrelated reasons: continued Jewish concern over the dangers of anti-Semitism
and the desire to lessen it where possible, the increasing importance of
collaborative political work with the black community and the fear of
undermining it, and the growing engagement with a universalist civil
rights struggle that made the contradiction between calls for equal treatment and continued racist practice less tenable.

By the mid-1950s the issue of black economic anti-Semitism had de-clined markedly. As Kenneth Clark observed in 1957, "The more obvious forms of verbal anti-Semitism, common among Negroes ten to fifteen years ago, seem to have been substantially ameliorated." He accounted for this by noting, among other factors, the increased and "important role" Jewish organizations had begun playing in the civil rights struggle. The continued exodus of Jewish businesses from inner-city neighbor-hoods and improved practices of those who remained no doubt contrib-uted as well. But if Jewish economic exploitation and black anti-Semitism declined, the Rev. James Robinson noted new arenas of conflict, including "an increased feeling of bitterness over the fact that Jews in better neigh-borhoods and suburban areas are often as hostile as other whites, when Negroes attempt to move in." [154]

"No Negroes present": Southern Jews and Civil Rights

Perhaps the greatest challenge to black/Jewish amity was the situation in the South, where most Jews sought invisibility when it came to ques-tions of race. Some southern Jews like Burnett Roth, who helped found Miami's active ADL office, did work hard and openly for civil rights. The NCJW's San Antonio chapter lobbied Congress to abolish the poll tax in 1943. Its Charleston chapter was the only Jewish group to join the effort to integrate the police force. In several cities Jews were promi-nent in Civil Rights Congress chapters. A black and Jewish-led CORE chapter in Miami desegregated local lunch counters in the late 1950s. A few rabbis, mostly Reform, spoke out against segregation and worked with black ministers and others, usually behind the scenes, to promote racial equality.[155]

But more often, southern Jews proved themselves little better than other whites around them. Relatively few in number, still perceiving themselves as vulnerable outsiders in a bastion of Christian fundamentalism, most southern Jews followed the segregation patterns set by their white gentile neighbors. A 1951 ADL survey revealed that unlike the common practice in the North, no southern Jewish Community Center accepted black members, and most barred them from any participation at all. A syna-gogue youth group "had an interracial week," noted the Chattanooga Tennessee Urban League in disgust, "—no Negroes present." Walter White neatly encapsulated the divergent behaviors within the southern Jewish community when he contrasted a Fort Lauderdale Jewish choir that sang in a black church despite being threatened with violence by the local police, and a Jewish-owned hotel twenty-six miles away in Miami that refused to accept African American guests.[156]

Most southern Jews attributed their silence to fear of anti-Semitism, and pressed their nationals to tone down their efforts. Nor were such fears unfounded. In 1958 AJC's Edwin Lukas warned, "Huge quantities of primitive anti-Semitic literature have been poured by organized . . . hate mongers . . . , blaming Jews for nearly everything that has happened in the South—from Lee's surrender and Sherman's march, to the Supreme Court decision [in *Brown*] itself."[157]

Not only did national Jewish groups therefore find it difficult to recruit local volunteers for southern projects, southern Jewish resistance limited action even on the national level, since these organizations relied on their membership for both financial support and policy decisions. Despite decades of involvement by the NCJW against restrictive housing covenants, for example, a southern delegate to its 1943 conference blocked passage of a resolution opposing them by insisting that racial integration, unlike religious, required further study.[158]

In deference to southern concerns the AJC pledged in 1949 "never to undertake activity in a local community against the opposition of the local community organization." As George Hexter explained, "Local communities in the South can not be expected to implement fully the national policy of all-out opposition to anti-Negro discrimination; but this . . . does not mean that any Southern chapter . . . has ever said that it opposed the policy nationally."[159]

Because ADL chapters weighed in on policy decisions, southern members managed to delay the ADL's filing of several amicus briefs. In *Briggs v. Elliott*, the ADL's Southern Regional Board advised the national against filing. "After much discussion" the ADL decided to file, but the Regional Board asked it to reconsider "with such vehemence and genuine sincerity" that the ADL agreed to postpone its decision until the next National Commission meeting. There, the southern representative, Alfred Smith, pleaded that while "[a]ll men of good will—and we are certainly in that category—want with utmost sincerity to see an extension of the democratic principle of equal civil rights in all fields," filing briefs was the wrong way to attain that goal. With southern opposition so strong, public identification with desegregation would identify Jews as a "disloyal minority" and reduce ADL workers "to a position of inertness." Other southern speakers reminded listeners of southern anti-Semitism. Ultimately the ADL did vote to proceed. Filing in the *Brown* case was similarly delayed. And even after the court decision, B'nai B'rith lodges in Louisiana, Mississippi, and Virginia asked the ADL to reconsider its position.[160]

Here, southern fears merely cost ADL a delay. In other cases, the League ended up compromising its program. In 1949 an ADL affiliate, the Institute for American Democracy, produced two sets of "brotherhood" comics for children. In one, a scene of children included a black boy. The other, for use in the South, depicted an entirely white crowd. As White noted in a letter of protest, "It seems to me that if members of the ADL living in the south cannot stand up for the brotherhood of all human beings, including Negroes, there is little point spending money to print 'brotherhood' literature at all." In his reply, Ben Epstein admitted being "as shocked as you were" and claimed that "we are vigorously opposed to what was done." But, he added, "This does not at all detract from the fact that some materials will be more acceptable in the South than others." Almost a decade later, the ADL, with more, and more active, southern offices than any other Jewish organization, was still playing down its civil rights activities, reassuring southern Jews that while it worked "in harmony" with the NAACP on issues of joint concern, "we probably have more projects going with chambers of commerce."[161]

The Garden of Forking Paths: Race, Religion, and Liberalism

The liberal consensus itself also contributed to black-Jewish strains in ways that would only become fully visible in the 1960s. Because liberals of the time posited racism as a moral problem and looked to individual action to remedy it, neither community fully recognized the structural underpinnings to racism. When liberal strategies failed to dislodge those deeper barriers, black activists would, far more quickly and more often than Jews, come to question the efficacy of the liberal vision. The roots of these future disagreements are visible even in cooperative political activities of the 1940s and '50s, and are nowhere more evident than in efforts to end employment discrimination against both blacks and Jews.

Take the struggle to convince employers not to inquire about religion or race on application forms. The Commercial Travelers Mutual Accident Association of America's application asked, for example, "Are you a male white person?" When challenged by the AJCongress in 1942, the Association explained this was not "discrimination against any particular class or creed, but . . . so that we would not be forced to accept applications of some undesirables where the question of color would be involved." Such inquiries were ubiquitous. Maslow reported that in 1946 "there was an increase in discriminatory help wanted ads . . . [of] almost 200 percent" and feared that "this type of discrimination was likely to increase as the years went on." The Bureau on Jewish Employment Problems in Chicago conducted a survey of four thousand firms in 1955. It found 27 percent requested non-Jewish placements and "as might be expected, discrimination by reason of race proved to be the most severe."[162]

Once employers agreed not to solicit racial or religious information, Jewish groups considered the problem largely solved; without knowing an applicant's background, employers would now hire on the basis of merit. And for many Jews, at least those without identifiable Jewish surnames, this was indeed the case. As Maslow observed, even if this change "does nothing but drive discriminatory practice underground, it still serves a useful function. It is much more difficult for a personnel manager to discriminate against Jews when he has no ready means of determining whether an applicant is a Jew."[163] But for African Americans writing one's race on a form is usually superfluous and most continued to be denied employment, housing, loans, and accommodations. For black organizations, unlike Jewish ones, theoretical race blindness was not enough. In fact one of the crucial differences between blacks and Jews in the United States is precisely that Jews, at least those who do not look or sound "Jewish," can "pass" in a way that most black people cannot. In other words, Jews' white skin gave them access to opportunities still determined by race. But when those determinations were no longer made explicitly, their operation became largely invisible to Jews and other whites. This was white privilege in operation, whether its beneficiaries recognized it or not.

Jews' belief that the discrimination problem was largely solved may be explained by the lesser resilience of anti-Semitism compared to racism. As Maslow explained in 1954, unlike racism, which was still "not only blunt and obvious but often . . . boasted of," anti-Semitic acts "are not considered respectable," and so eliminating questions on religion improved Jewish economic opportunity. During World War II, when anti-Semitism was more overt, Jewish groups recognized that firms, when barred from inquiring about religion, used other means to identify Jewish applicants.[164] But by the 1950s, Nazism had discredited active Jew-hatred, and religious differences muted as the migrants' children assimilated and civil rights protests diverted attention to race. Perhaps one reason many Jews did not see the limitations of their efforts to prevent queries on race or religion in the 1950s was that given lessening anti-Semitism, for Jews the strategy succeeded.

Even when discrimination continued against Jews, improved Jewish class status rendered it less significant. As the 1948 NCRAC study observed, for example, while certain Illinois department stores rarely hired Jewish clerks, "only a very small number of Jews seek employment in these fields." Similarly few sought membership in trade unions. Indeed, since most Jews there were "middle-class, self-employed and professional, . . . on the whole, discrimination in employment is not an immediate problem . . . since they are scarcely in the labor market."[165]

Furthermore, because religion never played the central role race did in defining American identity, the discrediting of public anti-Semitism meant that for Jews discrimination manifested itself almost exclusively in the private actions of individuals. Racism, by contrast, remained firmly rooted in the law and in economic practice. Maslow observed that because of these differences between racial and religious discrimination, Jews rarely required the legislative and legal strategies still employed by black agencies. Concluding that irrational prejudice explained bigotry, Jewish groups increasingly focused on public education campaigns to promote tolerance.[166] While they argued that these benefited African Americans as well, racism was far less responsive to such techniques. In any case, the roots of racism lay in the deep structures of society rather than solely in the minds of individuals.

Many Jews (and other liberals) failed to recognize the real and substantial benefits discriminators gained by their discrimination. Anti-Semitism and, even more so, racism were sustained not only by stereotypes but by white Christian self-interest. By limiting access to society's goods and services, those within the circle enjoyed a disproportionate share. While Jews, small in number and never legally restricted, posed little threat, black equality required the dismantling of exclusionary systems, from FHA guidelines protecting white neighborhoods to seniority rules that privileged those already inside. Educational programs could not accomplish this; institutional racism had to be tackled in very different ways. So long as these methods included legal and legislative work, Jewish groups continued to support civil rights efforts, even though they had little impact on anti-Semitism.

But the growing movement within the civil rights community toward mass action strategies that appeared to threaten the system of civic stability made liberal Jewish groups uneasy. Jews' relative safety in a society rooted in liberal ideals of civil order and obedience to the law, and their remarkable success in transcending discrimination and joining the middle class, inevitably led to a devotion to the American social system that had made that safety and success possible. Their success verified for them a commitment to liberalism. But it also made Jews wary of actions that might jeopardize their gains. In the words of Kenneth Clark, "Personal status needs and conformity pressures as they operate to perpetuate the racial status quo appear no less imperative for Jews than for other Americans."[167] With some trepidation, Jewish groups did come to support the tactics of the Montgomery bus boycott and even CORE's dignified civil disobedience, although they refused direct participation, and, when they could, still counseled patience and negotiation as preferable to public protest. Jewish organizations, happy and indeed eager to embrace the civil rights agenda of voting rights and antisegregation and discrimination legislation, remained more skeptical about tactics that rejected the value of moderation that they believed crucial for their own security.

Yet many Jews understood the divergence between black and Jewish political choices differently. Jews were not doing too little on behalf of black civil rights. "[O]ur organizational structure is completely committed to the elimination of all forms of prejudice," Nathan Edelstein of the AJCongress insisted in 1960. "We adhere to this position even though corresponding Negro support of Jewish objectives . . . has not been extensive. Faced with problems far more severe than those of the Jewish community, Negro defense activities have been shaped far more by their own immediate and pressing problems than by general principles. . . . If one views the situation in terms of striking a balance, there is a large Negro deficit." Roy Wilkins concurred. He lamented that while Jewish groups had served as resources "with respect to predominantly Negro problems . . . I would wish that it could be true consistently of Negro groups with relation to anti-Semitism." Edelstein concluded that the imbalance was irrelevant to the question of whether Jews should involve themselves in civil rights. "Jews are dedicated to the cause of justice and equality because it is best for all Americans. Jews as well as Negroes are the beneficiaries of a society that assures full equality for all."[168] Nevertheless, such differences of perspective and approach would sharpen in the next, more activist, mass-action phase of the civil rights movement. Liberalism, and with it the liberal black-Jewish coalition, would find itself under siege.

CHAPTER FIVE

Red Menace

Communism posed particular challenges for liberals engaged in civil rights. Communists as well as noncommunist leftists had long been active in antiracist and civil rights struggles as courageous and committed advocates at a time when few other allies were to be had. Their economic critique of racism and mass-action tactics brought something new and important to the civil rights struggle. But many desired revolution more than democracy. They were also targets of intense fear and antagonism, so collaboration with them intensified attacks from the right. These facts forced liberals into difficult choices.

If the question of whether to work with communists presented a dilemma, so did the means of repudiating them. Many steps taken against the Communist Party (CP) also diminished democracy by trampling on the civil liberties crucial for the free expression of difference. Furthermore, many of the most public opponents of communism were those who regularly denounced all civil rights and social reform programs as communist conspiracies. Thus if liberal black and Jewish groups were to continue their work, they believed they had to simultaneously fight communism and defend the civil liberties that protected its free expression. How they sought to strike that balance, and how they selected strategies and programs within these constraints, is the subject of this chapter.

The postwar history of civil rights is deeply embedded in the political struggles between liberals and leftists. Communists and socialists had embraced black civil rights long before most white liberals had, and in local communities, both North and South, they had provided the backbone of much civil rights organizing. They continued to do so in the postwar period.[1] But now, leftists faced two new challenges: liberals and the cold war. Liberals, newly strengthened by the New Deal and the war, newly energized to challenge racial discrimination and bigotry, opposed communist activity for reasons of both ideology and control. And the intensifying hatred, fear, and competition between the communist nations of the East and capitalist nations of the West rendered all American communist activity suspect and provided a potent weapon for conservatives to challenge progressive programs.

The postwar history of blacks and Jews was shaped by these political struggles. Liberal black and Jewish organizations fought for traction in this charged environment, and blacks and Jews figured prominently among both liberals and leftists, from Irving Howe and Sidney Hook to Paul Robeson and W.E.B. Du Bois.[2] The writings of black and Jewish intellectuals helped shape the goals and priorities of the organizations engaged in civil rights work. They had just as profound an influence on the political and tactical choices these organizations made regarding the parameters of that engagement. The complex and ambivalent relationships between black and Jewish liberal agencies and the left is central to our story.

Despite communists' history of contributions to antiracist and antidiscriminatory struggles, however, liberal (and most socialist) African American and Jewish groups opposed them, particularly after the Nazi-Soviet pact of 1939. They considered communism antidemocratic, both in theory and in its concrete expression in the Soviet Union and, later, China. Because democracy was the cornerstone for most black and Jewish appeals for justice, communism represented a threat to both groups' most deeply held goals. "Communism . . . rests upon the denial of democracy, . . . upon the suppression of the fundamental basis of human liberties," B'nai B'rith, the nation's largest Jewish fraternal order, resolved in 1938, before such a position was politically expedient. "[F]or all of these reasons, and more, Communism is abhorrent to the Jews." The NUL held the same view. "Everything that the League stands for and seeks to accomplish is within the democratic framework and devoted to the democratic principle," wrote executive director Lester Granger in 1956. "The Communist purpose is to destroy that framework and abort the principle."[3]

This appeal to democracy was certainly strategic. In an era where democracy provided the motivating rhetoric for war, both hot and cold, tying one's agenda to it elevated that agenda to one of national security. Anticommunism was also politically crucial. The right often equated Jews and communists, and portrayed African American civil rights activists as communist dupes. Black and Jewish organizations therefore had to establish their distance from communism, both to refute charges that could destroy their political viability, and to legitimize their civil rights positions. Certainly it did one's political agenda no good to be seen as linked to communism.[4]

But for these black and Jewish groups the commitment to democracy ran deeper than pragmatism. It was at the root of their commitment to liberalism. "Jewish welfare is bound up with the preservation of democratic principles and ideals," the AJC argued. "Jews have been traditionally in the forefront of every liberal movement. Communism is the negation of liberalism. We should fight it because it imperils those values that we deem essential to a good life."[5] Liberalism protected differences and grounded civil rights arguments. These organizations argued that a liberal democracy, which required a participatory citizenry and the dispersion of power, was crucial to the defense of civic equality. The opposites of democracy—dictatorship, fascism, totalitarianism—were notorious for their denial of equal rights, and their concentration of power within small groups, which, the AJCongress repeatedly noted, "inevitably corrodes and destroys those freedoms which must constitute the foundation for the peace and progress of mankind." Such attitudes were rooted in self-interest. As the AJC, B'nai B'rith, and JLC insisted in a 1935 statement, "Jewish emancipation has always gone hand in hand with the progress of democracy."[6] Granger made the same point for African American liberals in 1949: "[T]he Communist . . . seeks to destroy the democratic ideal and practice which constitute the Negro['s] sole hope of eventual victory in his fight for equal citizenship." Communist organizations supported civil rights efforts for their own reasons, Roy Wilkins insisted. "The CP boys are . . . liars and double-crossers and their true allegiance . . . is to the Soviet Union, not to the attainment of democracy for the Negro. . . . Their end objective is to do away with the American Constitutional system. . . . That is . . . basic Communist philosophy as everyone knows who can read."[7]

Power struggles also help explain the vehemence of the liberal opposition. When Frank Crosswaith of the Negro Labor Committee lambasted communists he was speaking, at least in part, explicitly about those whose efforts to organize Harlem labor challenged his own organization.[8] The NAACP resisted the efforts of the communists to defend the Scottsboro boys and opposed the National Negro Congress's antilynching campaign as much over turf as over politics.

For all these reasons, liberal black and Jewish organizations monitored and challenged communist groups and doctrines, publicized communism's dangers to their communities, and even cooperated with investigative bodies and committees they recognized as a threat to civil liberties. Crucial to this effort was the repeated assertion of their anticommunist convictions, particularly as the right linked their programs with the communist agenda they abhorred.

We Are Not Communists

"PROJECT BIG FOUR!" accused officers of the ADL, AJC, NAACP, and NUL of "belonging to Communist inspired or otherwise subversive groups." Its leaflets wondered, "WHY SHOULD YOU, A PATRIOTIC AMERICAN CITIZEN, PERMIT THIS CONSPIRACY AGAINST YOUR INDIVIDUAL FREEDOMS AND PRIVATE PROPERTY RIGHTS TO CONTINUE?" This "secret investigation committee," directed by Aldrich Blake from the right-wing "America Plus," was only one of a number of efforts to discredit and destroy the leading civil rights agencies.[9] It and like-minded organizations led campaigns in dozens of cities to challenge the groups' tax-exempt status, to convince local Community Chests to withdraw support from the Urban League, and to "whip up racial hysteria" in the South, to use Granger's words. In 1955, when Granger raised the matter, challenges to the NUL were underway in Richmond, Little Rock, Memphis, Fort Worth, St. Louis, Baton Rouge, and Washington, D.C.; "We are not fooling ourselves about the seriousness of this and similar movements." Following his suggestion, the four groups in question met to strategize against this latest attack. Blake's lawsuits failed, but the gathering noted with concern the link between his group and California state senator Jack Tenney. As chairman of his state's Committee on Un-American Activities Tenney had listed the liberal Institute for American Democracy and several departments of the ADL as subversive, and labeled his state's AJCongress a communist front. These sorts of attacks on the loyalty of black and Jewish Americans were commonplace, and the right used them to justify opposition to liberal programs.[10]

In 1952, for example, the Houston Council on Education and Race Relations invited Dr. Rufus Clement, president of Atlanta University, to speak at its annual interracial, interdenominational service. Eager to discredit the president of the largest African American university in the country, a small right-wing group began to circulate rumors against Clement. "There are many Methodists who do not object to the program of social mingling of Negroes and Whites," anonymous literature disingenuously asserted, but "there are many who will oppose an individual with a communist front record presiding over the brotherhood services." The accusations were false, the ADL intervened with the local American Legion to prevent protest demonstrations, and the service went on as planned. "*The smear attempt had failed*," gloated S. Thomas Friedman in his report to ADL counsel Arnold Forster.[11]

Other attempts proved more successful. Insisting the NAACP was a subversive organization, several southern states in the 1950s demanded the Association turn over its membership lists. It refused to do so. While the NAACP won each case in the end, its arguments reinforced by Jewish organizations' amicus briefs, there was little chapter activity in those states during the long months and years of litigation. The "Southern Manifesto," a 1956 declaration signed by more than ninety southern congressional leaders outlining their intent to resist desegregation, labeled civil rights a communist plot to destabilize the U.S.[12]

Black and Jewish organizations were therefore particularly concerned to rebut the accusation of disloyalty by publicizing their community's anticommunism. Such positioning began early among black liberals. In 1930 the NAACP publicized the testimony of Labor Department commissioner Charles Wood before a congressional committee investigating communism: "I do not think the Communist movement . . . is making any substantial headway into the ranks of the colored race. The colored race as a whole are pretty sound-minded, canny too; they are . . . honest-to-God Americans and they glory in that fact." At every opportunity, black leaders stressed the CP's failure to recruit large numbers of black people. When Granger testified before HUAC, the House Un-American Activities Committee, in 1949 he spent fully a third of his time providing evidence that few African Americans belonged to the CP. Rather, he insisted, racists claimed black people were communist merely to discredit civil rights.[13]

When Paul Robeson, outspoken on both civil rights and communism, suggested in 1949 that black people might not be loyal to the United States in a war with the Soviet Union, Walter White hastened to reassure the broader public. Despite anger over segregation, he maintained, African Americans would support the nation in any war. "We know of no authority delegated to Mr. Robeson to speak for the fourteen million Negro Americans. We are convinced that . . . he has not voiced the opinion of the overwhelming majority of colored citizens." Even whites got the message. After interviewing white people in Atlanta, Alexander Miller of the ADL's southern regional office reassured a concerned HUAC investigator that "the great majority believed that Robeson was wrong and that Negroes would be loyal."[14]

While the anticommunist right often charged that African Americans were communist dupes—that communist agitators stirred up otherwise contented black people to demand what they did not deserve—they accused Jews of being those agitators, directing the actions of the Soviet Union and all international attempts to destabilize (Christian) civilization. Jewish organizations took pains to rebut this longstanding canard and to ensure their community did nothing that might reinforce it in the minds of non-Jews. On the heels of the Russian revolution, Louis Marshall, then president of the AJC, publicly repudiated the charge made at a Senate Judiciary Committee hearing that Jews were Bolshevists. "Everything that . . . Bolshevism stands for is to the Jew detestable," he declared.[15]

Following Hitler's equation of Jews and communists in 1935 (which he used to justify the denial of Jewish civil rights in Germany), the AJC, B'nai B'rith, and the newly organized Jewish Labor Committee (JLC) issued a joint statement pointing to the low number of Jewish communists and arguing that his accusation was a smokescreen for the Nazis' suppression of civil liberties. They feared the same at home. As Rabbi Edward Israel of Boston observed in 1939, "The technique of the American Nazi and Fascist is to try to identify the Jew with Communism and thus use the anti-Semitic hysteria as an instrument to push America to the other extreme."[16]

Such concerns made Jewish statements even more forceful. "COMMUNISM NEVER WAS JEWISH! COMMUNISM CERTAINLY IS NOT JEWISH TODAY! COMMUNISM CAN NEVER BE JEWISH!" began a 1938 ADL "Fireside Discussion Group" pamphlet.[17] The AJC conferred with news editors "with respect to featuring pro-democratic activities . . . of Jews as well as their forthright anti-Communist positions" and widely distributed a Billy Rose column entitled "Yom Kippur in Korea."[18]

No Jewish organization remained silent. "The doctrines of Judaism have always been akin to the doctrines of democracy," insisted the Jewish War Veterans (JWV) at their 1939 convention. In 1940 *The Modern View* offered its readers "'Jewish Communism Is a Lie!': Communism Can Never Be Jewish—Jewish Representatives Speak Out," a compilation of anticommunist pronouncements of Jewish organizations of the past twenty years. Similar statements came from virtually every Jewish organization, individual rabbis and congregations, and from the Jewish press.[19]

The Korean War provided black and Jewish groups a public opportunity to portray their anticommunist credentials as well as attack the right on questions of domestic civil rights and civil liberties. The Synagogue Council of America viewed Korean "communist imperialism" as not only a threat to U.S. security but also "a threat to the spiritual values that are the foundation of the Jewish faith." It therefore supported American war aims. But, it warned, the United States "must [simultaneously] establish within our own borders a just and righteous society, based on vigilant protection of individual rights." Lester Granger likewise praised the military mobilization against a worldwide communist threat "more massive than any faced by the American people since the War of Revolution." But the U.S. could not win that struggle without addressing the "delayed starts, timid efforts and wasted opportunities" that marked race relations.[20]

But such avid anticommunism occasionally led to pragmatic alliances with the right. While it might "acquire . . . a number of unsavory allies in this fight," the AJC explained, "We are not joining forces with them."[21] That claim was belied in October 1950 when it voted to affiliate with the All-American Conference Against Communism, and make a substantial donation. This decision horrified most other Jewish groups. The Conference, the AJCongress pointed out, "is the group whose prime movers include such 'stalwart defenders' of civil rights and civil liberties as the Daughters of the American Revolution, the American Legion, the National Association of Manufacturers, Senators Mundt and Tenney of California." DAR members "are among the most rabid advocates and practitioners of segregation and discrimination" and many in the NAM "represent the industries in which discrimination in employment has been flagrant and unchecked." Although the NAACP believed the AJC sought by its participation to "direct its activities into more democratic channels," the AJCongress countered that "we Jews have learned by this time that our security is, in the long run, jeopardized less by the violent anti-Semitism of the hate mongers than it is by those who maintain the pattern of racist thought and practice in America, who cavalierly violate civil liberties and who resist any effort to make democracy meaningful." The ADL, which also considered joining the organization for the sake of a Jewish anticommunist presence, decided not to do so because of "the deep-rooted antipathy of the overwhelming mass of the Jews to sitting around the same table with the Mundts, and the Tenneys, and the others."[22]

Still, the AJC hardly staked out the most conservative position in the Jewish community on this question. The American Jewish League Against Communism (AJLAC), which posited communism as "a conspiracy aimed at God, the Ten Commandments and Judeo-Christian morality," worked closely with anticommunists like J. Edgar Hoover, Richard Nixon, and Roy Cohn (whom it honored for "outstanding Americanism and Judaism") to expose communists, fellow travelers, and "careless" or "naive" Jewish leaders who inadvertently supported the "Communist Line."[23]

AJLAC revealed its politics in its analysis of the civil rights struggle. In a letter to President Truman the group concluded that "much of the racial tension is artificial; and . . . has been deliberately fostered by the Communist party to divide the American people." That the group had little sympathy for liberals is evident; elsewhere it accused them of being dupes, intentionally or not, of communism.[24] Although AJLAC represented a tiny minority of the Jewish community, its high visibility and the company it kept made the group a concern for the mainstream Jewish organizations, who monitored its every move to provide damage control.

Despite such strenuous anticommunist avowals, white supremacists continued to cast blacks and Jews as communists, and all civil rights activity as communist-inspired. Granger believed the attacks and accusations "increasingly better organized" after the *Brown* decision. These attacks had real repercussions for southern black-Jewish collaboration. Edwin Lukas lamented that as a result, "communication between Negro and white groups, around a variety of urgent intergroup problems, has been almost entirely suspended in about eight . . . southern states, and is carried on desultorily in the others." Although cooperation among progressive groups was particularly urgent given the increased threat of violence, it appeared more risky than ever for groups to enter into such coalitions. As historian Ray Mohl noted in reference to the Miami bombings, "these attacks linked white racism, anti-Semitism, and anti-Communism—a powerful combination in the South and in the United States in the 1950s."[25]

The "quarantine treatment"

Given their pragmatic and ideological opposition to communism, liberal organizations generally shunned communist or front groups seeking to cooperate on civil rights. S. Andhil Fineberg of the AJC called this the "quarantine treatment." The Party's real goal, totalitarianism, "is utterly destructive of the spiritual, cultural and social values on which depend the security and free development of Jewish life no less than the survival of democratic civilization." Therefore, as Granger emphasized, "in order to defeat their long-range purposes we must reject their offer of support even for the cause which we ourselves serve." These groups were only reiterating the agenda of the CP itself. "We must orient our comrades to be active among the masses and main organizations of the Jewish workers and people and not to . . . leave the bulk of the people to the influence of reactionary leadership," John Williamson insisted on behalf of the CP National Committee. He cited the AJCongress as one instance of a "substantial united-front experience."[26]

Liberal black and Jewish efforts to block communist involvement began well before government loyalty programs. In August 1935 the AJCongress Governing Council debated "cooperation with the communists" on anti-Nazi efforts. During the ensuing debate, a Mr. Segal insisted that "the Communists had no moral right to participate in the anti-Hitler fight with Jews" and warned cooperating with them would drive noncommunists away. The council chairman disagreed. He argued such positions were "too narrow and tactically unwise" and noted that the Congress worked in coalition with other groups with whom it had no shared interests beyond anti-Nazism. A Professor Michael pointed out that refusal to cooperate with communists was disturbingly similar to the position of those who would not cooperate with Jews because they were Jews. The anticommunists won the day, and the group passed a motion agreeing to "cooperate with all organized groups of American citizens engaged in combating Hitlerism in Germany, with the exception of the Communists."[27]

Other Jewish groups shared these concerns. The NCJW president feared communist groups might "try to associate themselves with" its efforts. The Council chose to continue its program, "which we believed is so urgently needed," but sought to "exercise the utmost care in the selection of cooperating organizations." When, despite its precautions, the "Families of the Smith Act Victims" and National Committee to

Secure Justice in the Rosenberg Case "fraudulently used and/or referred to" the NCJW "for their own political purposes" in 1952, the president made prompt and strong objection.[28]

Certainly these organizations were mindful of the danger of witch hunts. In 1950 the Jewish Peoples Fraternal Organization (JPFO), "an organization of proven Communist affiliation," was expelled from the Los Angeles Jewish Community Relations Council (JCRC), and the local AJC asked the national office for guidance "as to what position it should take within the [J]CRC on this matter." The national agreed, "relationships with such [communist-affiliated or led] organizations cannot in the first instance be developed . . . and whenever . . . attempted, cannot be continued." But it tried to balance fear of communism with concern for civil liberties. "Such a determination however should not be made by mere association, by rumor, or by anonymous accusations. It should be made only on the basis of adequate evidence and fair procedures." Several ADL leaders also warned against "overreaction" to the communist threat. "I wonder if we are not giving aid and comfort to the purveyors of hysteria and fear by magnifying the danger?" mused Oscar Cohen.[29]

The NAACP also struggled with the question of cooperation with communists. Both had been deeply engaged in the antilynching struggle for many years, and leftists had provided much of the muscle and energy in local campaigns. The NAACP therefore agreed to CP requests to distribute the Association's antilynching petitions. In 1939, however, White raised concerns with George Murphy who had passed the petitions on. The May 4 *Daily Worker* headline, "'Harlem C.P. Shows How to Lead Anti-Lynch Drive' . . . confirmed my feeling that the Communists would try to appropriate the entire issue." The issue was not one of credit, he insisted, but pragmatism. "This clipping in the hands of Bilbo, Connally, Russell, Smith or Carter Glass would practically ruin any efforts to secure passage of the bill." He pressed Murphy "to be much more selective in the future . . . because the work of thirty years can be and may be destroyed."[30]

Murphy emphatically disagreed. "Frankly, I think it is a little fantastic to suppose that the whole work of the N.A.A.C.P. could be destroyed, as you put it, by the mere fact that the Communist Party distributed a large number of our anti-lynching petitions." In any case, he pointed out, the communists had issued their own antilynching petitions before the NAACP did. "In this respect I agree with Heywood Broun, who says, and quite logically, are we to be branded because we believe in a number of things that the Communists also believe in? And, must we cease to believe in those things because the Communists believe them too?" He acknowledged White's position as "a practical lobbyist" and agreed to follow White's instructions. Nonetheless, he questioned White's reasoning, since "the Bilbo's are going to filibuster no less because the Communists are not going our way than they would if the Communists are going our way." No one "can frighten the N.A.A.C.P. . . . unless we ourselves, allow ourselves to be frightened," he concluded, "and I want to believe that you still stand up to the opposition as you have done in the past." But despite such internal disagreements, the NAACP remained steadfast, some believed overzealous, in its refusal to work with communist groups, excluding them from all its programs and coalition efforts, since "the Communist philosophy precludes of necessity a consistent stand of civil rights."[31]

The NUL was equally clear about the dangers, both ideological and pragmatic, of cooperation with communist and communist-front organizations. Beyond the "social danger" communism posed, "It would also destroy our effectiveness . . . since the groups that we depend upon for collaboration are themselves as strongly anti-Communist as we," explained Granger.[32] Given the number and ferocity of right-wing attacks and smear campaigns against it, the NUL had reason to be concerned about the political danger of apparent collaboration with communists. Nevertheless, such choices, as Granger himself admitted, meant rejecting the help of one of the handful of organizations working on civil rights in this era.

Concerns that cooperation with communists would jeopardize their own organization extended even, or perhaps especially, to more progressive black groups. On the grounds that the CP's highest goal was not civil rights but the promotion of Soviet interests, the 1948 CORE convention voted unanimously against allowing "Communist-controlled" organizations to affiliate, and to expel chapters that had become dominated by them. CORE chapters were urged not to cooperate with front groups.[33]

"We want none of that unity"

The refusal of liberal groups to cooperate with the CP or perceived front organizations on civil rights issues sealed the fate of the National Negro Congress; the story of the NNC and its offspring, the Civil Rights Congress (CRC) illustrates another component of liberal/communist conflict. The NNC and CRC employed tactics and styles offensive, if not antithetical, to liberals. The incompatibility between the two, that is, extended to differences of approach as well as substance.

A national committee led by John Davis, Secretary of the Joint Committee on National Recovery, formed the NNC in 1936 as an umbrella for progressive civil rights organizations. Davis served as its executive secretary, and A. Philip Randolph as its president (succeeded, upon his resignation, by Max Yergin and then Davis). Independent of the CP but always friendly to it (and economically supported by it), the NNC provided a vehicle for communist activists seeking to join mainstream civil rights efforts. Both the Nazi-Soviet pact and Hitler's invasion of the USSR, however, forced communist NNC members to make dramatic swings in crucial positions. This alienated other activists and provided an opening for anticommunists to challenge the NNC's methods. In 1940 Randolph left the organization in disgust, and the NNC more openly embraced communist positions. By the end of World War II the NNC had diminished in numbers and force, and much of the momentum of a leftist civil rights effort had been lost. But from the start liberal black organizations, particularly the NAACP, had kept a suspicious distance.

Walter White and Charles Houston had worried about communist involvement in the NNC's 1936 founding convention. The NAACP refused to endorse the convention, White explained, "because we are not certain of its sponsorship and where it is going." He did agree to send Wilkins to observe, but warned Randolph, "Do hope Congress is not permitted to be 'sold down the river' to any political group. Have heard many disturbing rumors." Randolph replied, "I assure you that so far as I have any power, the Congress will not be 'sold down the river' to any political group, and I think this is the sentiment of numerous forces in it." Still, he acknowledged, "it is well to be ever vigilant."[34]

At the convention itself, held February 14–16 in Chicago, Wilkins reported close to a thousand delegates in attendance. The sessions focused on labor and civil liberties. "With the exception of the distinct trade union . . . discussions, practically the rest of the program might be classified as an N.A.A.C.P. program." He noted several politicians and the many prominent African American leaders from the NUL, Chicago Interracial Committee, and even the NAACP who were present or held leadership positions within the Congress. Wilkins described with admiration the many young people at the conference who "owed their allegiance only to organizations committed to a militant fight for the Negro. . . . Unquestionably the Congress was an expression of the willingness of masses of the people to sacrifice and fight." The NAACP, he observed, had been criticized for its lack of vigor in addressing the problems of the race, and its top-down, undemocratic structure, criticisms that "would be intensified a hundredfold if we held off and refused to take any part in this movement." William Hastie likewise supported a formal endorsement of the NNC. The NAACP board, however, remained undecided.[35]

To Houston, Wilkins voiced concerns about communist involvement in the NNC. "There are key Communists in every discussion" at the convention, he noted. "Not actually leading, but always with their hands in." He closed: "Saw John and he looks in the face as though he had been drawn through a knothole."[36]

Cooperation between the two organizations began cordially, if uneasily. One of the first causes the NNC embraced was antilynching, and it sought to hold a joint mass meeting in 1936 with the Chicago NAACP. According to Davis, the NNC hoped to gather three thousand people "to work for the support of the NAACP's fight against lynching and the fight for the Scottsboro boys." Too suspicious to endorse mutual action, but willing to accept help, the NAACP board agreed to let Wilkins speak at the meeting. For two years the two collaborated, holding conferences, passing resolutions, sharing strategies, and providing mutual support. Although it still refused to formally affiliate, the NAACP sent an observer to each NNC conference. NNC monthly bulletins implored its members to aid in the NAACP's fight for an antilynch law, and in April 1937, White thanked Davis for the NNC's help on one such bill.[37]

But in February 1938 the relationship soured. The NNC proposed a demonstration to protest the Senate's failure to pass the Wagner–Van Nuys antilynching bill. White replied that the NAACP's behind-the-scenes effort to save the bill would be jeopardized by a public demonstration. The NNC offered to hold off for two weeks. White proposed instead that the NAACP determine the appropriate moment for protest. Ten days later Davis wrote to White again. The NNC board had concluded that waiting any longer would diffuse momentum. "We realize the NAACP, which has done such a good job thus far in the fight for the anti-lynching bill, must proceed with care," Davis explained. "It is our judgement, however, that the calling of a conference of leaders of organizations . . . will be of aid to the NAACP in its valiant fight" by publicly registering "the deep resentment of all decent people to the slurs hurled at the Negro people by the filibusterers." Davis assured White that the NNC "has only one desire: the passage of the anti-lynching bill. It intends that in all the dealings on this matter to see to it that full credit for leadership . . . be given you and the NAACP.[38]

If the NNC considered the NAACP too hesitant, the NAACP believed the NNC too self-serving. White viewed the conference as an effort to "chisel in for the National Negro Congress and the Communists on the fight." He drafted a reply to Davis's letter and passed it to Wilkins and Houston. "You may probably think that I am too blunt," he told them. "You may be right. But I am convinced that if we pull any punches dealing with as determined and as unscrupulous a person as John, we will make a serious mistake."[39] After receiving their input and conferring with Max Yergin, a revised version was sent. The changes were small but significant in their tone: "My dear Mr. Davis," became "My dear John," a paragraph opposing spending time and money "for ballyhoo purposes" was deleted, and a sentence reaffirming the importance of the issue and the freedom of each organization to act as it saw fit was added. "Let me . . . reiterate,"

White's letter continued, "that neither is the Association nor am I personally the least bit interested in, to quote your phrase, 'full credit for leadership in the fight for the bill.' We are interested solely in one thing—getting the bill passed and enforced." That, however, required "certain steps" which would be derailed by the NNC's proposed conference. Nor could the NAACP "divulge the nature of these steps since to do so would almost certainly forewarn enemies of the bill and insure defeat." The letter repeated, "We take no proprietary interest in the bill but you will understand our position when I say to you quite frankly that having worked for more than a quarter of a century against lynching . . . we cannot jeopardize all that has been accomplished by taking ill-advised action."[40]

Clearly the NAACP *did* take a proprietary interest in the bill, if the tone of White's response to Davis is any indication. The NAACP fully intended to call the shots in this game. But beyond turf battles, tactical differences underlay the tension. The NAACP's more cautious legislative strategy conflicted with the more public, mass approach of the NNC. In explaining why the NNC decided to hold the conference in the end, Davis wrote, "Press commentators have said that administrative leaders are waiting to see if there is really sufficient sentiment in the country at large to warrant their making a fight on the anti-lynching bill," so "we felt it necessary . . . to take steps to increase the number of telegrams demanding passage of the bill and to arrange for public demonstrations in a number of cities." Although Davis tried to mend fences by adding "[m]y own sincere belief is that such activity cannot help but improve the possibilities of success of any plans which the NAACP might have," White remained angry. He insisted that the local antilynching committees the NNC called for were "needless duplication of organization already existing, . . . and which has brought the fight for anti-lynching legislation up to its present point." Monies raised for these new committees would likewise bleed support from longstanding and hard-working antilynching groups. "What purpose can it serve except to split the forces supporting the Anti-Lynching Bill?" White's letter closed with the familiar refrain that the issue was not who received credit, along with the reminder of where credit actually belonged: "As I have said to you previously, we assume no proprietary interest in this legislation, irrespective of the fact that the N.A.A.C.P. has worked . . . incessantly for many years to bring the fight up to this point." As White explained to his colleagues, "John's letter is very cleverly written and is obviously designed to create the impression that his motives are of the purest and that it is we who are at fault."[41]

In Davis's eyes, the NAACP was compromising its effectiveness by its caution. Indeed, the NAACP's efforts came to naught, although it is not clear whether more public protest could have succeeded since the main obstacle to passage of the bill remained the intransigence of southern racists. In White's view, NNC tactics could be explained only by Davis's ambition to establish the NNC's centrality in the civil rights struggle. Wilkins believed that since the bill had no real chance of passage, Davis held the meeting only for money and publicity.[42] Of course, if passage was in fact hopeless, White's opposition to the meeting was equally self-serving.

Not surprisingly, the head of the NUL and other liberal black leaders concurred with the NAACP's assessment. White described conversations with "Max Yergin, Lester Granger and others who are now or formerly were active in the National Negro Congress. I find them disgusted with some of John's trickery. Lester Granger told me that he resigned from the National Negro Congress last year because of this." When White told him of the antilynching fracas, Arthur Huff Fauset replied, "I see your point only too clearly—have seen it—and understood it—and appreciate it—how sorry I am about the whole business I can hardly express in words."[43]

And in a parallel to Jewish warnings of the dangers of godless communism, a group of black church leaders issued a statement "in opposition to the Program of the NNC." While applauding the NNC's agenda, "we deplore . . . that no well known church leaders" appeared on NNC lists of "persons to strike key notes or champion causes," nor on its planning board. Church support was crucial for success, and "neglect" of church leadership could cause resentment. Those who "neglect God" fail, they warned, as "Russia and Germany . . . are now learning."[44]

Relations between liberal groups and the NNC worsened further when the Nazis invaded the Soviet Union. The NNC shifted its priority from racial equality to the war effort, belying its claim to be a civil rights advocacy group. Both NNC's style and its policy flip-flops cost it virtually all of its following. The group's collapse, however, did not end such conflicts.

In 1946, out of the ashes of the NNC and several other organizations emerged the Civil Rights Congress (CRC), one of the most successful Communist-front organizations of the period. It took on legal cases involving race and communism, and intersected with mainstream black and Jewish programs in several ways. It involved itself in cases pursued by the NAACP. Its defense of those indicted under national security laws overlapped with efforts of organizations such as the Civil Liberties Clearing House, a coalition of black, Jewish, and other liberal groups. And it repeatedly stressed the crucial and fundamental similarity of the black and Jewish struggles and the importance of joint efforts to overcome barriers to full civil rights. "The anti-Negro attack at Cicero, Illinois, is evidence that 'fascism in America is concentrating its attack upon the Negro people in the precise manner followed by Hitler against the Jews of Germany,' " read a CRC press release following the 1951 housing riot.[45]

The CRC's embrace of the Trenton Six brought them into direct conflict with the NAACP. Despite shaky evidence, six black men were convicted and sentenced to death in a New Jersey court for having murdered a white man. The CRC took the cases to the state Supreme Court and launched a publicity and fund-raising campaign. The NAACP, which represented two of the defendants, organized a parallel effort and protested the CRC's involvement. William Patterson, CRC executive secretary, insisted that while it withdrew from the case's "legal phases" after a conversation with NAACP counsel Thurgood Marshall, "I did not surrender the right of our organization to continue to develop the mass pressure which had saved these men from the electric chair." Indeed, "as the April, 1949 'NATION' says, 'had it not been for the CRC, the men would today be dead and buried.' "[46]

The NAACP, of course, saw the situation rather differently. Even after the CRC agreed to withdraw from the case, and despite NAACP protest, it continued fund-raising and publicity. Rejecting the CRC's offer of "co-operation" on future cases, Marshall commented in a draft letter to Patterson in 1949, "Your offer of 'cooperation' must be measured in the light of past 'cooperation.' " He questioned the group's motives in the Trenton Six case, and called the CRC's conduct in the Martinsville case (seven black men ultimately executed for the rape of a white woman) "disgusting to say the least." While the CRC notes " 'its consistent work over the years . . . in the fight to end discrimination, segregation and Jim-Crow' . . . [w]e are not aware of this long and consistent program and as a matter of fact do know that you and your associates were conspicuous by your absence in the fight . . . during the period of our last World War and especially after Russia's intervention."[47]

The final version of the letter to Patterson added more detail about what the NAACP considered unwarranted intrusion into its cases, and the CRC's close ties with communists. "We remember . . . that in the Scottsboro case the NAACP was subjected to the most unprincipled vilification [by a CRC predecessor, the ILD]. We remember the campaign of slander in the Daily Worker. We remember the leaflets and the speakers and the whole unspeakable machinery that was turned loose upon all those who did not embrace the 'unity policy' " that communists declared. "We want none of that unity today." During the war, "when Negro Americans were fighting for jobs on the home front and fighting for decent treatment in the armed services" they received no support from the "extreme Left." Indeed, "[d]uring the war years the disciples of the extreme Left sounded very much like the worst of the Negro-hating southerners." All this, "American Negroes, and especially the NAACP, cannot forget."[48]

The debate between the CRC and NAACP, suffused in bitterness and recrimination, again involved turf and a struggle over tactics and the depth of commitment to the cause of black equality. In 1951 Patterson contacted the NAACP again regarding the plight of the Martinsville Seven, who by then had lost their case and been sentenced to death. The Supreme Court, having refused review of the case, "are following the example of Pontius Pilate," Patterson charged. Because there was "no 'due process of law' in these cases," only concerted public protest could save the men now. "If the Martinsville Seven are to be saved we must act . . . as one to move people— the tens of thousands whose concerted mass action alone can reverse that decision of death." He urged that the two organizations work together.[49]

Thurgood Marshall would have none of it. "In the first place, I . . . am unalterably opposed to characterizing the Supreme Court of the United States as 'following the example of Pontius Pilate.' I believe that if all lawyers would spend more time on preparing their cases than in finding characterizations for the courts, we would make more progress." The NAACP had always proceeded "in a lawful . . . manner within the lawful machinery of our Government" and would continue to do so. "We have never been convinced that the Civil Rights Congress is primarily interested in the protection of the rights of Negroes. . . . We therefore have no intention whatsoever of permitting you to interfere in any of these cases."[50]

Marshall's view of the CRC's strategy and intent was clear. But Patterson's reply offers an alternate perspective. He pointed out that Marshall's letter did not actually "deal with the issue" of joint action. The question was "shall we arouse the justifiable wrath of decent Americans against the most arrogant violation of the constitutional liberties and human rights of the Negro people, which reflects itself so callously and grossly in this case?" Patterson stressed, "the important factor here remains, in my opinion, that: THE LIVES OF THESE INNOCENT MEN CAN BE SAVED!" He urged citizen petitions, used in the Scottsboro and Trenton Six cases, which surely met Marshall's criterion that all actions be legal. As for criticizing the courts, "Certainly that court's decisions which have failed to meet the grave constitutional issues repeatedly raised by the Negro people indicates the existence of deep-rooted political and economic prejudices, and not any inadequacies of counsel who represented those Negro clients." This, of course, referred to the NAACP, whose pleas had been rejected by that court time and again. For the NAACP to reject this criticism of the court would be to admit its own inadequacy. "But that is not the issue here," Patterson continued, returning to the high ground. "This is no time for petty bickering or name-calling. The attacks on the Negro people under the terrible heat of a cold-war are mounting in all sections of our country." He reminded Marshall that the NAACP's own literature made these same points, as did President Truman's Civil Rights Committee, and concluded with a ringing reminder of the failures of NAACP strategies to this point. The Association had lost the case and the men "have been condemned to death. Yours has been a hush-hush policy without regard to the overwhelming strength which derives from the support of the people." So, "I beseech you" to join in a "struggle for the lives of these men, whose terrible condemnation is symptomatic of the oppression of Negro Americans throughout our great land."[51] The Martinsville Seven were executed.

Later correspondence became more heated still. Patterson accused the NAACP of pursuing "joint action . . . with the Klan and every reactionary element in America."[52] Beyond insults, the issues between the two groups were clear, and remained until the CRC's demise in 1956. To the NAACP, the CRC was tactically irresponsible and its motives suspect. To the CRC, the NAACP had so compromised its programs in reaction to anticommunist hysteria as to reject legal and effective approaches to problems it wanted solved. Further, that narrowness of perspective had blinded it to the structural impact of racism, the ways in which all social institutions, including the courts, had been compromised. Both claims have merit, and in the conflict between the organizations, racial justice was the loser.

But mutual antagonism was not the whole story. Alongside liberal public condemnation of leftist groups came occasional behind-the-scenes cooperation, or at least agreement to proceed in parallel. The NAACP aided a black San Francisco man accused of rape despite the fact that his defense committee was "largely made up of Left-Wingers," for example, and filed briefs in Southern Tenant Farmers Union and Workers Defense League cases.[53] Because leftist and communist groups often had a substantial impact on local civil rights struggles, liberals could not ignore them altogether.

The contradictions are apparent in the story of United Nations petitions regarding racism. The NNC issued a ringing denunciation of the evils of legal discrimination and racial violence in a 1946 petition to the UN written by the (heavily Jewish) National Lawyers Guild and (Jewish) Herbert Aptheker. Discredited by its communist taint, the NNC was unable to move the indictment forward despite both incontrovertible evidence and enormous effort, and the NAACP took up the challenge. Authored by Du Bois, whose own leftist activities would increasingly anger and alienate the Association's leadership, the NAACP's petition to the UN, "An Appeal to the World," documented and elaborated on the NNC's claims. It asserted that racism undermined the American commitment to democracy and justice, encouraged American sympathy with imperialism, and threatened to plunge the nation into "oligarchy or even fascism. . . . It is not Russia that threatens the United States so much as Mississippi; not Stalin and Molotov but Bilbo and Rankin."[54]

Still, when the CRC less than a decade later presented a similar petition, "We Charge Genocide," white leaders and much of the liberal black establishment rejected its central claims. Despite the NNC's use of the NAACP's own evidence, the Association pronounced the petition communist propaganda. The abuses, while significant, did not constitute genocide, it insisted, and racial progress was being made. Allies, antagonists, competitors: the facts of segregation heightened the intensity of the contradiction. Roy Wilkins lived across the hall from William Patterson in a Harlem apartment building.[55]

Boring from Within

The possibility that individual communists might infiltrate their own organizations also worried many liberals.[56] While some groups took a harder line than others, ultimately no liberal black and Jewish organizations allowed communists to serve on their boards or participate in their programs. This was far more difficult than refusing to cooperate with known communist organizations, since infiltration occurred, by definition, by those not readily identifiable as communist. Exclusion therefore raised serious internal debates about the balance between defending civil liberties, crucial for civil rights advances, and protecting the organization.

In 1946 the NAACP took up the question of communist membership because, as White noted, "fellow travelers and sympathizers . . . have succeeded in placing the NAACP in an embarrassing situation" by joining the San Francisco branch and voting to participate in a CP picket line against a local theater that refused to hire African Americans. Both the local press and the state (Tenney) Committee on Un-American Activities then linked the NAACP with the CP, and branch membership plummeted. "The CP boys . . . damn near wrecked the Philadelphia branch," Wilkins lamented. "They have completely wrecked the San Francisco branch." As board member Alfred Baker Lewis observed, "My experience in the N.A.A.C.P. . . . is that the Commies are busy and fairly effective in infiltrating. . . . It takes a good deal of smoking out, once they are in. . . . It is a lot easier . . . to stop it before it gets going fully."[57]

In June of 1950 the annual convention passed a resolution to do just that. "WHEREAS, it is apparent . . . that there is a well-organized, nationwide conspiracy by Communists either to capture or split and wreck the NAACP," the Association resolved to "investigate the ideological composition . . . of the local units" in order to "eradicate such infiltration, and if necessary . . . suspend and reorganize, or . . . expel any unit which in the judgement of the Board . . . comes under Communists [sic] or other political . . . domination." As the covering memorandum reminded local branches, "The resolution does not give branches the right to call anybody and everybody a Communist [or to] eliminate members just because those members disagree with the branch or its officers." Using punctuation for emphasis, the memo warned, "DO NOT BECOME HYSTERICAL AND MAKE WILD ACCUSATIONS. We do not want a witch hunt in the NAACP, but we want to make sure that we, and not the Communists, are running it."[58] The NAACP struggled to balance civil liberties with the conviction that, if unchecked, communists could destroy the organization. But the line between fair investigation and witch hunts, between legitimate disagreement and communist subversion, would prove difficult to locate.

In 1952 Dr. Henry Bibby applied for membership in the Ulster County, New York, branch. The branch secretary queried the national about allowing "communistically inclined people" into the NAACP. The director of branches responded that CP members could not join. Given a suspicious applicant, he advised, "do not accept their membership and if they insist, have them apply directly to the National Office." The branch then informed Dr. Bibby, without explanation, that the national office had rejected his application. Bibby complained to the national, calling the decision "outrageous, perverse and completely unfounded," and "an absolute negation of the principles upon which your organization was founded." The national queried the branch secretary regarding the evidence against him. She replied that Bibby's name appeared on the California Attorney General's list "as having subversive activity. Several of our well-known citizens . . . have made it known to us that they will have nothing to do with the organization if he remained a member." Indeed, "all of the prominent white citizens of Kingston . . . 'cold-shouldered' " him. "We have also returned the memberships of Miss Margaret Easton and Mrs Dorothy Wilson of Woodstock, N.Y. whose families are known for their subversive activity," she added, observing, "Woodstock, N.Y. is a mecca for Communists."[59]

The board instructed the branch to reconsider his application using proper procedure, which included a hearing and the ratification by the entire branch of any expulsion. In a tacit admission of the unfairness of such local decisions, the process allowed rejected applicants to then apply directly to the national. "In several other cases where Branches have rejected members, the members have applied for membership to the National Office and their applications have been accepted. This entitled them to membership in the National Association, though not in the Branch."

The difference between this investigation of Bibby and a witch hunt is small indeed; the local board used the AG's list of subversive organizations as a determining factor in his case, and in the case of the two women, rejected them not even for their own membership in suspicious organizations but for family members' activities and their town's leftist reputation.

While the national returned Bibby's case to the local, it did not deny the legitimacy of those grounds. Furthermore, putting dismissals to a vote allows rumor and innuendo to affect decisions. To the NAACP, the risk of overzealousness was outweighed by the importance of securing loyal membership and creating an atmosphere of trust for local activists. "The NAACP's non-Communist policy, while seeking to protect the civil rights of its members, is a difficult one, at best, to enforce," White acknowledged. Although branches did not always proceed "as well as we would like . . . most of our leaders know, personally, those . . . whose presence and membership would make it difficult for the unit to carry out our program."

The ADL, perhaps because of the delicate nature of its investigative work, felt equally uneasy when political questions were raised about members. Although as an organization it opposed the presumption of guilt inherent in any case of suspected disloyalty, it nonetheless became concerned when an FBI investigation was launched against one of its own lay leaders. In 1952 Seymour Carmel, chairman of a Washington, D.C., B'nai B'rith Lodge, learned from neighbors that he was under investigation. He concluded that he was under suspicion because he had attended leftist meetings for the ADL, and suggested that the FBI confirm with the League that he had been there on assignment. ADL leaders did confirm it, but asked the agent whether the FBI had any other concerns regarding Carmel. The FBI officer refused to answer. The agent's supervisor also hedged, saying only that the FBI was "not interested in Carmel because of his ADL activities." ADL staffer Herman Edelsberg then turned for advice to Lou Nichols, an FBI agent with whom ADL had worked in the past. "A B'nai B'rith lodge leader is questioned by the FBI about a member who is a committee chairman. The leader indicates that everything he knows about the subject is commendable, but suspicion remains because the FBI is investigating. The leader is tempted to tell his colleagues not to let the subject advance up the line of BB offices. What to do?" Nichols answered, "a routine investigation should raise no suspicions against the subject. It is unfortunate if people jump to unjust conclusions." As Edelsberg explained to Forster, "we have been put in a spot. We would assume . . . that any . . . employee still in the government was perfectly loyal and would feel free automatically to call on him to work with us. Now a question has been raised and we would like to know how to handle Carmel in the future. . . . [A]ll we can do is make the best guess we can in the circumstances and sweat it out." He added in a P.S., "Let me say that we have absolutely no intimation . . . that there is any question about Carmel, other than the FBI investigation." The reply of the ADL's Domestic Intelligence Division equivocated. "It seems to us that the best we can do in the case of utilizing volunteers is to be absolutely certain in your own mind that the guy is clean."[60]

Less concerned with the niceties of civil liberties was the Urban League. It kept "a careful compilation of the background and activity of everyone of our 450 employed staff throughout the country," as well as "the connections and community activities of members of our local boards. When there appears to be evidence of pro-Communist collaboration this evidence is promptly brought to the attention of the responsible officials." Such board members were dropped, and staff required to resign. Perhaps because its surveillance was more ubiquitous to begin with, the NUL worried less about the danger of false accusations. "Pro-Communist sympathies are fairly simple to detect if every effort is made . . . to keep abreast of the issues. . . . Fortunately, the frequent and sudden changes in the Communist Party line, particularly with respect to the race question, provide handy reference points for checking attitudes and sympathies of individuals."[61]

Even the progressive and egalitarian CORE banned communists from membership and investigated all allegations of infiltration. Division over such procedures led at least one chapter to disband. Not that black and Jewish organizations were unusual, or unusually suspicious, in their exclusion of communists. The ACLU, which defended communists' right to speak and to organize, nonetheless barred them from serving on its governing board. "We have a creed," Roger Baldwin explained. "Whether you are Communists . . . or Rightists . . . if you are regarded as qualifying your support of the democratic principle of rights for all, you cannot help make our policy."[62]

Cooperation or Collaboration?

The three most visible bodies fighting communism were J. Edgar Hoover's FBI, HUAC, and the machinery of Senator Joseph McCarthy. While, as we shall see, black and Jewish groups challenged each one, they also selectively cooperated with these agencies in hopes of advancing their own interests. The NUL boasted, "The record of . . . assistance . . . is very clear." When asked to testify before HUAC, both the NUL and NAACP complied, and used their time to underscore the persistent racial discrimination that left some black people open to communist appeals. "Testifying before a committee does not imply approval of the Committee," Alfred Baker Lewis explained to Granger. "It is simply taking advantage of an opportunity for publicity for the Urban League . . . and gives you a chance to tell the committee what you think it should do."[63]

The only way to truly combat communism, both groups argued in their testimony, was to strengthen civil rights, and to challenge racist organizations as energetically as communist ones. As Granger argued in his 1949 statement, HUAC must pursue foreign-directed communists, "but at the same time *it must strongly fight against the native-born proponents of a brutal racism.*" While "reactionaries" unfairly label "every Negro spokes-man who offers a protest against the injustices perpetrated upon his people" a communist, "the Ku Klux Klan . . . indulges in floggings, lynching or other forms of intimidation of Negroes" which are "tolerated without protest, or are even tacitly approved by representative leader-ship." Meanwhile, "on the floor of Congress, duly elected representatives . . . express obscenely racist sentiments regarding the legitimate aspira-tions of Negro citizens." All this fueled communists' arguments. "The obvious way to block such strategy is for the anti-Communists of this country to deprive our enemies of their propaganda weapon by moving with equal vigor and more honesty to eliminate these fester-spots from our national life." The Commission on Interracial Cooperation had made the same point as early as 1934: "revolutionary movements among the people of any race can be best combated by correcting the ills and injus-tices upon which revolution thrives."[64]

Seeing an opportunity to press their agenda, several Jewish groups also accepted invitations to appear before HUAC. More problematic, the ADL, AJC, and AJLAC also exchanged complimentary notes or shared information with J. Edgar Hoover, HUAC, and even Senator McCarthy. A 1951 ADL meeting with McCarthy at the senator's request "for the purposes of consideration of matters of mutual interest" raised eyebrows in the rest of the Jewish community. That same year ADL chairman Meier Steinbrink expressed to Hoover his "appreciation of the great work done by the Bureau under your devoted and inspired direction. In a period of grave national crisis, you faced the awesome task of guarding at once the security of our beloved nation and the constitutional liberties of our peo-ple. The record of your discharge of your stewardship has earned an hon-ored and secure place in our history." Steinbrink was also "delighted with the manner in which Mr. Louis Nichols of your staff has handled the relationship with our office. It is a joy to work with him." He concluded, "I wish you many years of good health and the continuance of your matchless service. In this I know I am joined by the officers and staff of the Anti-Defamation League, of whose continued cooperation in your great work you may rest assured." By cooperation, Steinbrink referred to the regular sharing of information the ADL gathered regarding suspicious organizations and meetings by sending observers and collecting printed materials and statistics.[65]

The year following, Steinbrink wrote to congratulate Hoover on "35 years of loyal and patriotic service to our country." When queried in a 1991 interview, Arnold Forster insisted such contacts were both genuine, given their mutual interest in fighting communism, and strategic. Certainly, each glowing letter to Hoover praised him for his commitment to protecting democracy and constitutional liberties, a subtle (if ineffective) reminder of the importance of observing due process and rights of privacy.[66] Nevertheless, it is difficult to escape the conclusion that, in the end, such cooperation and support encouraged witch hunts and legitimized the use of threat and character assassination which would later be used against civil rights leaders themselves.

The Crime of the Century

Perhaps no case captured the minds of Americans as that of the Rosenbergs. Convicted of conspiracy for passing atomic secrets to the Soviets, Ethel and Julius Rosenberg were executed in 1952, the first such peacetime execution in American history. Because these parents of young children protested their innocence to their deaths, the case attracted not only the widespread attention afforded spy trials, but also a surprising level of sympathy. Given the anticommunist hysteria that surrounded the trial, it was inevitable that the Rosenbergs' defense would be spearheaded by communist and front groups. Because the accused were Jewish, it was likewise inevitable that Jewish organizations would be pulled into the fray. The latter's reactions offer a window into their political position in this anxious time.

Many communists suggested the Rosenbergs' Judaism played a pernicious role in the case, claiming that the Jewish judge, Irving Kaufman, "leaned backward" in order to prove he could be a good American and not let sympathy for his coreligionists cloud his patriotic judgment. As Albert Vorspan of NCRAC, the umbrella group for Jewish organizations, warned in a 1951 memo, "this could be an extremely dangerous development since it will open avenues of impairing public confidence in the ability of Jewish judges to deal with cases involving Jews on a fair and impartial basis." Communists, however, were hardly the first to point out the potential link between an unjustly harsh verdict and the religion of the judge. The editor of the noncommunist *Jewish Day* opined, "The death sentence which Judge Kaufman issued left the feeling that precisely because he is a Jew, he went to an extreme. . . . [It] perhaps unconsciously motivated him to issue a verdict which, in the opinion of many, is considered to be unjust and brutal."[67]

Nevertheless Jewish groups refused to link their name in any way to efforts to defend the Rosenbergs (and later, Morton Sobell), or appeal for clemency. Most did not believe any miscarriage of justice had occurred. As Steinbrink explained to the ADL's National Commission, "We studiously examined the record. There was no anti-Semitism in the Rosenberg case, except perhaps that which the Communists may have provoked later while parading as its opponents!"[68]

Others feared protesting as Jews would give credibility to the alleged link between Jews and communism, which they recognized as political suicide. When the Progressive Party sought to hold a meeting in Chicago for the National Committee to Secure Justice in the Rosenberg Case (NCSJRC, which included among its sponsors numerous Jews and Du Bois), it approached Temple Judea, a local Reform synagogue. Temple Judea agreed to provide space, but withdrew its offer when the ADL, the AJCongress, the JLC, and AJC objected. Although the temple admitted it had previously allowed the JPFO and others to hold meetings there ("we assume unwitting[ly]," noted the ADL), they promised to be more circumspect in the future.[69]

All the major Jewish organizations agreed. In a joint press release that May, the AJC, AJCongress, ADL, JLC, JWV, UAHC, and NCRAC agreed that "[a]ny group of American citizens has a right to express its views as to the severity of the sentence in any criminal case. Attempts are being made, however, by a Communist inspired group called the National Committee to Secure Justice in the Rosenberg Case, to inject the false issue of anti-Semitism. . . . We denounce the fraudulent effort to confuse and manipulate public opinion for ulterior political purposes." These liberal groups were struggling to position themselves as the only legitimate spokesmen for their community. If those favoring clemency "desire to express their point of view, they should do so as individual Americans," A. Abbot Rosen warned local offices, and "be careful to avoid association with communist or communist-inspired organizations."[70]

Clemency appeals did have resonance in the Jewish community, a partial explanation for the vehemence of organized Jewry against involvement. At the *Jewish Daily Forward*, "When we editors got the news that Julius and Ethel Rosenberg were sentenced to death, a shudder passed through all of us. . . . From our hearts came the word, 'Death sentence, too horrible.' " Not only were many protest meetings on behalf of the Rosenbergs well populated by Jews (and, interestingly, by African Americans), but numerous rabbis and congregations pleaded for clemency.[71] Nevertheless, liberal Jewish groups held to their position. They, not communists, spoke for the Jewish community.

Most Jewish leaders appeared satisfied that justice had been done. "We have been particularly shocked by the outrageous statements . . . made by the attorney for the Rosenbergs that their execution amounted to murder," wrote ADL's Henry Schultz to President Eisenhower and J. Edgar Hoover. "No one who knows your record can possibly place any credence in such wild charges. The judicial process as it operated in this particular case is exactly the opposite of what occurs in totalitarian countries." Such responses were shaped as much by Jews' liberal anticommunist ideology as by their concerns about an anti-Semitic backlash. Certainly, non-Jewish liberal groups drew similar conclusions about the case. Even the ACLU found no civil liberties violations in the trial or penalty.[72]

As with the wartime incarceration of Japanese Americans, American Jewish organizations were so focused on their own agenda, in this case to demonstrate their deep moral and patriotic opposition to communism, that they were unable to recognize the possibility that, regardless of the Rosenbergs' guilt, hysteria and improper conduct affected the trial. They themselves acknowledged that the sentence, which exceeded that of any other peacetime espionage conviction, might be excessive, and possibly violated the law. Yet they did nothing. While they argued that, absent overt anti-Semitism, the Rosenberg case was not "a Jewish issue," they nonetheless took up the issue of Jewish civil servants dismissed for disloyalty because of their activities or membership, not their Jewishness. The Rosenberg case was different because of its high profile and the severity of the crime. Jews, so often equated with communists, must not be seen as involved in any defense. Jews who had criticized German non-Jews for not resisting Hitler, and American white Christians for remaining silent in the face of racial and religious bigotry, had failed in precisely the same way.

By refusing to challenge the harsh sentence, those Jews who believed in clemency abrogated their responsibility. Arnold Forster admitted as much in a 1991 interview. "I bemoan . . . the cowardice of the general Jewish community and the organized infrastructure of Jewish defense work in not speaking out against the death penalty imposed upon the Rosenbergs. It was one thing to remain uninvolved in [questions about] their . . . communist activities. This was not within the orbit of ADL's interest. But when they were . . . sentenced . . . to death, clearly in the judgment of many of us, this was excessive punishment."[73]

"Sterile and barren": Consequences of Anticommunism

This refusal by liberal agencies of all congress with communists had a dramatic and limiting impact on civil rights activity. It seemed too threatening, too communistic, to raise questions of economic equity when communists made class so central an issue. Their opposition to most public forms of militancy rested explicitly on their similarity to communist tactics. The result was "sterile and barren" programs, in the words of Judge Jane Bolin, who in 1950 resigned from the NAACP board in disgust. She accused the Association of "blind[ing] the public to its lack of a positive and alive program by continuing to yell 'Communist' and 'fellow-traveler' about every Board member and branch" which wanted from the "NAACP less talk and more action."[74]

W.E.B. Du Bois offers a case in point. In 1951 he and other members of the leftist Peace Information Center were indicted for failure to register as "foreign agents." Despite the advocacy of several individual members and branches, the national NAACP, Du Bois's offspring, offered only luke-warm support. The board did pass a resolution of protest, over some objection that Du Bois "went ahead . . . into the present difficulty without consulting the Association." But the resolution refused comment "on the merits of the . . . indictment," simply noting that Du Bois's prominence as a civil rights advocate led many to conclude that "efforts are being made to silence spokesmen for full equality of Negroes." Indeed virtually the entire liberal establishment made him persona non grata, despite his decades of forceful civil rights activism and his scholarly preeminence in the field of race relations. "It was a bitter experience and I bowed before the storm," Du Bois wrote in his autobiography. "I lost my leadership of my race. . . . The colored children ceased to hear my name."[75]

As they demonstrated in San Francisco in 1946, and on similar occasions elsewhere, national NAACP leaders often opposed participation in civil rights protests not because the allegations were incorrect or the action too militant, but simply because communists had organized them. As Manning Marable, Gerald Horne, Carol Anderson, and other scholars have reminded us, fear of communism and the exclusion of leftists from civil rights programs moved liberal organizations to narrower ground, concentrating on civil rather than economic equality, and on compromise rather than confrontation.[76] The loss to the cause of civil rights was both significant and avoidable.

Tactically, such decisions robbed civil rights of some of its hardest-working advocates. In 1952 the NAACP decided not to pursue a work stoppage to protest racism because, as White "regretted to report . . . only one of the non-communist unions has agreed to go along."[77] Other black and Jewish groups similarly declined to take up discrimination cases because of the "leftist tendencies" of those involved, although they acknowl-edged the civil rights issues at stake. In 1950, for example, the ADL learned that a New York landlord had evicted a Sidney Tobias from his apartment after learning he had sublet to a black man. The Chelsea Ten-ants Council protested and its representative, Rose Bloom, asked for sup-port from other community groups, including the ADL. The presence of the American Labor Party, the consideration of picketing as a means of protest, and "other indicators" revealed the coalition's "left wing tenden-cies," the ADL concluded; although it "found the facts to be as Miss Bloom states . . . the ADL could not involve itself in this particular situation."[78] By avoiding engagement with leftists, liberal civil rights organizations failed to challenge instances of racism. Nor could they solidify or build on the successes leftist groups did achieve.

The JLC, NAACP, AJCongress, NUL, and Workmen's Circle all refused to join an effort to integrate housing in Parkchester, New York, because it was spearheaded by, in the JLC's words, a "Cominform apologist." In a memo filled with exclamation marks the JLC noted that the organization offered the victims "sympathy . . . , increased agitation for the removal of the discriminatory rental policies—but nothing else!" Ironically, given the Jewish presence in communist and leftist politics, liberal groups not only lost willing workers, but discredited the very arenas where black-Jewish collaboration was particularly strong. As Irvin Mollison observed in a 1935 letter to White, "in the minds of most Negroes . . . the one redeeming thing about the Jewish people is that most of the communistic Jews have unequivocally stood for equal rights for all Americans without regard to color."[79]

The unwillingness to work with communists meant more than a loss of colleagues. It also meant the loss of their emphasis on the structures of oppression. Recognizing early on the institutional benefits white skin provided, communists offered an important critique of the presumption that black and Jewish experiences, and therefore agendas, were the same. The communist John Williamson argued that while Jews suffer from anti-Semitism, African Americans also lack "equal rights and full economic, social and political equality." This meant a substantively different struggle: "Oppression and discrimination against the Negro workers takes place 24 hours a day. It affects the Negro workers in relation to where they can sleep, where they can eat." Because of Jews' different class position, the "imperialist ruling-class poison of white chauvinism has penetrated also among the Jewish people and even finds expression in their progressive and Left circles." As a result, many Jews, even activists, show a "lack of sensitivity to expressions of white chauvinism."[80] Had the liberal Jewish community heeded such warnings earlier, it is possible the divisions of the 1960s might have played themselves out differently.

On a more pragmatic level, the efforts of liberal agencies to prove themselves anticommunist, challenge their constituents to resist communist blandishments, or jockey for position as community spokespersons, took time and resources away from the civil rights task at hand. Judge Bolin warned, "Our organization has blown the Communists up to such fantastic proportions that we give them more of our attention and time than we do the American Negro." That same year Ben Herzberg of the AJC complained that by concentrating "energy and resources on" programs to distinguish Jews and communism, "the attention of the staff was diverted from other programs of greater urgency." ADL's Harold Lachman acknowledged later, "that fear was in our minds and actually did not exist in fact."[81]

Liberal activists felt torn. If the paucity of allies and the many shared goals of communists and liberals pulled in one direction, competition, fear of smear campaigns, and genuine distaste for communism pulled in the other. "I have to work with whomever is willing to pursue those goals of racial understanding and good will," Eugene Holmes wrote to Leonard Finder in a critique of what he called ADL's "redbaiting," and its desire to "deal only with 'safe' . . . organizations." "If we desire to preach democracy . . . it is obvious that we cannot use those who are . . . out of sympathy with that philosophy," Finder responded. "In the long run, any cause is helped or injured by the character and reputation of those who espouse it. . . . If the average citizen should ever come under the impression that racial understanding is a theory advocated primarily by communists . . . then it will be a lost cause." Historians will doubtless continue to debate whether civil rights would have been better advanced with greater collaboration between liberals and communists, or more completely derailed. From this vantage point, however, the "inevitable result of things unsaid," to quote James Baldwin,[82] the lost opportunities, the narrowed agendas, and the tacit legitimation of a politics of suspicion and intimidation, seem more significant than the dangers posed.

Defending Civil Liberties

Liberal black and Jewish organizations certainly understood that the right used anticommunism to knock the legs out from under liberalism and undermine its goals of integration and equality. How far, then, should their own anticommunism go? The 1948 AJC leadership was divided between those who believed Jewish agencies should launch "an all-out, clear-cut attack on communism" and those who "take an equally strong position that the whole Jewish cause would be hurt by such an attack because it would serve to weaken the liberal movement, and liberals in general, as well as the fight for preservation and extension of civil rights for all."[83]

Such debates between anticommunism and defense of civil liberties wracked every liberal organization. With their own programs and goals labeled communist or subversive, they had little choice. In a 1948 letter to President Truman, the NAACP warned of "an increasing tendency on the part of government agencies to associate activities on interracial matters with disloyalty." Not only had individuals under investigation been asked whether they had social relations with those of another race, "many colored government employees, who are now being charged with disloyalty, have such accusations brought against them because they have actively opposed segregation and discrimination." As White explained to the NAACP board, "the most dramatic case is that of twenty-seven postal employees in Cleveland who have been cited on charges of disloyalty. All of these men are colored with the exception of four Jews and one who is a white Protestant."[84] Ultimately, black and Jewish organizations tried to have it both ways, maintaining anticommunist policies while defending civil liberties against anticommunist critics. But balance proved elusive.

Jews, historically a vulnerable minority, were particularly concerned with civil liberties. As the ADL argued, "We as Jews cannot ignore the spreading suspicions against all those who are different or those who advocate changes, because we can only exist in an atmosphere which accepts cultural, religious and ethnic diversity." An AJC poll revealed, "opposition to McCarthyism among Jews is far greater than among others. . . . Anti-Communist activities in which Jews, as a rule, are willing to engage are limited to those wherein they are certain nothing detrimental to civil liberties will occur."[85]

Some gloried in the right-wing attacks they received. When California senator Tenney labeled its state chapter a "Red front group," the AJCongress issued a public statement. "We are proud that our contribution to American democracy has become significant enough to be recognized by Mr. Tenney." It noted that the President's Committee on Civil Rights had incorporated AJCongress's agenda. "If such company as that of the President's committee be un-American, Mr. Tenney has honored us by his charges."[86]

These activists were under no illusion about the motivations behind the anticommunist "smear attacks" (to use the ADL's term). Law professor Thomas Emerson argued at the AJCongress convention that "the attack upon subversives was one form of an attack [by Republicans] upon the New Deal." But Republicans were not alone in using anticommunism to play politics. Especially after Roosevelt's death, Emerson continued, "the Democrats apparently considered it wise policy to steal the thunder of the Republicans and put out a Loyalty order, in an attempt to establish their loyalty." These loyalty programs were not designed to ferret out those planning espionage or sabotage, for which ample legislation already existed. Their agenda was to circumscribe civil liberties and to tar all progressives with the same anticommunist brush. Similarly HUAC's attacks on Hollywood suggested a "dangerous trend" to Walter White; its "real objective is to terrorize the industry into fear of presentation of thoughtful, intelligent pictures on domestic or international matters."[87]

Their concerns were not just theoretical. The Attorney General and federal, state, and local agencies compiled lists of allegedly subversive organizations. For the purpose of determining loyalty, anyone involved in groups named there was legitimately suspect. These lists were generally not vetted or subject to challenge prior to their issuance, and conservatives often placed progressive civil rights organizations on them. Tenney's list in California was but one example. In the same state, the NAACP appeared on the Army's list. The AG's 1950 list included, among others, Shinto Temples, the CRC, International Labor Defense, Michigan Civil Rights Federation, NNC, and several other civil rights groups that were, like the Southern Negro Youth Congress, fronted by communists but attracted noncommunist supporters. As the AJCongress pointed out regarding the McCarran Act, which required registration of all "Communist-front" organizations, "the looseness with which these groups are defined makes it possible for an organization to be designated as 'Communist' solely because one of its policies or objectives is the same as that of admittedly Communist groups or governments. . . . The result is that once avowedly Communist bodies have endorsed liberal or civil rights legislation, every other group can endorse such legislation only at its peril." Furthermore, fear that one might be added to that list would "discourage many people from engaging in any liberal activities whatever. In effect this would leave the Communist groups the sole spokesmen for liberal and civil rights legislation in America."[88]

The NUL and NAACP made precisely that point to HUAC. One reason communism had failed to do better in the black community was the presence of successful—but vulnerable—liberal coalitions. "They have failed" in Detroit, Turner testified, "because there exists in this community a positive alternative to the hollow claims of the Communists. . . . The NAACP, together with . . . the Michigan Committee on Civil Rights, the Catholic Interracial Council, the Council of Churches, the Jewish Community Council, the Urban League, the CIO . . . and many, many others, has demonstrated that . . . civil rights can be achieved within the framework of the American Constitution." David Dubinsky of the Jewish-dominated ILGWU agreed. "The best way to fight Communists and their Left Wing Allies," he declared, "is to begin a wide campaign of organization among the unorganized." In other words, as Granger observed, "The honest alliances increasingly being established with Americans who may be liberal or conservative . . . but who are agreed that race, color and creed must not be allowed to condition a person's chances" were the nation's best weapon against communism. "To . . . check this alliance . . . would be to encourage Negro Americans to seek support from other sources."[89]

In the view of every black and Jewish liberal organization, loyalty oaths and congressional investigating committees acted as such checks. Thus, despite their recognition of government's legitimate interest in ensuring the loyalty of workers in sensitive positions, and despite their own conviction of the dangers communism posed, they opposed these programs. A government using "any of the techniques of totalitarianism in resistance to it," the AJCongress warned, "immediately and surely, negates the purpose for which that resistance is carried on. Nor can democracy be preserved . . . by any measures which would limit democracy." The NAACP warned of "the dangerous error of labeling 'subversive' honest American Doctrines of freedom, justice and equality."[90]

Black and Jewish groups considered civil liberties and civil rights inextricable. In a 1947 policy statement NCRAC decried anticommunists' "interference with the exercise of the freedom of speech, press and assembly" arguing this was "a first and dangerous breach in the protecting citadel of civil rights erected by the Constitution. Denial of the rights of one minority leads inevitably to the denial of such rights to others and finally to the disintegration of democratic freedom itself."[91]

Thus despite their opposition to communism, which they reiterated at every opportunity, every major Jewish and black organization went on record to oppose presidential loyalty orders, state and local loyalty tests, book and speech bans, HUAC tactics, and broad-brush anticommunist legislation, although they differed in their approach. After substantial debate, AJCongress, for example, advocated the abolition of HUAC and repeal of Truman's Executive Loyalty Order, while the NAACP instead called for the order's revision to prevent "biased informants from using the loyalty program to persecute members of minority groups or persons sympathetic to the program of civil rights."[92]

The NAACP, ADL, AJCongress, and NCRAC investigated disloyalty allegations for such bias. They found plenty. They also found evidence that civil rights activity made employees suspect. Raymond Lieberman of Highland Park, Michigan, for example, was brought up for questioning because his name "appeared on the active indices of the National Federation for Constitutional Liberties," for having "spoken in favor of . . . the Michigan Civil Rights Federation."[93] A NCRAC subcommittee found "a disproportionately high number of Jews and Negroes have been accused by the Post Office Department of disloyalty." In eleven cities, the Post Office conducted seventy-five investigations of African Americans, at least fifty-three of Jews, and sixteen of white Christians. Anecdotal evidence was more frightening still, including a case of mistaken identity in which the wrong Puerto Rican worker was accused of disloyalty. "Loyalty Board officials refused to look into the matter, stating to the Attorney for the accused, 'What are you worried about? He is just a poor Puerto Rican. He will get another job.' " When a white non-Jewish employee appeared before the board to answer charges against him, "the clerk is said to have exclaimed, in effect, 'What are you doing here? This is for Jews and Niggers!' " NCRAC pledged opposition to all loyalty programs lacking civil liberties safeguards, and involvement in cases reflecting racial or religious discrimination.[94]

These organizations opposed much of the proposed anticommunist legislation on these grounds. The investigative and enforcement provisions of these bills seemed to be such a grotesque violation of civil liberties and the traditional presumption of innocence, such an unwarranted invasion of privacy, and to create such a chilling effect on speech that groups who themselves banned communists rejected them as draconian. As the ADL boasted, "actions taken by our national organization have been far more aggressive than our statements of policy."[95]

The NAACP filed amicus briefs in several court challenges arguing the unconsitutionality of the Smith Act. It investigated whether jury selections in Smith Act prosecutions evidenced racial discrimination. It also, of course, challenged state attempts to coerce submission of membership lists, although its defense included distinguishing the NAACP, which ought not be investigated, from the CP, which could be.[96]

The AJCongress, one of the most outspoken defenders of civil liberties, urged the "outright repeal" of the McCarran Act. Its CLSA filed briefs in cases challenging public and private loyalty procedures. In New York it supported a CP suit against a state listing of subversive organizations, and in New Jersey it sided with the Progressive Party by opposing loyalty oaths for candidates for public office. It also joined the case of the "Hollywood Ten" who refused to answer political questions posed by HUAC. Its staff drafted bills to regulate investigating committees, testified before state and congressional committees, and prepared background materials on other civil liberties issues including wiretapping. The NCJW opposed the Mundt bill to prevent subversion on the grounds that it "proposes to 'control' dangers to democracy by totalitarian methods; and thus it allies itself with the . . . very forces it purports to expose." The NAACP concurred, arguing the vagueness of its language made it "a threat to all organizations engaged in the effort to obtain full civil rights for American citizens."[97]

Finding a satisfying balance between civil liberties and protection against subversion proved difficult. The NAACP, for example, opposed loyalty oaths but would not defend individuals fired for refusing to take them. As Thurgood Marshall explained, the latter was not properly an NAACP issue, but rather a ploy by communists to "blackjack" the Association into taking on their battles. The NCJW opposed outlawing any political party, but believed communists and fascists should properly be barred from government employment. Therefore it opposed the Smith Act, which outlawed membership in the CP, but supported Truman's loyalty program. It opposed local "anti-Communist ordinances" and advocated working against them, but warned "the Council section should not be the spearhead of such activity."[98]

Still, while most liberal organizations recognized the threat to civil rights and civic freedoms inherent in the current atmosphere of intolerance, black and Jewish groups were among the few to confront its dangers head on. "McCarthyism has cast a pall of unreasoning fear over weak-kneed Washington officials," the NAACP complained. "And we . . . repudiate the argument that approval of McCarthy's politics is in any way a correct test of anti-Communism." Every major black and Jewish organization issued pointed statements, held public forums on constitutional rights, and provided public platforms for distinguished advocates of civil liberties. It was at one such ADL venue that President Eisenhower issued his first public denunciation of Senator McCarthy.[99]

Generally the groups based their opposition on the threat to civil liberties, not concern for racism or anti-Semitism. In fact McCarthy was neither particularly anti-Semitic nor racist, and the ADL publicly rejected claims to the contrary as "narrow and untenable." Rather, his methods hurt "the total American democracy." After reading pro-McCarthy mail received by Senator Fulbright, Herman Edelsberg concluded, "Only a tiny fraction of the letters contained any overt anti-Semitism. What I've seen, however, is more nauseating and I think more dangerous than the anti-Semitic junk we regularly see." The letters were filled with "sadism and smut," and "the terrific amount of misinformation and illogic is a sad commentary on our educational system and our newspapers." Virtually every liberal black and Jewish organization publicly rebuked the senator for inappropriate and unfair accusations and maintained a steady stream of public criticism.[100]

To a few, McCarthyism was even to blame for the degenerating moral standards of young people. In his sermon at New York's Temple Rodeph Sholom, Rabbi Louis Newman blamed the senator for the recent "dormitory raids" by college students. "A vast silence has descended upon young men and women today in the colleges of our country, and they find an expression for their bottled-up energies in foolish and unseemly 'raids' upon dormitories. . . . Instead of channeling this vitality into healthy argument on the vital issues of the times, they grow restless and inhibited."[101]

These organizations opposed the worst elements of anticommunist measures; some, like the AJCongress, proved acutely aware of the threats posed by any attempt to silence speech. Others, either tacitly or actively, agreed that certain views were in fact dangerous enough to suppress, and endorsed limitations on speech or activity so long as they were not egregious. Their willingness to engage in public debate and criticism, based on both the need to defend their own positions and their liberal convictions about the importance of civil liberties, was laudable. But their acceptance of the need to limit speech or political activity in certain cases helped provide legitimacy for all campaigns of political suppression or harassment.

"United Opposition"

Given the political sensitivity of the issues, acting in coalition proved particularly attractive. While black and Jewish groups recognized their obligation to monitor loyalty programs for racial or religious discrimination, most maintained they should deal with broader civil liberties questions as Americans rather than as blacks or Jews. They and other liberals therefore helped organize the National Civil Liberties Clearing House in the spring of 1949. By that fall over fifty groups had signed on, including the Friends Committee on National Legislation, NCJW, Americans for Democratic Action, National Education Association, National Jewish Welfare Board, Southern Regional Council, ACLU, Japanese American Citizens League, Congregational Christian Churches, Textile Workers Union, the Board of Missions of the Methodist Church, and the National Farmers Union. Linking civil liberties and civil rights, NCLCH chairman E. Raymond Wilson and advisory board chairman Francis Biddle explained, "The Clearing House is an informational agency established and conducted by . . . representatives of national organizations which share a common interest in civil liberties and civil rights, for the purpose of pooling their joint experience, information, ideas and effort."[102]

Clearing House organizations issued a joint statement protesting the civil liberties failures leading to the Peekskill riot, for example, organized communications to Congress and the president, and sent informational bulletins regarding civil liberties issues to hundreds of governmental and private organizations. In 1950 the cooperating organizations issued a joint statement outlining their opposition to the Mundt-Ferguson-Johnston and Nixon bills. As Shad Polier noted with punctuational vehemence in a memo to AJCongress and CLSA chapters, "THIS STATEMENT IS AN EXTREMELY IMPORTANT ACHIEVEMENT BECAUSE IT PLACES ON RECORD THE UNITED OPPOSITION OF THESE MOST IMPORTANT CIVIL ORGANIZATIONS TO THIS HIGHLY DANGEROUS LEGISLATION." Polier urged chapters to lobby, organize "community rallies, delegations and visits . . . to your Congressmen and Senators and community-wide statements." The usual caution prevailed regarding cooperation with communists. "These suggested actions should be undertaken in cooperation with other signatory groups, he noted, "AND WITH NO OTHERS." Still, in a few cases, urgency overrode caution. Just as state-sponsored lists and loyalty oaths compelled AJCongress to cooperate with the Communist and Progressive Parties, the Mundt bill posed enough of a threat that in New York the NAACP organized an opposition committee with the CRC.[103]

In 1953 eighteen leading liberal organizations also combined forces in a "liaison group" on civil liberties designed to complement the Clearing House by performing functions outside the latter's scope. Many belonged to both. This liaison group met informally to share resources and ideas "when infringements of civil liberties were threatened in local communities, . . . that some semblance of coordinated action might be instituted."[104]

The liaison group proved an effective mechanism for advancing both civil liberties and civil rights. At a January 1954 meeting the ACLU representative described efforts by the American Legion, Minute Women, and others to prevent the formation of a branch in Indianapolis. Because the local Council of Churches, NAACP, CIO, and Jewish Community Council provided support to the ACLU, a branch was established. The NUL representative at the meeting lamented that his group had been unable to establish a branch there, given the intensity of opposition. Some supporters had even been threatened with the loss of their jobs. Perhaps a similar joint effort might succeed? Edwin Lukas of the AJC responded, this "is exactly what the group is concerned with, and . . . if, episode by episode, these situations were dealt with and the attacks of the Legion and related groups neutralized, a real contribution would be made." If the national organizations made their positions in defense of democracy and civil rights better known, he reasoned, "in time" locals would "spring into action." Indeed, this was precisely the strategy used by northern-based nationals to prod local southern chapters to engage in civil rights. The liaison committee demonstrated once again the potential strength of that model. Meanwhile, liberal women's groups explored ways they might "work together to further civil liberties" on the local level.[105]

Ultimately, black and Jewish liberal organizations saw their civil liberties and anticommunist commitments not in conflict but rather mutually reinforcing. In Wilson Record's words, "American Negroes, more than any other group in our society, have a deep appreciation of the promises inherent in the American radical tradition and the egalitarian potential of the Constitution and the Bill of Rights. . . . [T]hese 'bourgeois' documents represent a liberating force such as the Communist Manifesto could never possibly be. Negroes are aware of this, even if it has been forgotten at times by the white community." Not all whites had forgotten. The ADL's mission, its Mr. Zara pointed out, "was designed to assure an equal opportunity to all to enjoy the benefits of a democratic society and that . . . was the most effective answer to Communism."[106]

When black and Jewish organizations fought communism while defending communists' right to speak, they saw themselves as true liberals, and liberals as true Americans. As Dore Schare argued at the 1948 ADL National Commission meeting, "From the very start of our nation, Americans always have been liberals. . . . Our history, our training, our love for our country, has insisted that we be and remain liberals. And because we Jews are Americans and human beings, liberalism has been terribly attractive to us, too." Although communists often masqueraded as liberals, "the Communist philosophy has not extended a tenth of the freedoms to its people that our democracy enjoys." Nevertheless, "as Liberals, as Americans, Jews and human beings, we must protect the rights of the American Communist until that very time he is proved to be dedicated to the overthrow of our democracy. We must do this without becoming confused or letting the Communist confuse us as to why we are protecting his rights." His conclusion could have been uttered by any of his black or Jewish colleagues. "So, politically, the drive still is toward Liberalism—which is American, which is Judaic, which is human. And, once again, the truth of Liberalism is a sustained truth because it is Justice."[107]

Noble as such sentiments sounded, and outspoken as these organizations were on civil liberties and civil rights, they also bear some responsibility for the marginalization or suppression of unpopular views. Anticommunism provided a rationale for conducting a campaign of threat, intimidation and character assassination that would ultimately be used against civil rights activists like Martin Luther King Jr. While black, Jewish, and other liberal groups opposed its most extreme forms, they hedged (some more than others) over whether it was ever legitimate to suppress liberties or prosecute ideological differences. And they themselves generally chose exclusion and marginalization of those farther to the left. Such choices not only contributed to the poisoned atmosphere of distrust, but lost them allies and foot soldiers, narrowed their choice of strategies and goals, limited the situations in which they were willing to intervene, distorted their perspective and priorities, and deprived them of crucial insights regarding race and class. To liberal black and Jewish organizations, the threat justified such choices. In hindsight, the benefits seem outweighed by the costs.

CHAPTER SIX

Things Fall Apart

> The Negro community is completely dissatisfied with the pres-
> ent rate of progress toward quality. . . . Negroes are . . . re-evaluat-
> ing their alliances. . . .
>
> One of its results has been a mistrust of "liberals" in the strug-
> gle for civil rights. And we must recognize, for good or ill, that the
> Jews, more than any other group, are generally so identified. . . .
>
> . . . [T]he willingness of Jewish and other groups to accept, on
> occasion, a partial victory (because of the danger that demanding
> too much will result in getting nothing) has caused resentment in
> Negro ranks. They often feel that this compromises their position
> and demonstrates a lack of understanding on our part. . . .
>
> The new militant Negro demands his rights; he will not accept
> patronizing assurance of future action.[1]

This prescient observation at a 1960 NCRAC meeting came just after the
first student sit-ins and the formation of the Student Nonviolent Coordinating Committee (SNCC), before the Freedom Rides and the urban riots
of those "long hot summers," before Black Power. The same forces that
had brought blacks and Jews together in the preceding two decades would
divide them in the decades following. Black enthusiasm for international
anticolonial freedom movements, which had earlier brought support for
the fledgling Jewish state, led many in the 1960s to sympathize with Palestinians and to castigate Israel as a European-style imperial power. The
Jews' shift from economic and social outsiders to insiders took decades
to complete, but the impact on Jewish attitudes toward the evolving civil
rights agenda was profound. Once united by shared oppression, the two
communities became increasingly divided by perspectives fundamental to
their social and class differences. Jews' satisfaction with their success, and
the system that made it possible, could not easily coexist beside African
Americans' frustrations that the promise of America continued to be denied them. Many African Americans rejected old partners and old
agendas as they proved inadequate to the task; inevitably those rejections
offended and angered Jews. Each group felt betrayed by the other.

The rise of identity politics, with its emphasis on group membership
and its rejection of pluralism and even of cross-cultural coalition, dealt
black-Jewish relations another blow as both communities turned inward.

Beyond the hurt and anger, their interests and concerns had diverged. At the same time, ironically, civil rights successes contributed in their own way to the demise of coalition politics. With many of the fundamental legal and legislative civil rights protections in place, many well-intentioned coalitions that acknowledged that there was more work to be done nonetheless floundered for lack of specific and broadly agreed-upon goals.

The 1960s, then, brought a new set of issues to the fore, issues nonetheless determined in part by earlier struggles between blacks and Jews. Jews had largely embraced the status quo. To their black colleagues Jewish leaders recommended patience, moderation. This was not condescension or a withdrawal from their political commitments. Rather, Jews' faith in liberalism and their blindness (along with that of most other whites) to what scholars call white skin privilege, the often invisible benefits that being white provides in American society, allowed them to believe they had risen on their own merits; they felt confident black people were capable of doing the same. Jews' success, in turn, made them more accepting of compromise, and less conscious of the limits of liberalism than were many in the black community who continued to bump up against those limits. It was precisely along this liberal fault line that black-Jewish political collaboration foundered in the late 1960s. While individual Jews remained in the civil rights coalition, black and Jewish agencies publicly parted company on several occasions. Most often cited as points of division were the Ocean Hill–Brownsville controversy and affirmative action. Other analysts point to the rise of black nationalism and radicalism, which alienated many white supporters, including most Jews. While all these do reveal the growing division between blacks and Jews, they were symptoms, not causes, of the fraying of the coalition, which was rooted in the struggle over liberalism.

Already suspicious of mass action, most Jewish organizations grew more uneasy in the 1960s as grassroots civil rights groups increasingly challenged the liberalism they had embraced. CORE and SNCC criticized Kennedy, the Democratic Party, and the establishment more generally. First SNCC, then Martin Luther King Jr., publicly opposed the Vietnam War. This was not simply a foreign policy disagreement but a critique of the entire power structure. Many in the black community, dispirited by white recalcitrance and liberal inaction, turned to nationalism. And when the civil rights movement moved North, into the neighborhoods of these liberal Jews, the question of integration took on a different character. With concerns now couched in class rather than racial terms, most Jews fled to suburbs almost as quickly as white Christians to avoid what they perceived as the deterioration of their schools and neighborhoods. They pointed to riots as evidence of civil rights agendas run amok. And although Jews still expressed less racism than other whites, they nonetheless engaged in the same social segregation of blacks that white Christians had made a tradition.

This process of divergence developed over several decades, and occurred more in fits and starts than as a smooth progression, with some issues pulling the old coalition back together as others pulled it apart. Furthermore, different segments of the black and Jewish community moved away from coalition at different times. The NCJW and AJCongress steadfastly continued their civil rights work long after the AJC had turned to the right, for example; black leaders from the NAACP, NUL, and Negro American Labor Council continued to work with Jewish allies as CORE and SNCC embraced nationalism and rejected white partnerships. As historian and activist Clayborne Carson has pointed out, this was as much a split between liberals and leftists as it was between blacks and Jews.[2]

The 1960s, in other words, also intensified differences within the black and Jewish communities as the liberal consensus unraveled. Within the black community, the programs of older organizations seemed conciliatory and weak to younger and more militant groups like SNCC and the Revolutionary Action Movement. While the NAACP supported many of the legal efforts of these newer groups, it, and even more so the NUL, disparaged their tactics, their impatience, and their enthusiasm for the urban riots. Many historians have argued that the two approaches were in fact complementary, that the demands of more radical groups strengthened the negotiating position of those black leaders such as Martin Luther King Jr. and Whitney Young whom whites now perceived as moderates. Still, these were polarizing divisions within the black community as new voices that rejected liberal values and strategies gained legitimacy in a community frustrated by the limits of liberal gains.

Meanwhile, in the Jewish community divisions largely along generational lines led many young Jewish activists to reject the organizations their parents had established, and to join black-led grassroots civil rights groups. By and large, these young people were also less likely to be affiliated with congregations or other Jewish organizations. And within the religious community, generally speaking, the Reform movement's commitment to civil rights proved far more extensive and durable than that of the Conservative or Orthodox, whose engagement was more limited and less central to their members or their organizational structures. Class too divided Jews, as an economically and educationally successful Jewish community left its working-class compatriots behind.[3] At the same time, longstanding differences between black and Jewish organizations, and among Jewish organizations themselves, widened until they found themselves on opposite sides of civil rights issues ranging from affirmative action to improving ghetto communities. In the last decades of the twentieth century the interests of the various Jewish agencies would reconverge. Whether a similar reconvergence will occur between black and Jewish organizations no one yet knows.

And yet, a great deal of black-Jewish cooperation endured through these difficult times, and work on specific projects proceeded. Both communities maintained their staunchly liberal voting patterns, and the bitter public exchanges, while real, were never the dominant style of interaction. Rumors of the death of black-Jewish relations have been greatly exaggerated. If the pattern between blacks and Jews in the first two-thirds of the twentieth century was one of growing cooperation with an undertone of persistent conflict, the pattern in the last third of the century might be characterized as one of growing conflict that did not erase the possibilities of cooperation.

The Sit-ins and the Jewish Problem

In February 1960 a small group of African American students in Greensboro, North Carolina, planned and executed a protest against segregation. Entering a local Woolworth's, they bought school supplies, then sat down at the lunch counter. Denied service, they remained seated and returned the next morning. When they were arrested for violating segregation and trespass laws, others took their place.

The strategy spread like wildfire. Within three months fifty-three cities in nine states saw similar actions. Demanding the right to be served, the demonstrators called for boycotts to support their protest. Generally targeting all offending stores in the area, these protests had a substantial economic impact. Jewish merchants in Nashville estimated that boycotts there were "95% effective." Of ten communities studied by a NCRAC committee, such pressures succeeded in integrating dining facilities in six; the committee concluded that for the other four "it is only a question of time."[4]

The sit-in efforts were initiated and coordinated in virtually every city by students, who organized themselves into the Student Nonviolent Coordinating Committee (SNCC). SNCC, in turn, reinvigorated more established local black organizations such as churches or branches of the NAACP. While they had their differences with the students, these groups sustained the boycotts, bailed out protesters, and provided other forms of support. (Both the NAACP and SCLC also tried, unsuccessfully, to bring SNCC under their own wings.) A few local black leaders expressed reservations. Still, in the words of a 1961 NCRAC report, "the differences between the various forces in the local Negro community were becoming blurred," as both a "so-called militant leader or a conservative leader" gave "basically the same answers, though in different language and tone."[5]

Most of the national Jewish organizations endorsed these protests relatively quickly. In early April 1960 the AJCongress urged presidents of chain stores facing sit-ins to serve black customers. "It is believed this marks the first declaration of support for the Negro sit-down strikes in the South by a national Jewish organization," the *Pittsburgh Courier* noted, although the JLC had already been providing support. The 1960 NCRAC plenum, while not endorsing the sit-ins per se, reaffirmed its commitment to the goals of equal opportunity and equal rights the sit-ins sought. And hundreds of younger (northern) Jewish activists endorsed these protests directly with their bodies. Many of these were so-called red diaper babies raised in progressive and leftist families, whose commitments emerged naturally from their politics. But others described their motivation in religious and ethnic terms.[6]

Few southern Jews shared their enthusiasm. A special NCRAC committee surveyed Jewish leaders in ten southern communities that had both sit-ins and CRCs in late 1960 and early 1961. No Jewish merchants "voluntarily desegregated," the report found, but "[t]here was virtual unanimity among those interviewed that the reasons were basically economic"; they feared they would lose white customers. Once compelled to desegregate, however, none reported a drop in white patronage. Nevertheless, Jewish merchants repeatedly expressed resentment that the sit-ins had placed them in the front lines of the civil rights battle.[7]

For their part, southern Jewish communal leaders resisted any suggestion the sit-ins had any special resonance as a "Jewish issue." Rather, "there is deep resistance among CRCs to taking any planned or organized approach to these problems. There is virtually no discussion . . . but simply the almost *a priori* decision to avoid involvement, as a community." While many rabbis privately professed to civil rights convictions, virtually all in the Deep South remained silent, lest they antagonize the white gentile community or, for that matter, their own congregants. Little had changed in the South from earlier years in this regard. NCRAC reported that while "Negro leaders were believed to have higher expectations of Jews . . . almost no sustained relationship exists between Jews and Negroes, and virtually no thought had been given to the longer range questions of relationships between the Jewish community and the emerging Negro community."[8]

As before, of course, there were the courageous exceptions, such as Rabbi Jacob Rothschild of Atlanta, whose long and public advocacy of desegregation won his synagogue the dubious honor of being dynamited by white supremacists in 1958. A member of the Southern Regional Council, he helped found a community group to prepare Atlanta for school desegregation in 1961, and organized a well-attended testimonial dinner for Martin Luther King Jr., following the latter's receipt of the 1964 Nobel Prize. Rabbi Charles Mantinband of Hattiesburg, Mississippi, worked openly with local NAACP activist Medgar Evers (later assassinated by a white supremacist) and defended Clyde Kennard, framed for trying to enroll at Mississippi Southern College. Liberal rabbi Levi Olan of Dallas, Texas, praised the *Brown* decision publicly, pressed his congregation into accepting an African American member, and marched with his family in civil rights demonstrations. Most southern Jewish leaders did not have that sort of outsized courage. Though they claimed to be supportive of desegregation and racial equality in their hearts, they rarely translated those sentiments into public action. In the words of historian P. Allen Krause, "they have not done what it was within their power to do."[9]

Still, although Jewish merchants and leaders resisted taking a formal role in the struggle, the NCRAC committee found "the extent of involvement of Jews in the sit-in conflict is remarkable." Jews, disproportionally represented among the affected merchants, "played leadership roles behind the scenes in discussions with the mayor, business leaders, other merchants and Negro leaders." A few rabbis intervened in similarly quiet ways, as did several local CRC leaders. Perhaps, the NCRAC committee speculated, these Jewish leaders might be persuaded to increase their private activities in what Krause described as "a minimal program."[10]

As before, the southern Jewish rank and file were more reluctant still to get involved, something Rabbi Rothschild "regretted." Paradoxically, he found the more secure Jewish communities tended to be the least active, perhaps because they had the most to lose by antagonizing their white Christian neighbors. Nor did most southern Jewish college students join the sit-in movement. The NCRAC committee noted with dismay "the apparent apathy of Jewish students generally about the issues involved"; a Hillel director insisted the students simply feared the same white backlash their parents did.[11]

Nevertheless, Jewish leaders understood that the sit-ins had transformed the civil rights movement. At a February 1961 meeting of southern Jewish leaders, Harold Fleming, executive director of the Southern Regional Council, "emphasized the critical urgency of the situation today. . . . The problems can no longer be dealt with on a leisurely basis, he said; forces are pushing for solutions one way or another." What changed was not only the speed but the focus. "There has been a dramatic emergence of Negro cohesiveness and leadership," he observed. As a result, the agenda of the sit-ins gradually broadened, from lunch-counter desegregation to employment opportunity, which NCRAC leaders considered a more significant but also more challenging goal. Fleming also predicted that "pressures by Negroes to vote would come sooner than these states anticipated."[12] He was correct. On the heels of these early efforts came CORE's Freedom Rides and SNCC's first foray into Mississippi in 1961 to register black voters. SCLC, SNCC, and CORE, often aided by the NAACP, expanded the desegregation campaign, bringing protests and demonstrations to southern cities and towns and to the 1964 Democratic National Convention. The civil rights movement had intensified beyond anyone's imaginings ten years earlier.

The Freedom Rides, modeled on the 1947 Journey of Reconciliation, used white and black bus riders to test the 1961 Supreme Court decision desegregating services at terminals of interstate travel. Across the South white mobs who met the buses threw bricks, set fire to the buses, and assaulted riders, drivers, and the federal agents accompanying them, until state officials and President Kennedy struck a bargain: the riders would be protected until they could be arrested for violating the now-unconstitutional segregation laws. Unlike its 1947 precursor, however, the Freedom Rides made the news. Freedom rider and veteran JOR participant James Peck, so badly beaten that he spoke from a hospital bed, vowed to get back on the bus so as not to let the segregationists win. Constitutional violations, secret deals, and white violence had become public knowledge.

SNCC, too, continued to make national news throughout the early 1960s. Expanding on their sit-in tactics, SNCC workers led demonstrations and marches, brought black citizens to courthouses to register to vote, and staged read-ins at libraries, wade-ins at swimming pools, and kneel-ins at white churches. King's SCLC followed suit. Civil rights workers were attacked by fire hoses and police dogs in Birmingham, Alabama, and by mounted police with tear gas in Selma; they were threatened, shot at, bombed, imprisoned, and beaten in the tiny hamlets and quiet towns in which they doggedly pursued their programs. SNCC in particular attempted the dangerous, difficult work of organizing in rural Deep South communities, establishing Freedom Schools to teach black children and adults about their rights and their history, and launching voter registration campaigns. The most ambitious, Mississippi Freedom Summer in 1964, mounted a full-scale challenge to the lily-white state Democratic Party. SNCC and its allies brought northern college students into the state to join local black activists in a summer-long campaign to organize a parallel state party structure, the Mississippi Freedom Democratic Party (MFDP). Despite the well-publicized disappearance and presumed deaths early that summer of volunteers Andrew Goodman, Michael Schwerner (both Jews), and veteran activist James Chaney (African American), the effort went on. Electing an integrated slate of delegates, the MFDP demanded Mississippi's seats at the Democratic National Convention in 1964 as the only state party organization that had followed the Democrats' rules against discrimination. Fearful of antagonizing southern (and even some northern) Democrats, and unwilling to put the civil rights struggle front and center, Lyndon Johnson proposed a compromise of two at-large seats and a promise to change the rules for future conventions. ("We didn't come all this way for no two seats," MFDP leader Fannie Lou Hamer argued in rejecting the offer.)[13] Again, the battle played out in full view of the public.

One dramatic consequence of the sit-ins and demonstrations was the escalating white backlash. This concerned many Jews. Fleming "warned that the resistance movement was becoming more extremist and showing signs of incipient anti-Semitism."[14] Such fears were not misplaced. The White Knights of the Ku Klux Klan planned to kill Jews in Jackson and Meridian, Mississippi, believing they were instigating civil rights action. In 1966 and '67 they murdered two NAACP leaders, bombed a Meridian synagogue and the home of an outspoken rabbi. The next year they targeted a Jewish businessman for assassination and a synagogue for bombing, although the plot was foiled and the would-be assassins shot by police in an ambush. For this reason the ADL kept southern hate groups under "constant . . . surveillance" and cooperated with FBI and local law enforcement to infiltrate and undermine them. In fact it was the ADL that raised funds to pay the informants who set up the ambush.[15]

Such events help explain why southern Jews continued to avoid public engagement in civil rights. The Rabbinical Assembly sent northern rabbis to march in Birmingham in 1963 to counter the silence of local Jews. Damning with faint praise, the Rev. Fred Shuttlesworth of SCLC suggested in 1966 that the southern Jewish response to the civil rights movement "compares favorably with that of numerous other white groups"; Aaron Henry of the MFDP was more blunt. "Sorry, they are not with it."[16]

Even among the national Jewish leadership, there was considerable uncertainty about the civil disobedience strategy the sit-ins and similar protests employed. Jewish groups at a 1961 NCRAC meeting debated whether breaking the law, even for a good cause, was justifiable. While those who answered affirmatively cited the Nuremberg trials and appealed to the higher call of moral law, most believed the best hope for both racial equality and Jewish security lay in the absolute rule of law. Segregationists could use the same arguments civil rights workers did, they pointed out. Better to pass and enforce fair laws everyone must obey. This deeply held Jewish faith in the rule of law, of course, ran directly counter to the experience of African Americans in the Jim Crow South, where equal protection rulings held no force, where white juries routinely acquitted violent white supremacists, and where even elected officials advocated resistance to constitutionally mandated school integration. A few Jewish leaders also expressed concerns that the politics of the more activist civil rights groups might be too far to the left. The ADL, for example, worried about communist influences in groups like SNCC, and monitored it as closely as it did the Klan.[17]

Jewish organizations nonetheless remained firm supporters of civil rights through the decade, fighting for stronger legislation, sending northern rabbis and Jewish lay leaders to southern marches, and maintaining their traditional coalitions. Rabbi Joachim Printz of the AJCongress addressed the March on Washington in 1963; Rabbi Abraham Joshua Heschel, one of the greatest modern Jewish theologians and a leader in the Conservative movement, marched with King in Selma. Rabbi Arthur Lelyveld of Cleveland participated in Freedom Summer. Asked by King to support a demonstration in St. Augustine, Florida, in June 1964, the Reform Movement's Central Conference of American Rabbis, meeting nearby, joined the protesters in the streets and in prison. "We came because we could not stand silently before our brothers' blood," the rabbis declared in a statement. "We came as Jews who remember the millions of faceless people who stood quietly, watching the smoke rise from the crematoria."[18] Jewish groups remained central actors in the Leadership Conference on Civil Rights; helped lobby for civil rights bills including, of course, the pivotal Civil Rights Act of 1964, the Voting Rights Act of 1965, and the Fair Housing Act of 1968; and continued to file amicus briefs in civil rights cases. And numerous local branches of these organizations, primarily in large cities, cooperated on civil rights and antidiscrimination problems closer to home.

These Jewish liberals continued to exploit traditional cold war arguments to defend their positions. Educational integration was crucial, Shad Polier insisted, because "[t]oday we are faced by an enormously greater and no less dangerous gap [than the missile gap]—the educational chasm that separates the Negro child from the white child and that threatens our viability as a nation and our future as a leader of the free world. In the face of this challenge, the Federal government must play its proper role."[19]

The mainstream black and Jewish organizations continued to monitor racists and anti-Semites. Individual Jews, including the religiously observant Kivie Kaplan, the secular Jack Greenberg, and the leftist Herbert Hill continued to work for, and materially aid, black organizations. A substantial portion of SCLC's, CORE's, and SNCC's budgets came from Jewish donations. Leftist Jews, like many of the attorneys in the National Lawyers Guild, defended jailed protesters. Younger Jews, particularly those with more secular and leftist leanings, continued to swell activist ranks, from the hundreds engaged in SNCC and CORE projects, to Stanley Levison, one of King's closest advisors. And this engagement operated even on the most intimate of levels. As the editor's introduction to Albert Gordon's study of interracial and interreligious intermarriage observed,

"It is a fact that young American Jews are unusually active in the civil rights struggle, are especially devoted to the attainment of a racially egalitarian society. . . . It follows, then, that of the relatively few white-Negro marriages . . . a relatively high percentage involves Jews."[20]

Black leaders also continued to support human rights issues of special concern to American Jews, although as Christians, they were not invited to join Jewish organizations. The NAACP protested Abdel Nasser's discrimination against Jews in Egypt. "Injustice to any people is a threat to justice to all people—and I cannot stand idly by," King explained to Jewish leaders honoring him for his work on behalf of Jews persecuted in the Soviet Union. King proved one of the most outspoken of black leaders in his opposition to all forms of anti-Semitism. But he was not alone. Roy Wilkins, Whitney Young, Dorothy Height, Vernon Jordan, John Lewis, and many others expressed their support of Jews and Jewish interests. Bayard Rustin, longtime civil rights strategist and democratic socialist, insisted that nothing could stop him from discussing anti-Semitism. Even "if every Jew told me to get out, I would still accept every invitation to go and speak about this. And if I didn't get invited, I would speak to people in buses and trains" because "I am not going to get out of the movement which I am dedicated to, the movement against injustice."[21]

Liberalism Tested

Still, tensions between blacks and Jews simmered below the surface. By the end of the decade, once the great legal and legislative battles had been won, these tensions replaced joint civil rights projects at center stage. This came about in part because the escalating war between liberals and their critics was often overlaid with and rewritten as a series of black-Jewish conflicts.

The intensity of white resistance led civil rights activists of both races to confront liberalism head on. They questioned the efficacy of nonviolence, and the government's commitment to constitutional rights. They pointed to the lack of federal protection during the entirely legal Freedom Rides, and the flawed compromise that had resolved it. Police attacks on civil rights marchers had gone unpunished, and murders of civil rights workers unsolved. Of what use were liberal tactics?

SNCC's Freedom Summer project had also raised the question of whites' place in the movement. The project's strategy—bringing in well-connected white northerners to direct national attention to racial discrimination—proved the point of its critics, and its successes only highlighted the extent of American racism. Reporters and news cameras followed whites, not blacks. Freedom Summer did publicize white racial violence, but largely because white civil rights workers were among the victims.

When the FBI dredged rivers in search of Chaney, Goodman, and Schwerner, they discovered black bodies, victims of lynchings the police had never seriously investigated. Tensions emerged between northern, generally better-educated but often paternalistic whites, and veteran southern black activists.

Nor were these merely southern problems. That summer's crowning achievement, the MFDP's challenge of the traditional "Dixiecrat" delegation, was rejected by the allegedly liberal national Democratic Party. And as the integration struggle moved North, whites who called themselves civil rights supporters aped the arguments and strategies of the most ardent southern segregationists. White liberals had proven themselves either hypocritical or weak, too willing to compromise with the forces of segregation.

One might argue that it was not liberalism but liberals who were at fault, unwilling in the end to live up to their ideals, unwilling to yield the power they unfairly held. And certainly in this period, many who had voiced liberal positions regarding southern segregation refused to confront problems in their own back yards. Others simply never meant the words of racial justice they had mouthed. But this was more than the personal moral failings of self-proclaimed liberals. These instances revealed the limits of liberalism as an ideology. Most liberals had not abandoned their principles; rather they too frequently found themselves caught between competing liberal positions: civil rights versus respect for law and the democratic process, immediate equality versus working within the system.

Such dilemmas were not new. In the war years, liberals were forced to choose between building needed wartime housing and accepting segregation in them. In the 1950s and early '60s, they debated how closely to tie desegregation with federal aid to education. Whenever Congress considered education bills, Representative Adam Clayton Powell Jr. would propose an amendment to prohibit segregated schools from receiving aid. If that amendment passed, everyone understood, southern opposition would torpedo the entire bill. Which value had the higher priority, government support of public education or racial justice? Consistently, liberal groups pleaded with Powell to withdraw his amendment and avoid the conflict, although when he refused, they endorsed the amended bills. In subsequent years such dilemmas proved no less stark.[22]

These liberal failures were not simply about race. Black liberals too had proven disappointing to many activists. King turned back in Selma rather than confront Alabama state troopers; Rustin supported the Democratic Party's proposed compromise with the MFDP. Many activists complained that the SCLC and the NAACP employed top-down campaigns rather than listening to and relying on poor black people. SNCC lambasted the March on Washington for its celebratory stance regarding the progress of civil rights; only his deep respect for A. Philip Randolph, whose dream the march had been since 1941, convinced SNCC's chairman, John Lewis, to tone down his fiery speech there. Still, these struggles over liberalism spilled inevitably into struggles over race and, therefore, over the role of Jews, the most prominent whites in the liberal civil rights coalition. And as a community psychologically invested in a black-Jewish partnership, Jews certainly felt their impact.

The labor movement proved one of the most bitter battlegrounds. Soon after its founding in 1959, Randolph's Negro American Labor Council found itself at odds with the JLC, after which it had been modeled. For years, and especially after the silencing of leftist organizers, the JLC and the AJC's National Labor Service (NLS) were among the most prominent white voices against racism within the labor movement. Their style, which coupled pressure for improvement with abundant praise for tiny gains, was, however, far more conciliatory than the NALC was comfortable with. One NALC member complained in 1961 that the JLC "is too eager to see progress where it ain't." Herbert Hill, then labor secretary for the NAACP, advised the NLS and JLC that they "would do well if they ceased to apologize for the racists in the American labor movement, and instead of attempting to create a desirable public image for the AFL-CIO, join with Negro workers and the NAACP in directly attacking the broad pattern of discrimination." The head of the NLS retorted that constant confrontation "discourages good guys from pushing civil rights. Why do it at all if all you're going to get is blame for tokenism anyway?"[23]

The JLC in turn denounced the NAACP as anti-Semitic in 1962 after the Association criticized the Jewish-led ILGWU. In a reply, Roy Wilkins highlighted the continuing problem of paternalism as well as the difference in style of these organizations. "When you declare . . . that the NAACP's continued attack upon discrimination . . . by trade union bodies and leaders places 'in jeopardy' continued progress towards civil rights goals or rends the 'unity' among the civil rights forces, or renders a 'disservice' to the Negro worker . . . you are, in fact, seeking . . . to force us to conform to what the Jewish Labor Committee is pleased to classify as proper behavior." As to anti-Semitism, "We do not deign to defend ourselves against such a baseless allegation." These were differences of style and approach, coupled with instances of Jewish paternalism and black resentment at having Jews serve as their self-appointed spokespersons. Jews' differential success in the labor movement, and their long experience there, led them to a more conciliatory, more deliberate approach, a balancing act of pressuring and placating those with power. African Americans, tired of waiting, tired of empty promises, could no longer accept what seemed to them tokenism or empty symbolism. For them the dilemma was how much they could afford to alienate irritating but still useful allies.[24]

Certainly Jewish liberals understood black resentment and the need for self-assertion. And they frequently reiterated the need to work against the Jewish tendency toward paternalism, even if they remained unwilling to move beyond the boundaries of liberalism as they understood it. As Nathan Edelstein, chairman of the AJCongress, argued, "The maturing Negro of today is through with his former inferior status and will no longer allow others to speak for or lead him. With full recognition of his new and proper status, Jews and Negroes can and must forge a partnership of equals." The AJC came to a similar conclusion, critiquing certain of its own longstanding tactics. As its Community Relations consultant wrote, "I would oppose the idea that the Jews should in a special brochure show what they have done for Negroes. The repercussions are not what might be expected. This summary would emphasize the position of the Jew as a benefactor, a role that usually brings resentment rather than appreciation."[25]

Black Power

Many civil rights activists felt this increasing frustration with liberals or the liberal agenda. Black SNCC and CORE workers had begun employing nationalist and militant rhetoric by the mid-1960s, fed in part by the charismatic preachings of Malcolm X and the Nation of Islam. Even Adam Clayton Powell Jr. embraced both Malcolm and his arguments, criticizing the NAACP, CORE, and SCLC in 1963 because they had white members and leaders. Black stalwarts of the liberal coalition fired back. Wilkins called Powell an "opportunist"; labor leader Frank Crosswaith defended the integrated movement in the *Amsterdam News*. Powell did not help his case when he identified the owners of the *New York Times*, who criticized his views, as Jews. But as Cleveland Robinson, African American union leader, observed in 1966, "Today the Negro is calling the shots; the Negro is making the demands."[26]

Not just the rhetoric but the issues themselves were changing. The dismantling of legal Jim Crow had little impact on the life of southern tenant farmers or the residents trapped in northern black ghettos. As Rustin stressed in 1966, "*Negroes today are in worse economic shape, live in worse slums, and attend more highly segregated schools than in 1954.*" Black unemployment was greater than white, the wage gap between black and white workers remained substantial. The housing in poor black neighborhoods was deteriorating, and their schools poor. Because of in-

"Take my picture next to this sign," Malcolm X told Laurance Henry. "I like it."
Reproduced by permission of the estate of Dr. Laurance G. Henry.

sufficient funding, "[t]he promise of meaningful work and decent wages once held out by the anti-poverty programs has not been fulfilled."[27]

Nonviolence seemed as ineffective a tactic against these ills as it had proven to be against southern vigilantes, and many advocated greater militance. Stokely Carmichael (whose first political demonstration had been in support of Israel) insisted that "rampaging white mobs . . . must be made to understand that their days of free head-whipping are over. Black people should and must fight back. Nothing more quickly repels someone bent on destroying you than the unequivocal message, 'O.K. fool, make your move, and run the same risk I run—of dying.' "[28] These were controversial views. Rustin, for example, countered that while no one disputed the right to self-defense, making whites feel fear was more likely to generate hostility than respect. Furthermore, it allowed white conservatives to deflect the national conversation from civil rights to law and order. Still, even he, a democratic socialist, understood the impulse. Carmichael, he noted, had not always opposed integration. "It took countless beatings and 24 jailings—that and the absence of strong and continual support from the liberal community—to persuade Carmichael that his earlier faith in coalition politics was mistaken."[29]

Rustin understood that Black Power constituted a "Negro revolution" against "liberals . . . who . . . offer only a philosophy of integration with whites and a program of 'opportunity' which can have relevance only for the few." That program "was and is essentially concerned with the structure of law and social justice; its goals were equality before the law and equality of individual opportunity," in other words, modern liberalism. Black people, in coalition "with the forces of labor, humanism, religious radicalism, and political liberalism," produced remarkable results: civil rights laws, executive orders, legal decisions. And it reshaped liberal ideas, including "the reconstruction of the legal basis of civil rights," recognition of federal responsibility for civil rights enforcement, and the identification of equality before the law as an explicit public policy goal. Yet these successes also signaled the end of the liberal civil rights movement, Rustin argued, for "virtually everything that was envisaged by the liberal as legal 'civil rights' has either already been done, or been accepted (at least in principle) by the federal government as its responsibility." The LCCR and the Conference on Religion and Race "have atrophied or all but vanished from the scene, along with their once prominent white civil-rights leaders." In its place has come "*the Negro movement*. The difference between the two can be summed up in the contrast between the coalition's belief that what is good for democracy is good for the Negro, and the Negro movement's belief that what is good for the Negro, is good for democracy." This new movement "is a self-interest movement which is for civil rights because it serves Negro welfare." Like Jews, then, "Negroes when acting collectively as a group are . . . motivated predominantly by self-interest." That interest now lay not only in an improvement in "material welfare" but also in "a rediscovery of pride and confidence."[30]

Even integrationist groups like the NAACP increasingly insisted on having African Americans fill their top positions, and pressed a 1966 White House conference on civil rights to focus exclusively on black issues. Black Democratic congressmen began meeting as a bloc within the Party (something, arguably, they might have done before had they had sufficient numbers). Black Power was one embodiment of a wider sense of group solidarity that had emerged over the past two decades of civil rights efforts, and reached into liberal and mainstream groups as well as more militant ones. As Rustin observed, " 'Black power' is the slogan for those Negroes who know that their destiny as individuals will be ruled by the fate of their group as a whole" and argued it was simply the most recent expression of pluralism. Still, his was by no means an embrace of the militants' position. "That solidarity entails a certain degree of 'separatism' goes without saying, but the separatism of a strengthened and enriched Negro community need be no more absolute than that, say, of the Jewish community," Rustin cautioned.[31]

Most young nationalists disagreed. Not only were white liberal allies vacillating and weak, not only were liberal methods inefficacious, they argued, but the liberal struggle for full public integration—penetrating existing political, economic, and social structures—was simply covert assimilationism into a value system blacks ought instead to repudiate. As Carmichael and political scientist Charles Hamilton explained, "The values of this society support a racist system; we find it incongruous to ask black people to adopt and support . . . those values. We also reject the assumption that the basic institutions of this society must be preserved. The goal of black people must *not* be to assimilate into middle-class America."[32]

Integration, they insisted, required cultural genocide. To fully succeed in the existing system blacks had to become, for all intents and purposes, white, something not only undesirable but in any case made impossible by personal and structural racism. As James Farmer wrote in 1965, "America would become color blind when we gave up our color. The white man, who presumably was no color, would have to give up only his prejudices. We would have to give up our identities."[33] Such critiques moved Black Power advocates and others inspired by them not only from liberalism to nationalism but also from pluralism to identity politics, the belief that one's background or group identity determined one's interests.

A few went further, insisting that individuals must be recognized as inevitable members of their biologically determined group. This essentialist view, while not a new one, further troubled traditional liberals. In fact, few who claimed the fixity of race considered it simply biological. Rather, they argued that race had been *treated* as an inescapable and hereditary category and that race therefore had reality based on the widely divergent historical experiences of populations whose ancestors came from different continents, and who enjoyed differential access to power based on that ancestry. Nevertheless, their rigidity on questions of racial identity seemed to liberal critics disturbingly akin to those of white racists, and suggested both a lack of understanding of historical change and a decidedly unliberal willingness to ascribe social and political definitions to phenotypical traits.

Rather than seek integration, these nationalists contended, black people must redefine themselves and their goals, organizing themselves separately in order to free themselves from the definitions and limits imposed by whites. Such arguments resonated powerfully with many in the civil rights movement who were frustrated with its slow gains. By the late 1960s new militant nationalist groups had seized the momentum from the moderates, and SNCC and CORE had redefined themselves as all-black. The expulsion of whites from these organizations was hotly contested. When SNCC voted on the question in 1967, nineteen voted for expulsion, eighteen opposed, and twenty-four abstained. The decision dismayed many black as well as white SNCC activists; Fannie Lou Hamer resigned in protest. Those who supported it argued that it was not antiwhite. Each race had its own job to do. Nevertheless, for most white liberals, this separatism was not only a tactical error, but a wound to the heart.[34]

On this point, at least, Jewish activists and their more moderate parents in Jewish mainstream organizations agreed. The latter argued that this militancy was rhetorical rather than substantive, and simply alienated white moderates needed to pass further civil rights legislation. In any case, given these groups' more confrontational tactics and heated rhetoric, organized Jewry's distaste was a foregone conclusion.[35] For most Jewish (and other white) organizations, hurt by their exclusion and convinced they had contributed a great deal to the civil rights effort, both black militancy and separatism confirmed their sense that African Americans were moving away from the political vision they had shared. Furthermore, if historian Hasia Diner is correct that Jews considered African Americans a test case for American democracy—if black people can be accepted, so can Jews—then the shift to a black particularism made many Jews uneasy because it implied that America had failed the test.[36] At the same time, however, Jews failed to recognize their own particularism, in the form of support for Israel and Jewish institutions generally, and thus incorrectly concluded that they and African Americans were moving in completely different and incompatible directions.

However, not all African Americans had embraced these new political views. Both black and white liberals believed that Black Power threatened hard-won civil rights gains. Samuel Lubell, public opinion pollster and political analyst, warned that southern conservatives might ally with skittish northern whites to form a new conservative majority. Rustin insisted that the movement could not advance further unless it moved "From Protest to Politics." Ultimately, he concluded, Black Power "diverts the movement from a meaningful debate over strategy and tactics, it isolates the Negro community, and it encourages the growth of anti-Negro forces." The better alternative for this longtime leftist was "a liberal-labor-civil rights coalition which would work to make the Democratic party truly responsive to the aspirations of the poor and which would develop support for programs . . . aimed at the reconstruction of American society in the interests of greater social justice." Black Power advocates, on the other hand, seek merely "the creation of a *new black establishment*." While seemingly progressive, Black Power had both capitalist and conservative tendencies.[37]

A few Jewish progressives considered the new nationalist militance a positive development for Jews. Leonard Fein argued in 1969 that "the new Negro assertiveness is . . . an audacious effort to force America to come to grips with real diversity. . . . If the effort is now successful, we ourselves are likely to be among its unintended beneficiaries, for in an America prepared, at last, for pluralism, there will be more elbow room for Jewish assertiveness." He pointed to greater Jewish activism on campuses and the demands to establish Jewish Studies programs, developments emerging directly out of the contemporary civil rights movement.[38]

But most Jewish leaders strongly disagreed. They viewed Black Power as antithetical to pluralism, not its most recent manifestation, as Fein and Rustin would have it. To them, pluralism had always been about culture, ideas, and social access, not about political power based on one's ancestry. Rather, they considered Black Power a direct threat both to civil rights advances dear to Jewish hearts and to Jews more directly. Nathan Perlmutter, for example, countered that given "the militancy of . . . those who would tear our system down, . . . [w]e will be, intended or otherwise, its earliest victims."[39] Much of this fear entered on the link they perceived between black militancy and anti-Semitism. In 1960 Nathan Edelstein found "distressing indications of active anti-Semitism among Northern Negroes and seemingly deliberate efforts to fan its flames by some of their leaders"; they intensified as the decade proceeded.[40]

Within the nationalist Black Arts movement, for example, poet and playright Amiri Baraka, who had married a white Jewish woman in his earlier life as LeRoi Jones, by the late 1960s had not only repudiated his family and his name, but had penned lines like "Smile, jew. Dance, jew. Tell me you / love me, jew. . . . I got the / extermination blues, jewboys." He called for "poems / like fists" to make the "Liberal / Spokesman for the jews clutch his throat / & puke himself into eternity. . . . Another bad poem cracking / steel knuckles in a jewlady's mouth." Nationalist intellectuals like Harold Cruse singled Jews out explicitly for attack; nationalist "buy black" efforts occasionally transmogrified into anti-Semitic campaigns to expel Jewish merchants and landlords from black neighborhoods. During a passionate argument in 1966 about education in Mount Vernon, New York, a black CORE member burst out, "Hitler made a mistake when he didn't kill enough of you." Such offensive and aggressive acts drowned out the voices of black moderates and made less visible the good will toward Jews most African Americans continued to report.[41]

Build or Burn?

Those in the Jewish community sympathetic to black frustrations tried to mitigate the damage. Black Power was a "natural by-product" of resentment and disappointment, Shad Polier argued in 1964, likening black militants to the vigilante Stern Gang in Israel. He believed that as most Jews rejected the Stern Gang, most African Americans rejected the nationalists for "the responsible heads of the Negro struggle for civil rights," and that nationalism itself was unlikely to last. Nevertheless, he warned, "We are in for a period of increasing anti-Semitism among Negroes," especially given the longstanding economic tensions. A Jewish landlord or employer, Polier reminded his readers, "represents to the Negro the white exploiter who lives and battens upon the Negro's helplessness. . . . In striking . . . out against the Jew, the Negro is assaulting a white world which he believes has shortchanged him and which he believes is determined to take advantage of him."[42] This was not a justification for black anti-Semitic attacks on Jewish merchants, but rather a plea to understand their source, and separate issues of religion from economic exploitation. Other Jewish leaders strove to separate the issues as well. "I am in no mood to protect any slumlord who is a Jew," S. Andhil Fineberg of the AJC wrote in 1963. "All people have a right to hate them. My only concern is that their activity be not catalogued as Jews." Liberal black leaders made the same point. The exploitative "Jewish landlord or shopkeeper is not operating on the basis of Jewish ethics; he is operating on the basis of a marginal businessman," Martin Luther King Jr. insisted. The solution "is for all people to condemn injustice wherever it exists."[43]

If anti-Semitism coupled with nationalism led some African Americans to blame too much of their exploitation on the Jews, it was nonetheless true that Jewish merchants remaining in black ghettoes had done little to improve their perceptions. As Inge Gibel, progressive Jewish activist married to a black man, observed, "for every Negro who has heard of

Kivie Kaplan [NAACP president] and Jack Greenberg [NAACP counsel] there are hundreds more who can tell of being cheated by a grocer named Cohen or exploited by a housewife named Levy." One can understand "the bitter frustration" of poor black ghetto dwellers "who find it ludicrous when what looks and talks like an American white man tells them that *he* understands their problem because *he* is a Jew." Black New Yorkers interviewed in 1969 had a far worse opinion of Jewish businessmen than did local whites.[44]

Because a large number of business owners in Philadelphia's black neighborhoods were Jewish, Philadelphia's race riots in 1963 and 1964 brought the scrutiny of the local Jewish Community Relations Council. It concluded that "the riots were anti-white and not anti-Jewish," but recognized the danger Jewish merchants were in because they were white. It found no business associations in these neighborhoods, nor any "communication or contact whatever" between the merchants and the community they served. A black minister brought together with Jewish merchants by the JCRC "confessed that while he had been with his church for twenty years, this was the first time he sat in the same room with any of the white merchants." Landlord-tenant relationships were equally poor. As Polier had hypothesized, here Jews stood in for all whites. The JCRC held meetings with Jewish business and property owners, warning of the seriousness of the situation. They turned out at the meeting in force and discussed the dangerous combination of political tensions they faced: black nationalist efforts to oust white businessmen, post-riot tensions, pickets, claims of consumer fraud, civil rights demonstrations in other northern cities, and anti-Semitic rhetoric by white supremacist groups. As the ADL had done earlier, the JCRC urged the formation of activist business groups that would work with residents to address complaints and concerns and contribute to the improvement of local neighborhoods. Jewish business owners embraced these ideas. "The process may still blow up in the face of the JCRC, but thus far, to the accompaniment of some brickbats, it is proceeding extremely well," Jules Cohen exulted. One "brickbat" was the NAACP's skepticism that any programs could compensate for continued high prices that hurt poor black customers. Another, which Cohen shared, was a fear the momentum would not last. Nevertheless, faced with a choice of "Build or Burn?" and with the livelihood of Jewish business owners at stake, the JCRC continued to engage in civil rights efforts after the riots had chased more fainthearted sympathizers away.[45]

Several other northern cities saw similar cooperative programs, from the Boston office of the AJCongress, which supported the local Urban League and black rent strikers in 1964 to an Interracial Council for Business Opportunity begun in 1963 by the New York branches of the same two organizations, which offered loans and advice to black entrepreneurs. Within a year Newark and Los Angeles adopted councils of their own. But outside the large, and largely coastal, cities, conflicts and tensions far outran cooperative ventures to ameliorate them.[46]

The 1967 riots produced much the same findings and similar responses among Jews. A NCRAC study of thirty-six communities across the country (mostly in the North) found Jews owned 25 percent or more of ghetto businesses in twenty-one of them, and at least 75 percent in four. And again, "CRCs were active during the riots in trying to help restore order . . . and, after the riots, in relief of distress and efforts to restore or create sounder community and intergroup relationships . . . and in . . . preventive programs . . . for jobs, better housing, slum improvement, etc." Still, if this was an effort to ease Jewish flight or minimize anti-Semitism, it was a holding action at best. Despite the fact that no merchants reported the targeting of Jewish stores in the riots, local JCRCs depicted these ghetto businessmen "as fearful and anxious," and eager to leave, although that proved as true in cities without riots as in those that experienced them. The future of these businesses "is dim," the report suggested. A 1970 survey of Jewish business owners confirmed these findings: half were "very anxious to sell their places of business"; one in five had been held up at gunpoint. Most were older Jews "whose children . . . are unwilling to carry on the family business."[47]

The entrepreneurs who took Jews' places when they left "are most often not Jewish," they discovered. Over half the communities reported that a large number were "Negro" (which presumably included West Indians as well as African Americans). This was not a full nationalist victory, however; others were newer immigrants like Puerto Ricans, Cubans, or Koreans. In terms of economic conflicts, only the players had changed.[48]

The Northern Jewish "Street"

Black-Jewish divisions extended beyond economic tensions or political disagreements over strategy. Liberal Jewish agencies and leaders, who evinced hesitation about the direction the movement was taking, were still more progressive than most of their constituents on matters of race, as the economic interactions made clear. As Edelstein warned in 1960, "Despite the deep commitment of Jewish community relations agencies and their genuine efforts to preach and teach equality, there is a wide and alarming gap between the leadership and the rank and file in the Jewish community; and in the Negro community too." Jewish liberal Charles Silberman concurred. When Jewish involvement in civil rights "consists mainly of symbolic trips to Selma," he wrote in 1965, "the result may be to reinforce the Negroes' cynical view that our moral indignation and sense of commitment vary inversely with our distance to the scene of conflict." Regarding the broader Jewish community, the difference between southerners and northerners in on-the-ground engagement in civil rights may have been less than it first appeared.[49]

Class differences between the vast majority of blacks and Jews had widened. Economic success also brought social success, and by the 1960s large numbers of Jews were moving to the suburbs, "gilded ghettos," to use Judith Kramer's term, joining or building country clubs, and enjoying the privileges of their new status.[50] Most black people remained trapped by poverty and discrimination within disintegrating cities. And while both remained liberal politically, Jews' racial attitudes increasingly resembled those in the larger white community. In 1969 Leonard Fein wondered whether Jews had made themselves more securely "American by being bigots?" Sociologist Bernard Zvi Sobel and historian May Sobel suggested instead that Jewish attitudes had not changed, that popular Jewish support for civil rights had always extended to civil rights legislation but never to integration.[51]

Whatever the explanation, Edelstein lamented that "prominent Negroes have been excluded from predominantly Jewish clubs and . . . the best known builder of 'whites only' suburban developments is William Levitt," a Jew. "When Negroes start to move into predominantly Jewish areas, they often encounter resentment. Genuine social acceptance by Jews is at a minimum and, generally, we find the usual fear, panic and flight to the suburbs. In such situations Jews act, in the main, like other whites." As one black leader commented, although Jews and blacks served together on local NUL and NAACP boards, "when five o'clock comes, they go to their country clubs for dinner and never invite us."[52]

In fact most Jews who remained in inner-city neighborhoods were no more committed to integration than those who left; rather, they were less mobile. Poor, elderly, and often both, these Jews expressed a strong desire to leave their newly integrated neighborhoods for the perceived security and improved services of more suburban, more Jewish areas. Many cited concerns over rising crime, escalating violence, and deteriorating schools, the Philadelphia JCRC noted. "Many view community efforts to maintain racial stability as hopeless." So opposed were they to school integration plans that "a [1968] public hearing . . . on how to desegregate the schools was thrown into . . . a near-riot by angry . . . demonstrations." These Jewish protesters criticized Jewish agencies for being more concerned about black interests than their own.[53]

Meanwhile, mystified African Americans watched as Jews turned white before their eyes. In 1963 Irving Howe criticized Ralph Ellison, Richard Wright, and James Baldwin for producing more heat than light in their political writing. Ellison shot back that Howe, a Jew, was trying to pass for white. As Cleveland Robinson observed in 1966, "The American Negro is confused by the Jewish community. You initiated many of the programs against segregation and fought for the equal rights of all citizens. Now, in the areas of housing and education, we see many Jews blocking our progress. . . . That is the reason for the Negro's confusion and resentment." NCRAC concurred. A 1967 report found "Jewish backlash" in virtually every city it studied. This "varied in intensity from 'indifference' . . . about civil rights . . . to resentment and hostility toward Negro demands. On balance," it concluded, "the responses indicate a definite and substantial withdrawal of rank and file Jewish support" from the objectives Jewish organizations still sought. Sociologist Jonathan Reider found the same mix of fear, racism, and frustration in his study of Canarsie, New York. A study of Brooklyn Jews found "repugnance toward what they think Negroes typically represent: poverty, violence, crime, welfare, family disintegration, property deterioration, and low educational standards." The AJC reported a surge in membership for the militant Jewish Defense League, a right-wing nationalist organization willing to use force to press its agenda.[54] These middle- and lower-middle-class Jews, like other similarly placed whites, concluded that liberals had capitulated to unfair black demands, and passed the costs on to them.

A few Jewish leaders agreed with them and reconsidered their racial liberalism. A few anticommunist liberals like Irving Kristol had already begun the trend in the late 1950s. Then, in February 1963, the AJC's *Commentary* gave them new visibility by publishing Norman Podhoretz's "My Negro Problem—And Ours." Reflecting on his own, negative boyhood experiences with African Americans in a neighborhood where racial lines were drawn early and reinforced by parents, Podhoretz concluded that he, and all whites, "are sick in their feelings about Negroes." As "the good liberal I have grown up to be," he felt guilt and "self-contempt" for "the twinges of fear and the resentment they bring." He confessed "disgusting prurience . . . at the sight of a mixed couple" and argued "it cannot be so very far away" from what other white liberals felt. Therefore he despaired of integration, especially at the pace at which African Americans demanded it. Black impatience will meet white stubbornness and "blood may yet run in the streets." Since African Americans had no heritage to cling to, and because "[h]is past is a stigma, his color is a stigma, and his vision of the future is the hope of erasing the stigma by making color irrelevant," Podhoretz theorized that the only hope was to make color "*in fact* disappear" through "miscegenation. . . . [I]n my opinion the Negro problem can be solved in this country in no other way."[55]

While James Baldwin (whom Podhoretz approvingly discussed) raised no objections to what he perceived as "honest" comments, Justine Wise

Polier and Shad Polier were horrified. The article was "[s]uffused with self-pity, infantile self-appreciation, and fear," their tirade began. "As one reads it one is reminded of the hideous writings of the early Nazis." Furthermore, *Commentary*'s publication of it "makes Podhoretz's problem a problem for the Jewish community." They criticized his insensitivity, his lack of historical understanding, and his offensive resort to the basest of racial stereotypes. His solution, "the surrender of individual and group contributions to human development[,] is apparently not too high a price . . . to pay for individual physical comfort," they sneered, echoing James Farmer. "Only a man forgetting the . . . immortal value of the human spirit could so degrade the meaning of life." Beyond fratricide, this was a battle cry from the progressive liberal wing of the organized Jewish community, who considered the AJC's retreat from the front lines of civil rights a moral error. Their essay did not go unnoticed in the black community. "Congratulations and commendations for your excellent rebuttal," wrote Whitney Young. "I confess I was most disturbed by his article, but I should have known that as long as there are people like the Poliers such illogical thinking would not go unchallenged. . . . Bless you both!"[56]

Podhoretz's were among the first visible stirrings of what is now commonly called neoconservatism.[57] Within a very few years, as liberalism appeared to move toward radicalism and identity politics, a number of former liberals, mostly Jews, would move away from it, rejecting their old ideology as they claimed it had rejected them. This emerging critique would challenge liberalism from one direction while leftists and nationalists pressed it from the other. While neither would unseat the liberal coalition for several more years, seeds of that discontent were already visible. But neoconservatives had not yet had their moment. Their ranks would grow dramatically after a series of tense confrontations and in the debates over affirmative action.

"We need a Mau Mau"

Events around the world drove the black and Jewish communities farther apart as American black nationalists self-consciously linked their struggle with those of other nonwhite peoples resisting white oppressors. African Americans from Martin Luther King to Eldridge Cleaver followed the fate of African colonies with great concern; many saw models for their own struggle. "You and I can best learn how to get real freedom by studying how [Jomo] Kenyatta brought it to his people in Kenya," Malcolm X insisted. "In fact that's what we need. . . . In Mississippi we need a Mau Mau. In Alabama we need a Mau Mau. In Georgia we need a Mau Mau. Right here in Harlem . . . we need a Mau Mau."[58] Recognizing parallels between imperialist oppression and their own experience, many concluded that their ghettos were similarly colonized and advocated similar solutions. Such militance horrified and frightened many whites, including Jews. Meanwhile, the Vietnam War not only put more poor and nonwhite men on the front lines than better-educated middle-class whites, it also pitted a white oppressor nation against an independence-seeking nonwhite population.[59] First the MFDP, then SNCC, and finally King publicly condemned the war in Indochina as morally as well as strategically indefensible. Jewish progressives, especially young Jewish activists, applauded the announcements. But for conservatives they verified the un-American nature of the black struggle, and angered the Democratic Party, whose president was conducting the war. It also alienated many liberal moderates, Jews and non-Jews alike.

In the case of the Middle East, commitments to indigenous freedom movements dovetailed with the nationalist push to oust Jews (as whites) from civil rights coalitions. Members of radical black groups criticized Israel as a European-style oppressor of the nonwhite Palestinians, often employing anti-Semitic rhetoric that went beyond criticism of Israel and thus infuriated even the staunchest of Jewish civil rights supporters.

At the National Convention for New Politics in 1967, the black caucus, led by SNCC chairman H. Rap Brown, successfully pressed for the adoption of an anti-Israel resolution. Meanwhile the June–July 1967 SNCC newsletter blasted Israel for massacring Palestinians, accompanied by a vivid photo whose caption read, "This is Gaza Strip, Palestine, not Dachau, Germany." SNCC leaders explained this as an embrace of liberation movements by oppressed people: "Perhaps we have taken the liberal Jewish community . . . as far as it can go. If so, this is tragic, not for us but for the liberal Jewish community. For the world is in a revolutionary ferment." Black nationalists were doing nothing others on the left were not. As progressive journalist Jack Newfield explained, in the 1960s and '70s, "people on the Left were becoming more anti-Zionist, anti-Israel, and anti-semitic, which were all on some level interchangeable." Martin Luther King Jr. agreed. In response to a hostile question about Zionism during a 1968 speech, he observed, "When people criticize Zionists they mean Jews, you are talking anti-Semitism." Other black leaders also tried to reassure skittish Jewish colleagues. "The views expressed . . . are not those held by the great majority of blacks in this country," claimed Samuel Jackson.[60]

Meanwhile, Shad Polier and other progressive Jews continued to insist that black expressions of anti-Semitism were "essentially the result of a search for a scapegoat," and part of an effort to gain leadership roles for black people.[61] Certainly there was a political incentive for nationalist anti-Semitism; discrediting integration's staunchest advocates reinforced the separatist position. It also helped mask the internal divisions between nationalists and leftists that rendered SNCC's domestic program inert after 1967. In fact SNCC never formally adopted an anti-Semitic or anti-Israeli position, and the New Politics resolution explicitly denied anti-Semitism. Nevertheless, many Jews saw black nationalists' criticism as dangerous and offensive. Harry Golden lambasted SNCC for "echoing the ideas found in the Ku Klux Klan and the American Nazi party." Rabbi Harold Saperstein, the JLC, and others issued their own angry statements, as did Bayard Rustin and the NUL's Whitney Young. Jewish contributions to SNCC fell dramatically.[62] These Jews believed their fears confirmed by the events in Ocean Hill–Brownsville the year following.

Ocean Hill–Brownsville

The conflict in Brooklyn's Ocean Hill–Brownsville school district in 1968 pitted a primarily black community against a primarily Jewish teachers' union.[63] It began as a struggle over community control of schools. The local schools poorly served the impoverished black district, and parents demanded more decentralized community control. The Ford Foundation offered a grant for three experimental schools to be run by local school boards, in East Harlem, the Lower East Side, and Ocean Hill–Brownsville. At first the United Federation of Teachers (UFT), headed by Albert Shanker who had picketed segregated restaurants in college and marched in Selma, partnered with local parents and pressed the central school board for greater support. Fearful of losing its authority, the central board resisted, and the school principal, Rhody McCoy, called the experiment in local control a "fraud." McCoy, asserting his authority to act with the approval only of the local board, transferred to other districts nineteen teachers and administrators he considered unsupportive or ineffective. The teachers' union protested, insisting this occurred without due process and violated both civil service laws and the union's contract. Each side, seeing this as a test of its power, refused to budge. When the union won in court, Mayor John Lindsay refused to enforce the decision, and in September Shanker called the first of three strikes, which closed 85 percent of New York's schools for fifty-five days. Strikers and community leaders hurled insults and threats at each other across the picket lines.[64]

Although this was a fight between a community and a union, the fact that most of the teachers were white and Jewish, and most of the parents black and poor, turned the struggle into one involving class and race. It also became a struggle over allegations of anti-Semitism. During the protests, the UFT discovered and publicized anti-Semitic pamphlets that it claimed had been widely circulated. This, of course, provided the teachers with the moral high ground, linking advocacy of community control with anti-Semitism. Meanwhile, on radio station WBAI in New York, Julius Lester, former SNCC worker and author of *Look Out, Whitey! Black Power's Gon' Get Your Mama*, invited a black teacher to read his student's anti-Semitic poem on the air. On another show a black student lamented that "Hitler didn't make enough lampshades out of them." Not surprisingly, Jewish groups protested and the newly organized Jewish Defense League picketed the station. Despite the ADL's assurances six months earlier that there was no organized anti-Semitism in New York, and its even more recent report that African Americans were less anti-Semitic than whites, it now claimed that "[r]aw, undisguised anti-Semitism . . . is at a crisis level in New York City schools where, unchecked by public authority, it has been building for more than two years."[65]

For most Jews, the issue was either anti-Semitism or anti-white sentiment, with Jews, as usual, the victims. For most local residents, Jewish teachers represented the unresponsive and racist power structure: villains or puppets but certainly not victims. The "issue is not black anti-Semitism," Lester insisted. "This issue is what it has always been: racism." Ira Glasser, a Jew, the head of the New York Civil Liberties Union, and a local parent, insisted the incident was a power struggle between the union and the community, and "I have always blamed Shanker for whipping up the anti-Semitism issue" as a ploy to discredit the educational experiment. These community-based schooling advocates, in turn, criticized the liberalism of the existing structure. The local black teachers' organization, the African-American Teachers Association, condemned as racist the pluralist teaching methods of the white UFT teachers, insisting they ignored relevant cultural differences.[66]

Whether or not anti-Semitic sentiment was exaggerated, it became the dominant theme of the story and, in the perhaps overstated words of the *New York Times* almost twenty years later, "Ocean Hill-Brownsville came to stand as a symbol of hifalutin good intentions gone awry" which split "previously rock-solid" black and Jewish allies "into warring camps."[67] Although a few black leaders sympathetic to labor such as Rustin supported the UFT, and a few Jewish parents like Glasser supported McCoy, the media images of African American residents and Jewish union members screaming at each other across the barricades epitomized to many the then-current state of black-Jewish relations.

Liberal Dilemmas

Through these difficult times liberal Jewish organizations struggled between their commitment to civil rights and their distaste for many of the

movement's new tactics. At the 1969 National Black Economic Development Conference in Detroit, James Forman of SNCC called on black people to "seize state power. Do not hedge." He was clear this struggle would
"be an armed confrontation and long years of sustained guerrilla war-
fare." The "Black Manifesto" issued from the conference demanded $500
million compensation for slavery and racism from churches, synagogues,
and religiously based community agencies, which it threatened to obtain
through the disruption of worship services, and force if necessary.

NCRAC and the Synagogue Council of America agreed that the "gap
between principle and performance is lamentably large; we have fallen
short of our responsibilities in working for racial and economic justice,"
and that "it is entirely in order for our religious and communal institutions—no less than other segments of our society—to be challenged,
both from within and from without, to face up to their own shortcomings and responsibilities." Nevertheless, they insisted that this was not
the proper mechanism for doing so, "on both moral and practical
grounds." They favored the A. Philip Randolph Institute's "Freedom
Budget" and the NUL's "Domestic Marshall Plan" proposals, both of
which advocated massive government investment and action in employment, education, and welfare. NCRAC and the Synagogue Council thus
found themselves simultaneously erecting defenses against the Manifesto's proposed onslaught yet advocating for its basic goals. They "urge[d]
congregations and communal institutions to . . . redouble their efforts"
to ensure sufficient funding for civil rights and equal opportunity initiatives, "strengthen communication with local black communities," and
"contribute to . . . indigenous self-help projects." At the same time, they
issued guidelines for synagogues on how to defuse disruptions if they
occurred. Acutely aware that any critique of black activists could be
interpreted as further retreat from civil rights, the memo concluded, "We
recognize that Americans can no longer speak of 'violence' and 'extremism' without the terrible knowledge that their most destructive manifestation in American life is to be found in the violence done to the lives,
the hopes and aspirations of our Negro citizens. It is equally true, however, that even in pursuit of desirable ends, violence does not contribute
to the fashioning of a better society." Such threats must not "divert our
attention from the hard tasks which require our efforts and resources if
our moral and religious professions are to be taken seriously."[68] On that
much, at least, liberal black and Jewish organizations agreed.

Whipsawed by such cross-tensions, liberalism seemed to be self-de-
structing. Edmund Muskie lamented the "failure of American liberalism"
at a 1971 dinner of the Liberal Party: "The blunt truth is that liberals
have achieved virtually no fundamental change in our society since the
end of the New Deal." But many liberal Jews would have none of it. Given

civil rights advances, that statement was incredible, Ben Wattenberg and Richard Scammon insisted. "Thanks to . . . [liberal] Presidents, thanks to a liberal impulse in the Congress in the mid-1960's, thanks to the tireless efforts of liberals all over America, the legislation was passed [for] . . . manpower programs, poverty programs, and a stunning array of health, education, and legal services. Now, more than a decade later, we can look back and see—results . . . ; in particular, a better deal has been given to the poor and the black. . . . Liberalism worked." By shifting toward racialized appeals to victimhood and entitlement, they argued, liberals had abandoned their principles in order to sustain their leadership positions.[69] Here was the newly potent critique of the neoconservatives; it was time to move beyond liberalism.

Progressive Jews acknowledged the continued shift of Jews away from liberalism, but explained it differently. They viewed neoconservative critiques as merely a way to justify Jewish withdrawal from the fight for racial justice. Too many of their coreligionists had turned inward, self-absorbed, parochial, they warned, forgetting the prophetic call to justice and their own self-interest. "Are American Jews Turning to the Right?" wondered Bernard Rosenberg and Irving Howe in *Dissent*, although they could not provide a definitive answer. Such a turn, they warned, would be "a moral and practical disaster" for Jews. Arnold Wolf, a Reform rabbi from Chicago, saw many Jewish organizations making this shift. He called ADL's "flip flops" on black anti-Semitism during the Ocean Hill–Brownsville debacle "quite incredible . . . even from the point of view of public relations" and theorized that Jews have "been put on by our defense organizations (who . . . perhaps . . . seek to find a new enemy against whom they can now rally the Jewish community)."[70]

Neoconservatives were certainly working hard to discredit their liberal colleagues. Challenging those Jews who disagreed with him that the recent black-Jewish tensions constituted a crisis, Milton Himmelfarb warned that although "Anne Frank would not yet be forty," Jews had already become complaisant about anti-Semitism. These Jews not only played the Holocaust card against black challengers, they played it against their Jewish colleagues in the community relations field.[71]

Many liberal Jews who formerly saw their self-interest in advancing civil rights now believed it lay in sustaining the status quo that had contributed to their newly established well-being. The militant nationalism they saw in the contemporary civil rights movement, as well as its anti-Semitism, seemed to pose a threat to everything they held dear. In 1973 Murray Friedman concluded, "The heart of the matter is that today Negroes and Jews are meeting each other in head-on collisions for the first time." He argued that earlier convictions that they shared a common enemy and a common goal had now shriveled, replaced by competition at work, ongoing and reciprocal resentments, a Jewish turn toward conservatism following economic and social success, and increasing black militance and rising anti-Semitism in the face of insufficient black advancement.[72]

Repairers of the Breach

Mutual engagement had not ceased in this tumultuous period. "Jewish Community Activities in the Urban Crisis," a 1968 report by the Council of Jewish Federations and Welfare Funds, described cooperative charitable, economic, and political projects in Baltimore; Cleveland; Detroit; Essex County, New Jersey; Los Angeles; Philadelphia; Pittsburgh; Buffalo; Cincinnati; Dallas; and Kansas City. "We hereby commit ourselves and the resources of our respective organizations to advocacy and support of a program of legislative and executive action by government and correlative action by private institutions to attain the goals to which Dr. King dedicated his life," NCRAC pledged after King's assassination. And progressive leaders in both communities pleaded to hold on to old allegiances and heal the wounds. Dorothy Height, president of NCNW, and Pearl Willen, president of NCJW, gave a joint news conference in 1966 appealing for unity between their two communities. "The founder of the American Jewish Congress was a founder of the NAACP seventeen years before he started the Congress," Shad Polier reminded his audience that same year. "I came to the NAACP defense fund eight years before I joined the Congress." Still, the rhetoric had changed. The AJCongress fought for civil rights "not because we're a 'liberal' organization but because we're a Jewish one," Polier insisted, despite the fact that ten years earlier, he had made precisely the opposite argument.[73]

Other mainstream liberal organizations also fought to shore up their relationships. In 1968 Sterling Brown, president of National Conference of Christians and Jews, urged other cities to copy the "interracial colloquy" meeting monthly at his home since 1966, involving (among others) Wilkins, Whitney Young (NUL), and John Slawson (AJC). The same year, the president of United Jewish Appeal urged fifteen hundred assembled Jewish leaders not to withdraw from "the battle for equal rights and Negro justice." Following the divisive fight in Ocean Hill–Brownsville, a group of rabbis and African American clergy began meeting to air disagreements and ease tensions. The AJCongress established an Information Center on Jewish-Negro Relations in 1970; more than three hundred groups asked to participate in its activities. Alvin Poussaint issued "Blacks and Jews: An Appeal for Unity" in the July 1974 issue of *Ebony*, reminding readers of Jewish civil rights commitments and downplaying their differences. He even speculated that the FBI, having infiltrated black groups to discredit them, may also "have been at work to divide blacks and Jews in order to weaken the thrust of the human rights movement." Whatever the cause, any "serious split between them would work to the advantage of conservative forces."[74] Former coalition partners published articles and convened symposia on black-Jewish tensions. Even *Time* devoted a cover story to the black-Jewish split and attempts to repair the breach.[75]

Nor did the conservative movement or Republican Party offer viable alternatives for most black or Jewish people during this liberal crisis. Allied with the religious and anticommunist right, many conservatives continued to advocate for the ideal of the United States as a white Christian nation. Long a Republican, Jackie Robinson left that Party's 1964 convention, which nominated Barry Goldwater, commenting, "I had a better understanding of how it must have felt to be a Jew in Hitler's Germany." James Farmer, who had agreed to serve in the Department of Health, Education and Welfare under President Nixon, soon resigned his position in opposition to its policies. Both blacks and Jews remained firm in their support of the Democratic Party.[76]

By the middle 1970s, as black advances halted and in some cases even reversed under the Nixon administration, signs emerged of a thaw between black and Jewish leaders, and a renewed optimism that liberal coalition politics could work and that universalism could still coincide with self-interest. Black Power had lost some of its allure; SNCC, the Black Panthers, and CORE had self-destructed. As Carl Gershman of the Social Democrats argued in 1976, "the fact that Black nationalism has largely spent its force has removed the most disruptive element in the relationship." Cognizant that significant problems remained between blacks and Jews, he did acknowledge that attempts to revive the coalition "have a certain strategic deliberateness about them, which is to say that the alliance is perceived to be a desirable thing but no longer flows naturally from the dynamics of the situation. It can be revived around specific issues, but it will take constant care and attention to sustain even immediate tactical coalitions." Still, "[a] strategy of forming alliances, with the goal of influencing national economic and social policies, is now accepted almost universally among Black leaders. Toward this end, Jews remain a natural ally of Blacks, whatever differences now exist between the two groups on particular issues." Meanwhile, Israel's perennial vulnerability reminded Jews of their continued need for allies. "Blacks and Jews Viewed as Drawing Closer Again," read a 1975 front-page headline in the *New York Times*.[77]

A few Jews even reengaged with former black militants. Phil Bronstein described one such group in San Francisco in early 1977 who responded to Kathleen Cleaver's plea for funds to get her husband Eldridge out of jail. These meetings, "a prototype of a scene that would be repeated . . . all over the country," included a "whole stratum in the Jewish community— lawyers, doctors, communal leaders—[who] suddenly began to take notice of Eldridge Cleaver." Jewish lawyers defended him, Jewish leaders spoke out on his behalf. In Bronstein's view, however, the motive was less rooted in altruistic Jewish ethical precepts than the participants claimed, and "says more about expediency than it does about respect." These Jews argued that Cleaver was now outspokenly supportive of Israel, and to the extent that he might influence other former black radicals, supporting him could only be good for the Jews. Now rejecting violence, repudiated by many of his former Panther colleagues, and embraced by Bayard Rustin, Cleaver seemed to many to offer a new way back into a black-Jewish partnership. Only a few leftist Jews remained aloof, suspicious of his new patriotism as well as his switch on the Middle East.[78]

The hopeful return to coalition was mutual. In a 1977 article Roy Wilkins rehearsed the long history and substantial successes of black-Jewish cooperation and urged "these two great minorities of similar experiences" to "come closer together in their common campaign for humanity." Three years later Vernon Jordan, head of the NUL, issued an "Appeal to Blacks and Jews to Seek Unity." In an attempt to ease tensions over black criticism of Israel and to reassure edgy Jewish leaders, Rustin formed BASIC, the Black Americans to Support Israel Committee, in September 1976. Among its founding members were the heads of all the major black organizations, black politicians, Ralph Ellison, Hank Aaron, and other luminaries. Its founding statement declared, "We believe Blacks and Jews have common interests in democracy and justice."[79]

Affirmative Action

This tentative return to partnership was tested by the affirmative action cases of the 1970s. Marco DeFunis, a Sephardic Jew, was denied admission to the University of Washington Law school; Allan Bakke was a white Vietnam veteran denied admission to the University of California Medical College at Davis. Both sued, arguing that accepting nonwhites with lower scores constituted reverse discrimination. In both *DeFunis v. Odegaard,* 1974 and *University of California Regents v. Bakke,* 1978, black organizations filed amicus briefs on behalf of the university's affirmative action policies while most Jewish agencies filed briefs in opposition. It was the first time black and Jewish organizations had publicly and formally positioned themselves on opposite sides of a civil rights question. As Mayor Coleman Young of Detroit claimed in 1980, "You know, Jews and Blacks used to be part of a great coalition on many social causes. But it's fallen apart. Affirmative Action divided them."[80]

The divide did not run entirely along racial or religious lines. Again, internal divisions separated Jews from one another on this question, although all the liberal black organizations endorsed affirmative action. The AJCongress, CCAR, and NCJW filed briefs in support of affirmative action in the *DeFunis* case against their more conservative Jewish colleagues (although they declined to do so in *Bakke*), and Irving Howe and Bernard Rosenberg defended the idea of quotas in the pages of *Dissent*, as did Leonard Fein in *Midstream*.[81]

Nor did division on these cases mean an end to black-Jewish cooperation. After the *DeFunis* filing, Bertram Gold, executive vice president of the AJC, insisted that "Jews and blacks have many more issues in common than those that might separate them. The climate has never been more receptive . . . than it is now for us to work together on common agendas." The leaders of the NAACP, NUL, ADL, AJC, AJCongress, and Puerto Rican Legal Defense and Educational Fund cosigned a letter to Caspar Weinberger, secretary of HEW, urging him to "direct the issuance of non-discriminatory guidelines clarifying how educational institutions can best develop appropriate tools for special efforts to recruit persons from previously excluded groups."[82]

Still, affirmative action went straight to the heart of black-Jewish differences. For the majority of Jews, those who supported Bakke and DeFunis, the issue was clear. Not only were affirmative action programs that involved set-asides or quotas reminders of many colleges' earlier Jewish quotas, they were wrong for the same reason: such programs violated the spirit of the race-blind liberalism Jews endorsed. The ADL brief in *De-Funis* argued, "A racial quota creates a status on the basis of factors that have to be irrelevant to any objectives of democratic society, the factors of skin color and parental origin. A racial quota denigrates the human dignity and individuality of all to whom it is applied." They viewed numerically based affirmative action programs as a retreat from the faith that in the absence of discriminatory rules, all individuals would enjoy full and equal access to the rights and privileges of American life.[83] Jewish leaders trusted that once rules and incentives were in place, those in power would operate in good faith. If that good faith was violated, the remedy lay in penalizing the offending individual, not setting quotas. Affirmative action rules, they argued, required explicit consideration of group membership, an idea as offensive to Jews in this instance as it had been when such considerations had been used to exclude them. Such rules represented the antithesis of liberalism.

This position on affirmative action was entirely consistent with Jews' view of the goal of civil rights: the equality of all individuals. Committed to the right of black (or any other) candidates to embrace any aspect of their cultural heritage free of persecution, Jewish organizations nonetheless insisted that in any application process heritage could play no role. Thus they continued to file supporting briefs in desegregation and voting rights cases, and to promote intercultural understanding through aggressive programming, while steadfastly opposing any return to strategies which formally identified race or assigned individuals to inherited and fixed categories. They did not, however, oppose affirmative action programs which sought to broaden applicant pools or otherwise level the playing field. To put it in current terms, they supported rules designed to achieve equality of opportunity but opposed those designed to produce equality of outcome. They acknowledged that historical patterns of discrimination hampered black opportunity, but insisted the solution was not what they considered preferential treatment, but rather remedial training, outreach, and education programs.[84]

Such a race-blind, liberal stance was understandable for a community whose members had been themselves persecuted and excluded on the basis of fixed racial categories. It was also a political strategy that had proven successful for them. Most members of the Jewish community had moved into the middle and upper classes while maintaining whatever level of religious or cultural distinctiveness they chose. While anti-Semitism remained, barriers to full acceptance were coming down everywhere. By any measure of middle-class status—levels of education, earnings, proportion in professional and managerial ranks—by the end of the 1960s Jews outperformed most other groups in the United States. Jewish family incomes in 1970, for example, were 72 percent higher than the national average; among men ages 35–44 with a college degree, Jews earned 75 percent more than the average. Now, argued Howe and Rosenberg, Jews felt less insecure about entering mainstream America, and concluded instead that their greatest threat came from "urban blacks who . . . are pressing to undo Jewish positions and accomplishments—pressing, especially to undermine the merit system that has made possible Jewish positions and accomplishments." Rabbi Wolf put it more starkly: "The system which has admitted us, . . . promoted us, protected us is the very system which the black sees as the enemy. . . . For the black, the enemy is . . . the liberal establishment itself, which for them is American racism incarnate. So we defend, quite against our own real interests, a system in which we have a place and they have none."[85]

African Americans could not feel as sanguine as Jews about white good will once discrimination became illegal. This division over affirmative action was in many ways a reprise of the 1950s disagreements over whether deleting race questions from applications was sufficient. They knew from bitter experience that whites in power, who had historically discriminated against black people, had not suddenly become race blind because the laws had changed. Affirmative action, including set-asides, was crucial to close the gap between the rhetoric of race blindness and the reality of continued discrimination. For African Americans, whose community remained largely mired in poverty, the liberal vision had proven far less effective than it had for Jews, as well as less morally persuasive. In any case, so long as whites determined the standards for admission to social goods, it was not clear those standards were race blind at all. They set as requirements information and skills most whites had greater access to (such as standardized tests that—for a fee—could be coached), and protected white privilege (for example, college admissions preferences for alumni children or nepotism in union hiring). In other words, the meritocracy in which Jews (and others opposed to affirmative action) placed their faith was itself a myth.

Some rejected liberalism's focus on individual behaviors and attitudes. They argued that the racial divide was perpetuated by institutional or structural barriers, and these must be challenged by refocusing the civil rights struggle on group rights, including affirmative action. As scholars Michael Omi and Howard Winant have argued, many racial theorists, arguing from an ethnic paradigm or immigrant analogy, believed that once discriminatory barriers fell, black people, like white immigrants, would be able to rise. These theories ignored or denied the effects of structural racism and therefore rested on the false assumption that individual action was the only significant variable in overcoming disadvantage. As the authors point out, "Many blacks (and later, many Latinos, Indians and Asian Americans as well) rejected *ethnic* identity in favor of a more *racial* identity which demanded group rights and recognition." Because the notion of an individual meritocracy was so patently false, many affirmative-action advocates insisted, remedies must consider blacks as a community, not as disparate individuals.[86]

The multiculturalism movement of the 1980s and '90s made many of the same claims, and faced many of the same objections. A critique of pluralism's assumed deference to European values and cultures, multiculturalism celebrated global diversity and nonwestern contributions to American culture. It insisted on the centrality of race and racism as explanatory agents in history and the ongoing reality of discrimination and bigotry. But most public versions of multiculturalism played down the importance of religion, region, class, or ethnicity, thereby narrowing difference to race. And, unlike most pluralist conceptions, this racial divide was often depicted as biologically determined and permanently unbridgeable. This troubled not only many Jewish (and non-Jewish) neoconservatives, who saw multiculturalism as an attack on traditional values, but also liberals, who saw a far more complex and fluid picture of what constitutes identity. While African Americans and Jewish Americans were hardly the only players in these debates, they were among the most out-spoken on both sides.[87]

These multiculturalists and affirmative action supporters believed that Jews had revealed their true social position as insiders by virtue of their class and their race. Jews might still view themselves as outsiders but to most on the outside, the Jewish establishment had become cozy with power. They had embraced, wittingly or unwittingly, the attitudes and values of the dominant society. They confused meritocracy with white privilege, attributing their own success solely to hard work and personal commitment and ignoring the structural constraints race imposed on op-portunity. Jews were now portrayed—and many saw themselves—as a model minority, and suspected African Americans' failures lay, at least in part, with themselves. As *Time* magazine's 1969 article on the black-Jew-ish split reminded its readers, "On the scale of achievement in the U.S., the Jews rank as the most successful minority, the blacks as the least." Jewish audiences repeatedly wondered why African Americans could not follow in their footsteps. Only a few, like Jewish economist Eli Ginsberg, recognized the temporal and structural differences that, beyond racial im-pediments, had given earlier white immigrants greater opportunity for advancement, like the greater availability of federal loans, the possibilities for mobility from unskilled labor, and the emergence of unions.[88]

Unlike their black counterparts, then, Jews had moved solidly into the middle class and if their voting patterns remained far more liberal than those of white gentiles (evidence of Jews' continued sense of vulnerability and distrust of Republican evangelical language and social conservatism), they nonetheless began to express more conservative economic and politi-cal views. Neoconservatism had at last arrived, with former liberals, often Jews, opposing quotas, government commissions that blamed white rac-ism for black problems, and entitlement programs that seemed to perpetu-ate helplessness rather than foster self-sufficiency.[89]

Such dramatically divergent viewpoints produced a theory of identity politics, the conviction that people's political interests were inevitably de-termined by their identities (racial, class, gender, or the like).[90] While based on real divisions as well as exaggeration, such a political position lessened the likelihood of coalitions between whites and racial minorities. And identity politics fostered nationalist impulses not only in the black community; it had its counterpart among Jews (and others). Especially following the Six Day War, assertive Jewish pride and an increasingly inward focus took Jews away from coalitions almost as decisively as na-tionalism had for African Americans. As Jews feel more " 'at home' . . . the messianic strand of Jewish sensibility . . . keeps dimming," Fein warned in 1969.[91]

To put it bluntly, then, some of the explanation for the growing estrangement of blacks and Jews lay in the fact that by virtue of their increased security Jews had become more "white," or in any case, decidedly less "other." Herbert Hill made precisely this point regarding the JLC. "By the 1960's," he noted, "Jews in America had become 'white,' that is, they had become assimilated and successful enough in a society sharply divided by race that they regarded themselves as 'white' and by and large they were accepted as such." Now living primarily in suburbs, generally well educated and professionally employed, "many Jews," Nathan Agran of the Philadelphia JCRC observed, "are not in sympathy with the . . . efforts of community relations agencies to help solve the problems of the urban crisis."[92] In other words, Jews moved away from the civil rights coalition in part because they no longer perceived it as personally useful. Although self-interest is hardly unusual, the anger of black Americans was particularly acute because Jews had so rarely explained their involvement in terms of political or economic self-interest, preferring to employ the moral and altruistic rhetoric by which liberal Judaism characterized itself. Thus when Jews were revealed to be narrowly self-interested, it seemed a betrayal. "We expect more of him and when it's not forthcoming that love turns to rage," explained Daniel Watts, African American editor of the *Liberator.* "The Jew has been a hypocrite. The liberal Jew has been in the forefront telling the South to integrate, while he lived in lily-white communities in the North. That hurts more than a Wallace, who is at least honest." This was precisely the argument the neoconservatives had been advancing—Jews would be better off once they rejected their automatic liberalism and began voting in their own, more politically conservative, self-interest.[93]

These growing divergences between black and Jewish concerns reflected larger, national truths. By the 1980s the gap between black and white incomes and life chances, which had begun to shrink in the 1960s, had widened again. A backlash against black advances resulted in a weakening of civil rights laws, greater educational and residential segregation, and a frighteningly familiar racist rhetoric of "us" and "them" that cast African Americans outside the boundary of American society. Even had the two communities remained committed to the same political agenda, black organizations now faced very different problems than did their Jewish counterparts.

But a growing number did not remain committed to the same agenda. As Nathan Perlmutter, national director of the ADL, put it in 1981, "The two groups are simply not as relevant to each other as they were during the civil rights era" in part because, in his mind, the civil rights movement had succeeded. "In short, sympathy based on color will no longer come as automatically as it once did" to Jews or their organizations. The rightward drift of Jews continued, and at least some pointed to a coincident rise in black anti-Semitism.[94] Virtually every public sphere saw new, sharp confrontations between blacks and Jews, from the academy to the courts, from the streets to electoral politics.

Flashpoints

In August 1979 Andrew Young, U.S. ambassador to the United Nations, and the first African American in that post, was forced to resign. He had met with a Palestine Liberation Organization leader, despite U.S. policy barring contact with any organization that did not recognize Israel's right to exist. Although (with the exception of the American Zionist Federation) the organized Jewish community did not publicly demand Young's resignation, many in the black community, from the SCLC leadership to Jesse Jackson and Gloster Current, accused it of engineering it behind the scenes. Linking the Young affair with affirmative action conflicts, some charged Jews with blocking all programs for improving the lives of nonwhite peoples anywhere in the world. Both Roy Wilkins and Young himself raised once again the issue of Jewish paternalism. While acknowledging past contributions by Jews and Jewish groups, a meeting on the Young incident, sponsored by the NAACP and attended by more than two hundred black leaders, issued a statement blaming continued black-Jewish tensions on Jewish withdrawal from the civil rights movement, Jewish opposition to affirmative action, and Jewish condescension. It accused Jews of acting as "apologists for the racial status quo." Kenneth Clark called the statement "our Declaration of Independence." Jewish leaders, while publicly maintaining their commitment to black-Jewish cooperation and their faith that the tension would soon fade, felt betrayed again. UAHC president Rabbi Alexander Schindler lamented that "the Administration which let Andrew Young go has also failed blacks and Jews and all who believe in economic justice and compassion for the poor. Instead, the black and Jewish communities have been entrapped into squaring off against each other—a result that can only delight our common enemies."[95]

This was more than simply a disagreement over Israel's treatment of Palestinians. A few Jewish voices like New Jewish Agenda criticized Israeli policies, while many African American leaders like Rustin continued to publicly support Israel. The "Declaration of Independence," signed by black leaders across the political spectrum, reflected deeper and longer-standing differences. Nevertheless, for most of organized Jewry, and for many of their African American counterparts, support for Israel remained a flashpoint for the remainder of the century.[96]

Conflicts in both local and national electoral politics also divided Jews and African Americans. In 1981, for example, Detroit's black mayor fought with his state's Jewish Democratic Party chairman. Black and Jewish leaders sparred in Miami; Washington's black mayor alleged that authorities cared more about Jewish than black children. The black mayor of Gary, Indiana, tried to replace a Jewish member of the Democratic National Committee with an African American. Zionist organizations clashed with black congressional candidates in California and Louisiana.[97]

Most public were black-Jewish conflicts over Jesse Jackson's 1984 presidential candidacy. A colleague of Martin Luther King Jr., Jackson still worked within the civil rights community. While some on the left viewed him as an opportunist, and some on the right considered him a rabble-rouser, Jackson nonetheless brought activist credentials to his run for the Democratic nomination. He also brought a view of Jews that was at best insensitive and at worst anti-Semitic. He had close ties to Nation of Islam (NOI) leader Louis Farrakhan, who had himself made numerous disparaging references to Jews. And in a remark he thought was off the record, Jackson referred to Jews as "Hymies" and New York as "Hymietown." When criticized in print, he lashed out at the black reporter who "betrayed" him by reporting his remarks, before apologizing for inadvertently giving offense. Jackson denied any bigotry, insisting "Hymie" was "just an expression." Few Jews believed him, and argued that even if his anti-Semitism was unconscious, it was no less dangerous for that. Jews had not changed their minds about him by the time of his second run in 1988. Ed Koch, Jewish mayor of New York, publicly insisted Jews "would be crazy to vote for Jackson." And they did not. In the Democratic primaries, while 41 percent of self-professed liberals and 92 percent of African Americans voted for Jackson, only 8 percent of Jews did. Once again the familiar themes of black-Jewish conflict played out: members of the black community were angry that Jews opposed a civil rights leader and could not forgive a trivial and unintended insult while members of the Jewish community were appalled that a black leader could serve up such callously bigoted statements without any real repercussion, and a small segment of Jews proudly wore "Jews for Jesse" buttons in defiance of the rightward movement of mainstream Jewry.[98]

Jackson's were not the only controversial comments. Farrakhan criticized Israel in 1984 for practicing a "dirty religion," a reference many understood as an indictment of Judaism rather than of Israeli policies. He pointed to Alan Greenspan, Jewish chairman of the Federal Reserve Board, as evidence that Jews controlled American finance. In 1988, Steve Cokely, an aide to Chicago mayor Eugene Sawyer, accused Jewish doctors of deliberately infecting black babies with the AIDS virus, a charge repeated by NOI speakers and Professor Griff of the rap group Public

Enemy. Stokely Carmichael, now Kwame Toure, lectured extensively about the "International Zionist Movement" that controlled everything from financial institutions to local slums.[99]

"Kill the Jew!"

On August 19, 1991, Yosef Lifsh was driving a car in a convoy escorting the Lubavich (Hasidic) Rebbe Menachem Schneerson through Crown Heights, Brooklyn. Losing control of the vehicle, Lifsh plowed into two children, killing one, Gavin Cato, and wounding the other. Two communities cohabited in the neighborhood: Hasidic Jews, of whom Lifsh was one, and West Indian immigrants, including both victims. Although a grand jury would subsequently decline to bring any charges against Lifsh, the crowd that gathered was far less forgiving. Leveling accusations (ultimately proved false) that a Jewish ambulance tended to Lifsh but not the children, mobs surged through the streets crying, "Kill the Jew" and attacking Jewish passersby and property. The Jew one youth managed to kill was Yankel Rosenbaum, a student from Australia. Other bias attacks were reported, but the police did little to restrain the rioters until Mayor David Dinkins finally ordered them to intervene directly and end the violence three days after it had begun.

For several days, neither the media nor Jewish groups focused on the anti-Semitic nature of the violence, until the ADL broke the silence. Jews, generally embarrassed by the old-fashioned, conservative Hasidim, and African Americans, feeling their own ambivalence toward the immigrant West Indian community, believed at first that the conflict did not involve them. But with the open anti-Semitism of black activists Sonny Carson and Al Sharpton, and with many Jews concluding that the riots constituted a "pogrom," the familiar battle was rejoined.[100]

In many ways, American blacks' and non-Hasidic Jews' original perceptions were correct. Crown Heights was an anomaly. The tensions that fanned this outburst were largely based on the particularities of that Hasidic/West Indian, lower-class/middle-class urban community. Most Jews were not only better off than the Lubavitch, they lived in more racially segregated communities. And the West Indians in Crown Heights were by and large newer immigrants, both temporally and spatially removed from the experiences of most African Americans.

Nevertheless, to dismiss these black-Jewish tensions, or the violence that ensued, as irrelevant would be to miss the fallout from the collapse of liberalism and of any black-Jewish understanding. The Jews in Crown Heights had organized neighborhood patrols after numerous complaints about crime and assault went unanswered by authorities. The West Indian community considered these groups vigilantes who unfairly and often aggressively targeted black people. Eager to house their growing families, the Lubavitch pushed up real estate prices in a neighborhood with a limited supply of decent housing, and received city money to renovate old buildings. Better organized politically (and U.S. citizens as well), they used political pressure to ensure that their interests were given priority over others', from traffic control on the Sabbath and Jewish holidays to the redrawing of district lines. Class, cultural, political, and religious differences had inflamed passions before the car accident sparked physical violence.

By the time of the riot, of course, black-Jewish conflict had become the norm rather than the exception; blaming the Jews for Cato's death fit the prevailing mind-set, and dangerous black anti-Semitism had become headline news again.[101] The Crown Heights attacks also followed several racist incidents involving not Jews but other whites. In 1986 white teens had viciously attacked and killed a twenty-three-year-old black man, Michael Griffith, in Howard Beach, Queens. Three years later, sixteen-year-old Yusef Hawkins was senselessly murdered by another mob of white boys in Bensonhurst. And in March 1991 Los Angeles white police officers were caught on videotape beating Rodney King, a black man in handcuffs. The fury of Crown Heights's black residents and the doomsaying Jewish response were both tangible expressions of longer-standing resentments not only between blacks and Jews but about race relations in general.

Fear and Loathing in the Ivory Tower

At the end of 1993 black-Jewish antagonism intensified again. That November, NOI's Khalid Muhammad attacked Jews during a public lecture at Kean College in New Jersey. He called them "bloodsuckers" and suggested they had brought the Holocaust on themselves. After a short journalistic silence, the *New York Times* reported the story on the front page of its Metro section. And as it had in Ocean Hill–Brownsville, the ADL broadcast the remarks widely, this time in a full-page newspaper ad in January 1994.[102] Such anti-Semitic comments from the NOI were certainly not new. And its speakers routinely targeted a wide variety of enemies, from gays and lesbians to Catholics. But this talk's vicious anti-Semitism, and its highlighting by the *Times* and the ADL, raised both the NOI's public profile and the public's condemnation. Because a Jewish group attacked the speech and demanded a response, the struggle became a black-Jewish one, even though Muhammad had also insulted many others.

Although black as well as white public figures condemned Muhammad's bigotry, Jewish groups demanded that all black leaders, whether or not they had any relationship to Farrakhan, publicly repudiate the

NOI. Many African Americans bridled at what seemed once again to be racist paternalism. Had white leaders been required to publicly repudiate white racists and anti-Semites like the Reverend Pat Robertson or David Duke, to demonstrate that not all white people believed as they did? Even those most forcefully opposed to Farrakhan criticized this as an unfair and imbalanced test of loyalty.

Meanwhile Farrakhan offered lukewarm criticism of his lieutenant. "I found the speech . . . vile in manner, repugnant, malicious," he declared. "While I stand by the truths that he spoke, I must condemn . . . the manner in which those truths were presented," and suspended him from his position. Because he had endorsed Muhammad's "truths," his comments convinced many Jews of the Nation's pervasive anti-Semitism. But his repudiation of the speech and of Muhammad himself reassured many black people who supported the NOI's advocacy of pride and self-help that anti-Semitism was a distasteful but marginal part of the Nation's program.[103]

Though that first speech was a tragedy, each repetition proved to be a farce. Black student groups in universities around the country invited Muhammad and others to speak, counting on white, and especially Jewish, anger (and resulting publicity) in response. And Jews rose to the bait, protesting these speeches before, during, and after their occurrence. Stung by what seemed to them the explicit and wilful endorsement of anti-Semitism by a community they believed to be an ally, Jewish students reported feelings of betrayal as well as anger. Yet on most campuses, there had been no joint black-Jewish action or even dialogue for at least a decade, and black students noted in disgust the long absence of an organized Jewish student presence in support of black struggles.[104]

These simmering black-Jewish tensions among students exploded on several campuses in the 1990s, from UCLA to Howard University. At the former, the black student magazine *Nommo* asserted the validity of the anti-Semitic forgery, *The Protocols of the Elders of Zion*. At Howard, a law student led an audience in a chant blaming Jews for the death of Nat Turner and the prosecution of Marcus Garvey. *The Protocols* and the NOI's new book, *The Secret Relationship between Blacks and Jews*, which distorted and exaggerated Jewish involvement in the slave trade, slavery, and other forms of exploitative racism, could readily be obtained at student rallies and through campus organizations.[105]

It was hardly surprising that the academy offered fertile ground for black-Jewish conflict. Not only was it a public site of political discourse, but a disproportionate number of academics were Jewish. Most of them identified themselves as politically to the left of mainstream Jewry and still concerned with issues of race. They were now joined by a new, and newly visible, group of black scholars, many of whom came directly from the civil rights movement. Meanwhile, black and Jewish students, a generation younger, may have heard stories of coalition from their parents, but had themselves encountered only enmity or disregard.

Political tensions between integrationists and separatists, between liberals and critics to their left and right, were therefore mirrored in this rarefied intellectual sphere. In 1984 James Baldwin gave a talk at the University of Massachusetts, Amherst, about Jesse Jackson and black-Jewish relations. Some Jewish students heard his critical comments about Jews as anti-Semitism. Julius Lester, who twenty years earlier had hosted the radio program featuring black anti-Semitic poetry, agreed. That and a number of other conflicts, coupled with Lester's conversion to Judaism, led to irreconcilable conflicts between himself and the Afro-American Studies Department in which he taught; he moved into the Department of Judaic Studies in 1988. The charges and countercharges produced by those events created such a furor that *The Black Scholar* devoted its November/December issue to the subject.[106]

Tony Martin, a professor at Wellesley College and specialist on Marcus Garvey, offered an analysis of Jews' role in black life so controversial that he entitled his account of the attacks upon him *The Jewish Onslaught: Despatches from the Wellesley Battlefront*. In 1991 Leonard Jeffries, a black City College of New York professor of African-American Studies, publicly accused Jews (and their Italian partners) of perpetrating every system that hurt black people either culturally or economically. Several years before, a politically conservative Jewish CCNY professor, Michael Levin, had asserted in print that science demonstrated black intellectual inferiority. While both were investigated by City College, Levin was spared disciplinary action on the basis of academic freedom, with little protest from the Jewish community, while Jeffries was attacked from within the college and from Jewish leaders outside it, losing his chairmanship in the process. In 1992 Henry Louis Gates of Harvard wrote an op-ed piece for the *New York Times* about black anti-Semitism that earned him the appreciation of the Jewish establishment and the resentment of numerous black activists who considered the presentation unfair and one-sided. Where was any discussion of Jewish racism? And in 1995 Cornel West, also of Harvard, was the subject of a critical review in the *New Republic* by the Jewish critic Leon Wieseltier that many believed strayed beyond intellectual criticism into mean-spirited ad hominem attacks. The details of these fracases, fascinating though they are, and the legitimacy of their accusations, are less important than the frequency of their occurrence and the intensity of their rhetoric. Black-Jewish conflict had followed blacks and Jews into the ivory tower.[107]

Meanwhile, other leftist academics sought healing, or at least clarity. As in the 1940s, a flurry of intellectual activity centered around the creation of texts and dialogues on black-Jewish relations. Black and Jewish lesbian feminists lamented finding themselves "Between a Rock and a Hard Place," while Jonathan Kaufman returned to the scene of the crime in *Broken Alliance*, a study of of Ocean Hill–Brownsville and other sites of black-Jewish interaction, and wondered in another essay, "What's a Jewish Liberal to Do?" David Theo Goldberg examined relations from the perspectives of philosophy and political science, and Adam Newton from a literary angle. Jack Salzman's historical examination of blacks and Jews through documents and analysis accompanied a museum exhibition on that topic; Michael Rogin and Jeffrey Melnick considered black-Jewish relations within the artistic world. Joseph Washington Jr. edited a volume on *Jews in Blacks' Perspectives*. Michael Lerner, who left the academy to publish the leftist Jewish magazine *Tikkun*, devoted a substantial number of its pages to the topic. Paul Berman examined the intellectual discourse itself, through its presentation in journals and magazines. Many of these scholarly works, whether anthologies, articles, or monographs, offered titles emblematic of their theses—*Bittersweet Encounter*; "Parallels and Divergences"; *In the Almost Promised Land*; "Ambivalent Allies"; *An Unillustrious Alliance; Strangers and Neighbors; What Went Wrong?*; "The Other and the Almost the Same"; *Alliances and Arguments; Bridges and Boundaries*.[108]

Some offered sharp critiques of one side or the other, others were generalized laments. But all shared the sense that the disintegration of liberal black-Jewish coalitions had proven a loss for the advancement of civil rights. Gates, whose annual "Working Groups" bring academic specialists together on topics related to African American Studies, devoted one to the subject of black-Jewish relations. It focused almost entirely on ways to both understand and heal the wounds, and included leading journalists and writers, as well as academics. That followed a scholarly conference on the same subject organized by historian Nancy Grant at Washington University, and numerous panels at scholarly conventions. Many black and Jewish professors offered courses and lectures on the subject; others discussed it in public journals from *The Center Magazine* to *The Progressive*, from *Commentary* to *Dissent*, from *New York* to *The Nation*, from *Tikkun* to *Transaction*, from *USA Today* to the *Economist*, from *Esquire* to the *New York Review of Books*. And in 1997 Nathan Glazer made a truce, if not a lasting settlement, in another fractious debate, with his critique of theories of race-blind melting pots and his reluctant endorsement of affirmative action programs in *We Are All Multiculturalists Now*.[109]

Black and Jewish political organizations and leaders joined discussions as well, from the Reform movement's *Common Road to Justice: A Programming Manual for Blacks and Jews*, to *CommonQuest, a Journal of*

Black-Jewish Relations whose occasional appearance on the newsstands between 1996 and 2000 was underwritten by Howard University and the AJC.[110] Perhaps black-Jewish relations were seen as a problem, but both blacks and Jews still considered it a relationship worth engaging over.

Y2K

Black-Jewish tensions persisted through the end of the century, as the NOI continued its rhetoric of black uplift and anti-Semitism, as the situation in the Middle East worsened with the first and second intifadas, and as black and Jewish organizations continued to disagree over affirmative action. Perhaps more problematic than such direct disagreements, black and Jewish groups maintained their inward focus, directed toward their very different problems. For African American groups, still frustrated with the slow pace of meaningful integration or even—given entrenched de facto segregation—achieving equality across largely separate institutions, poverty, discrimination, education, crime, and their attendant problems dominated their agendas. More socially and economically stable, the organized Jewish community refocused its attention on church-state separation, civil liberties and privacy issues, and the security of Israel.

Additionally—and ironically—by the 1990s some Jews concluded that assimilationist pluralism had proved too much of a good thing. As intermarriage rates continued to rise and synagogue affiliation to drop, as more Jews chose not to live their lives as Jewish in any communal way, many called for a self-conscious promotion of Jewish self-identification, or "continuity." This is in some sense a separatist or nationalist position, although Jews have not budged on their commitment to the other component of liberal pluralism: voluntary or self-chosen identity.

Furthermore, the absence of collaborative political engagement left only personal relationships between blacks and Jews, while segregation and continued class distinctions ensured that these encounters occurred between virtual strangers of different economic and social status. Without the more egalitarian, productive interactions blacks and Jews experienced as coalition partners, the same anti-Semitism that has long been a part of the African American community and the same racism that has long existed in the American Jewish community have taken center stage in the debate over the nature of black-Jewish relations.

Yet the black-Jewish split, understandable as it is, bodes ill for further progress on still shared goals. If blacks and Jews, staunchest defenders of liberal civil rights, have abandoned their faith in the liberal vision, is there hope for race relations? And might the conflicting critiques of liberalism by blacks and Jews serve as the proverbial canary in the coal mine, heralding the ideology's imminent collapse?

I think these concerns are based on a faulty premise. In fact, most blacks and Jews have not abandoned liberalism. Rather, the two have shifted their attention to different sets of liberal issues, and narrowed their understanding of what liberalism means. For black groups, whose nationalism has largely shifted from political to cultural, traditional liberal concerns about poverty and discrimination continue to dominate their political agenda, and they feel betrayed by Jews' move away from these issues. But while the current agenda of the organized Jewish community—church-state separation, concern about anti-Semitism, Jewish self-determination, and Israel as a safe haven from persecution—is arguably narrower in its focus, these are still liberal issues as well. Since blacks and Jews no longer share priorities, and have largely discarded the rhetoric of universalism in favor of self-assertion, it is not surprising their partnership has withered. But that does not mean that either has abandoned liberalism.

While more Jews now express conservative views, most still look a lot like traditional liberals. They can still be distinguished from other white people at least in their lesser level of racism, their continued commitment to traditional civil rights, their stance on social and gender issues, and certainly in their self-perception. As Arthur Hertzberg commented in 1989, "I believe that most . . . [American Jews, whether religious or not] sense that being Jewish is somehow connected to moral responsibility." Justice Ruth Bader Ginsberg agreed. "The demand for justice runs through the entirety of Jewish history and Jewish tradition," she wrote. "I hope in all the years I have the good fortune to serve on the bench of the Supreme Court of the United States, I will have the strength and courage to remain steadfast in the service of that demand."[111] When Jewish agencies and synagogues host lectures and discussions about Jews and civil rights (and the fact that these remain such popular topics is itself worth noting), they still identify themselves as liberals, and they too feel betrayed—by black folk they believe have abandoned the liberal vision Jews still endorse for a narrow and anti-Semitically tinged nationalism. And Jews still tend, in the words of the old joke, to earn like Episcopalians and vote like Puerto Ricans.

Milton Himmelfarb lamented in 1989 that while the Irish and other deeply committed Democrats had shifted toward Republicanism, "[p]ractically alone among white voters, American Jews have changed hardly at all." And despite their higher average incomes, Jews still called themselves liberal far more often than non-Jews. In the 1988 election, for example, 25 percent of all voters accepted that label, compared with 46 percent of Jewish ones. While 43 percent of voters considered themselves conservatives, only 25 percent of Jews so identified themselves. Twelve years later,

49 percent of Jews (and 42 percent of African Americans) called themselves liberals, and 19 percent "conservative" (25 percent of black respondents). Jews continue to vote Democratic in significantly higher proportions than any other comparably earning group. This proves equally true
for congressional elections. In 1998 the two populations that voted Democratic by the highest proportions were African Americans (89 percent)
and Jews (79 percent). Hispanics came in at 63 percent, Catholics at 53.[112]
It is not blacks and Jews so much as postwar liberalism that has splintered.
The Jewish community, still liberal on race and on social issues, has become more conservative economically. The black community, by contrast,
remains liberal on economic issues but far less unified on traditional liberal approaches to civil rights.

Encouraging also is continued political cooperation between liberal
black and Jewish organizations. Nationally as well as in states and municipalities, black and Jewish groups continued to work together through
the 1980s and 1990s on aid to public education; antipoverty, hunger, and
homelessness programs; women's rights, hate crimes legislation; voting
rights; civil liberties, and similar causes. Like black organizations, Jewish
groups continued to monitor cases of bigotry and continued their tolerance work. The AJCongress's president, executive director, and a senior
vice president were arrested in a 1984 demonstration against apartheid
in South Africa. The Jewish-dominated UFT remained committed to organizing and defending the interests of black and Latino workers in New
York even after its antagonistic engagement with African Americans in
Ocean Hill–Brownsville. In 1985 Murray Friedman noted "the strong
bonds between Jewish and black politicos on Capitol Hill" where Jews
"have been in the vanguard of legislative attacks on apartheid in South
Africa" and African Americans "have given consistent backing for economic and military aid to Israel." Socialist Jewish congressional representative Bernie Sanders echoed this point in 1998.[113]

There has certainly been a black-Jewish confluence of interests on the
individual and local levels as well. A majority of Jewish Los Angelenos
supported black mayoral candidate Thomas Bradley over white mayor
Sam Yorty in 1969, despite the latter's playing on racial fears to win the
Jewish vote; in New York both blacks and Jews overwhelmingly opposed
the conservative senatorial candidate James Buckley in 1970. Although
Jews were less unified in their support of David Dinkins in 1989, they
supported him in larger percentages than any other group of whites. Jews
along with blacks strongly supported Harold Washington's Chicago mayoral campaign. And locally organized black/Jewish coalitions that call
themselves the Black-Jewish Economic Roundtable or the African-Ameri-
can/Jewish Coalition for Justice continue to operate programs of mutual
interest and cooperation from Boston, Massachusetts, to Seattle, Wash-

ington, to Tidewater, Virginia.[114] If persistent tensions challenged the growing cooperation between blacks and Jews over the past century, persistent cooperation has challenged the black-Jewish tensions of the past thirty years that have been threatening to turn them into enemies.

The Lessons of History

Both those who claim that blacks and Jews are "natural" allies and those who insist that the two have never shared values or goals have missed the lesson of history. Neither identity nor political feeling is fixed and unchanging; they are contingent on the historical context in which groups find themselves. In the middle of the twentieth century both Jews and blacks, long considered by others as outsiders in the United States, and facing social, economic, and political restrictions, recognized the potential of postwar liberalism to challenge those restrictions while proving they too were fully American. This liberalism, though ill-defined, understood equality as both indivisible and individual. It therefore advocated full public integration while it defended private differences and individual rights. Within this ideological framework, and in pursuit of their shared goals, blacks and Jews worked together on broad civil rights issues.

While the marginality of African Americans and the attraction of a liberalism that would redefine them as fully American are evident, American Jews' choices seem less obvious. But although it has been difficult for many black people to understand, even after they had begun to "make it" in America, Jews still perceived themselves as vulnerable. It is this sense of their own marginality, alongside a postwar distrust of radicalism, that led so many of these Jews to liberalism. Jews, for reasons of both self-interest and their understanding of their ethnic and religious heritage, embraced the cause of civil rights more energetically than any other white group. Many communities experienced persecution; only Jews chose to devote a large proportion of their own agencies' agendas to issues of African American equality. And Jews made up a disproportionate number of the white contributors to and activists in the civil rights movement. If their commitment was less avid than many now like to claim, certainly it was greater than that of other white communities.

Yet beneath blacks' and Jews' apparent unity of program and purpose lay divisions based on class, race, religion, historical experience, and access to white privilege. These divisions, always problematic, came to a head in the 1960s and '70s, once formal barriers finally fell. Given structural racism, the two components of liberal civil rights now appeared to many to be a contradiction: equality for all could not be achieved by focusing only on individual rights. African American organizations, frustrated by the seeming permanence of racism, challenged the goal of integration and pointed up the limits of liberalism while Jews continued to hold fast to it.

Blacks and Jews held their divergent positions for the same reason: the impact of liberal programs on their community. Jews had benefited from policies designed to enforce blindness to race and religion, while African Americans enjoyed far more limited success and at greater cost. Furthermore, Jews' class position made them wary of challenges to the vision of meritocracy and moderation they had embraced. Their participation in civil rights lessened as the agenda moved from legislation to economics, from education to confrontation, from equal access to numbers and timetables. As liberalism lost its footing, so too did black-Jewish cooperation, replaced by disillusionment, resentment of former partners, and rejection of the process—or even the possibility—of coalition. Although both scholars and activists have been eager to naturalize the situation in which they found themselves by claiming it reflected timeless truths, black-Jewish divisions, just like black-Jewish cooperation, were and are a product of their moment, an embodiment of liberalism's travails.

Jews, by and large, have been unable to see the extent to which postwar liberalism, operating within a racialized state yet denying its existence, constrained both black identity and black access to political and economic advancement. Structural barriers play a greater role than most white liberals have been willing to acknowledge. African Americans remain "the other" in the most profound sense. America's ostensible race-blind pluralism, while proving an effective challenge to legal racism, after the 1964 Civil Rights Act could no longer serve as a useful guideline for achieving an egalitarian society because it did not recognize the depth and intractability of America's racial divide. Jews fundamentally misunderstood the frustration and anger of many black activists in the 1960s; those activists in turn exaggerated the failures of liberalism to deliver meaningful civil rights, and perhaps exaggerated its potential to deliver what it never could, a truly egalitarian society. The collapse of black-Jewish political cooperation had less to do with specific incidents than it did with a divergent set of political beliefs and visions.

Yet critics of that liberalism must resolve issues of their own, including problematic claims of fixed and single racial identities. And the nationalist retreat from the liberal ideal of multiracial equality (even if historically honored only in the breach) narrowed a universalist movement for justice into one of parochial self-interest. Even in the era of greatest cooperation, blacks and Jews had embraced coalition out of self-interest. But this was a *spacious* self-interest that recognized that security for one meant security for all, that if any were denied equality, all were vulnerable. This was liberalism at its finest. While that liberal vision alone could not provide an egalitarian society, its critics were too impatient to appreciate the gains it did achieve, or to resolve its contradictions in a way that maintained the movement's momentum.

These concerns are not merely academic. The many misperceptions and even self-delusions that fuel the debates over black-Jewish relations threaten the stability of the American polity. The fact is that Jews have moved to the inside in a society that still has an outside. Yet most Jews still perceive themselves as at least partly outside.[115] That apparent contradiction lies at the heart of American race relations, and it helped throw American liberalism into chaos. It must be addressed, and it can be by remembering that time when liberal notions were indeed spacious, when African Americans, Jews, and other marginalized or vulnerable communities understood they had a common interest in promoting political agendas that are inclusive and that protect all minority interests.

As persistent poverty, poor education, urban decay, and the growing disparities of wealth threaten the well-being of the nation as a whole; as right-wing Christian evangelicalism erodes church-state separation and the respect for difference that separation has permitted; as the weakening of civil rights laws and remedies turn American society increasingly segregated even as it becomes increasingly multicultural demographically, it is possible a liberal politics based on that sense of spacious self-interest could return. That coalition would be different, but those liberal values of mutual respect, democracy, the protection of individual rights, and the responsibility of the state to protect those rights and ensure equal opportunity would remain at its heart. If it does not return, we will have abandoned liberalism's noblest goals while leaving intact its deepest contradictions.

New Birth?

The 2000 election, held at the very turning point of the millennium, was itself punctuated by black-Jewish moments. When Democratic presidential candidate Al Gore announced Joseph Lieberman, an observant Jew, as his running mate, Jesse Jackson opined, "When that wall came down . . . it opened up space for all minorities."[116] Perhaps. But perhaps it revealed not the openness of the process to outsiders, but rather the dramatic extent to which Jews had become insiders. A poll conducted at the time asked respondents if they would vote for qualified individuals of their party who were female, gay, or of various racial and ethnic groups. Gays and atheists fared worst; only 59 and 49 percent of those polled, respectively, reported they would vote for such people. Both blacks and Jews did far better; such theoretical candidates could count on receiving 95 and 92 percent of their party's vote. (The slight edge theoretical black candidates enjoyed over

Jewish ones is both interesting and a change from earlier decades.)[117] What people report does not always coincide with what they do; nevertheless, the poll is remarkable for how far we as a nation have come. Still, Gore invited a Jewish and not an African American man to join him on the ticket, and despite Jackson's euphoria, the ambiguity of Jews' status as both insider and outsider remains, and the message the selection communicates about race relations is equally unclear.

The election closed with blacks and Jews firmly, if fleetingly, united. At the New Birth Baptist Church in North Miami, Florida, angry black and Jewish voters joined Jesse Jackson to protest what they perceived as their mutual disenfranchisement by Republican state officials. Jackson, joined by Kweisi Mfume, president of the NAACP, and Rabbi Steven Jacobs of a Los Angeles synagogue, hosted another interracial meeting at Miami's Temple Israel, sponsored by the newly organized Black-Jewish Civil Rights Coalition. In Florida, as in the rest of the country, blacks and Jews had again voted overwhelmingly Democratic, continuing their almost seventy-year pattern of staunch allegiance to the more liberal party. "Once again, the sons and daughters of slavery and Holocaust survivors are bound together by their hopes and their fear about national public policy," intoned Jackson. Rabbi Jacobs agreed, calling this an "opportunity for Jews and blacks to come back together."[118] Probably wishful thinking, certainly opportunistic, the comments and the gathering offered some important reminders to the two communities of once and future possibilities.

ABBREVIATIONS

AM—Annual Meeting*
AR—Annual Report
A-S—Anti-Semitism
BB—B'nai B'rith
  WSC—Women's Supreme Council of BB
C—Newspaper clipping
CF—Clippings file
CIC—Catholic Interracial Council
CL—Civil Liberties
CR—Civil Rights
EC—Executive Committee*
ED—Executive Director
ES—Executive Secretary
JCRC—Jewish Community Relations Council(s)
NEC—National Executive Committee*
NJR—Negro-Jewish Relations
PR—Press release
Schomburg—Schomburg Center for Research in Black Culture, New York, N.Y.

JOURNALS AND NEWSPAPERS

AHR—American Historical Review
JAH—Journal of American History
AJH—American Jewish History
AJHQ—American Jewish Historical Quarterly
AJYB—American Jewish Year Book
AJCW—[AJ]Congress Weekly
JAC—Jews Against Communism
JNH—Journal of Negro History
NHB—Negro History Bulletin
NQ—Negro Quarterly
NYT—New York Times

ARCHIVAL COLLECTIONS

AJC—American Jewish Committee papers, AJC Library, New York, N.Y.
  AO—Area Offices
  CJ—Communists and Jews
  DAC—Domestic Affairs Committee*

IVF—Inactive Vertical Files
OH—Oral History Collection, Jews in Civil Rights (at New York
    Public Library, Jewish Division)
RR—Race Relations
VF—Vertical Files
WD—Women's Division
AJCong—American Jewish Congress papers, AJCongress Library, New York,
    N.Y. Used with permission.
    AC—Administrative Committee*
    AEC—Administrative and Executive Committee*
    BC—Biennial Convention*
    C&C—Conferences and Conventions*
    DAC—Domestic Affairs Committee*
    GC—Governing Council (sometimes called Governing Board: GB)*
    WD—Women's Division
ADL—Anti-Defamation League microfilms and papers, ADL Library, New York,
    N.Y. Used with permission.
    Chisub—"Chicago subjects" microfilm (listed by file topic and reel number)
    CIRR—Committee on Inter-Racial Relations*
    CRC—Civil Rights Committee*
    CRD—Civil Rights Division*
    D—Microfilm "Dittos" (by year)
    EFC—Executive Finance Committee*
    I:McC—Individuals: McCarthy
    I:R—Investigations: Rosenberg
    MP—Motion Pictures
    NAC—National Administrative Committee*
    NC—National Commission*
    NRP—"Negro Race Problems"
    NWD—"Not the Work of a Day: An Oral History of the Anti-Defamation
        League," 1983, oral memoirs, typed and bound by ADL
    RO—Regional Offices
    Y—Microfilm "Yellows" (by year)
    YD—Microfilm "Yellows and Dittos" (by year)
    WB—warehouse box
AB—Algernon Black papers, Columbia University Rare Book and Manuscript
    Library, New York, N.Y.
Bearden—Bessaye Bearden papers, Schomburg.
Bolin—Jane Bolin papers, Schomburg.
Crosswaith—Frank Crosswaith papers, Schomburg.
FDR—Franklin D. Roosevelt papers, Hyde Park, N.Y. Official Files (OF) named
    and numbered by topic; boxes follow colon.
JLC—Jewish Labor Committee papers, Tamiment Library, New York, N.Y. Mi-
    crofilm reels and box numbers separated by colons.
NAACP—NAACP Papers, Manuscript Collections, Library of Congress, Wash-
    ington, DC. Chronological series noted with roman numerals, boxes with
    letters and Arabic numbers.

MMBD—Minutes of the Meeting of the Board of Directors*

ROS [Month] —Report of the Secretary for the [Month] Meeting of the Board

NCRAC—National (Jewish) Community Relations Advisory Council papers, American Jewish Historical Society, Center for Jewish History, N.Y. Boxes follow colon.

NCJW—National Council of Jewish Women papers, Manuscript Collections, Library of Congress, Washington, D.C.

    NCSL—National Committee on Social Legislation*

    TC—Triennial Convention*

    WO—Washington office

NCNW—National Council of Negro Women papers, Manuscript Collections, Mary McLeod Bethune Museum and Archives, Washington, D.C. Series and boxes separated by colon.

NUL—National Urban League papers, Manuscript Collections, Library of Congress, Washington, D.C. Series and boxes separated by colon.

    BT—Board of Trustees*

    EB—Executive Board*

    FC—Finance Committee*

    SRO—Southern Regional Office (separate collection)

Polier—Shad Polier papers, American Jewish Historical Society, Center for Jewish History, New York, N.Y.

SCA—Synagogue Council of America papers, American Jewish Historical Society, Center for Jewish History, New York, N.Y.

UNIA—Universal Negro Improvement Association papers, Schomburg.

*Citations from these files are minutes, unless otherwise specified

INTRODUCTION

1. Friedman, *What Went Wrong?* (New York, 1995).

2. Cruse, *The Crisis of the Negro Intellectual* (New York, 1967).

3. E.g. Lewis, "Parallels and Divergences," *JAH* 71, no. 3 (December 1984): 543–64; Hill, "Black-Jewish Conflict in the Labor Context," *Race Traitor* 5 (Winter 1996): 72–103. Also see Adolph Reed Jr., *The Jesse Jackson Phenomenon* (New Haven, Conn., 1986).

4. Diner, *In the Almost Promised Land: American Jews and Blacks 1915–1935* (Westport, Conn., 1977).

5. Melnick, *A Right to Sing the Blues: African Americans, Jews, and American Popular Song* (Cambridge, Mass., 1999); *Black-Jewish Relations on Trial: Leo Frank and Jim Conley in the New South* (Jackson, Miss., 2000); Rogin, *Blackface, White Noise: Jewish Immigrants in the Hollywood Melting Pot* (Berkeley, Calif., 1996).

6. There are no reliable figures but detractors and enthusiasts alike acknowledge that Jews, less than 3 percent of the population, constituted a significant proportion of the CR community, whether SNCC activists, NAACP contributors, coalition partners, or integration supporters.

7. Throughout my study, "Jews" refers to Euro-Americans. There are non-white Jews and Jewish communities; I do not mean to erase them but to provide a shorthand for what is, essentially, a study of black/Euro-Jewish relations.

8. Quoted in P. Allen Krause, "Rabbis and Negro Rights in the South, 1954–1967," *American Jewish Archives* 21, no. 1 (1969): 31.

9. See, e.g., Melanie Kaye-Kantrowitz, "'Stayed on Freedom': Jews in the CR Movement and After," in *The Narrow Bridge*, ed. Marla Brettschneider (New Brunswick, N.J., 1996), 105–22, esp. 107; Paul Berman, "The Other And the Almost the Same," in *Blacks and Jews*, ed. Berman (New York, 1994), 1–30, esp. 9–13; Samuel Klausner, "The Religious 'Other' in Black-Jewish Relations," *Society* (September–October 1994): 51–57, esp. 52.

10. Data from J. J. Goldberg, "Portrait of American Jews," *Jewish Journal*, May 5, 2000. Fewer than one-fourth attend services weekly. Sixty percent reported encounters with discrimination, higher than any other group except African Americans, 3. This helps explain a peculiarity of American-Jewish civil rights involvement: the most committed activists came from both the most secular and the most religious of backgrounds. For more on ethical Judaism as historical product see, e.g., Douglas Rushkoff, "Judging Judaism by the Numbers," *NYT*, November 20, 2002, 23.

11. On biology and race see, e.g., American Anthropological Association, "Statement on 'Race,'" adopted May 17, 1998; Michael Blakely, "Ideologies of Race and Ethnicity," paper presented at "Race and Ethnicity: Relations between

African Americans and Ethnic Groups in American Society," German Historical Institute, Washington, D.C., September 22, 1994. On the changing U.S. definitions of race, see F. James Davis, *Who Is Black? One Nation's Definition* (University Park, Pa., 1991). Consider also the many language shifts referring to individuals of African descent.

12. Omi and Winant, *Racial Formation in the United States from the 1960s to the 1990s* (New York, 1994), 55.

13. See, e.g., Karen Brodkin, *How Jews Became White Folks and What That Says about Race in America* (New Brunswick, N.J., 1998); Eric Goldstein, *The Price of Whiteness* (Princeton, N.J., 2005); Matthew Frye Jacobson, *Whiteness of a Different Color* (Cambridge, Mass., 1998); Rogin, *Blackface, White Noise*; David Roediger, *Towards the Abolition of Whiteness* (London, 1994), chap. 11.

14. Danzy Senna, *Caucasia* (New York, 1999), 140. Novels and memoirs about black-Jewish families include Katya Gibel Azoulay, *Black, Jewish and Interracial* (Durham, N.C., 1997); Jane Lazarre, *Beyond the Whiteness of Whiteness* (Durham, N.C., 1996); Philip Roth, *The Human Stain* (Boston, 2000); James McBride, *The Color of Water* (New York, 1996); Rebecca Walker, *Black, White and Jewish* (New York, 2000).

15. Baldwin, "The Harlem Ghetto: Winter, 1948," *Commentary* 5, no. 2 (February 1948): 170.

16. Kurt Lewin, Alf Marrow, Charles Hendry, AJCongress, "Accent on Action: A New Approach to Minority Group Problems in America," 5 (portion written by Lewin), n.d. [1945?], NAACP IIA360.

17. There were hundreds of such groups, varying in political orientation, strategy, size, and structure, including political and self-help groups, women's clubs, trade union groups, religiously based organizations, fraternal orders, and Democratic and Republican clubs.

18. Harlem women's charity was reported in the *NY Age*, March 20, 1920; the quotations are from *Amsterdam News*, February 12, 1930, both cited in Isabel Price, "Black Response to Anti-Semitism" (Ph.D. diss., University of New Mexico, 1973), 92. See also Alexander, "Meeting of the Committee of One Hundred in Defense of Human Rights," December 12, 1938, 1–2, NAACP IC208.

19. Quoted in Diner, *Almost Promised Land*, 71. See also Hollander to David Robinson, December 18, 1947, ADL Y1947: NRP; Diner, chap. 4.

20. For more regarding communist and socialist black-Jewish relations, see Gerald Early, especially "Black, White and Red," in Brettschneider, *Narrow Bridge*, 123–35; Paul Buhle and Robin Kelley, especially "Allies of a Different Sort," in *Struggles in the Promised Land*, ed. Jack Salzman and Cornel West (New York, 1997), 197–230.

21. Other tensions include use of confrontational tactics, southern Jewish behaviors, concerns over communism, and sometimes different goals. The book explores these at length. Leadership Conference: Walter White of the NAACP, and Arnold Aronson of NCRAC.

22. This discussion highlights only a few types of class interaction. I describe public and relatively formal grievances, e.g., but rarely face-to-face interactions or class tensions between groups within each community (e.g., labor and middle-class organizations), or between races within each class (e.g., black and white trade

unionists). While these are important, I only discuss locations of class conflict most directly linked to the larger political story.

CHAPTER ONE
Settling In

1. For American Jewish population estimates, see Abraham Karp, *Haven and Home* (New York, 1985), app. 1; Jacob Rader Marcus, *The American Jew 1585–1990* (Brooklyn, 1995), 385; National Jewish Population Study (2000–2001), North American Jewish Data Bank, United Jewish Communities.

2. For Jews' role in the slave trade and system, see David Brion Davis, "Jews in the Slave Trade," and Jason Silverman, "'The Law of the Land Is the Law,'" both in Salzman and West, *Struggles in the Promised Land*. Still, given their tiny population, Jews made up a small number of those directly involved in slavery or slave trading (Davis, 71) According to Silverman, 25 percent were (75).

3. On spirituals, see e.g., William Barton, "Recent Negro Melodies," *New England Magazine*, 1899, reprinted in *The Social Implications of Early Negro Music in the United States*, ed. Bernard Katz (New York, 1969), 111; Thomas Wentworth Higginson, "Negro Spirituals," *Atlantic Monthly* 19 (June 1867): 688; *Harper's Magazine* 19 (1859): 859–60; Leonard Dinnerstein, *Anti-Semitism in America* (New York, 1994), 198; Fredric Jaher, *Scapegoat in the New Wilderness* (Cambridge, Mass., 1994), 241. On the durability of attitudes toward Jews, see, e.g., Horace Mann Bond, "Negro Attitudes toward Jews," *Jewish Social Studies* 27 (January 1965); Dinnerstein, 198–203; Richard Wright, *Black Boy* (New York, 1945), 53–54.

4. The "acomidation" letter is from Emmett Scott, "Letters of Negro Migrants of 1916–1918," *JNH* 4 (July 1919): 333. The "husband" and "principle" letters are from Scott, "Additional Letters," *JNH* 4 (October 1919): 413, 415–16, 456–62. The "entrance" quotation is from the *Chicago Defender*, January 19, 1918. All quotations reproduce original spelling and grammar.

5. Scott, "Additional," 459. Du Bois, *Address to the Country*, Niagara Movement leaflet, 1906. *Defender*, October 7, 1916.

6. For black population changes in selected cities, see U.S. Dept. of Commerce, *Negroes in the United States, 1920–1932* (Washington, D.C., 1935), 55. For white complaints see James Grossman, *Land of Hope* (Chicago, 1989), 40.

7. For migration studies see, e.g., Nell Painter, *Exodusters* (New York, 1976); Allen Ballard, *One More Day's Journey* (Philadelphia, 1984); Albert Broussard, *Black San Francisco* (Lawrence, Kans.,1993); Peter Gottlieb, *Making Their Own Way* (Urbana, Ill., 1987); Farah Jasmine Griffin, *"Who Set You Flowin'?"* (New York, 1995); Grossman, *Land of Hope*; Alferdteen Harrison, ed., *Black Exodus* (Jackson, Miss., 1991); Earl Lewis, *In Their Own Interests* (Berkeley, Calif., 1991); Carole Marks, *Farewell—We're Good and Gone* (Bloomington, Ind., 1989); Kimberley Phillips, *AlabamaNorth* (Urbana, Ill., 1999); Milton Sennett, *Bound for the Promised Land* (Durham, N.C., 1997); Joe Trotter, ed., *The Great Migration in Historical Perspective* (Bloomington, Ind., 1991); Trotter, *Black Milwaukee* (Urbana, Ill., 1985); Lillian Williams, *Strangers in the Land of Paradise*

(Bloomington, Ind., 1999). On Caribbean migrants see Irma Watkins-Owens, *Blood Relations* (Bloomington, Ind., 1996); Philip Kasnitz, *Caribbean New York* (Ithaca, N.Y., 1990); Ira De Augustine Reid, *The Negro Immigrant: His Background, Characteristics, and Social Adjustment, 1899–1937* (New York, 1939); Louise Kennedy, *The Negro Peasant Turns Cityward* (New York, 1930); W. A. Domingo, "The Tropics in New York," *Survey Graphic* 53 (March 1, 1925): 648–51; and "Gift of the Black Tropics," *The New Negro*, ed. Alain Locke (1925; repr., New York, 1968): 341–49.

8. Adam Clayton Powell Sr., *Against the Tide* (New York, 1938), 185.

9. On early-twentieth-century urban black neighborhoods see, e.g., Broussard, *Black San Francisco*; St. Clair Drake and Horace Cayton, *Black Metropolis* (New York, 1945; repr., Chicago, 1970); Gottlieb, *Making Their Own Way*; Grossman, *Land of Hope*; James Weldon Johnson, *Black Manhattan* (1930; repr., New York, 1968); Kenneth Kusmer, *A Ghetto Takes Shape* (Urbana, Ill., 1976); Lewis, *In Their Own Interests*; Gilbert Osofsky, *Harlem* (New York, 1963); Thomas Philpott, *The Slum and the Ghetto* (New York, 1978); Alan Spear, *Black Chicago* (Chicago, 1967); Quintard Taylor, *The Forging of a Black Community* (Seattle, 1994); Trotter, *Milwaukee*; George Wright, *Life behind a Veil* (Baton Rouge, La., 1985).

10. Quoted in Drake and Cayton, *Black Metropolis*, 74; Ovington quoted in Judith Weisenfeld, *African American Women and Christian Activism* (Cambridge, Mass., 1997), 78; the Detroit Urban League director is quoted in Marks, *Farewell*, 160. See also Grossman, *Land of Hope*, chap. 5.

11. Watkins-Owens, *Blood Relations*, 51, 61, 80–81, 128, 152, 173; McKay, *Home to Harlem* (1928; repr., Boston, 1987), 155, 134.

12. Watkins-Owens, *Blood Relations*, 49. For postwar interaction among economic classes in black neighborhoods, see Norman Fainstein and Susan Nesbitt, "Did the Black Ghetto Have a Golden Age?" *Journal of Urban History* 23, no. 1 (November 1996): 3–28. For interclass tensions, see Franklin Frazier, *Black Bourgeoisie* (New York, 1957), 235–36; Frazier, *The Negro in the United States* (New York, 1949), 283–305; Drake and Cayton, *Black Metropolis*, vol. 2; Kasnitz, *Caribbean New York*, 45–49; Jervis Anderson, *This Was Harlem* (New York, 1981), 137, 299–304; Roi Ottley and William Weatherby, eds., *The Negro in New York* (New York, 1967), 193; Cheryl Greenberg, *"Or Does It Explode?"* (New York, 1991), 17; Kennedy, *The Negro Peasant Turns Cityward*, 222; Domingo, "Gift of the Black Tropics," 343, 346, 348.

13. Morris, *Origins of the Civil Rights Movement* (New York, 1984).

14. UNIA Constitution preamble; Powell, *Against the Tide*, 71.

15. Garvey, "The Negro's Place in World Reorganization," *Philosophy and Opinions of Marcus Garvey*, ed. Amy Jacques-Garvey, vol. 2 (1925; repr., New York, 1992), 35. UNIA claimed it aided 10,000 in Harlem alone. See UNIA Central Division, UNIA papers, boxes 6, 7.

16. Briggs, "Race Catechism," *Crusader*, September 1918; "African Blood Brotherhood," *Crusader*, June 1920, both reprinted in *Modern Black Nationalism*, ed. William Van Deburg (New York, 1997), 38, 36.

17. Terrell, "First Presidential Address to the NACW," 1897, in Beverly Jones, *Quest for Equality* (Brooklyn, 1990), 134. For the women's club movement, see Dor-

othy Salem, *To Better Our World* (Brooklyn, 1990); Ida B. Wells, *Crusade for Justice* (Chicago, 1970), 242–43; Charles Wesley, *The History of the NACW Clubs* (Washington, D.C., 1984), esp. 112–29; Elizabeth Davis, *Lifting as They Climb* (NACW, 1933); Terrell, *Colored Woman in A White World* (Washington, D.C., 1940); Terrell, "History of the Club Women's Movement," *Aframerican Women's Journal* (Summer–Fall 1940): 34–38; Jones, *Quest for Equality*; Salem, "NACW," in *Black Women in America*, ed. Darlene Clarke Hine, Elsa Barkley Brown, and Rosalyn Terborg-Penn (Bloomington, Ind., 1993), 842–51; Deborah Gray White, *Too Heavy a Load* (New York, 1999). For black women and uplift, see Brown, "Womanist Consciousness," *Signs* 14 (1989): 610–33; Gertrude Marlowe, *A Right Worthy Good Mission* (Washington, D.C., 2003); Weisenfeld *African American Women*. The NACW's middle-class orientation is illustrated by the fact that in the organization's first five years, of fifty officers for whom there is information, thirty had college degrees, and thirteen of those had graduate or professional degrees (Jones, 22).

18. Terrell, "Address," 136.

19. Wesley, *History*, 42; see also, 31–43, 57, 63; Jones, *Quest for Equality*; 28, 33; Salem, *To Better Our World*, 36, 52, 224, 232.

20. Louise Daniel Hutchinson, *Anna J. Cooper* (Washington, D.C., 1981), 88.

21. Card distributed by Chicago UL, n.d. [1917?] cited in Grossman, *Land of Hope*, 147. The *Defender*, the YMCA, and others produced similar advisories. See Grossman, 144–150 and the *Defender* for additional examples.

22. Nancy Weiss, "Long-Distance Runners of the Civil Rights Movement," in Salzman and West, *Struggles in the Promised Land*, 143. Six of twenty-eight whites (of known religion) on the NUL board 1911–21 were Jews; ten of twenty-eight in the 1920s (ibid., 137–39).

23. The "Call's" Jewish signers were Wald, Wise, Hirsch, and Henry Moskowitz. On the general committee were Jacob Mack, Schiff, Moskowitz, Edwin Seligman, Wald, Wise, and Rita Morgenthau. On the board were Rabbi Joseph Silverman, Wald, Walter Sachs, Spingarn. Note the overlap with NUL donors. See NAACP ARs; Charles Kellogg, *NAACP*, vol. 1, *1909–1920* (Baltimore, 1967); Weiss, "Long-Distance Runners," 130–31, 136; Diner, *Almost Promised Land* 119–24. Du Bois's comment on Spingarn comes from, *Dusk of Dawn* (New York, 1940), 255.

24. Tushnet, *The NAACP's Legal Strategy against Segregated Education, 1925–1950* (Chapel Hill, N.C., 1987), 11; John Kirby, *Black Americans in the Roosevelt Era* (Knoxville, Tenn., 1980), 181.

25. For photos of the parade, see Osofsky, *Harlem*, 148. For an account of the NAACP conference, see Jonathan Rosenberg, "For Democracy, Not Hypocrisy," *International History Review* 21 (May 1999): 601–2. Du Bois, "Returning Soldiers," *Crisis* 18 (May 1919): 14.

26. See Jervis Anderson, *A. Philip Randolph* (New York, 1973); Brailsford Brazeal, *Brotherhood of Sleeping Car Porters: Its Origin and Development* (New York, 1946); Melinda Chateauvert, *Marching Together* (Urbana, Ill., 1998); William Harris, *Keeping the Faith* (Urbana, Ill., 1977); Theodore Kornweibel, *No Crystal Stair* (Westport, Conn., 1975); Paula Pfeiffer, *A. Philip Randolph* (Baton

Rouge, La., 1990); Jack Santino, *Miles of Smiles, Years of Struggle* (Urbana, Ill., 1991); Joseph Wilson, ed., *Tearing Down the Color Bar* (New York, 1989).

27. For communists in unionizing struggles, see below.

28. For African American churches' community work and political activism, see Randall Burkett and Richard Newman, eds., *Black Apostles* (Boston, 1978); John Brown Childs, *The Political Black Minister* (Boston, 1980); James Cone, *Black Theology and Black Power* (New York, 1969); Cone, *For My People* (Maryknoll, N.Y., 1984); W.E.B. Du Bois, ed., *The Negro Church* (Atlanta, 1903); Arthur Fauset, *Black Gods of the Metropolis* (Philadelphia, 1944); Ralph Felton, *These My Brethren* (New York, 1950); E. Franklin Frazier, *The Negro Church in America* (New York, 1964); Frazier and, C. Eric Lincoln, *The Negro Church in America: The Black Church since Frazier* (New York, 1974); Charles Hamilton, *The Black Preacher in America* (New York, 1972); James Harris, *Black Ministers and Laity in the Urban Church* (New York, 1987); Evelyn Brooks Higginbotham, *Righteous Discontent* (Cambridge, Mass., 1993); Joseph Jackson, *A Story of Christian Activism* (Nashville, 1980); C. Eric Lincoln and Lawrence Mamiya, *The Black Church in the African American Experience* (Durham, N.C., 1990); Lincoln, *Race, Religion and the Continuing American Dilemma* (New York, 1984); Benjamin Mays and Joseph Nicholson, *The Negro's Church* (1933; repr., New York, 1969); Morris, *Origins of the Civil Rights Movement*; Ida Mukenge, *The Black Church in Urban America* (New York, 1983); Hart Nelsen, Raytha Yokley, and Anne Nelsen, eds., *The Black Church in America* (New York, 1971); Peter Paris, *The Social Teaching of the Black Churches* (Philadelphia, 1985); Albert Raboteau, *A Fire in the Bones* (Boston, 1995); Milton Sennett, *Afro-American Religious History: A Documentary Witness* (Durham, N.C., 1985); Sennett, *Bound*; William Walls, *The African Methodist Episcopal Zion Church* (Charlotte, N.C., 1974); Joseph Washington Jr., *Black Religion* (Boston, 1964); Washington, *Black Sects and Cults* (New York, 1972); Robert Weisbrot, *Father Divine and the Struggle for Racial Equality* (Champaign, Ill., 1983); Weisenfeld, *African American Women*; Gayraud Wilmore, *Black Religion and Black Radicalism*, 3rd ed. (Maryknoll, N.Y., 1998); Robert Wilson, *The Northern Negro Looks at the Church* (New York, 1968); Carter Woodson, *The History of the Negro Church* (Washington, D.C., 1972).

29. Hundreds of books describe eastern European Jewish immigration, including Jack Glazier, *Dispersing the Ghetto* (Ithaca, N.Y., 1998); Susan Glenn, *Daughters of the Shtetl* (Ithaca, N.Y., 1990); Andrew Heinze, *Adapting to Abundance* (New York, 1990); Jenna Joselit, *The Wonders of America* (New York, 1994); Deborah Dash Moore, *At Home in America* (New York, 1981); Gerald Sorin, *A Time for Building* (Baltimore, 1992); Sorin, *Tradition Transformed* (Baltimore, 1997); Sydney Weinberg, *World of Our Mothers* (Chapel Hill, N.C., 1988). These informed this discussion. For Jewish community studies, see e.g., Gerry Cristol, *A Light in the Prairie* (Fort Worth, 1998); Steven Hertzberg, *Strangers within the Gate City* (Philadelphia, 1978); Kenneth Kann, *Comrades and Chicken Ranchers* (Ithaca, N.Y., 1993); Abraham Lavender, *Jewish Farmers of the Catskills* (Gainesville, Fla., 1995); Carolyn LeMaster, *A Corner of the Tapestry* (Fayetteville, Ark., 1994); Ewa Morawska, *Insecure Prosperity* (Princeton, N.J., 1996); Leonard Rogoff, *Homelands* (Tuscaloosa, Ala., 2001); Peter Rose, *Strangers in Their Midst*

(Merrick, N.Y., 1977); Jonathan Sarna and Ellen Smith, eds., *The Jews of Boston* (Boston, 1995); William Toll, *Making of an Ethnic Middle Class* (Albany, 1982). New York Jewish immigrants have been studied most often (sometimes with the assumption that New York defined the American Jewish experience), including Stephen Birmingham, *"Our Crowd"* (New York, 1967); Ruth Gay, *Unfinished People* (New York, 1996); Arthur Goren, *New York Jews and the Quest for Community* (New York, 1970); Jeffrey Gurock, *When Harlem Was Jewish* (New York, 1979); Irving Howe, *World of Our Fathers* (New York, 1976); Hutchins Hapgood, *The Spirit of the Ghetto*, ed. Moses Rischin (Cambridge, Mass., 1967); Jenna Joselit, *New York's Jewish Jews* (Bloomington, Ind., 1990); Thomas Kessner, *The Golden Door* (New York, 1977); Egon Mayer, *From Suburb to Shtetl* (Philadelphia, 1979); Rischin, *Promised City* (New York, 1962); Daniel Soyer, *Jewish Immigrant Associations and American Identity in New York 1880–1939* (Cambridge, Mass., 1997); Michael Weisser, *Brotherhood of Memory* (New York, 1985); WPA Yiddish Writers Group, *Jewish Hometown Associations and Family Circles in New York* (Bloomington, Ind., 1992).

30. Sorin, *Building*, 1:12.

31. On Jews "becoming" or "not-yet" white, see, e.g., Brodkin, *How Jews Became White Folks*; Melnick, *A Right to Sing the Blues*; Jacobson, *Whiteness of a Different Color*; Goldstein, *The Price of Whiteness*; Rogin, *Blackface, White Noise*; Roediger, *Towards the Abolition of Whiteness*, chap. 11 (Roediger attributes the term "not-yet-white" to John Bukowczyk, 184).

32. Numerous, often conflicting, analyses of the Frank case and black-Jewish relations abound; see, e.g., C. P. Connolly, *The Truth about the Frank Case* (New York, 1915); Leonard Dinnerstein, *The Leo Frank Case* (New York, 1968); Harry Golden, *A Little Girl Is Dead* (New York, 1965); Albert Lindemann, *The Jew Accused* (New York, 1991); Nancy MacLean, "The Leo Frank Case Reconsidered," *JAH* 78 (1991): 917–48; Melnick, *Black-Jewish Relations on Trial*; Steve Oney, *And the Dead Shall Rise* (New York, 2003). Also see Eugene Levy, "Is the Jew a White Man?" *Phylon* 35, no. 2 (Summer 1979): 212–22; Philip Foner, "Black-Jewish Relations in the Opening Years of the Twentieth Century," *Phylon* 36, no. 4 (Winter 1975): 359–67.

33. Elazar, *Community and Polity* (Philadelphia, 1976), 59.

34. Golden, "The Jews of the South," *AJCW* 18 (December 31, 1951): 9–11. Also see Foner, "Black-Jewish Relations," 365; Stephen Whitfield, "Commercial Passions: The Southern Jew as Businessman," *AJH* 71 (March 1982): 342–57. Rogoff, in *Homelands*, observes that despite anti-Semitism, gentiles in Durham and Chapel Hill, N.C., liked local Jews because they fit in.

35. Sorin, *Building*, 9, 239; Dinnerstein, *Anti-Semitism*, chap. 5, esp. 85–86. See also Carey McWilliams, *A Mask for Privilege* (Boston, 1948), chap. 5.

36. Morawska, *Insecure Prosperity*, 243; Johnson, *Autobiography of an Ex-Colored Man* (New York, 1990), 116. Also see Stella Suberman, *The Jew Store* (Chapel Hill, N.C., 1998) regarding Concordia, Tenn.

37. Sorin, *Building*, 28. On Jews and the left, see, e.g., Arthur Liebman, *Jews and the Left* (New York, 1979); Paul Buhle, "Themes in American Jewish Radicalism," in *The Immigrant Left in the United States*, ed. Buhle and Dan Georgakas

(Albany, 1996), 77–118; and below. Many socialist and communist Jews rejected religious rituals altogether.

38. "Declaration of Principles Adopted by a Group of Reform Rabbis at Pittsburgh, 1885," (Pittsburgh Platform) in CCAR *Yearbook* 45 (1935): 189–200; Moore, *At Home*, 15. Many scholars have noted American Jewish commitment to universalism, e.g., Seymour Lipset and Earl Raab, *Jews and the New American Scene* (Cambridge, Mass., 1995), 1–8, 13; Whitfield, "The 'Bourgeois Humanism' of American Jews," *Judaism* 29, no. 2 (Spring 1980): 160–66; Charles Silberman, *A Certain People* (New York, 1985); Fred Strodtbeck, "Family Interaction, Values and Achievement," and Nathan Glazer, "The American Jew and the Attainment of Middle-Class Rank," both in *The Jews*, ed. Marshall Sklare (Glencoe, Ill., 1958); Robert Park, *Race and Culture* (Glencoe, Ill., 1950), 354–55.

39. Whitfield, "Bourgeois," 160. See also Marc Dollinger, *Quest for Inclusion* (Princeton, N.J., 2000).

40. "Polish" (and others) cited in Sorin, *Building*, 51, 68; "Asiatics" and "darkened" cited in Birmingham, *"Our Crowd"* (345 no bibliographic details provided), Isaacs cited in Naomi Cohen, *Encounter with Emancipation* (Philadelphia, 1984), 327). See also Ande Manners, *Poor Cousins* (New York, 1972); Rischin, *Promised City*, chap. 6.

41. UAHC, quoted in Elias Tcherikower, *The Early Jewish Labor Movement in the United States*, trans. and revised by Aaron Antonovsky (New York, 1961), 108–9. For uplift, see Sorin, *Building*, 62. For the Jewish press, see Cohen, *Encounter with Emancipation*, 311.

42. Hannah Solomon, *Fabric of My Life* (New York, 1946); Faith Rogow, *Gone to Another Meeting* (Tuscaloosa, Ala., 1993); Linda Kuzmack, *Women's Cause* (Columbus, Ohio, 1990); Monroe Campbell and William Wirtz, *The First Fifty Years* (New York, 1943); Beth Wenger, "Jewish Women and Voluntarism," *AJH* 79, no. 1(Autumn 1989): 16–36; Charlotte Baum, Paula Hyman, and Sonya Michel, *The Jewish Woman in America* (New York, 1977), 48–52, 165–70, 172–78, 213. On the NCJW's voice, see Rogow, 37.

43. Quoted in Manners, *Poor Cousins*, 112.

44. Yezierska, "My Own People," in *Hungry Hearts and Other Stories* (New York 1985), 243, 232, 248. *Forward* quoted in Manners, *Poor Cousins*, 113. Also see Cohen, *Encounter with Emancipation*, 325.

45. Rogow, *Another Meeting*, 43.

46. Rogow, *Another Meeting*, 4, 35, 43–53, 163–65, 242–43; Solomon, *Fabric of My Life*, 43.

47. Rogow, *Another Meeting*, 159–66. Men's organizations did so in the 1920s and 1930s. Two significant exceptions, Stephen Wise and Emil Hirsch, were also signers of NAACP's "Call."

48. Kuzmack, *Women's Cause*, 3, 30, 172.

49. Stephen Wise, *Challenging Years* (London, 1951), 203.

50. Marshall to Adolph Kraus, June 12, 1915, in Sorin, *Building*, 212.

51. "Aims of the AJCongress," AJCongress *Courier* 1, no. 1 (April 21, 1933): 15.

52. Quoted in Dinnerstein, Roger Nichols, and David Reimers, *Natives and Strangers*, 2nd ed. (New York, 1990), 188.

53. Israel Zangwill, *The Melting Pot* (1908), in *From the Ghetto to the Melting Pot: Israel Zangwill's Jewish Plays*, ed. Edna Nahshon (Detroit, 2005).

54. *Bataan*, 1943, MGM, directed by Tay Garnett. On pluralism, see Philip Gleason, *Speaking of Diversity* (Baltimore, 1992); Werner Sollors, "A Critique of Pure Pluralism," in *Reconstructing American Literary History*, ed. Sacvan Bercovitch (Cambridge, Mass., 1986), 250–79; Daniel Greene, "The Crisis of Jewish Freedom: The Menorah Association and American Pluralism, 1906–1934" (Ph.D. diss., University of Chicago, 2004); John Higham, *Send These to Me* (1975; rev. ed. Baltimore, Md., 1984), chap. 9; Higham, *Hanging Together* (New Haven, Conn., 2001); Omi and Winant, *Racial Formation*; Milton Gordon, *Assimilation in American Life* (New York, 1964), 88–114; Charles Lippy, *Pluralism Comes of Age* (Armonk, N.Y., 2000); Stanford Lyman, *Color, Culture, Civilization* (Urbana, Ill., 1995). Interestingly, blacks and Jews were compared directly even in these early discussions of race relations. Ezra Park, e.g., recognized similarities between African American and European Jewish experiences as minorities, but also contrasted blacks as primitive and Jews as sophisticated people (*Race and Culture*, 186, 264).

55. Inherited: Kallen, *Culture and Democracy in the United States* (New York, 1924), 122–23; Johnny Washington, *Alain Locke and Philosophy* (Westport, Conn., 1986), 194; Locke, "The Legacy of the Ancestral Arts," in *The New Negro*, 254. Voluntary: Kallen, *Cultural Pluralism and the American Idea* (Philadelphia, 1956); Locke, "The Concept of Race as Applied to Social Culture," reprinted in *The Philosophy of Alain Locke*, ed. Leonard Harris (Philadelphia, 1989), 191–92. Popular depictions of pluralism continued to reflect essentialist assumptions even as the concept metamorphosed into multiculturalism.

56. Bond, "Temperament," *Crisis* 30, no. 2 (June 1925): 83–86; Locke, "Frontiers of Culture," 1949, in Harris, *Locke*, 233–34.

57. Benjamin Epstein, ADL NWD, vol. 1, 82–83. The ADL also produced a film on appropriate dress. See also chap. 2, below.

58. Frazier, *Negro in U.S.*, 680–81. See also Harris, *Locke*, 235; Wright, "The Literature of the Negro in the United States," 1957, in *Black Expression*, ed. Addison Gayle Jr. (New York, 1969), 228; Gunnar Myrdal, *An American Dilemma*, 20th anniversary ed. (New York, 1962), 927–30.

59. Forman, correspondence with author, March 17, 1997.

60. Brandeis quoted in Whitfield, "Bourgeois," 158. See ADL Program Division, ADL WB178; AJC programs in AJC library. Regarding community, also see Christopher Sterba, *Good Americans* (New York, 2003).

61. Lloyd Garrison, "Progress Report of the Committee on Urban League Policy," July 22, 1954, NUL 11–15. See also Marshall, quoted in *AJYB 1924–25* (Philadelphia, 1924), 640.

62. *Morgen Journal-Tageblatt*, September 1, 1933, 4, quoted in Diner, *Almost Promised Land*, 68. See also, *The Messenger*, editorial, August 1923, 781.

63. Terrell, *Voice of the Negro* (August 1905): 566–68; Domingo, "Gift," 345. Garvey, "Racial Reforms and Reformers," 9, 10 (sympathetic); "The Negro's Place," 35–36 (admiring); "Speech Delivered at Madison Square Garden, New York, N.Y., U.S.A. Sunday, March 16, 1924," 121 (envious), all in *Philosophy and Opinions*. See also Bond, "Temperament"; Kelly Miller in *Amsterdam News*,

April 16, 1930; *AME Church Review,* 9 (1892–93): 8; Jones, *Quest for Equality,* 216, 249.

64. Pauline Angell, "Julius Rosenwald," *AJYB* 34 (1932): 160–61. Adler, "Louis Marshall," in *Louis Marshall, A Biographical Sketch by Cyrus Adler* (New York, 1931), 65. For other examples of individual or organizational Jewish antiracism, see Weiss, "Long-Distance Runners," 135; 142.

65. *Forward* quoted in Diner, *Almost Promised Land,* 38, 43, 77; *Tageblatt,* July 31, 1917. On the Chicago press, see Grossman, *Land of Hope,* 63; cites translations of 1912, 1917, 1919 articles, 322 n. 5. On the English-language Jewish press, e.g., *American Israelite* 69 (May 11, 1922): 3; regarding the antilynching bill, see Diner, 96–100. Diner offers comprehensive examination of these issues.

66. On Hostess House (1917), see Salem, "NACW," 210; Weisenfeld, *African American Women,* 140. On Chicago, see Rogow, *Another Meeting,* 186.

67. NCJW and NCJ Juniors, "Social Betterment through Legislation," n.d., and "Resolutions: Social Legislation," May 1943, list resolutions, NCJW:142. The list dates the anti-lynching resolution as 1935; Henry Feingold, *A Time for Searching* (Baltimore, 1992), 45–46, reports NCJW lobbying for anti-lynching laws by 1923. Possibly local chapters acted in advance of the national.

68. Ford, *A-S and the Struggle for Democracy,* pamphlet, National Council of Jewish Communists (New York, 1939), 19, 8. Even if inflated, this number suggests the attraction of the left for Jews. AJCongress claimed 400,000 members in 1933. Also see Whitfield, "Bourgeois," 163–64; Whitaker Chambers, *Witness* (Chicago, 1952), 204–5. For leftist and union organizing among African Americans, see, e.g., Frank Adams, *Unearthing Seeds of Fire* (Winston-Salem, N.C., 1975); James Allen and Philip Foner, eds., *American Communism and Black Americans: A Documentary History* (Philadelphia, 1987); Anthony Dunbar, *Against the Grain* (Charlottesville, Va., 1981); John Egerton, *Speak Now against the Day* (Chapel Hill, N.C., 1995); Philip Foner, *American Socialism and Black Americans* (Westport, Conn., 1977); Michael Honey, *Southern Labor and Black Civil Rights* (Urbana, Ill., 1983); Robin Kelley, *Hammer and Hoe* (Chapel Hill, N.C., 1990), esp., 48; William Maxwell, *New Negro, Old Left* (New York, 1999); Mark Naison, *Communists in Harlem during the Depression* (Urbana, Ill., 1983); Bruce Nelson, *Workers on the Waterfront* (Urbana, Ill., 1988); Nell Painter, *Narrative of Hosea Hudson* (Cambridge, Mass., 1979); Wilson Record, *The Negro and the American Communist Party* (Chapel Hill, N.C., 1951); Theodore Rosengarten, *All God's Dangers* (New York, 1974); Mark Solomon, *The Cry Was Unity* (Jackson, Miss., 1998); Patricia Sullivan, *Days of Hope* (Chapel Hill, N.C., 1996); Theodore Kornweibel Jr., *Seeing Red* (Bloomington, Ind., 1998).

69. On inclusive unions, see Nancy Green, *Ready-to-Wear and Ready-to-Work* (Durham, N.C., 1997), 224–26, 235–36; Sterling Spero and Abram Harris, *The Black Worker* (1931; repr., New York, 1974), 338, 341; Steven Fraser, *Labor Will Rule* (Ithaca, N.Y., 1991), 291. On racial bars in unions, see, e.g., Eric Arnesen, "Like Banquo's Ghost, It Will Not Down," *AHR* (December 1994): 1601–33. These workers believed self-interest lay in white supremacy.

70. *Defender,* February 11, 1928; *Messenger* 2 (July 1919), 6.

71. Lewis, "Shortcuts to the Mainstream: Afro-American and Jewish Notables in the 1920s and 1930s," in *Jews in Black Perspectives*, ed. Joseph R. Washington (Rutherford, N.J., 1984), 84.

72. On Hillquit, see Murray Friedman, *What Went Wrong?* 84. White to Joel Spingarn, October 26, 1928, quoted in Diner, *Almost Promised Land*, 126. On Rosenwald, see Weiss, "Long-Distance Runners," 140–41.

73. Rosenwald quoted in Weiss, "Long-Distance Runners," 139. Himmilfarb quoted in Jonathan Reider, *Canarsie* (Cambridge, Mass., 1985) 48.

74. Washington quoted in Weiss, "Long-Distance Runners," 126; "Prejudice Minus Discrimination," *New York Age*, January 28, 1915.

75. Early papers of the ADL, AJCongress, AJC, NCJW, NAACP, and NCNW reveal virtually no sustained discussion of problems facing the other. On the size and weakness of the organizations, see, e.g., Arnold Forster, *Square One* (New York, 1988); Du Bois, *Autobiography of W.E.B. Du Bois* (New York, 1968); B. Joyce Ross, *J. E. Spingarn and the Rise of the NAACP* (New York, 1972); Shad Polier, "Law and Social Action," *AJCW* 17 (November 27, 1950): 3; Forster, ADL, interview with author, August 13, 1993, New York, N.Y.

76. On racism and A-S, see, e.g., Eleanor Wolf, Vin Loving, and Donald Marsh, *Negro-Jewish Relationships*, pamphlet (Wayne State Studies in Intergroup Conflicts in Detroit #1, 1944), 7, AJC IVF:NJR; Wolf, Loving, and Marsh, "Some Aspects of Negro-Jewish Relationships in Detroit, Michigan," Part 1, 1943, ADL Y1944:NRP; L. D. Reddick, "A-S among Negroes," *NQ* (Summer 1942): 113–17; Elmo Roper, "The Fortune Survey," *Fortune* (November 1942 and October 1947); H. L. Lurie, "Introductory Report on the Study Project of NJR," December 9, 1943, 1, AJC VF:NJR:AJC 1938–1969, and ADL Y1943:NRP; Laurence Thomas, "The Matrices of Malevolent Ideologies," *Social Identities* 2, no. 1 (February 1996): 107–33.

77. See, e.g., Morawska, *Insecure Prosperity*, 90–91; Sorin, *Building*, 5; Whitfield, "Commercial," 353–54; Louis Schmeir, "A Jewish Peddler and His Black Customers Look at Each Other," *AJH* 73 (September 1983): 39–55; Suberman, *Jew Store*.

78. ADL Y:NRP and AJC VF:A-S and IVF:NJR contain examples from around the country. Also see Reddick, "A-S," 116; Wolf, Loving, and Marsh, "Aspects"; Kenneth Clark, "A Positive Transition," *ADL Bulletin*, December 1957, 6. On the South, see, e.g., Golden, "Jews of the South"; Greenberg, "The Southern Jewish Community and the Struggle for Civil Rights," in *African Americans and Jews in the Twentieth Century*, ed. V. P. Franklin et al. (Columbia, Mo., 1998), 123–64. See also chaps. 3 and 4 below.

CHAPTER TWO
Of Our Economic Strivings

1. Literature on Depression-era African Americans includes national studies: Harvard Sitkoff, *A New Deal for Blacks* (New York, 1978); Nancy Weiss, *Farewell to the Party of Lincoln* (Princeton, N.J., 1983); Kirby, *Black Americans in the Roosevelt Era*; Myrdal, *American Dilemma* (condensed in Arnold Rose, *The*

Negro In America [New York, 1944]); Bernard Sternsher, ed., *The Negro in Depression and War* (Chicago, 1969); Raymond Wolters, *Negroes and the Great Depression* (Westport, Conn., 1970); Melvyn Dubofsky and Stephen Burwood, eds., *Women and Minorities during the Great Depression* (New York, 1990). For local studies, see Dominic Capeci Jr., *The Harlem Riot of 1943* (Philadelphia, 1977) and *Race Relations in Wartime Detroit* (Philadelphia, 1984); Drake and Cayton, *Black Metropolis*; Egerton, *Speak Now Against the Day*; Nancy Grant, *TVA and Black Americans* (Philadelphia, 1990); Greenberg, *"Or Does It Explode?"*; Kelley, *Hammer and Hoe*; Naison, *Communists in Harlem during the Depression*; Painter, *Narrative of Hosea Hudson*; Rosengarten, *All God's Dangers*; Patricia Sullivan, *Days of Hope* (Chapel Hill, N.C., 1996). Even black self-help rhetoric invoked Jews, praising their accumulation of power and wealth to benefit their own community. For an example, see Mark Solomon, *Red and Black* (New York, 1988), 583–84.

2. Sorin, *Tradition Transformed*, 167; Feingold, *Searching*, 148. On Jews in the Depression see, e.g., Beth Wenger, *New York Jews and the Great Depression* (New Haven, Conn., 1996); Neil Cowan and Ruth Cowan, *Our Parents' Lives* (New York, 1989); Moore, *At Home in America*. The Depression's differing impact on the two communities is reflected in the imbalance in attention it receives. Feingold's bibliographic essay does not even contain a section on the Depression per se.

3. See, e.g., Charles Hamilton, *Adam Clayton Powell, Jr.* (New York, 1991). On church activism see Ottley and Weatherby, *Negro in New York* 290–91; Mays and Nicholson, *Negro's Church*, 9, 279–88.

4. Feingold, *Searching*, 149–50; Wenger, *New York Jews*, chap. 6.

5. Feingold, *Searching*, 219.

6. Cited in Weiss, *Farewell*, 155.

7. On the NCNW, see Tracey Fitzgerald, *The NCNW and the Feminist Movement 1935–1975* (Washington, D.C., 1985). The NNC quotations come from the call to form the NNC, 1935, cited in *Black Protest*, ed. Joanne Grant (New York, 1968), 243. No book-length study of the NNC exists, but there are several dissertations, including Hilmar Jensen, "The Rise of an African American Left" (Cornell University, 1997); Cicero Hughes, "Toward a Black United Front" (Ohio University, 1982); John Streater Jr., "The NNC, 1936–1947" (University of Cincinnati, 1981). Also see Lawrence Wittner, "The NNC: A Reassessment," *AQ* 22, no. 4 (Winter 1970): 883–901.

8. Feingold, *Searching*, 221–23; Whitfield, "Bourgeois," 164–65; Wenger, *New York Jews*, chap. 5. On New Deal liberalism, see, e.g., Sidney Milkis and Jerome Mileur, eds., *The New Deal and the Triumph of Liberalism* (Amherst, Mass., 2002); Gary Gerstle and Steve Fraser, eds., *Rise and Fall of the New Deal Order* (Princeton, N.J., 1989); William Chafe, ed., *The Achievement of American Liberalism* (New York, 2003).

9. Wilkins, *Standing Fast* (New York, 1994), 210, referring to the period around 1950.

10. On blacks in the Democratic Party, see Weiss, *Farewell*; on liberalism and Jews see Feingold, *Searching*, 220; Whitfield, "Bourgeois," 164–65; Moses Rischin, "The Jews and the Liberal Tradition in America," *AJHQ* (September

1961): 4–29; Benjamin Halpern, "The Roots of American Jewish Liberalism," *AJHQ* (December 1976): 190–215; Liebman, *Jews and the Left*; Moore, *At Home in America*, 200–230; Marc Dollinger, *Quest for Inclusion*; Lloyd Gartner, "The Midpassage of American Jewry," in *The American Jewish Experience*, 2nd ed., ed. Jonathan Sarna (New York, 1997), 258–67; Leonard Dinnerstein, "Jews in the New Deal," *AJH* 72 (June 1983): 461–76; Rieder, *Canarsie*, 48–51; Wenger, *New York Jews*, chap. 5.

11. The JLC bibliography is limited; see Arieh Liebowitz and Gail Malmogren, eds, *The Papers of the JLC* (New York, 1993). There is disagreement regarding the scope, effectiveness, and motivation of JLC antibias efforts; the most prominent critic is Herbert Hill; see, e.g., "Black-Jewish Conflict in the Labor Context."

12. See Dan Carter, *Scottsboro* (Baton Rouge, La., 1969); James Goodman, *Stories of Scottsboro* (New York, 1994). Goodman cites "Jew money" from trial transcript, 143. The NAACP and ILD fought over control of the case. See chap. 5, below.

13. See, e.g., Friedman, *What Went Wrong?* 94; Diner, *Almost Promised Land*, 80–81; Jacob Weinstein, "Behind the Harlem Riots," *Jewish Frontier* (May 1935), C, AJC IVF:NJR:NYC.

14. See "NAACP Publicity Moves," n.d. [September 1932?], 2; White to Will Alexander, September 20, 1932, both NAACP IC219. See also, NAACP, *The Lynching of Claude Neal* (NAACP, 1934); Paul Gilje, *Rioting in America* (Bloomington, Ind., 1996), 153–54.

15. Brundage, *Lynching in the New South* (Urbana, Ill., 1993), 245, 249.

16. For NAACP strategies, see "Private Attorneys-General: Group Action in the Fight for CL," *Yale Law Journal* 58 (March 1949): 584; Tushnet, *NAACP's Legal Strategy*, esp. 10–11. On challenges, see B. Joyce Ross, *J. E. Spingarn*, chaps. 6–8; Sitkoff (*New Deal for Blacks*, 249–58) does see change within the NAACP. There were complex reasons for Du Bois's resignation.

17. Forster, *Square One*, 43.

18. AJCong GC, April 6, 1937, 4, AJCong box GB 1935–38.

19. Fineberg, interview by Isaiah Terman, January 30, 1974, 54, AJC OH. AJCongress, "Development and Work of the AJCongress," AJCongress *Courier* 1, no. 1 (April 21, 1933): 15. See also ADL *Bulletin*, November 15, 1938, 3, ADL Y1938:Literature.

20. ADL, EC, August 25, 1941, 1, ADL WB178. Note the controversy between the ADL and the more public AJCongress. See also, regarding the New York State Employment Service, ADL, AC, April 28, 1941, 2–3, ADL WB178.

21. Gutstadt to Finder, September 27, 1937, ADL Y1937:Investigations.

22. Finder to Milton Grunauer, August 11, 1937; Gutstadt to Finder, November 19, 1937. See also Finder to Ben G., August 3, 1937; Finder to "Sir and Brother," August 4, 1937; Gutstadt to Finder, June 24, 1937, all ADL Y1937:MP; Epstein to NBC, August 27, 1941, ADL Y1941:National Broadcasters; Gutstadt to Finder, October 15, 1937, ADL Y1937: Investigations; Philip Chasin to Finder, March 8, 1940; Finder to Gutstadt, March 15, 1940, both ADL Y1940:Native Son. There are many more examples in MP, "Magazine and pamphlets," "Books, undesirable," and "Literature" Y files for 1937–42. Similar examples appear in

AJC and AJCongress records, e.g., "Anti-Jewish Materials in Christian Text Books," AJCongress *Courier* 1 (April 21, 1933): 16.

23. Finder to I. A. Davis, November 10, 1939; Horace Marston to David Robinson, September 25, 1939, both ADL Y1939:MP. Also see Gutstadt to "Friends," March 10, 1938, ADL Y1938:MP.

24. Williams to Epstein, March 31, 1941, ADL Y1941:books:undesirable; Finder to Frederick Jay, February 3, 1938, ADL Y1938:Magazines and pamphlets. See also E. T. Browne to "Sir" [ADL], n.d. [October 1937?], ADL Y1937:Investigations; Alvin Gardner to Finder, January 24, 1938; Finder to Gutstadt, January 24, 1938; Francis Wurzburg to Finder, January 26, 1938; Finder to Wurzburg, January 26, 1938, January 27, 1938; Miles G to Finder, January 27, 1938, all ADL Y1938:Magazines; ADL, *Bulletin*, November 15, 1938, 6–7; Philadelphia Anti-Defamation Council, "Report of Activities 1/1/39–8/30/39," 7, AJC VF:Community Files:Philadelphia.

25. White to Dodd, Mead and Co., October 28, 1932; H. Dodd to White, November 1, 1932, NAACP IC219. White persisted: see his letter of November 2, 1932. There are similar examples in NAACP IC217, 219, 220. See especially White to Hesseltine, September 27, 1937, regarding *Gone with the Wind*; reply October 8; Thelma Collier to NAACP, February 22, 1939; list of troubling books, n.d.; Charles Houston, manuscript review, 1933; Ira deAugustine Reid to White, February 2, 1935; Mrs. Callie Browne to James Weldon Johnson, September 13, 1933; White to Superintendent R. K. Smith, September 26, 1933. For investigations, see, e.g., "Report of Miss Ovington on Textbook Investigation by Mr. Reddick," April 11, 1938, NAACP IA18.

26. RWB [Robert Wellington Bagnall], Director of Branches, to Harper and Brothers, March 7, 1930; Eugene Reynal, Harper and Brothers, to Bagnall, March 10, 1930, both NAACP IC219. On promoting positive materials, see, e.g., "Books by and about Negroes Not Included in Bibliography on the Negro Published by the NYPL in February, 1930"; Ruth Raphael to White, July 24, 1930, both NAACP IC219; Robert Hass, Random House, to White, January 3, 1937; White to Alfred Knopf, January 25, 1937; White to Macmillan, February 17, 1937; White to Harcourt Brace, May 11, 1937; White to *Atlantic Monthly*, May 24, 1937; to *Harpers*, September 8, 1937; to Viking, September 10, 1937; White to Houston, Marshall, Wilkins, A. Spingarn, Charles Russell, Charles Thompson, Robert Vann, Ralph Bunche, James Weldon Johnson, Robert Weaver, Otto Klinberg, November 1, 1937; "Sterling" [Brown] to White, August 10, 1939; White to Mr. Selee, Longman's, Green and Co, December 5, 1939, all NAACP IC217.

27. Advertisement for *Prejudice* by Doris Benson, with the word "darkies" circled; White to M. Lee, Fortuny Publishers, June 24, 1939; reply (and agreement to change word): June 26, 1939, all NAACP IC217.

28. Golden, "No Opium in the Elevator," in *For 2¢ Plain* (New York, 1960), 75.

29. Fineberg, OH. "Self-interest" phrase supplied by interviewer. See also Finder to Jack Cohn, Columbia Pictures, December 27, 1939, ADL Y1939:MP; Philadelphia Anti-Defamation Council, 7.

30. Mallach, "Factors Contributing to A-S in Harlem," AJC report, June 11, 1941, 1, AJC VF NJR:NYC; Harry Schneiderman and Nathaniel Goodrich, February 20, 1941, "Report on Ownership of Property in Harlem Areas Where Negro

Population Is Densest," February 20, 1941, 2, AJC IVF:NJR:NYC:AJC. See also Marie Syrkin, "Anti-Semitic Drive in Harlem," *AJCW* 8, no. 35 (October 31, 1941): 7.

31. Wolf, Loving, and Marsh, "Aspects" (partially funded by NAACP and JCC); AEB [Berland] to REG [Gutstadt], September 1, 1943, Memorandum re "Jewish Merchants in Chicago's Negro Community," ADL Y1943:NRP; Hughes, "Poetry," *The Big Sea* (New York, 1940). See also Dan Dodson, [New York] Mayor's Committee on Unity, to Frank Trager, ADL, March 1, 1948, ADL Y1948:NRP.

32. On the desperation of Jewish merchants, see, e.g., Wenger, *New York Jews*, 99. On the tensions surrounding credit, see, e.g., Mollison to White, December 12, 1935, NAACP IIL7.

33. *Frontier*: Weinstein, "Harlem Riots," 3 [C]. On cheating see, e.g., Irving Horowitz, *Daydreams and Nightmares* (Jackson, Miss., 1990), 20.

34. Greenberg, *"Or Does It Explode?"* chap. 5; Gary Hunter, "Don't Buy from Where You Can't Work" (Ph.D. diss., University of Michigan, 1977); William Muraskin, "The Harlem Boycott of 1934 and Its Aftermath" (M.A. thesis, Columbia University, 1966); Melville Weiss, "Don't Buy Where You Can't Work" (M.A. thesis, Columbia University, 1941); Vere Johns (yes), George Schuyler (no), "To Boycott or Not to Boycott," *Crisis* 41, no. 9 (September 1934): 258–60, 274.

35. Epstein to Finder, Memo regarding "Situation in Harlem," November 14, 1939, ADL D1939: NUL. ADL files: NRP each year. After 1941 the files also contained ADL CR activities. AJC data in VF and IVF "NJR." By the late 1930s AJC minutes discussed little except threats to European Jewry. Kenneth Janken, *White* (New York, 2003), 212.

36. NAACP IC208. The "news" refers to Kristallnacht.

37. E.g., "A-S Among Negroes," editorial, *Crisis*, June 1938: 177; "The Heighth [*sic*] of Something," editorial, *Pittsburgh Courier*, August 27, 1938, 1; "Negroes and Jews," *Amsterdam News*, August 22, 1942; "Southern Exposure," *Chicago Defender*, December 15, 1956.

38. Mollison to White, December 12, 1935. Lurie, "Introductory Report," 2–4. See also White to Hastie, July 26, 1939.

39. ADL, "Memo on the Negro Situation: The Chandler Owen Project," n.d. [1941?], ADL Y1941:NRP. See also Lurie, "Introductory Report" 2–4; AJC, "The Truth about Baltimore," report, January 1949, 36–38, AJC Department of Scientific Research, IVF:PR and Reports.

40. Data from Wolf, Loving, and Marsh, "Aspects."

41. Ibid. Emphasis theirs. Similar findings for domestic workers in Jewish and white gentile homes.

42. Ibid., 7. Emphasis theirs.

43. Bearden, handwritten speech fragment, n.d. [1942?], Bearden, box 1; Reddick, "A-S," 116. See also Murphy to White, memorandum to "Mr. White (for the Committee Studying A-S in Harlem)," September 30, 1939, NAACP IC277. Many Jews, especially those on the left, made similar arguments. See, e.g., Weinstein, "Harlem Riots," 3. Whitfield finds anecdotal evidence southern blacks believed Jews would treat them better ("Commercial," 354).

44. ADL Y1938:Magazines and pamphlets.

45. McCallister, "Memorandum of Proposed Study of Southern A-S," August 8, 1938, 1; NAACP to AJC: Brendan Sexton, WDL, to Morris Waldman, AJC, June 10, 1938. Also see McCallister, "General Observations," Report, n.d. [1938]; McCallister, "Report on Survey of A-S in the South," 1939. All NAACP IH11.

46. White to Earl Dickerson, June 25, 1938; reply, July 5, 1938; reply, July 14, 1938 (quotation), NAACP IC208. See also "League Names 5-Man Board to Study A-S in the South Side Area," *Defender* June 25, 1938, NAACP IC208; A. L. Foster to Benjamin Epstein, November 10, 1947, ADL Y1947:NRP.

47. "A Word to Dr. Preston Bradley," *Dynamite*, May 21, 1938, 1. Capitals in original. ADL, response: ADL *Bulletin*, November 15, 1938, 2.

48. Syrkin, "Anti-Semitic Drive," 6–7; L. Vogelman, "Complaints of Negroes against Jews," *Forward*, ADL copy, with "?," in ADL D1939:Negroes. See also Marston to Gutstadt, August 15, 1940, ADL YD1940:NUL (regarding Pittsburgh); Greenfield to Marston, August 9, 1940, ADL YD1940:NRP (Harlem).

49. "Heighth." It didn't help that the editorial also called Jews "Shylocks" and claimed "Jewish shopkeepers suck out the lifeblood of [local] Negroes." See also Houston to Ovrum Tapper, December 5, 1938; White to Claude McKay, December 23, 1938, both NAACP IC208.

50. White to Mrs. David Alter, October 9, 1940, NAACP IIA325; Houston to Tapper, December 5, 1938; editorial, *Amsterdam News*, August 27, 1938, cited in James Ford, *A-S and the Struggle for Equality*, pamphlet, National Council of Jewish Communists (New York, 1939), 4. See also Morel Fuchs to Forster, memorandum "Re: A-S in Harlem," July 26, 1943; Sidman to Max Kroloff, September 1, 1943, "Interview for Negro Analysis," both ADL Y1943:NRP; Dickerson to White, July 5, 1938, NAACP IC208.

51. Lurie, "Introductory Report," 2–4. See also Maurice Rosenblatt to B.R.E. (Epstein), memo, "Re: Harlem Situation, Report to A.D.L. from M. R., April 23, 1939," 3, NAACP IC277; "Complaints of the Negroes and A-S in Harlem," *Jewish Morning Journal*, October 30, 1939, from AJC "Jewish Press and the Jewish-Negro Problem,"12, AJC VF:NJR.

52. Dan Gardner, "Jews in the South Must Stop Practices of Discriminating [against] Negroes in Stores," *Carolina* [NC] *Times*, May 28, 1943, 4. Barber, 1939 interview, in *First-Person America*, ed. Ann Banks (New York, 1980), 254–57. All *sic*.

53. AEB to REG, memo. See also Rosenblatt to BRE, "Harlem."

54. Mallach, "Factors," 1.

55. The story appeared in Wilkins's syndicated "Watchtower" column in 1941. *In Fact* 4 (November 3, 1941) quotes the store memo. Both C, ADL Y1941:NRP.

56. Finder to Irving Maxon, New York City attorney, November 7, 1941; Berland to Finder, memo re "Article by RW (NY Amst Star)," September 12, 1941. Also see David Sullivan, *NY Amsterdam Star News* to Louis Fabricant, August 25, 1941; reply, September[?] 2, 1941; Finder to Fabricant, September 9, 1941; Irving Maxon to ADL, November 11, 1941. All in ADL Y1941:NRP.

57. White to Ridder, November 29, 1938, NAACP IC208.

58. Gutstadt to Paul Richman, August 19 [10?], 1941; AJC, "Baltimore," 37. A similar defensiveness can be seen in Finder to Nathan Kaufman, October 30, 1942, ADL Y1942:NRP; Kroloff to Finder, December 6, 1941; Finder to Maxon, "Analysis of the Chandler-Owen Project," n.d. [1941?], both ADL Y1941:NRP; AJC, "Jewish Contributions to Negro Welfare," May 14, 1942, ADL Y1942:NRP; Lawrence Goldsmith, "Report of the [ADL] Committee on Inter-Racial Relations," July 7, 1943, ADL Y1943:NRP; J. Harold Saks to Nissen Gross, September 6, 1945, ADL Y1945:NRP. Some blacks acknowledged an imbalance between exploitation and targeting: e.g., George Schuyler, cited in Stanley Jacobs to ADL Staff, RO, CRCs, "Negro Press—Memo #2," April 17, 1942, 4, ADL Y1942:NRP; Reddick, "A-S," 115–17. The ADL occasionally intervened with Jewish owners: e.g., Finder to Louis Fabricant, September 9, 1941, ADL Y1941:NRP; Alex Miller to Lou Novins, August 16, 1945, ADL Y1945:NRP; Finder to Robinson, July 15, 1940, ADL YD1940:Nation; Gutstadt to Harold Cowin, February 19, 1942, ADL Y1942:NRP; see also below and chap. 3.

59. Cited in Jacobs, "Negro Press," 5.

60. George [Murphy] to White, memorandum "Re: Confidential Reports on A-S in Harlem," July 9, 1939, 1, NAACP IC277.

61. White to Houston, December 5, 1938 and December 7, 1938. See also White to Tapper, November 22, 1938; reply November 30, 1938; reply December 5, 1938; Tapper to Houston, December 2, 1938; reply December 5, 1938; Houston to White, November 21, 1938; White to Dickerson, July 14, 1938 and November 30, 1938; William Patterson, *Midwest Daily Record*, to Ira Latimer, Chicago CL Committee, July 11, 1938; reply, n.d.; White to Miss Randolph, July 15, 1938; White to McKay, December 23, 1938 [all but McKay described Chicago], all NAACP IC208; White to Ted Poston, September 15, 1939; White to Hastie, July 26, 1939, both NAACP IC277; White to Frank Crosswaith, December 2, 1941, NAACP IIA325.

62. Isadore Zack to Sidney Sayles, December 10, 1952, ADL Y1949–52:NRP.

63. AJC, "Contributions"; Rev. Ben Richardson, *This Is Our Common Destiny*, pamphlet, 1943, AJC IVF:NJR:Negroes; Vogelman, in *Forward*, October 27, 1939, from AJC, "Jewish Press," 6–7. See also Dingol in *Day*, September 24, 1939, "Jewish Press," 8.

64. Mollison to White, December 17, 1935, 2; Wright to White, December 30, 1935, NAACP IIL7. See also Weinstein, "Harlem Riots," 2.

65. "Julius Rosenwald," editorial, *Courier*, September 3, 1938. Protests regarded "Heighth."

66. Miller in *Defender*, April 20, 1935.

67. Twenty-eighth AM, NUL, February 8, 1939, 2, NUL 11:1.

68. Forster, *Square One*, 53. Emphasis his. This is corroborated in Epstein, NWD, 82–83, 87–88; ADL NC, 9/21–26/46, ADL WB176. It is also reminiscent of German-Jewish condescension toward eastern Europeans; e.g., Cohen, *Encounter with Emancipation*, 324 and passim.

69. Owen, ADL, "Memo on the Negro Situation," 4; White to Ridder, November 29, 1938. See also NUL draft fund-raising letter, in FC, June 18, 1940, 2, NUL 11:3.

70. A. N. Franzblau, "Objectives," n.d. [1930s], 2, AJC VF:A-S; ADL, *Bulletin*, November 15, 1938, 2. See also ADL EFC, March 3, 1941, 1, ADL WB178.

71. ADL, *Bulletin*, November 15, 1938, 3. There is no evidence of further action in the files.

72. On Hill see Epstein to Finder, April 2, 1940. The ADL did pursue contact: see Epstein to Hill, May 28, 1940; Robert Greenfield to Hill, May 31, 1940, all in ADL YD1940:NUL. See also Houston to Tapper, December 5, 1938; White to Poston, September 15, 1939; "Rosenwald," editorial, *Courier*.

73. Brown to White, December 16, 1935. See also Jas Gayle to White, December 20, 1935, both NAACP IIL7.

74. F. E. De Frantz to White, December 26, 1935. See also Schuyler to White, December 22, 1935 (regarding the South), both NAACP IIL7; McCallister, "Survey," 17–18, 54: McCallister, "Southern Conference for Human Welfare, Birmingham, Alabama, 11/20–23/38," 1, 3, NAACP IH11; White to MacNeal, December 16, 1935, NAACP IC208. Both positive and negative views from White's 1935 survey. On muted African American political activity, see, e.g., Richard Pierce, *Polite Protest* (Bloomington, Ind., 2005) regarding Indianapolis.

CHAPTER THREE
Wars and Rumors of Wars

1. A. N. Franzblau, "Objectives," 1. See also S. Andhil Fineberg, interview with Isaiah Terman, January 30, 1974, AJC OH, 47; ADL, *Bulletin*, November 16, 1938, 1, ADL Y1938:Literature.

2. See e.g., Walter White to Mayor LaGuardia, December 8, 1938, NAACP IC208; *Mass Meeting against Bigotry*, leaflet (for April 25, 1946); Bernard Harkavy, AJCongress, to NAACP, March 8, 1946, both NAACP IIA360.

3. Arnold Forster, interview with author, August 13, 1991; Lewis, "Shortcuts to the Mainstream," 91. Also see Diner, *Almost Promised Land*, 236–38, who suggests Jews embraced CR in part to demonstrate their own Americanness.

4. For increases in membership, see, e.g., Forster, *Square One*, 96; Rogow, *Another Meeting*, 173.

5. Richard Dalfiume, "The 'Forgotten Years' of the Negro Revolution," in Sternsher, *The Negro in Depression and War*, 306.

6. Forster, *Square One*, 40–42. Earlier, the AJC had resisted a public campaign for Leo Frank's defense: Oney, *And the Dead Shall Rise*, 346–48. For the quiet methods of the NAACP, see chap. 2. Harris et al. pressed for greater public activism and more emphasis on economic issues.

7. White, ROS, November 10, 1938, NAACP IA18, 1–4.

8. White to Lester Granger, December 3, 1943, NAACP IIA203. White, paraphrasing Granger.

9. NAACP, MMBD, October 13, 1942, 4, NAACP IIA134; White to Granger, December 3, 1943; "Memorandum for the N.A.A.C.P. Program," n.d. [1943], 2, NAACP IIA203. See Also NAACP, MMBD, September 14, 1942, 3, NAACP IIA134.

10. NCNW, "Report," November 18, 1944, NCJW WO:18. The conference, February 11, 1944, in Washington, D.C., included many women's organizations; see below. For other connections between groups, see NCJW, "Report of ED to EC," May 6, 1943, 3–4, NCJW:111.

11. Fineberg, OH, 55. See also Finder, "Memorandum Re: AJC-ADL joint meeting about NY Street Scene," July 23, 1940, esp. 1–2, ADL WB178.

12. Perlmutter, NWD, vol. 1, 45–50.

13. "The Difference between the Congress and the A.D.L.," editorial, *Jewish Post*, May 10, 1946. This incident occurred after the AJCongress established CLSA, but differences in style were visible earlier. See, e.g., ADL, EC, August 25, 1941, 1, ADL WB178.

14. AJC, *AJYB*, 1937–1938, 39 (1937), 76–77; Feingold, *Zion in America*, rev. ed. (New York, 1981), 282. Zionism, ironically, represented the opposite of the Jewish commitment to building alliances: a Jewish state was needed because Jews could not rely on others and had to "go it alone."

15. *AJYB*, 1937–1938, 76.

16. Siegel to Jeanetta Welch Brown, NCNW, April 26, 1944; reply May 4, 1944, NCNW 5:3. Siegel had already had contacts with the NCNW.

17. Sorin, *Tradition Transformed*, 190. AJC, *AJYB* 1937–1938, 78–79.

18. E.g., Lawrence Goldsmith to Finder, March 6, 1942, ADL Y1942:NRP.

19. Frankel to Richard Gutstadt, September 2, 1943, ADL Y1943:NRP; "Confidential Report from National Opinion Research Center: Trend of Semitic Question," March, 1944, 1, AJC IVF:Public Opinion Polls/NORC; Henry Pohly to Mr. [Arnold] Wallack, "Interracial Conference of the Council against Intolerance in America," September 27, 1943, ADL Y 1943:NRP. See also Louis Novins to Edward Meisler [illegible], June 2, 1943, ADL Y 1943:NRP.

20. Lurie, "Introductory Report," 10. Similar concerns voiced in the 1940s and 1950s offered different explanations. See below and chap. 4, as well as Taylor, *Forging*, 285 n. 67.

21. Lurie, "Introductory Report," 11. See also Gutstadt to Berland, Memo regarding "Jewish Merchants in Chicago's Negro Community," September 9, 1943, ADL Y1943:NRP; Frankel to Gutstadt, September 2, 1943.

22. Finder to Col. A. Ralph Steinberg, June 11, 1943, ADL Y1943:NRP.

23. Bernheim to Lurie, October 29, 1943, ADL Y1943:NRP; George [Murphy Jr.] to White, Memo "Re: Confidential Reports on A-S in Harlem," July 9, 1939, 5, NAACP IC277; "N.A.A.C.P. Program," 2.

24. Harap, "Anti-Negroism among Jews," *NQ* (Summer 1942); Miller to Lou Novins, Memo re "NJR," August 16, 1945, ADL Y1945:NRP. See also "Negroes and Jews," editorial, *Amsterdam News*, August 22, 1942; Miller to Abel Berland, July 12, 1946, ADL Y1946:NRP; Kelley, *Hammer and Hoe*, 88 (regarding Montgomery, Alabama). For more on southern Jews, see, e.g., Cheryl Greenberg, "The Southern Jewish Community," 123–65; Marc Dollinger, "'Hamans' and 'Torquemadas,' " *Quiet Voices*, ed. Marc Bauman and Berkley Kalin (Tuscaloosa, Ala., 1997), 67–94.

25. Silberman, "The Minority Problem," *HUC Monthly* (April, 1943): 21 and 6.

26. Gutstadt to Stanley Jacobs, June 28, 1943, ADL Y1943:NRP.

27. Richman to Finder, Memo re "Philip Randolph—Railway Porters' Brotherhood Union," September 3, 1942; Gutstadt to Finder, September 14, 1942. See also Stanley [Jacobs] to Finder, September 10, 1942; Finder to Richman, September 4, 1942; Abe Rosenfeld to Finder, July 22, 1942 (regarding Adam Powell); Lawrence Goldsmith to Finder, March 6, 1942 (regarding Algernon Black). All ADL Y1942:NRP.

28. Jacobs to ADL staff, RO, C.R.C., memo, "Negro Press," March 31, 1942, 2, ADL Y1942:NRP; Report or memo fragment, ADL, n.d. [1942], ADL Y1942:NRP. Dalfiume, "Forgotten Years," 302–3, finds black nationalist sympathy for the Axis, especially the Japanese. Also see Francis MacDonnell, *Insidious Foes* (New York, 1995).

29. This and other handbills in AJC IVF:A-S propaganda '30s–'40s. There was strong anti-Jewish sentiment throughout the 1930s and the war years (Dollinger, *Quest for Inclusion*, 61, 73).

30. The Memphis article was reported in *COUNTERATTACK*, National Committee to Combat A-S, newsletter, 1945, NAACP IIA325; "Harlems [*sic*] Jews vs. Negroes," *Crusader*, July 4, 1942, 5. Also see Abe Rosenfield to Finder, July 15, 1942, ADL Y1942:NRP. On monitoring, see, e.g., ADL, "QUOTES FROM THE COLORED ANTI-SEMITES IN HARLEM," n.d. [Fall 1941?]; Jacobs to ADL RO, C.R.C., Confidential memo, "Negro-Jewish Propaganda," June 12, 1942; Harold Cowin to Stanley Jacobson, May 27, 1942; reply June 2, 1942; Monroe Steinberg to Forster, memo re "Harlem street corner meeting," September 28, 1942, all ADL Y1942:NRP; M.R. [Maurice Rosenblatt], memo "In re anti-Semitic propaganda and sentiment among the Harlem Negroes," April 23, 1939, 2; Paul Saffron to NAACP, July 7, 1941, both NAACP IIA325; Memo, December 19, 1941; Forster to Finder, October 9 and 14, 1941; Forster to Gutstadt, October 17, 1941; anon. to Inspector Sutter, October 29, 1941; "Harlem Situation," October 7, 1941; Morel Fuchs, memo "Re: Frank Wolf," n.d.; Fuchs, "Report on Assignment #202," September 15, 1941; Goldsmith to Finder, memo re "Report of September 15, Assignment 202," September 19, 1941; Greenfield to Goldsmith, memo re Harlem situation, August 5, 1941, all ADL Y1941:NRP; Finder, "AJC-ADL"; Marie Syrkin, "Anti-Semitic Drive," 6–8; Goldsmith to Finder, 8/6/43, 1, ADL Y1943:NRP.

31. See, e.g., "REPORT ON THE ARTICLE IN THE PROPAGANDA SHEET 'THE HOUR' ENTITLED, 'PRO-AXIS PROPAGANDA IN HARLEM' ISSUE OF AUGUST 23RD, 1941 CONFIDENTIAL FOR MR. WALTER WHITE OF THE N.A.A.C.P.," September 11, 1941, NAACP IIA325; 1942 meeting regarding link between Nazism and A-S sponsored by NLC, JLC, BSCP, Council for Democracy, Friends of Democracy, Union for Democratic Action (see below): Frank Crosswaith and Rachel Corrothers to "Friends," November 28, 1941, NAACP IIA325; NLC et al. to "Friends," January 22, 1942; Jack [Baker?], to Cowin, February 9, 1942, both ADL Y1942:NRP; Arnold Johnson, Secretary, [Greater New York] Coordinating Committee for Employment, to Frank Karelsen Jr., May 5, 1942, ADL Y1942:NRP; White to Lewis Strauss, January 13, 1937; Ford, *A-S*, 3, 18; Dalfiume, "Forgotten Years," 302–3.

32. Steinberg to Harold Franklin, memo, "Factual Pamphlets for Harlem Situation," September 4, 1941, 1, ADL D1941:Negro. See also "Complaints of Negroes Against Jews," translation and summary of October 13, 1939 *Forward* article by ADL staffer, ADL D1939:Negroes; Lurie, "Introductory Report," 2; M.R.,

memo, 2, 3; Cowin to Finder, May 27, 1942; Syrkin, "Anti-Semitic Drive." On the nationalists, see "REPORT," 3, 5. The claim these were nationalists is further demonstrated by the speakers' dislike for black mainstream leaders and light-skinned blacks, e.g., "REPORT," 1; ADL "QUOTES."

33. Col Steinberg, NAC, April 28, 1941, 3, ADL WB178. See also Forster, *Square One*, 55–56. Many of these collaborations led to arrests.

34. Goldberg to Robinson, Zeisler, Coleman, [Benjamin?], [Bluestein?], Forster, October 15, 1942, re "Temple of Islam Raid," ADL Y1942:NRP. Thirty-two arrests resulted in convictions. The raid was described by the infiltrator (who was present during raid) in "Final Report on Temple of Islam Raids," September 20, 1942, ADL Y1942:NRP. There was criticism of the ADL, e.g., Arthur Garfield Hays, in Steinberg to Gutstadt, April 30, 1943, ADL Y1943:Misc.

35. Forster to K. P. Aldrich, June 17, 1941; Forster to Kroloff, June 27, 1941; Aldrich to Forster July 9, 1941. See also Ramsey Bloch [Black?], Third Asst. Postmaster General to Forster, June 27, 1941; Bloch [Black?] to Postmaster, Wichita, Kansas, June 27, 1941, all ADL Y1941:books, undesirable; ADL AC, July 8, 1940, ADL WB178 regarding the World's Fair bombing; Rabbi Theodore Lewis, "Rabbi Lashes Out at Obsolete Methods of Fighting Rising A-S," *Jewish Examiner*, May 17, 1946, AJCongress CF:racism, A-S. Elsewhere, the AJC, AJCongress, and other Jewish organizations defended the Nazis' right to free speech (Dollinger, *Quest for Inclusion*, 62, 69).

36. Lurie, "Introductory Report," 1.

37. Joseph Kleinfeld to Finder, memorandum "Re: 'Mr. Smith Goes to Washington,'" October 26, 1939, ADL Y1939:MP.

38. See Greenberg, "Black and Jewish Responses to Japanese Internment," *JAEH* (Winter 1995): 3–37. Roger Daniels reminds us that Japanese Americans were incarcerated, not interned: "Words Do Matter," in *Nikkei in the Pacific Northwest*, ed. Louis Fiset and Gail Nomura (Seattle, 2005), 183–207.

39. Robert Marcus, ES, Joint Boycott Council, to White, July 7, 1938, NAACP IC208. The AJC and B'nai B'rith opposed the boycott, fearing repercussions against German Jews (Dollinger, *Quest for Inclusion*, 47).

40. Rev. J. Raymond Henderson, W. J. Brown, and J. B. Bullock, Bethesda Baptist Church, to N.A.A.C.P., November 22, 1938, NAACP IC208. Du Bois quoted in Werner Sollors, "W.E.B. Du Bois in Nazi Germany," *Chronicle of Higher Education*, November 12, 1999, B4. The Crusader News Agency provided news of interest to black readers. Its papers are in the Schomburg. See also R.W.G. Alexander, "Meeting of Committee of One Hundred In Defense of Human Rights," December 12, 1938, Newark, N.J., 1–2, NAACP IC208; Ray Krimm, "Foulkes Defies Nazi Threat at Rally," *Newark Ledger*, December 13, 1938; Dollinger, *Quest for Inclusion*, 51 (black participation in 1934 AJCongress anti-Nazi rally); Jonathan Rosenberg, *How Far the Promised Land?* (Princeton, N.J., 2005).

41. Ames to White, telegram, November 17, 1938; Pickens, "Hitlerism's Challenge to Human Brotherhood," September 16, 1934, Pickens reel 27; NAACP, "NAACP SECRETARY DENOUNCES NAZI POGROMS," PR, November 18, [1938]. See also White to Ames, November 18, 1938; Charles Russell to White, December 14, 1938; White to William Robson, November 19, 1938; Max Yergin to White, November 25, 1938; reply, November 30, 1938; Roscoe Dunjee, "The Mob Pun-

ishes the Innocent," *Black Dispatch*, December 10, 1938; Inter-racial Committee of the District of Columbia, "Resolution," n.d. [1938], 1–2, all but Pickens NAACP IC208; Alexander, "Meeting of the Committee," 3–4; "Nazis, Negroes, Jews and Catholics," editorial, *Crisis* 42, no. 9 (September 1935): 273. Black communists made the same points: see, e.g., Ford, *A-S and Democracy*, 14, 17.

42. Jayne to White, November 25, 1938; reply, November 29, 1938; reply, December 2, 1938, all NAACP IC208.

43. Wilkins to White, memo, March 25, 1938; White to Hull, telegram, March 25, 1938, both NAACP IC208. Schuyler, "Abuses of Colored Citizens in U.S," *World-Telegram*, November 21, 1938. Many more in IC208.

44. "SEN. KING, SORRY FOR JEWS, URGED TO SUPPORT FED ANTI-LYNCH BILL," NAACP PR, November 18, [1938], NAACP IC208; Miller, "Race Prejudice in Germany and America," *Opportunity*, April, 1936, 102–5; Ford, *A-S and Democracy*, 17. See also White to Hon. William H. King, November 15, 1938; White to LaGuardia, December 8, 1938.

45. White to Roosevelt, September 14, 1940, NAACP IIA325.

46. Wilkins, "Watchtower," *Amsterdam News*, September 4, 1937; Draft letter, NUL FC, June 18, 1940, 2, NUL 11:3.

47. "N.A.A.C.P. Program," 1; Myron Harshaw, Transitads, Inc., to George Schuyler (ATA director), June 30, 1943, Schuyler papers, box 6, Schomburg. See also White to John Pew, Sun Shipbuilding and Drydock Co., June 1, 1942, ADL Y1942:NRP. Dozens of *Crisis* editorials made similar arguments.

48. Granger, speech at Wellesley Summer Institute, Briarcliff Junior College, Briarcliff Manor, N.Y., June 22, 1943, 3, NUL I:169. See also Eugene Knickle Jones, "The NUL in 1938," February 8, 1939, 5, NUL 11:1.

49. "N.A.A.C.P. Program," 1, 2.

50. [Baker?] to Forster, "Talk before [Merce?] Society," May 8, 1940, ADL YD1940:Negroes.

51. Finder to Thomas, September 20, 1943, ADL Y1943:NRP.

52. Bluestein to Gutstadt, May 20, [1942], ADL Y1942:NRP.

53. Gutstadt to ADL EC, February 10[?], 1941, ADL Y1941:NRP.

54. Gutstadt to Max Kroloff, November 4, 1941, ADL Y1941:NRP.

55. On the violence, see Gilje, *Rioting In America*, 156. The most serious riots were in Detroit (June 20–22) and Harlem (August 1). City and state unity committees (all founded 1943–45) with black and Jewish participation include Chicago (two), New Jersey, Minnesota, Cincinnati, Philadelphia, Denver, Columbus, New York City (two), Los Angeles, Seattle, Massachusetts, Pittsburgh, Illinois, Connecticut, Cleveland, Detroit (two), North Carolina, Texas, Rhode Island, Indianapolis, San Francisco. Also see ADL, "City and State Inter-racial and Good Will Commissions," June 1944, 2–5, ADL Y1944:NRP; Charles Collier Jr., Citywide Citizens' Committee on Harlem, to Finder, September 2, 1943, ADL Y1943:NRP; Jacobs to Gutstadt, June 24, 1943, ADL Y1943:NRP; AJCongress, CLSA, "Report of Activities 7–9/47," 2, NAACP IIA360.

56. Chicago Council against Racial and Religious Discrimination, "By-Laws." The City-Wide Citizens' Committee on Harlem and Council against Intolerance in America letterheads contain their names. CAI cooperated with AJC, AJCong, ADL, Women's Trade Union League, Sleeping Car Porters, NAACP, NUL, Harlem

YMCA, YWCA, and others: see, e.g., "Summary of Discussions at the Interracial Conference under the Auspices of the Council against Intolerance in America, 9/25, Hotel Edison, New York City"; John Becker to Finder, October 26, 1943; Wallack, memo re "Interracial Conference of the Council against Intolerance in America held at the Edison Hotel," September 29, 1943; Baker to Wallack, memo re "Interracial Conference," September 27, 1943; Henry Pohly to Wallack, "Interracial Conference"; Harold Schiff to Wallack, September 27, 1943, all ADL Y1943:NRP.

57. Wallack to President and ES, Jewish Community Council, Columbus, Ohio, September 8, 1943, ADL Y1943:NRP. Gutstadt to Finder, August 24, 1943, ADL Y1943:NRP.

58. Collier to Finder, September 2, 1943, ADL Y1943:NRP. On Indianapolis see Rabbi M. Goldblatt, Indianapolis, to CRC and ADL RO, memo re "Citizen's [sic] Council to promote better relations between the city's various racial and religious groups," August 13, 1943, ADL Y1943:NRP. On Chicago, see CCARRD PR, May 19, 1945, 3 ADL Chisub: 9.

59. CCARRD, PR, May 19, 1945, 1; Baker to Wallack, September 27, 1943, 2.

60. Otto Feldheim to White, April 22, 1940, NAACP IIA325.

61. Chairman, Jewish Anti-Defamation Council of Minnesota to Governor Harold Stassen, June 5, 1941, ADL Y1941:NRP. See also A. L. Foster to Epstein, November 10, 1947, ADL Y1947:NRP (Chicago UL); Jacobs to ADL RO, CRCs, May 15, 1942, "Negro Press—Memo #3," 3–4, ADL Y1942 (Chicago ADL).

62. On Oakland, see undated summary of 1942 ADL memos re black-Jewish relations, ADL Y1943. On the YWCA, see Jules Cohen (ADL) to Mortimer Brenner, Oscar Lewis, Rabbi Israel Levinthal, Finder, and George Hexter, July 26, 1943, ADL Y1943:NRP. On "recreation," see Milton [Chumauer?] to City Editor, PM, June 8, 1943, ADL Y1943:NRP. For more on race and YWCAs, see Weisenfeld, African American Women, esp. chap. 7.

63. Lurie, "Introductory Report," 10. For NCJW, see NCJW and NCJJuniors, National Committee on Legislation, "Social Betterment through Legislation," NCJW:142. According to Kenneth Janken, Jewish groups did provide "marginal" support to antilynching efforts (White, 212).

64. Beth Siegel to Wilkins, October 6, 1943, NAACP IIA325. For ADL, see Bluestein to Gutstadt, May 20, 1942.

65. White to Editor, Atlantic Monthly, August 15, 1941. Author was Louis Marshall's son, on NAACP's BD. See also White to James Marshall, August 7, 1941; reply August 14, 1941; reply August 15, 1941; White to Sidney Wallach, August 15, 1941. All NAACP IIA325.

66. In New York City, 43 percent of complaints alleged religious discrimination, 19 percent racial (Committee on Fair Employment Practice, First Report, 7/43–12/44 [Washington, D.C., 1945], 31, 37, 43, 118). Also see Lurie, "Introductory Report," 10. The AJCongress was most active in early black-Jewish FEPC coalitions. See, e.g., Malcolm MacLean, Chairman, President's Committee on FEP, "Prejudice and Fair Practice," AJCW 9, no. 20 (May 29, 1942): 5–8; J. X. Cohen, "A Denial of the President's Order," AJCW 10, no. 4 (January 22, 1943): 5–7.

67. On eradication of discrimination, see MacLean, "Prejudice and Fair Practice," 7–8. Perlman, "Anti-Discrimination Legislation," *AJCW*, 10, no. 7 (February 12, 1943): 9. On the wartime FEPC, see NCJW, "FEPC: Its Development and Trends," Report, n.d. [January 1944?], 2–3, NCJW:142. For the postwar period, see chap. 4. J. X. Cohen, *The Negro, the Jew and the FEPC*, pamphlet, 1944 (reprinted address to NAACP), 5, AJC VF:NJR:AJCongress. See also AJCongress, WD, "Resolution in Support of FEPC," June 2, 1944.

68. Bethune, transcript, National Planning Conference on Building Better Race Relations, February 22, 1944, Washington, D.C., 1, NCJW WO:4. See also Silberman, *A Certain People*, 21.

69. "The Klan is a threat today" included with ADL "Confidential memo re Anti-Semitic propaganda," 1941, AJC VF:A-S:ADL; Berman, AJCongress EC, transcript, December 11, 1949, 106, AJCongress box: "AEC, 1942–51." See also Siegel to Wilkins, October 6, 1943; Lester Guterman to NY ADL, Memo re Detroit riot, n.d. [June 22, 1943?], ADL Y1943:NRP; Gutstadt to Jacobs, June 28, 1943; Berland to Albert Kennedy, July 9, 1945, ADL Y1945:NRP.

70. "Timely Topics," *AJCW* 9, no. 31 (October 23, 1942): 3; Cohen, "Is This a White Man's War?" *AJCW* 10, no. 36 (December 17, 1943): 8–10, 14.

71. Silberman, *A Certain People*, 6; "ADL Vitally Interested in Welfare of the Negro Community," n.d. [1943], 1, ADL Y1943:NRP. See also Walter Plaut, "Question of the Month: The Negro-Jewish Problem," *Hebrew Union College Monthly* (April 1943), 8; Metropolitan Interfaith Committee, "Introduction, Discussion Outline on the Negro Problem," n.d. [December 18, 1945?], 3, NAACP IIA360.

72. Randolph, "Our Guest Column," American Press Associates, April 23, 1946, 1, 2, ADL Y1946:NRP.

73. Fauset, "A-S among Us," *Philadelphia Tribune*, August 19, 1944, AJC IVF:NJR:Negro. Pickens, "'Wolfing It' on Our Friends," July 8, 1935, article prepared for American Negro Press, Pickens, micro R996, reel 4, box 8; "The Danger of A-S," editorial, *Chicago Defender*, March 17, 1945; "The Way of Madness," *Opportunity* (October 1938), 292; "Jew Baiting Tactics Are Undemocratic," *Louisville Defender*, January 9, 1943.

74. White, statement for *Amsterdam News*, November 15, 1938; McKay, draft editorial [for unidentified journal], n.d. [December 23, 1938?], both NAACP IC208. Johnson quoted in Ford, *A-S*, 16. See also "NAZI POGROMS"; Yergin to White, November 25, 1938; White, "The Nazi Terror: My Reaction," November 27, 1938, NAACP IC208; White to Stephen Wise, telegram, August 30, 1943, NAACP IIA325; Randolph, rebuttal to "Indigestible Jew," reprinted in *COUNTERATTACK*; White, "Minority Problem," 22. See also Ibrahim Sundiata, *Brothers and Strangers* (Durham, N.C., 2003), 317–18.

75. Debrest, "Thou Shalt Not Defame," *Jewish Forum*, January 1941, C, NAACP IIA325; J. X. Cohen, *The Negro and A-S*, pamphlet, 1944, 9, AJC VF:NJR:AJCong; Plaut, Hughes (two articles, one title), "Question of the Month: The Negro-Jewish Problem," *HUC Monthly*, April 1943, 8, 9; White, Silberman (two articles, one title), "The Minority Problem from the Inside, Looking Out: A Frank Discussion of Negro A-S and Jewish Racism," *HUC Monthly*, April, 1943, 6–7, 21–22; Richardson, *Our Common Destiny*. See also Commission on Justice

and Peace of CCAR, "Justice for the Negro," February 8, 1942, AJC VF:NJR:Reform; NCJW, *Legislation Highlights 5*, no. 2 (November 1942), NCJW:142; ADL, "Vitally." On the *Amsterdam News*, see "Negroes and Jews." On the AJC, see "Contributions." On UNIA, see "IS THE UNIA ANTI-SEMITIC?" *Centralist Bulletin* 2, no. 9 (September 1944), UNIA Reel 2.

76. Weinstein, "Harlem Riots," 3; Ford, *A-S*, 19; Bronx Council, Jewish Peoples Committee, to NAACP, October 26, 1940, NAACP IIA325; Harap, "Anti-Negroism among Jews"; Reddick, "A-S"; Harap and Reddick, *Should Negroes and Jews Unite?* (New York, 1943). See also announcement, Frank Crosswaith speech for Dorchester Workman's Circle, 1938, in Yiddish and English, Crosswaith papers, box 1; Novins to Edward [Meisler?] June 2, 1948.

77. Steinberg to Finder, June 30, 1943, ADL Y1943:NRP. See also Novins to Jacobs, July 20, 1942, ADL Y1942:NRP.

78. Reddick, "A-S," 118–19.

79. Epstein to Charles Stelzle, March 7, 1940; Stelzle to A. Jackson, *Negro World Digest*, March 11, 1940, both ADL YD1940:Negroes; NAACP, "Resolutions Adopted at the War-Time Conference," July 12–16, 1944, NAACP IIA25. (More in NAACP IIA28.) On Johnson, see Verner [Cahnman?] to Vocational Service, B'nai B'rith, December 7, 1944, ADL Y1944:NRP.

80. Berland to Louis Sidman, memo re "Interviews for Negro Analysis," September 7, 1943, ADL Y1943:NRP.

81. AJCongress 1946 NC, panel, "The Struggle for Economic and Social Equality," May 30, 1946, 29–30, AJCongress box "NC 1946." Several rabbis contradicted him (30).

82. Earl Dickerson to White, July 5, 1938. NAACP, "Resolutions," 1944. Also see Arvarin Strickland, *History of the Chicago Urban League* (Columbia, Mo., 2001), 132–34.

83. White to Ridder, November 29, 1938, NAACP IC208. See also White to Crosswaith, December 2, 1941, NAACP IIA325.

84. Crosswaith and Rachael Corrothers to "Friends," November 28, 1941; NLC et al. to "Friends," January 22, 1942, JLC 2033:10. Also see "Statement Adopted by Conference," Crosswaith papers, box 1, bk. 3; Alfred Baker Lewis to "Friends," February 10, 1942, ADL Y1942:NRP. On the ADL, see Baker to Cowin, February 9, 1942.

85. Harold Franklin to Reddick, October 2, 1942, ADL Y1942:NRP.

86. "Agitation against the Jews in the Streets of Harlem,"*Forward*, October 18, 1939 (translated), ADL D1939:Negroes. See also Rosenblatt to B.R.E. [Epstein], memo, "Re: Harlem Situation, Report to A.D.L. from M.R.," April 23, 1939, 3, NAACP IC277.

87. Gutstadt to Cowin, February 19, 1942, ADL Y1942:NRP. See also Sherman to Gutstadt et al., memo re "Conditions in the South," April 23, 1946, 4, ADL Y1946:NRP.

88. Rosenblatt to B.R.E., 3; Jacobs to Novins, memo re "Chandler Owen Project," July 24, 1942, 2, ADL Y1941:NRP. For more on the project, see Jacobs to ADL RO, C.R.C., December 3, 1941, memo re "Chandler Owen Series," ADL Y1942:NRP; Jacobs to Berland, memo re "Negro activities Chandler Owens [*sic*] project," November 11, 1943; "Memo Of Negro Activities of National Office of

A.D.L.," n.d. [1943], both ADL Y1943:NRP; Gutstadt, "Analysis of the Chan-
dler Owen Project," n.d. [1941?], ADL Y1941:NRP. AJC, "Contributions." ADL,
"Vitally" (primarily on Chicago). Also see chap. 2; Wil Haygood, *King of the
Cats* (Boston, 1993), 79–80.

89. "Excerpt from Report of Meeting of National Legion of Mothers and
Women of America in Philadelphia, August 18, 1941"; Wallach to "Walter," September 3, 1941; reply September 6, 1941, both NAACP IIA360.

90. "Memo from Mr. White," n.d. [August 1939], NAACP IC277.

91. AJC, *He Practices Racial Tolerance*, pamphlet, 1944.

92. Granger, "Participation of Negroes in Radio," address, n.d. [1946], 7–8;
cover memo, J. Harold Saks to Frank Trager, October 15, 1946, ADL Y1946:NRP.
Granger does not cite religion. It is not certain the director was Jewish.

93. Finder to Louis Fabricant, September 9, 1941; Finder to Irving Maxon,
November 17, 1941, both ADL Y1941:NRP; Lurie, "Introductory Report," 6–
8. See also Franzblau, "Objectives," 2.

94. Jacobs to Cowin, June 2, 1942, ADL Y1942:NRP.

95. On mediation, see AEB [Berland] to MN[?]K, memo re "Pawnbrokers in
the Negro Community," April 13, 1944, ADL Y1944:NRP. On the chamber of
commerce, see Berland to Wallack, memo re "Negro Problem," November 4,
1943, ADL Y1943:NRP.

96. AEB to REG [Gutstadt], September 1, 1943, memo re "Jewish Merchants
in Chicago's Negro Community," ADL Y1943:NRP.

97. *Regarding SCA*, pamphlet, n.d. [1944?]; Berland to Harry Lyons, memo
re "SCA," November 9, 1944, ADL Y1944:NRP; "Industrial Program of SCA,"
report fragment, n.d. [1946], ADL Y1946:NRP; Berland to Epstein, November
12, 1947, ADL Y1947:NRP. SCA gives 1944 as its founding date but it apparently
predated that: see, e.g., ADL, "Vitally," 1–2; Maxwell Goldman to Trager, memo
re "SCA," September 26, 1949 (dates SCA from 1943), ADL Y1949–52:NRP.

98. AEB [Berland] to Trager, March 18, 1948. See also Stella Counselbaum to
Trager, March 18, 1948, memo re "Harry Englestein," both ADL Y1948:NRP.

99. Goldman to Trager, "SCA."

100. Stella Counselbaum to A A Rosen, July 16, 1952 (letter July 5); A A Rosen
to John Sengetacke, July 21, 1952; reply July 29, 1952; A A Rosen, memo re
"Chicago Defender," September 8, 1952 (Browning), all ADL Chisub 12.

101. White to William Hastie, July 26, 1939; White to [Thurgood] Marshall
and [George] Murphy, memo, September 21, 1939; White to Ted Poston, September 15, 1939; Hubert Delany to White, September 19, 1939; Granger to White,
September 19, 1939; Marshall to White, memo, October 12, 1939; White and
Walter Mendelsohn to Marshall, September 27, 1939; Murphy to White, memo
to "Mr. White (For the Committee Studying A-S in Harlem)," September30, 1939;
White to Wilkins, Marshall, and Murphy, memo, October 9, 1939; White to Marshall and Elmer Carter, December 4, 1939; NAACP PR, "YIDDISH PAPERS TELL
JEWS THEIR PROBLEM IS SAME AS NEGRO'S," December 8, 1939, all NAACP
IC277; White, ROS, October 5, 1939, 4, NAACP IA18; AJC, "The Jewish Press
and the Jewish-Negro Problem," November 6, 1939, AJC VF NJR:AJC 1938–
69; ADL, Untitled report on articles on black-Jewish relations in *Forward*, October 1939, ADL D1939:Negroes.

102. George [Murphy Jr.], "Confidential Reports," 1–2; White, ROS, October 1939, 4; NAACP PR, "YIDDISH"; Murphy, memo to "Mr. White," 1–2; Marshall: Marshall to Mr. White, "Memorandum," October 12, 1939, all NAACP IC277.

103. M. Danzis, untitled article, *The Day*, December 11, 1939, 1–2 (translation), NAACP IC277; L. Vogelman, "Negroes Complain About Jews" (ADL translation: "Complaints of Negroes against the Jews"), *Forward*, October [13], 1939, in AJC, "Jewish Press," 2–3. See also "Complaints of the Negroes and A-S in Harlem," October 30, 1939, 12; A. Glanz, "It Would Have Been a Great Misfortune," *Day*, October 29, 1939, in "Jewish Press," 9.

104. Arthur Alberts to Norton Belth, memo re "Harlem: Negro Grievances against Jews," October 17, 1939, 1; Belth to [Sidney] Wallach, memo re "Negro-Jewish Cooperation," October 17, 1939, both AJC IVF:NJR:NYC; Finder to Fagan, November 29, 1941; Goldsmith, "Report of CIRR," July 7, [1943?], ADL Y1943:NRP; CIRR, September 17, 1943, ADL Y1943:NRP. The Harlem Committee (later the CIRR) operated at least from the late 1930s. For ADL proposals, see Lawrence Goldsmith to Finder, March 6, 1942, May 28, 1942, August 6, 1943; Arnold Johnson to Forster, June 16, 1942; Goldsmith to Forster, June 26, 1942, all ADL Y1942:NRP. Tensions remained high: see Rosenblatt to Reeves, March 6, 1941; Jacobs, memo to ADL staff, RO, CRC, "Negro Press—Memo #2," April 17, 1942, 1, ADL Y1942:NRP. See also Rosenblatt to B.R.E., 3–4.

105. Finder to David Robinson, July 15, 1940; Epstein to S. Zlinkoff, September 24, 1940; Finder to Mr. Zeisler, February 1, 1941, ADL Y1941:NRP; Kramer, Hebrew Institute of University Heights, to "Friends," July 6, 1940, ADL Y1941:NRP. See also Carl Offord, "Slave Markets in the Bronx," *Nation*, June 29, 1940, 780–81; ADL AC, October 15, 1940, 3, ADL WB 178; Finder to Goldsmith, July 15, 1940. All but Zeisler and Kramer from ADL YD1940:Nation.

106. ADL EC, February 17, 1941, ADL WB178. They were later run by the city and New York State Employment Service. See Alberts to Belth (AJC), "Bronx Slave Market," October 17, 1939; Cara Cook and Bessie Grossman, CSCM, "NEWS FLASH! Job Agencies to Replace Bronx 'Slave Markets,'" n.d. [May 1941], both AJC IVF:NJR:NYC (also agency fliers); Minutes of Subcommittee, Committee on Street Corner Markets (CSCM), August 20, 1941, 1–2; Cook, Grossman, and Millicent Munn, "To Bronx Residents," n.d. [1941]; Finder to Fagan, November 29, 1941; Goldsmith to Finder, August 6, 1943, 1; ADL AC, October 15, 1941, 3, all ADL Y1941:NRP; Marvel Cook, "Hiring Hall Aimed at Slave Markets," *NYT*, April 27, 1941, 35; Gutstadt to EC, February 10[?], 1941; ADL EFC, March 3, 1941, all ADL WB178. For a similar situation in 1950 see I. Joel Komarow to Presidents and ADL Chapter Chairmen, memo, September 18, 1950, ADL Y1949–52:NRP.

107. Goldsmith to Wallack, report (3 parts): "Harlem Riots," 1; "First Day Survey of the Harlem Riots"; "Interviews in Harlem Area," August 6, 1943, ADL Y1943:NRP. For more on the riot, see Capeci, *Harlem Riot of 1943*; Harold Orlansky, "The Harlem Riot: A Study in Mass Frustration," *Social Analysis*, report #1, 1943; Greenberg, *"Or Does It Explode?"* chap. 8.

108. CIRR, August 5, 1943, ADL Y1943:NRP. CIRR, August 9, 1943.

109. Maurice Fagan to George Hexter et al., memo re "Dr. Mary Huff Diggs," June 10, 1942; Paul Richman to Forster, July 9, 1942; Holmes to Finder, July 24, 1940; all ADL Y1942:NRP; Harry Lyons, "Jewish-Negro Relationships in the Post War Period," 1943, 2, AJC VF:NJR:AJC 1938–69.

110. "Survey," report, n.d. [cover memo, Forster to Finder, July 20, 1943], ADL Y1943:NRP; "Interviews in Harlem Area," 2–3.

111. All meeting comments are from the transcript, CIRR, December 9, 1943, 1–5. Also see CIRR, November 22, 1943, ADL Y1943:NRP (code); Wallack to Goldsmith, September 10, 1943, ADL Y1943:NRP.

112. CIRR, August 9, 1943; September 14, 1943; September 17, 1943; November 22, 1943; Goldsmith to Archbishop Francis Spellman, September 28, 1943, ADL Y1943:NRP. On earlier ADL support for offices, see Goldsmith to Finder, March 6, 1942; Goldsmith to Wallack, "Riots," 3.

113. CIRR, December 2, 1943; untitled updates to CIRR, December 14, 1943, both ADL Y1943:NRP.

114. Minutes, "Special Meeting of EC of BBB of New York City," December 30, 1943, 1–7, ADL Y1944:NRP; Uptown Chamber of Commerce, "Tentative Program of the Committee for the Improvement of Race Relations," n.d. [November 1944]; "Proposed Program of the Expansion of the Activities of the UCC," n.d.; Harry Lyons to Martin Frank, July 12, 1944; Sachs to Lyons, November 18, 1944, all ADL Y1944:NRP.

115. ADL NC September 21–26, 1946, 19, ADL WB176; Lionel Bernstein to Trager, June 3, 1948; see also Saks to Sachs, February 4, 1948; Dan Dodson (ED) to Trager, March 1, 1948, all ADL Y1948:NRP; Bernstein to Saks, January 31, 1949, ADL Y1949–51:NRP. For more on the New York black-Jewish situation, see Roi Ottley, *New World A'Coming* (New York, 1943), chap. 10; James Baldwin, *Notes of a Native Son* (Boston, 1955), 66–72.

116. Local black coalitions also improved Harlem's employment situation by 1944, helping explain easing of complaints. See Greenberg, *"Or Does It Explode?"* 133–39.

117. Siegel to Bethune, July 7, 1941, NCNW:4:1; CIRR, November 22, 1943; White to William Hastie, July 26, 1939; White to Marshall and Carter, December 4, 1939.

CHAPTER FOUR
And Why Not Every Man?

1. Polier, "Law and Social Action," 3. On CLSA's disdain for community education methods, see Joseph Robison, "A Victory Over Discrimination," *AJCW* 18, no. 12 (March 26, 1951): 9. Also see "Private Attorneys-General," 589.

2. E.g., George Sanchez, "'What's Good for Boyle Heights Is Good for the Jews," *AQ* 56, no. 3 (September 2004): 633–62; Marshall Stevenson, "Points of Departure, Acts of Resolve" (Ph.D. diss., University of Michigan, 1988); Wendell Pritchett, *Brownsville, Brooklyn* (Chicago, 2002); Melissa Faye Greene, *The Temple Bombing* (Reading, Mass., 1996); Ray Mohl, *South of the South* (Gainesville, Fla., 2004); Greenberg, "Southern Jewish Community," and Joe Trotter Jr., "Afri-

can Americans, Jews, and the City," both in Franklin et al., *African Americans and Jews in the Twentieth Century*, 123–64, and 193–207. For the 1960s and beyond, see chap. 6.

3. For liberalism's pervasiveness see, e.g., Dore Schary, ADL NC Transcript, May 5, 1948, 26, ADL WB182; Louis Hartz, *The Liberal Tradition in America* (New York, 1955); Daniel Bell, *The End of Ideology* (New York, 1960); Arthur Schlesinger, *The Vital Center* (Boston, 1949); Samuel Lubell, *The Revolt of the Moderates* (New York, 1956). See also Gary Gerstle, "The Protean Character of American Liberalism," *AHR* 99, no. 4 (October 1994): 1043–73, and the introduction to this book.

4. Granger, "Commencement Address," Howard University, n.d. [1945?], 9–11, NUL 1:169. See also Schary, ADL CRC, May 5–8, 1948, 4, ADL WB176.

5. Frazier, *Negro in U.S.*, 681. See also Myrdal, *American Dilemma*, 927–30.

6. Polier, "Why Jews Must Fight for Minorities," AJCong PR, November 4, 1949, 5, Polier:14. See also Charles Liebman, *The Ambivalent American Jew* (Philadelphia, 1973), 136–59; Henry Feingold, "From Equality to Liberty," in *The Americanization of the Jews*, ed. Robert Seltzer and Norman Cohen (New York, 1995), 97–118.

7. Sidney Levine to Horace Marston, November 27, 1944; reply December 2, 1944, both ADL Y1944:NRP. The desire for a Jewish state was another check on assimilation, although not all Jews, or Jewish organizations, were Zionist.

8. Epstein, AR, ADL NC, May 14, 1949, 4. The pamphlet describing this is in ADL's 1947 AR, ADL library.

9. NUL, *Negro Churchmen Speak to White Churchmen*, pamphlet, 1944, 9, NUL SRO A:70. See also Polier, "Fight."

10. Edward Newman, "Philosophy Underlying the Socio-Legal Approach as a Technique in Dealing with Problems of Group Adjustment," memo of AJC staff discussion, March 25, 1947, 1, AJC IVF:CR-AJC. Emphasis theirs. See also "Statement on the Purposes, Structure and CL Interests of the AJC," September 17, 1953, NAACP IIA203.

11. See, e.g., Mary Dudziak, *Cold War Civil Rights* (Princeton, N.J., 2000).

12. See, e.g., Alexander Bloom, *Prodigal Sons* (New York, 1986); Russell Jacoby, *The Last Intellectuals* (New York, 1987); Neil Jumonville, *Critical Crossings* (Berkeley, Calif., 1991); Carol Polsgrove, *Divided Minds* (New York, 2001); Alan Wald, *New York Intellectuals* (Chapel Hill, N.C., 1987); Michael Staub, "Negroes Are Not Jews," *Radical History Review* 75 (Fall 1999), 3–27. Some, including Norman Podhoretz and Irving Kristol, would become the core of a neoconservative movement two decades later. Nonblack non-Jews like Reinhold Niebuhr and Arthur Schlesinger were also central players in these discussions.

13. Johnson, AJCong NC panel, "Safeguarding American Democracy," November 10, 1949, 16–17, AJCong box C&C.

14. Stampp, *The Peculiar Institution* (New York, 1956), vii–viii. Emphasis his. In a footnote Stampp observed he meant only to assert the absence of biological differences in emotion or intellectual ability. See also Robert Weaver, "Bucking the Color Line," *AJCW* 17, no. 31 (November 27, 1950): 23.

15. "Discrimination: Unresolved Problem of Democracy," *Legislation Highlights* 5, no. 2 (November 1942): 1, NCJW:142. See also NUL "Credo," Polier, "Law," 3; AJCongress, "Safeguarding," 7–10; Schary, NC, 18.

16. CJP, "Statement Issued by the Institute on Judaism and CR," April 17–18, 1948, pamphlet, AJC VF:CR and Jews; NUL, "Churchmen," 8. The CCAR was the Reform movement's rabbinical body.

17. Ruchames, "Parallels of Jewish and Negro History," *NHB* (December 1955), 63. See also Dollinger, *Quest for Inclusion*, 128.

18. Delany, AJCongress NC panel, "Integration: The Position of the Jewish Community in the South," April 13, 1956, transcript, 62, AJCongress box: NCs 1954–58. See also Doxey Wilkerson, *People's Voice*, to "B'nai Brith" [*sic*], October 1, 1946, ADL Y1946:NRP; Berman, AJCongress EC, December 11, 1949, 107, AJCongress box AC/EC 1946–50; Berland to Nathan Cohen, memo: "Race Problem in Kansas City," July 21, 1944, ADL Y1944:NRP; Forster to J. Harold Saks, April 30, 1946; A Philip Randolph, "Our Guest Column," American Press Associates (APA), April 23, 1946, 1, both ADL Y1946:NRP; Leonard Finder to Jacob Potofsky, Amalgamated Clothing Workers of America, August 14, 1942, ADL Y1942:Discrimination; Polier, "Fight," 2–3.

19. Toubin to Hyman Fliegel, *Bnai Zion Voice*, July 13, 1953, 1–3, NAACP IIA362. See also Berland to Albert Kennedy, National Federation of Settlements, July 9, 1945, ADL Y1945:NRP; Steinbrink fund-raising letter for NAACP, n.d., cover memo: "White to Mr. Wilkins and Mr. Moon," May 18, 1949, NAACP IIA363; White, "Equality Is Indivisible," *AJCW* 17, no. 31 (November 27, 1950): 6–7; Stephen Wise to Marshall, April 11, 1946, NAACP IIA360; Maslow, "Advancement of Community Relations Objectives through Law and Legislation," October 25, 1954, 4–7, NAACP IIA387.

20. ADL, *The Facts* (September 1954): 22–23; Miller to Lou Novins, "NJR," 2, August 16, 1945, ADL Y1945:NRP. See also ADL NEC, September 22–23, 1955, 11, ADL WB178.

21. Interview of Leon Bass by Pam Sporn and students for *Blacks and Jews*, Educational Video Center, 1992. For more on Black see Studs Terkel, *The Good War* (New York, 1984), 278–79. Both Bass and Black were also educators and community activists.

22. NAACP, "ROS December," 1, n.d. [1947], NAACP IIA145; Maslow to White, December 1, 1947, NAACP IIA360; "Congratulations to Dr. Bunche," editorial, *Crisis*, January 1948, 9; "Dr. Du Bois Criticizes Bunche," *California Eagle*, December 9, 1948, 1, 5. Also see Ben Keppel, *The Work of Democracy* (Cambridge, Mass., 1995): 32–33. On Du Bois and the Mideast, see Gerald Horne, *Black and Red* (Albany, N.Y., 1984), 283–84.

23. Herbert Wright, NAACP, to "Youth Leader," December 9, 1952; "Report on Initial Meetings," both NAACP IIE61.

24. White to Maslow, December 10, 1947, NAACP IIA360. On the UN and international concerns, see chap. 5; Carol Anderson, *Eyes Off the Prize* (New York, 2003); Brenda Gayle Plummer, *Rising Wind* (Chapel Hill, N.C., 1996); Dudziak, *Cold War*. On support for freedom struggles, see e.g., *Crisis* February 1948, March 1948, and December 1948, on Madgascar, Vietnam, and Indonesia; NUL, "The South African Question," PR, n.d. [4/53?].

25. Randolph, "Our Guest Column," 2; CJP, " . . [sic] To All the Inhabitants Thereof," Statement for Race Relations Sabbath, 1951, AJC VF:RR:CCAR. See also Edwin Embree, Rosenwald Fund, "All of Us," essay, n.d. [1946], 1–2, ADL Y1946:NRP.

26. Robinson to Gutstadt, June 27, 1944, ADL Y1944:NRP. How well outreach worked is another question; see below for NAACP's more skeptical assessment.

27. Minorities Workshop, PR, May 12, 1944; Wilkins to LaGuardia, telegram, April 27, 1944, NAACP IIA325; "Highlights of Conference on Interracial Cooperation," in "Pacific Coast Committee for American Principles and Fair Play," quoted in Roger Daniels, *Concentration Camps, North America* (Malabar, Fla., 1981), 158; Morton Grodzins, *Americans Betrayed* (Chicago 1949), 190. Socialist Party, NCJW also protested: "Mayor Protests Japanese in East," April 27, 1944, C; NAACP IIA325. For the JACL, see AJCongress, "Struggle for Economic and Social Equality," 9; "Survey of the Anti-Semitic Scene in 1946," *The Facts*, (April 1947), 25; ADL *Bulletin 5* (1948): 5. Black and Jewish groups joined with JACL for the first time partly because only then did JACL seek such activities. NCJW included other minorities earlier: see, e.g., "Discrimination," 1. For more on the NAACP, see Audrie Girdner and Anne Loftis, *The Great Betrayal* (New York, 1969), 412; JACL to Wilkins, May 17, 1948; Wilkins to Senator John Cooper, May 18, 1948, NAACP IIA325. See also Greg Robinson, *By Order of the President* (Cambridge, Mass., 2001).

28. Tajiri, "The Nisei Future," *Pacific Citizen*, April 22, 1943, reference provided by Greg Robinson. Alexander Miller to Leonard Schroeter, December 23, 1954, cited in Taylor, *Forging*, 285 n. 67. A similar fear might have motivated Philip Frankel's 1943 comment to the same effect (see chap. 3). See also "The Copy Desk," *Pacific Citizen*, November 13, 1943; "Stress JACL Must Work for All Minorities," *Pacific Citizen*, February 8, 1947. Robinson finds such concerns waning after 1950, as Japanese American attempts to integrate become more successful. If so, this provides an interesting contrast to Jews who, despite similar successes, remained far longer in the CR coalition. On multifaith coalitions, see, e.g., NCRAC Special Committee on Reassessment, "Advancement of Community Relations Objectives through Law and Legislation," December 11, 1954, 7, NAACP IIA387 (committee final report; same title as Maslow's initial report). See below for examples of broad-based coalitions.

29. Justine Wise Polier, AJCong NC, plenary session, transcript, November 9, 1949, 52, AJCong box C&C.

30. Polier, "Safeguarding," 8. Black and Jewish groups rejected arguments that CR struggles were counterproductive because they would provoke backlash. See, e.g., NCRAC, "Advancement," 4; Isadore Chein, "A Social Scientist's View of the Use of Law and Legislation for the Advancement of Community Relations Objectives" (delivered at meeting to write "Advancement" report, December 9–11, 1954), NAACP IIA387. Michael Klarman, "How *Brown* Changed Race Relations," *JAH* 81, no. 1(June 1994): 81–118, explores that backlash.

31. AJCong NAC, "Supreme Court Decision on Racial Segregation," Statement, May 22–23, 1954, AJCongress box: AC/EC 1951–54. ADL began filing amicus briefs in 1947: Jill Donnie Snyder and Eric Goodman, *Friend of the Court* (New York, 1983), 11. CLSA did so from its founding. By 1949 AJCongress had

nine full-time attorneys: "Attorneys-General," 589. CLSA had CR lawyers on staff, and directed action from its NO; NAACP, with branches staffed primarily by volunteers, generally hired lawyers for local cases, reserving only the most significant cases for its five staff attorneys. "Attorneys-General," 582–84. There were some differences also because of the tax-exempt status of Jewish organizations and the NUL. See, e.g., "Attorneys-General," 581, 589; ADL, AJC correspondence with NAACP re CR Mobilizations. More on strategy differences below.

32. AJCong, "Court"; NCRAC, "Advancement," 3.

33. See, e.g., NCRAC, "Advancement," 3; "Attorneys-General," 588. ADL, NCJW, NUL, and AJC were the most frequent promoters of such campaigns. See below.

34. AJCongress, "Safeguarding," 28. Efforts are chronicled in the NAACP files, especially IIA351, 353, 186; Chicago UL WD, "Because We Believe," n.d. [1946], NUL SRO: A78; AJCong, "CLSA Monthly Report June 22, 1946–July 19, 1946," NAACP IIA360.

35. NCPF, PR, March 28, 1947, NUL 4:10 lists members. Allan Knight Chalmers and Randolph cochaired. Minkoff quoted in "Minutes of Informal Dinner Meeting to Consider the Possibility of Establishing a National Confederation of Human Relations Agencies," December 27, 1951, 6, ADL Y1949–52 Pro-org:NCRAC. Also see Maslow, "The Fight for Job Equality," *AJCW* 17, no. 31(November 27, 1950): 13–15; AJCongress, AC, "Resolution on FEPC," May 13–14, 1950, AJCongress box: A&E 1946–50; "Catalog of Mimeographed and Printed Materials," June 15, 1945–December 31, 1949; "Discrimination in Employment," AJCongress library; AJCongress, Joint A&E, January 24, 1954, 3–4, AJCongress box: A&E 1953–56; AJCongress, "Equality," 8–12, 68–69; "Safeguarding," 11–21; AJC DAC, January 18, 1949, 3; February 28, 1950, 1–2; March 28, 1–2; AJC, "PR," 1946–52, all AJC library; CRC, May 25, 1950, ADL Y1949–52 Pro-org:CRC; NAACP, "Reports from Branches on Visits to Congressmen and Senators Reported at January 16 Session of the CR Mobilization in Washington, D.C," NAACP IIA186; MMBD, January 2, 1951, 9–10. One indication of the challenge: 85 percent of white workers surveyed in 1944 opposed equal employment laws; a majority opposed working alongside African Americans. NORC, "The Color Line in Industry," 2–6 (black views); 7–11 (white), AJC IVF:Negroes: employment.

36. Cohen, "The People vs. Discrimination," *Commentary* 1, no. 5 (March 1946): 18.

37. NAACP, MMBD, June 11, 1945, 2–3, NAACP IIA135. Slaughter believed "creed" extended protection to communists.

38. Many liberals believed the Progressive Party was a communist tool. See, e.g., "The Election—And After," *Crisis* (December 1948), 361. Earlier full employment bills received strong black and Jewish support.

39. Wechsler and Wechsler, "The Road Ahead for CR," *Commentary* (October 1948), 301–2, 304. Also see Eddie Cantor, "One-Track Liberals" for APA, May 25, 1946, ADL Y1946:NRP.

40. Epstein, "How We Work Together: A Critique," NCRAC plenum, n.d. [1949?], NAACP IIA386; Dorothy Nathan, AJC, to Oscar [Cohen?], ADL, July

6, 1950, ADL Y1949–52. In 1952 the AJC withdrew from NCRAC (AJC DAC, October 8, 1952, 5). See also Lewis, "Rabbi Lashes Out."

41. Wilkins to Maslow, July 14, 1950; reply, July 18, 1950, NAACP IIA361.

42. AJCongress, "Safeguarding," 45–46, 48–51, 52, 62.

43. Ibid., 68–72, 76–84.

44. AEB (Berland) to BG, memo, "Meeting of the Civic Service Committee," August 6, 1947, ADL Y1947:NRP; ADL, "Freedom of Speech: Censorship . . . Picketing of MPs," n.d. [May 1949?], ADL WB42. On the moderate stance of white liberals, see Walter Jackson, "White Liberal Intellectuals, CR and Gradualism, 1954–1960," in *The Making of Martin Luther King and the CR Movement*, ed. Brian Ward and A.J. Badger (London, 1995); Steven Gillon, *Politics and Vision* (New York, 1987). Some Jews had even opposed the anti-Nazi boycotts. For black liberal doubts, see, e.g., NUL EB, November 9, 1943, 3–4, NUL 11:5, and below.

45. NUL, "Portland Oregon," n.d. [1944], 4, NUL 3:2.

46. George Houser and Bayard Rustin, "Journey of Reconciliation," report, n.d. [1947]; "Negroes Cautioned on Resistance Idea," *NYT*, November 23, 1946, 17; Harrison to Saks, memo, March 20, 1947, 2. See also Bayard Rustin, "Beyond the Courts," APA, December 28, 1946; CORE, *CORELATOR*, March 1947, 1–2; Houser to George Harrison, June 23, 1947; Samuel Markle to William Sachs, December 28, 1946; Rabkin to Houser, November 13, 1947, all ADL Y1947:NRP; see also Frank Trager to Harrison, Miller, and Saks, memo, April 2, 1947, ADL Y1947:NRP. The SRC was established in 1944 by racial moderates inspired by the earlier Commission on Interracial Cooperation. By 1949, the SRC formally opposed segregation. NAACP BD often considered rallies or "monster mass meetings" against discrimination and segregation: see, e.g., MMBD, June 14, 1943, 6; April 12, 1948, 6; and for Israel: September 13, 1948, 2–6, all IIA134.

47. Rabkin to Houser, November 13, 1947; Sachs to Trager, June 16, 1947, both ADL Y1947:NRP. Also see FOR PR, "Judge Tries to Give Six Times Maximum Term in Jim Crow Bus Case," June 27, 1947, ADL Y1947:NRP; Rustin and Houser, FOR, to "Friend," February 13, 1948, ADL Y1948:NRP; "Attorneys-General," 585–86.

48. A. J. Muste, "NVDA Committee Minutes," February 15, 1945, 1, NUL SRO: A74. For the Committee against Jimcrow in Military Service and Training, headed by Randolph, see Rev. Shelton Hale Bishop, Rev. William Lloyd Imes, Winifred Lynn, Randolph, and Rustin, to "Friend," May 28, 1948, ADL Y1948:NRP. For excerpts of Randolph's testimony before Committee on Armed Services, see NAACP IIA370. On the NAACP's views, see "President Truman's Orders," editorial, *Crisis* (September 1948); MMBD April 12, 1948, 6. Like the NAACP, the ADL opposed both military segregation and violating draft laws (Steinbrink to Henry Ansbacher Long, September 16, 1948, ADL Y1948:NRP). The ADL did urge state governors to desegregate the National Guards (Epstein to Michigan governor G. Mennen Williams, March 1, 1950; Henry Schultz to Pennsylvania governor John Fine, December 17, 1952, ADL Y1949–52:NRP).

49. NAACP, MMBD, March 12, 1951, 1–2; Dickerson, "Meeting held 3/13/51," 1–2; MMBD, April 9, 1951, 3, all NAACP IIA143.

50. NAACP, MMBD, March 27, 1951, 6–11. Delany later amended minutes for clarity (MMBD, April 9, 1951, 1–3).

51. Robert Fitterman to CRC, March 6, 1952, ADL Y1949–52:NRP. These tactics were used effectively in Harlem by Adam Clayton Powell Jr., and by the NNC and NAACP in the early 1940s. "Attorneys-General," 581, considered the NAACP the most militant minority organization.

52. Granger to Gutstadt, March 7, 1947, 2, ADL Y1947:NRP; Maurice Fagan and Jules Cohen, "Memorandum for Informal Dinner Meeting of December 27, 1951 to Explore the Possibility of Establishing a National Confederation of Agencies Interested in Fostering Better Human Relations," December 21, 1951, 1; "Meeting of Ad Hoc Committee to Consider Formation of a New Federation of Human Rights and Community Relations Agencies," January 15, 1951 (NCRAC, JCRC, ADL, JLC, AJC, AJCong); "Minutes of Meeting of Ad Hoc Committee to Consider Formation of a New Confederation of Human Relations Agencies," September 21, 1951, and next note. Similar coalitions include American Council on Race Relations (NUL, AJC, NAACP, ADL, SRC, Social Science Research Council and several wartime governmental agencies); National Citizens' Council on CR (included AJC, ADL, Freedom House); National Federation for Constitutional Liberties; American Conference for Racial and National Unity; ongoing unity committees (see chap. 3). See, e.g., ADL Y1944:NRP; ADL Y1949–52 Pro-org:Freedom House; AJC IVF:CR:NCCCR; FDR OF 93 "Colored Matters," box 6; FDR OF FEPC 4245g:7; NAACP IIA186.

53. "Minutes of Informal Dinner Meeting," December 27, 1951, 4; Cohen to Hollander, Fagan, Edwin Lukas, Maslow, Saks, and George Silver, memo re "Second dinner meeting of the group of labor, religious and racial leaders who first met last December to explore the possibility of a national confederation of human relations agencies," April 9, 1952; "Summary of Informal Dinner Meeting to Consider the Subject 'Discrimination in Housing,' " April 30, 1952, all ADL Y1949–52:Pro-org:NCRAC. Representatives from National Council of Churches in Christ, AJCongress, NCRAC, JCRC, NUL, AFL, AJC, ACLU, AFSC, CIO, ADL, JLC, National Catholic Welfare Conference, and NAACP attended. Also see AJCongress Conference at Roosevelt School, August 14, 1949, 423–24 and below.

54. Weisman, "To NC Meeting of ADL of B'nai B'rith, Chicago, Illinois, 5/14/50," speech, ADL WB176. Male-led groups had women on staff or serving as lay leaders and volunteers; they did not ignore women per se, but rather women's groups that were not sororities or auxiliaries. There was also competition between women's groups. See, e.g., Mrs. Migdal, NCJW, to Mrs. Elfenbein, NCJW, July 30, 1953, memo re CL meeting in Washington, D.C. "to which we were not invited," NCJW:72.

55. Transcript, National Planning Conference on Building Better Race Relations, 1944, NCJW WO:4; "Report of Mrs. Irving M. Engel on the 1952 Women's Leadership Conference," April 29, 1952, 1–2, NCJW:72. The organizations at the Race Relations Conference included the NCJW, National Council of Catholic Women, NCNW, Women's Trade Union League, YWCA, Pan American Union (Mexican American), National Council of Women, and BB Women. Also see NCNW Coordinating Committee for Building Better Race Relations, memo., n.d. [May 1944?], NCJW WO:4.

56. NAACP MMBD, January 2, 1951, 2–3, NAACP IIA135; ROS May 14, 1951, 1, NAACP IIA145. The 1951 meeting was at least partly about Caldwell: see Earl Dickerson, Committee to Implement Board Decision on the Caldwell Appointment, "Meeting held 3/13/51," minutes, 3, NAACP IIA135.

57. "RESOLUTION ADOPTED BY 1952 LCCR, WASHINGTON, D.C., February 1918, February 18, 1952, NAACP IIA353.

58. LCCR, PR, June 29, 1952, 3; "Supporting Organizations" (lists fifty-one groups), n.d., AJC VF:CR:LCCR. Of the fifty-one, eighteen were union affiliates or labor organizations; six Masonic, fraternal, or sororal; at least fifteen African American; nine Jewish; eight other religious; and six women's (some fall under multiple categories). Other organizations included the JACL, ACLU, National Bar Association, ADA, Am Vets, and American Council on Human Rights. The list shifted slightly over time, but core organizations remained. Annual lists in NAACP IIA353, AJC VF, ADL Y1953–58:LCCR.

59. Wilkins to Rabkin, January 29, 1952, NAACP IIA352; "RESOLUTION ADOPTED"; Aronson, "To All Cooperating Organizations," October 17, 1952, December 23, 1952, December 26, 1952; "Suggested Letter to Members of and Candidates for the United States Senate"; all AJC VF:CR:LCCR. See also NCRAC, "Advancement," 9; AJCongress, "CR and Federal Responsibility," resolution adopted by BC, May 14–18, 1958, 2–3; "Safeguarding," 13, 19–20; CRC, May 25, 1950, 3–4; NAACP MMBD, January 2, 1951, 10; "Summary of Decisions by NCRAC Bodies," 3, ADL Y1949–52:Pro-org:NCRAC; NAACP, ROS, September 1951, 3, NAACP IIA145.

60. Paul Hartman to Rabkin, memo re LCCR Steering Committee, April 21, 1953; Aronson to "Cooperating," memo "Re: Report on Conference with Attorney General Brownell," n.d. [held 5/1/53]; "MEMORANDUM TO ATTORNEY GENERAL ON IMPLEMENTATION OF NON-DISCRIMINATION PROVISION IN GOVERNMENT CONTRACTS," n.d.; "MEMORANDUM TO ATTORNEY GENERAL ON ADMINISTRATIVE ACTION TO IMPROVE CR MACHINERY OF DEPARTMENT OF JUSTICE," all ADL Y1953–58:LCCR.

61. LCCR, PR, June 29, 1952. Also see LCCR, "CR Reform Plank," June 21, 1952, AJC VF:CR. For the LCCR's lobbying of Republican and Democratic Conventions, see NAACP, ROS, September 8, 1952, 1, NAACP IIA145.

62. LCCR, "Summary of EC Meeting, March 3, 1955," 1–3. Sanford Bolz, AJCongress wrote the controversial memo. The committee also debated, without resolution, whether to support a federal aid-to-education bill lacking a nonsegregation clause (3). Maslow supported the possibility of a sanctionless FEPC ("Advancement," 14–15).

63. LCCR, "Summary of EC meeting, 7/19/55, Washington, D.C.," 1–3, NAACP IIA353; LCCR, "EC 3/3/55," 2. LCCR never ceased its CR advocacy but its visibility diminished with grassroots challenges to segregation and the expansion of groups like CORE and SNCC that led them.

64. L.K.G. [Lloyd Garrison], Committee on UL Policy, "Recommendations," 3, n.d. [July 22, 1954?], NUL 11:5. On the NAACP and legislative struggles, see, e.g., "The Election—And After," editorial, *Crisis*, (December 1948), 361.

65. NCJW, NCSL, March 27, 1942, 2, NCJW:141.

66. "Summary of Resolutions on Social Legislation Adopted by the TC November 7–11, 1943," NCJW:142; "Positions of NCJW on Issues of the 1950 Congressional Election," August 25, 1950; NCJW, "Planks Recommended for Inclusion in the 1952 Platforms of the Democratic and Republican Parties," August 20, 1952, both NCJW:74. Readers may be interested to learn that the NCJW opposed the Equal Rights Amendment as a threat to women's protective legislation, and advocated the internationalization of Israeli holy places and a divided Jerusalem.

67. NCRAC, "Decisions." See also, e.g., George Mintzer, "Statement for AJC Delivered before the House Committee on Administration Subcommittee on Elections on H.R. 3199," May 12, 1949; "STATEMENT OF [AJC] . . . IN SUPPORT OF THE PROPOSED 'CR ACT OF 1949' (H.R. 4682; S. 1725, 81st Congress)," June 22, 1949; "Statement of Justice Meier Steinbrink before Subcommittee on CR of the Senate Committee on Labor and Public Welfare on S. 692 on behalf of ADL, AJC," February 24, 1954, all AJC IVF:CR:AJC: statements; CJP, "Colored Races in the Pacific," in "Judaism and Race Relations," 1945; "Judaism and CR"; "Inhabitants," all AJC VF:RR:CCAR; "Rabbis Ask U.S. Aid for All Oppressed," *NYT*, August 27, 1946, AJCongress CF; AJC, "PRs," 1946–52; AJC, "Purposes"; ADL, "Call on Federal, State and Local Administration to Eliminate Discrimination on Basis of Race, Creed or Color," resolution, November 20, 1953, ADL WB42; AJCong, "CR and Federal Responsibility"; AJCongress, "Catalogue of Mimeographed and Printed materials"; ADL NCs, in WB176. For examples of black/Jewish cooperation on the judiciary, see Rabkin to Forster, July 5, 1950; B. M. Joffe, JCC Detroit, to NCRAC, ADL, AJC, AJCongress, JLC, memo re "Cloture on FEPC, and Judge Hastie's confirmation," July 21, 1950, both ADL Y49–52:NRP. *Amsterdam News* and Granger endorsed Justine Wise Polier for presiding justice of the New York Domestic Relations Court (Granger, "Manhattan and Beyond," *Amsterdam News*, December 19, 1959, AJC IVF:NJR). Jewish groups were also engaged with nonblack CR: see, e.g., "Noted Witnesses [from AJCong and NCJW] Urge House to Grant Issei Citizenship," *Pacific Citizen*, n.d. [1948?], AJCongress, CF:Racism, A-S; CLSA, "Report of Activities April 16–May 15, 1948," 2; "Report of Activities 10/49," 4, both NAACP IIA361. AJCongress, NAACP, and ADL filed briefs in JACL cases: see "Role of JACL in Test Cases Hailed by Maslow," *Pacific Citizen* (June 2, 1949), C, "CLSA binder."

68. "A Look at the Candidates," editorial, *Crisis* (January 1948), 9. See also "Who Should Be in the White House?" *Crisis* (October 1948), 298–99, 313–17; "Attorneys-General," 588; NCJW's "Legislative Highlights"; ADL's *Bulletins*, *The Facts*, AJC's *Commentary*, NUL's *Opportunity*.

69. Epstein, *A-S in the US*, Pamphlet, ADL, 1957, 9, AJC VF:A-S. I have never found any white supremacist organization that is not also anti-Semitic.

70. Isaac Franck, JCC of Greater Washington, to Forster et al., memo re "Municipal Court of Appeals' Decision on 1872–1873 Anti-Discrimination Laws," May 28, 1951; Frances Levenson and Rabkin to CRCs, AJC AO, ADL RO, memo re "Washington, D.C. CR Statutes," June 13, 1951, both ADL Y49–52:NRP. The Supreme Court upheld the statute (1953). Also see Snyder and Goodman, *Friend of the Court*, 30. Jewish groups also testified before the D.C. Recreation Board

on desegregating playgrounds: see Rabkin to Herman Edlesberg, April 28, 1952, ADL Y1949–52:NRP.

71. Maslow to Marshall, January 8, 1947; Maslow to Marshall, December 27, 1946; reply, January 3, 1947; Maslow to Marshall, February 6, 1947; reply, February 11, 1947; Maslow to Marshall, February 17, 1947, all NAACP IIA360. See also Jules Cohn to Rabbi Israel Lovinthal et al., July 24, 1944, memo re "Race Relations," ADL Y1944:NRP; Carl Van Doren to Trager, May 14, 1948, ADL Y1948:NRP; Granger to Gutstadt, March 7, 1947, 2.

72. William Oliver to Rabkin, March 11, 1952; Rabkin to Oliver, April 14, 1952, April 15, 1952, ADL Y1949–52:NRP. For more on the ADL and CIO, see Epstein to Arthur Goldberg, CIO, June 1, 1950; Miller to Dorothy Nathan, AJC, March 11, 1949, both ADL Y1949–52:NRP.

73. Rabkin to Miller, memo, August 29, 1950, ADL Y1949–52:NRP. The AJC hired Clark in 1950 to research the impact of segregation on children for the White House Conference on Children (K. B. Clark and M. K. Clark, "Detailed Statement of Plan of Work," n.d., provided by Ben Keppel). These studies led the NAACP to invite Clark's participation in *Brown*. See also Friedman, *What Went Wrong?* 149–52. *Brown* fn. 11 cites Clark's work. Two AJCongress CCI studies directed by Dr. [Stuart] Cook and Isadore Chein are also cited. Also see AJCongress AC, May 23, 1954, 3–4; AJCongress A&E 1953–54; John Harding, CCI, "Social Effects of Segregation," 1948, AJC IVF:Negroes—Segregation—Psychological and Social Aspects; Maslow, "Advancement,"10. For *Brown* briefs see Snyder and Goodman, *Friend of the Court*, 18–20; AJC DAC, October 8, 1952, 5; "Attorneys-General," 590. On Hillel's involvement, see "Large Jewish Organization in Controversy" (*Kansas City, Mo.*) *Call*, March 31, 1950, 1, 5, cited in Maurianne Adams and John Bracey, *Strangers and Neighbors* (Amherst, Mass., 1999), 520–21. Hillel also donated scholarships for incarcerated Japanese American students to attend college (conversation between author and Michi Weglyn, March 2, 1993).

74. Rabkin to Tom Friedman, December 19, 1952, ADL Y49–52:NRP. The case involved Louisiana golf courses.

75. CJP, "Inhabitants." See also AJCongress, "Integration in the North," BC Resolution, May 14–18, 1958, NAACP IIIA196. For local battles, see below. There are also many hints of personal friendships, thanks for aid, information, advice. See, e.g., Granger to Gutstadt, March 7, 1947, 1; Trager to Louis Sidman, NUL, April 27, 1949, ADL Y1949–52:NRP; W. Miller Barbour, Denver UL to Sidman, December 29, 1948, ADL Y1948:NRP; Edward G [illegible] to Epstein, September 9, 1946, memo re "Color Line," ADL Y1946:NRP; Leonard Schroeter, ADL, to Seymour Kaplan, memo re "Negro A-S," February 6, 1953, ADL Y1953–58; Robinson to George Azumano, Portland JACL, November 6, 1947, ADL Chi-sub:12; Cohn to Lovinthal et al.

76. On SCAD (until 1945, known as SCADE: "Employment"), see Governor Herbert Lehman to FDR, June 9, 1941, FDR OF 76C:7; AJC DAC, January 18, 1949, 3. New York, New Jersey, Rhode Island, Connecticut, Massachusetts, Oregon, Washington, New Mexico had FEPC laws by 1949 (AJCong., "Safeguarding," 20). By 1952, eleven states had them. (ADL NC, October 24–25, 1952, transcript, 19). Perlman, "Anti-Discrimination Legislation," 7–9, offers a history of New York's CR

laws. Employment discrimination affected blacks and Jews, although both acknowledged blacks suffered more (Maslow, "Safeguarding," 74–75). Also see White, "Indivisible," 6; AJCongress, "Equality," 77–81.

77. Mrs. Murray Newman, Brooklyn AJCong WD, "Safeguarding," 56–58;
"Drive on Discrimination," *Jewish Examiner*, November 27, 1947; AJCongress
CF; Maslow, "Safeguarding," 74–75; AJC DAC, January 18, 1949, 3. Outside
New York, restrictive ads were more common.

78. William Issel, "Jews and Catholics against Prejudice," in *California Jews*,
ed. Ava Kahn and Marc Dollinger (Lebanon, N.H., 2003); 123–34, esp. 123, 125–
27, 132. The Council began, 1942, as SFBAC against Discrimination; the name
changed by 1944. For more on housing, see below. See also "S.F. Drive Begins
on Discrimination," *San Francisco News*, June 7, 1948, AJCongress CF. NUL,
"Portland," discusses local employment coalitions, including San Francisco. Also
see Dellums to Wilkins, January 13, 1960, NAACP IIIA179, on the December
12, 1959, *Pittsburgh Courier* article by managing editor Harold Keith claiming
difficulty between black and Jewish leaders over CR in labor movement. This
claim was repudiated by Granger, Emanuel Muravchik, Randolph, and Wilkins.
All in AJC IVF:NJR. The controversy was part of a larger question about the JLC's
role in the struggle against union racism: see, e.g., Hill, "Black-Jewish Conflict in
the Labor Context"; Esther Levine, "Southern Jewish Views on Segregation,"
Jewish Life, August 1956, 20; Nancy Green, "Blacks, Jews, and the 'Natural Alliance,'" *Jewish Social Studies* 4, no. 1 (Fall 1997): 79–104.

79. "Informal Dinner Meeting," December 27, 1951, 2–3; Victor Blanc, "Safeguarding," 52–55; Friedman, *What Went Wrong?* 145. For cooperation elsewhere, see William Valentine, Seattle UL, to Samuel Holcenberg, Seattle ADL,
October 17, 1946, ADL Y1946:NRP; Taylor, *Forging of a Black Community*,
171, 186–87, 202; Fitterman to CRC, March 6, 1952; Sidney Sayles, Milwaukee
Jewish Council, to Nissen Gross, memo, "Door County situation," ADL
Y1948:NRP; NUL, "Portland." Enforcement was equally crucial; black and Jewish groups were active, especially CLSA ("Attorneys-General," 591). Employment
discrimination continued to affect all minority groups, although none so exten-
sively as African Americans (see ADL PR, n.d. [May 3, 1948], 1; ADL PR, April
18, 1949, 1–2; AJCongress, "Equality," 8–13, 76–81; "Statement of . . .
Steinbrink," February 24, 1954, 2–11, with data from numerous cities). On anti-
Jewish employment discrimination, see David Rose, NCRAC Committee on Overt
A-S, *Outlook for A-S in the US*, pamphlet, NCRAC, 1947, 5, AJC VF:A-S:US.
Elsewhere local JCRCs and other groups joined (failed) efforts to pass fair employ-
ment laws, e.g., Indianapolis: see Pierce, *Polite Protest*, 94–100.

80. On restrictions, see AJCong., "Equality," 45–66, 70–75, 87–90; AJCong.,
"Safeguarding," 28–33, 55–56; Ina Sugihara, "Curbing Discrimination in Education," *Crisis 55*, no. 5 (May 1948): 144–45; Steinbrink, "Legacy," 12–14, 20–21.
Northern public schools were also segregated due to housing segregation: see,
e.g., AJCongress, "Integration," 1. On the NAACP's intervention with the medical school, see White, "Indivisible," 6. The Quinn-Olliffe Act made it illegal for
any New York nonreligious postsecondary school to discriminate on the basis of
race, religion, or national origin. New York was the first state to pass this. The
legislation failed to pass twice, until CR organizations shifted their argument from

discrimination to equal opportunity for veterans. See Edward Saveth, "Democratic Education for NY," *Commentary* 6, no. 1 (July 1948): 46–52; Sugihara; Jewish Telegraph Agency, "Gov. Dewey Asked to Support Bill Outlawing Restrictive Covenants on Real Estate" [*sic*] n.d. [1946], C, ADL Y1946:NRP; "Steinbrink Urges State University for NY," ADL *Bulletin* 9 (November 1947): 5; *AJYB, 1947–48*, 49 (1948), 825–26; Steinbrink, "Legacy," 12–14; "Attorneys-General," 590–91; David Petegorsky, AJCongress, *On Combating Racism*, pamphlet, 1948, 13; Mrs. Newman, "Safeguarding," 58–59. The agencies also joined New York State Committee for Equality in Education. Massachusetts FEP legislation is discussed by Mr. Berlin in AJCongress, "Safeguarding," 42–49. Also see Rose, "Outlook for A-S," 5–6; ADL PR, April 18, 1949, 2–4.

81. Lorna Marple, President, Portland NAACP, "Statement to the Press, Radio and TV on Bill of Rights Day, 12/15/55"; Marple, "Organizations with whom NAACP will cooperate—*LCCR List*. Portland, Oregon, Branch," December 5, 1955, 1–2, both NAACP IIA353. For other examples, see NCJW, "Report of National Committee to Abolish the Poll Tax Meeting on May 10, 1943," NCJW:74; Wilkins, LCCR, to Participating Organizations, November 20, 1959.

82. Michael Freed to Rabkin, LCCR, December 19, 1955, memo re "Bill of Rights Day Rally—Denver," 1, 2, NAACP IIA353.

83. Philip Burton, NAACP, to E. Albert Morrison, Assistant AG, September 9, 1954; Lewis Watts, Seattle UL, to Della Urquhart, Department of Licenses, September 21, 1954; Burton to Morrison, September 22, 1954, all ADL Y1953–58.

84. Myron Schwartz and Isaiah Terman, "Community Relations Study of Illinois," July 11, 1949, 26–27, NAACP IIA386.

85. "Nazis in Washington," *Crisis* 54, no. 10 (October 1947): 297. On the Supreme Court decision (actually three cases), see *Shelley v. Kraemer*, 334 U.S. 1 (1948), *Sipes v. McGhee*, 334 U.S. 1 (1948), *Hurd v. Hodge*, 334 U.S. 24 (1948); "No Support for Covenants," editorial, 169; "Along the N.A.A.C.P. Battlefront: Supreme Court," 179–81, both *Crisis*, June 1948; Loren Miller, "Supreme Court Covenant Decision," *Crisis*, September 1948, 265–66, 285; "Attorneys-General," 587, 590. On the aid, and briefs provided, see Meier Steinbrink to Mr.___, May 18, 1949, NAACP IIA363; "'Covenants' Hit by Jewish Groups in Court Brief," ADL *Bulletin* 4 (December 1947): 1; AJCong., CLSA, "Monthly Report," July 1946, NAACP IIA360; AJCong., "Equality," 91–93; AJC, "Socio-Legal Approach," 4; Snyder and Goodman, *Friend of the Court*, 13–14 (ADL); "Calls for New Laws to End Racial Bias," *Los Angeles Daily News*, June 3, 1948, AJCong CF.

86. NAACP, AJCongress, and NUL raised these concerns at the time; see e.g., NAACP, "ROS," June 9, 1952, 2–3; AJCongress, "Integration," 1; "Equality," 94–95. So did leftists. See also Stephen Meyer, *As Long As They Don't Move Next Door* (Lanham, Md., 2000); Thomas Sugrue, *Origins of the Urban Crisis* (Princeton, N.J., 1996).

87. Saks to ADL RO, August 6, 1947, Memo re Fernwood Park, ADL Y1947:NRP. Also see Arnold Hirsch, *Making the Second Ghetto* (Cambridge, 1983).

88. ADL, "Racial Violence at Fernwood," confidential report, n.d. [1947] 1, ADL Y1947:NRP; Gilbert Gordon, CLSA Midwestern office, "Excerpt from

Weekly Report of Chicago Division . . . (For period ending—8/18/47)," 1, ADL Y1947:NRP.

89. Gordon, "Excerpt," 1; "To the Citizens and Public Officials of Chicago," September 10, 1947, 2; Gordon, "Excerpt," 3. The coalition expanded following the riot.

90. William Pinsley, "Tension Situation at 5643 South Peoria Street," November 17, 1949; Berman, AJCongress EC, December 11, 1949, 95–107. Also see Aaron Bindman (CIO host), Chicago-4 to NNG (Nissen Gross), memo re "Giant Protest Rally Coliseum— . . . Friday, November 18—8:15 P.M.," 2–4 (organized by Progressive Party). Both ADL Y1949–52:NRP.

91. ADL, "Trials of Defendants in Peoria Street Disturbances" (includes decision), Judge Joseph McGarry, March 13, 1950, 4–6; Gross to Forster, March 21, 1950, memo re "Peoria Street Riot Cases," 1–2, both ADL Y1949–52:NRP. Also see Pinsley to Forster, March 16, 1950; Berman, AJCongress EC, 111–12. The AJCongress criticized CCARD for not being outspoken enough: see AJCongress EC, 104.

92. The Cicero riots were widely chronicled. This discussion is drawn from ADL sources. All but *The Facts* come from Y1949–52:NRP. Mrs. Babcock to Illinois Interracial Commission, memo re "Cicero Riot," n.d. [July 14, 1951?]; Paul Annes and Waitsill Sharp, CCARRD, to Governor Adlai Stevenson, July 18, 1951; Homer Jack, CCARRD, "Cicero Riots of 1951," July 22, 1951; Gross to Forster, July 19, 1951, memo re Cicero through July 18 (Gross also CCARRD), 4; Lukas and Forster to CRC, AJC AO, ADL RO, joint memo, "Interim Report," July 27, 1951; J. I. Fishbein to Editor, *National Jewish Post*, August 30, 1951; Pinsley to Monroe Steinberg, September 5, 1951; ADL, "Cicero Riots," *The Facts* 6, no. 9/10 (September–October 1951):1–4; Robert Weaver to "Cooperating Agencies and Friends of the National Committee against Discrimination In Housing," "Cicero Demands Immediate Action by All Responsible Americans"; CCARRD, PR, September 27, 1951; NCRAC, PR, "Jewish Organizations Ask Federal Inquiry in Cicero Rioting," September 26, 1951; Levenson and Rabkin to CRC, AJC, ADL, memo re "Cicero Indictments"; NAACP, ROS, June 11, 1951, 6; September 1951, 1–2.

93. ADL, "Cicero Riots," 4; Weaver, "Cicero Demands Immediate Action," 1; Levenson and Rabkin, "Cicero Indictments," 2.

94. Jack, "Cicero Riots," 7; Gross to Foster, 5; Jack, "Cicero Riots," 9.

95. "Summary of Informal Dinner Meeting to Consider the Subject 'Discrimination in Housing,'" April 30, 1952, 2–5. The meeting included ADL, NCRAC, JCRC, NUL, AJC, AJCongress, JLC, CIO, National Council Churches of Christ, NCCJ, AFSC, AFL, CIC, ACLU, Philadelphia Fellowship Commission. See also Abrams, "Freedom to Dwell Together," *AJCW* 17, no. 31 (November 27, 1950): 15–17; ADL PR, n.d. [May 3, 1948], 1; PR, April 18, 1949, 2; "Safeguarding": Maslow, 34–36, George Johnson, 36–37; Stuart Cook, AJCongress, 37–41. On covenants, see David and Adele Bernstein, "Washington: Tarnished Symbol," *Commentary*, November 1948, 398–99.

96. Marston to Epstein, April 12, 1944; Marston to Epstein, memo re "Japanese Relocation," April 27, 1944, ADL D1943:"Int-Kap." Others present at the New Jersey meeting included Goodwill Commission, Japanese-American Com-

mittee for Democracy, YMCA, War Relocation Authority, Postwar World Council. See also Forster to Nathan Perlmutter, July 19, 1950, memo on cooperation with JACL and UL on housing; I. H. Gordon, JACL, to Bernard Simon, ADL, March 1, 1949, both ADL Y1949–52:Pro-org: JACL. On Bayside, see Marvin Jager to Arnold Wallack, May[?] 9, 1945, ADL Y1945:NRP. See also Monroe Sheinberg to I. Joel Komarow and Morris Sass, August 25, 1952, ADL Y49–52:NRP [Laurelton, N.Y.]; Milwaukee JC AR, 1954–55, "Report of the Committee on Fact Finding," AJC VF:communities:Wisconsin. On Levittown, see C from *Levittown Times*, n.d. [August–September 1957], provided by Bud Schultz. Christians from Levittown, Pennsylvania, also placed an ad supporting integration. The black family moved away.

97. Oscar Cohen to Trager; Fineberg, AJC; Walter Lurie, NCRAC; Maslow; Irving Salert, JLC; memo, January 30, 1948, ADL Y1948:NRP. See also Thomas Keene, "Information" memo re "Anti-Negro Housing Propaganda Circulated in Jewish Community," July 30, 1946, Detroit Commission of Community Relations Collection, 3:27, Archives of Labor and Urban Affairs, Walter P. Reuther Library, provided by Tom Sugrue; Robinson to Saks, memo: "Case Report," December 20, 1948. ADL Y1948:NRP.

98. Maslow, "Safeguarding," 34, 36. Charles Abrams, Polier, and Maslow represented the plaintiffs. For AJCongress material, see "Catalog of Mimeographed and Printed Materials" and the bound volume "Stuyvesant Case." The campaign was led by the New York State Committee on Discrimination in Housing (included AJCongress, ADL, NAACP, NYCLU, N.Y. Board of Rabbis, and Episcopal and Congregational groups); CLSA served as counsel. By 1954 it also included NCJW, AJC, UL, and JLC. Stuyvesant Town was owned by Metropolitan Life Insurance Co. See also Robison, "Victory," 7–9; Maslow, "Advancement," 12; NYSCDH, "Battle of Stuyvesant Town—Renewed," n.d., AB box 9; "Attorneys-General," 590, 592. Hamilton, *Adam Clayton Powell, Jr.*, notes the mayor's support reflected the "liberal's dilemma": balancing wartime housing needs and racial justice, 129–30. CORE leafleted and picketed: See "Report of Interracial Workshop, May 14–15" [1948], 1–2, ADL Y1948:NRP. For the follow-up, see ADL Y1949–52:NRP. AB box 9, also has more on the NYSCDH. See also "Discrimination Hit in Mortgage Bill," *NYT*, February 11, 1947, 30; Rabkin to Benjamin Greenberg, August 20, 1948, ADL Y1948:NRP (Los Angeles); Sam Rhinestine to Forster, memo re "NCRAC *Ad Hoc* Committee meeting on (a) Levittown, (b) American Bowling Congress," May 17, 1949, ADL Y1949–52 Pro-org:NCRAC Ad hoc (Levittown). (Levitt was Jewish). The FHA stopped restrictive policies, but permitted acts that prevented neighborhoods from becoming "less desirable" (Abrams, "The Segregation Threat to Housing," *Commentary*, February 1949,123).

99. Rabkin and Levenson to CRCs, ADL RO, AJC AO, joint memo re "Integration Achieved in Public Housing in Sacramento, California," April 23, 1952; 1–2, ADL Y1949–52:NRP. Cicero and similar outbreaks suggest their optimism was misplaced. See also Perlmutter to Cohen, July 10, 1950, ADL Y1949–52:Pro-org:JACL (on Denver).

100. LCCR, "CR Groups Call on President to Establish Anti-Discrimination Commission," PR, November 9, 1959, AJC VF:CR.

101. Gross to [ADL] Fact Finding Department, memo re "South Shore Beating Cases," March 21, 1952; Pinsley to Gross, memo re "Attacks in the South Shore Area of Chicago," March 20, 1952, both ADL Y1949–52:NRP. The Tuskegee Institute, NAACP, and ADL tracked lynchings: see, e.g., Joseph Robison, "Statement Before a Sub-Committee of the Committee on Judiciary Holding Hearings on H.R. 3488 and other Bills to Curb Lynching," February 4, 1948, 5, AJC IVF: Negro-lynching. Hundreds more were hurt or threatened. Not all targets were activists, but most such violence correlated with CR activity.

102. E.g., following a police shooting of a youth in Detroit, the Michigan Committee on CR (Detroit Council of Churches, CIC, JCC, ADL, JLC, JACL, Detroit UL, WILPF, several union locals, UAW, NAACP, ADA, YWCA) pressed the city regarding responses. The NAACP, JCC, and others contributed legal counsel (Cohen, JCC, to NCRAC[?], memo, July 6, 1948, 2; William Sperry, President, Detroit MCCR to "Co-worker," "Bulletin," June 24, 1948, and undated [July 1948?], all ADL Y1948:NRP). On southern violence, see below.

103. "Consultants' Interim Report on Peekskill, NY," December 7, 1949, 4, AJC IVF:Riots:Peekskill NY; Gloster Current to "Co-Worker," September 8, 1949, NAACP IIA369. See also AJC, "The Peekskill Story," n.d. [1949 or 1950], AJC IVF: Riots:Peekskill NY; Howard Fast, *Peekskill USA* (CRC, 1951); National CL Clearing House, "Joint Statement," 1, n.d. [September 1949], NCJW, WO:15; Wilkins to Dewey, telegram, August 31, 1949, NAACP IIA369. For more on liberal black and Jewish groups, CL, and anticommunism, see chap. 5.

104. AJCongress, 1949 NC, Resolutions Committee, transcript, November 11, 1949, 43–48, AJCongress box: "NC 1949"; NCRAC, "Suggestions for the Guidance of Jewish Organizations in Connection with the Paul Robeson Concert Tour," n.d. [cover memo, October 19, 1949], ADL Chisub:12:CRD; AJC DAC, October 4, 1949, 5–6, AJC library, vol. 1947–53; Fineberg to John Slawson, memo re "Preventing Rioting Incident to Communist Meetings," September 20, 1949; AJC, "Avoiding Clashes at Communist Rallies," n.d. [cover memo, October 19, 1949], (Chicago) Commission on Human Relations (included ADL, AJC, AJCongress, CIC, Chicago Metropolitan Council of Negro Women, UL, Conf. Jewish Women's Organizations, NAACP, South Central Assoc.), memo, "Paul Robeson Meetings in Chicago, September 23 and September 24, 1949," n.d. [October 1949?], all AJC IVF:Riots:Peekskill NY; NYC CRC, September 9, 1949, 1–4, ADL Y1949–52:pro-org:CRC; NCRAC Committee on CL, Violence and Defamation, December 18, 1952, 3–4, NCRAC:67; Current to New York branch officers, September 2 ,1949, NAACP IIA369. See also, "On CL," n.d. [1949], NAACP IIA386; Executive Chamber, New York State, PR, "Statement by Governor Dewey," September 14, 1949, NAACP IIA467; ACLU, ADA, AJCongress, AVC, Council Against Intolerance, and NAACP, "Statement on Grand Jury Inquiry into Peekskill Riots," September 22, 1949, NAACP IIA467; AJCongress EC, October 5, 1949, 8, AJCongress box:EC; White, "Robeson: Right or Wrong?" draft for *Negro Digest*, n.d. [1949], NAACP IIA467. Dewey blamed CP for provoking violence (as did most black and Jewish groups), but promised to investigate the riots and free speech violations.

105. Miller to Forster, memo, December 27, 1950, 2, ADL Y1949–52:NRP.

106. On the ADL and lynching, see Joseph Rainey, Philadelphia Branch NAACP, to "Friends," November 19, 1946; Beatrice Harrison, Philadelphia Anti-Defamation Committee to Epstein, November 21, 1946; Epstein to Harrison, November 22, 1946, all ADL Y1946:NRP; Robison, "Statement." On AJCongress activity regarding anti-lynching bills, see "Catalogue . . . on CR, CL and Public Accommodations," August 1, 1945–December 31, 1949: A. Masks; ADL NEC, May 14, 1949, 8–9, ADL WB178; Gilbert Balkin to Saks, memo re "Negro-White Relations—Miami Area," July 16, 1947, ADL Y1947; CLSA, *KKK and State Action*, pamphlet, September 4, 1946, AJCongress library; Morris Abram and Alex Miller, "Federal Anti-Klan Legislation," report, May 5, 1949; Forster to CRC, memo re "Anti-Mask Legislation, Free Speech, Group Libel. . . ," May 20, 1949, both ADL Chisub:12; Murray Friedman, "One Episode in Southern Jewry's Response to Desegregation," *American Jewish Archives* 33, no. 2 (November 1981): 172. Stetson Kennedy infiltrated the KKK and offered grand jury testimony: see *I Rode with the Ku Klux Klan* (repr. as *The Klan Unmasked* [Boca Raton, Fla., 1990]).

107. White to ADL [and others], telegram, July 31, 1946; Harold Cowin, ADL, to Forster, memo re "NAACP Meeting, Re: Lynchings in Monroe, GA," August 6, 1946; PR, August 1, 1946; Miller to Forster, memo, August 5, 1946, all ADL Y1946:NRP; Atlanta JCC, Committee on Community Relations, "Review of Minutes, Decisions and Policies, 1946–1953," AJC VF: "Communities: GA." The forty-three agencies present at the NAACP meeting included CIO, AFL, NCCJ, AVC, Negro Elks, YMCA, YMHA, AJCongress, AJC, Freedom House, and ADL. Miller's assessment proved wildly optimistic.

108. White to ADL, telegram, November 9, 1951; Forster to White, November 14, 1951; AJC, AJCongress, ADL, JLC, JWV, UAHC, and NCRAC, to Attorney General J. Howard McGrath, telegram, n.d., all ADL Y1949–52:NRP. For similar cooperation, see Miller to Forster, memo, January 7, 1952, ADL Y1949–52:NRP, re GA "anti-Negro rampage"; Miller to Herman Edelsberg, December 2, 1948; Edelsberg to Miller, December 6, 1948, memo re "Mallard case" (lynching in Georgia), all ADL Y1948:NRP; NAACP PR, "Will Defend Columbia Riot Victims to Utmost Limit: 19 Organizations Pledge to NAACP," March 14, 1946, ADL Y1946:NRP; NAACP, ROS, September 1951, 5 (violence in Alabama, Texas); ROS, June 9, 1952, 8 (SRC statement, with NUL, NAACP, ADL, NCNW, Georgia Committee on Interracial Cooperation and others, on over forty southern bombings in eighteen months); AJCongress, "Southern Bombings," Resolution, BC, May 14–18, 1958, NAACP IIIA196; Maslow and Joseph Robinson, *A CR Program for America*, pamphlet, AJCongress, 1947 (reprinted from *Lawyers Guild Review* 7, no. 3 (May–June 1947); Greene, *Temple Bombing*. Each *CR in the US: A Balance Sheet of Race Relations* AR describes racial violence. In 1955 the AJCongress and BSCP established a committee to aid southern victims, the "In Friendship" Coordinating Committee (including AJCongress, AVC, BSCP, JLC, NAACP, United Hebrew Trades, WDL, several unions); see "Memo on 'In Friendship,'" n.d. [February 20, 1956]; Randolph to "Dear Friend," February 17, 1956; Reverend James Robinson, Ashley Totten, and Rabbi Edward Klein to Granger, December 19, 1955; Granger to Executive Staff, memo, December 29, 1955 (regarding NAACP hesitation); Nelson Jackson to Granger, memo re "Your sched-

uled meeting on January 5, 1956," December 30, 1955 (NUL reservations), all NUL 1:49.

109. AJC, "Strengthen Justice Department's CR Power to Repair Damage to American Prestige Abroad Because of Till Case, Congressional Leaders Urged by AJC," PR, October 22, 1955; "Abroad," 1; Wilkins quoted in a follow-up AJC PR, November 22, 1955, 1. See also Harry Fleishman, National Labor Service, to "Brother," October 13, 1955; AJC Paris office to NO, memo re "European Reaction to Emmett Till case in Sumner, Mississippi," October 7, 1955, all AJC IVF:Negroes—Lynching. Stephen Whitfield, *Death in the Delta* (New York, 1988) details the Till lynching.

110. Fineberg to Slawson, memo re "Situation in Miami." See also Mrs. Irving [Katharine] Engel, NCJW, to J. Howard McGrath, February 8, 1952, NCJW:73; ADL PR, n.d.[1952], ADL Y 49–52:NRP; NUL Board of Trustees, resolution, January 17, 1952, NUL 11:4; NUL PR, January 23, 1952, NUL 5:35.

111. CJP, "Judaism and Race Equality," [1948]. See also Berland to Epstein, memo re "Queens Borough Realty Corporation," August 27, 1942, ADL Y1942.

112. Petegorsky, *Combatting Racism*, 8, 10. See also "Statement of . . . Steinbrink," February 24, 1954, 9–10; ADL, "To the Discussion Leader," 4, n.d. (cover memo, May 14, 1948), ADL Y1948:NRP.

113. N.Y. Council of Church Women, Interfaith Affairs Committee; AJCongress WD; NCNW Metropolitan Section, "Interracial and Interreligious 'Caravan'" announcement, March 8, 1945, Broadway Tabernacle Church, New York City, NAACP IIA360. See also AJCongress and AJCongress WD, "Mass Meeting Against Bigotry," broadside, April 25, 1946, New York City; Bernard Harkavy, AJCongress to NAACP, March 8, 1946, NAACP IIA360; "Adopt Plans for Bias Fight: 2,000 at Rally Hit Growth of Bigotry," *New York Post*, April 26, 1946, AJCongress NCs; *Blueprint for Freedom—1949*, production script for ADL NC performance, May 15, 1949; White to Mr. Wilkins and Mr. Moon, memo, May 16, 1949, both NAACP IIA363.

114. Moon, "Use of the Media of Communication for Community Relations Purposes," NAACP statement, for NCRAC Special Committee on Reassessment, draft, August 3, 1955, 2, NAACP IIA387. NCNW created material for the Chicago public schools: see "NCNW Report," November 18, 1944, NCJW WO:18. BB WSC provided books, films, workshops, discussion materials to public schools and civic groups in Ohio, Massachusetts, Pennsylvania, California, Georgia, Wisconsin, Mississippi: see Gertrude Weisman, "To NC Meeting of the ADL of B'nai B'rith," May 14, 1950, 1–3, ADL WB176. For more on public relations efforts, see Leonard Dinnerstein, "A-S Exposed and Attacked, 1945–1950," *AJH* 71 (September 1981): 134–49; Dollinger, *Quest for Inclusion*, chap. 3; Stuart Svonkin, *Jews Against Prejudice* (New York, 1997).

115. "Report of Program Committee Activities to NEC Delivered by Hon. Henry Epstein, 9/10/55," ADL WB178; similar materials are also in WB42; Richard Steele, "The War on Intolerance," *JAEH* 9, no. 1 (Fall 1999): 9–35, esp. 26–28. See also Moon, "Media"; ADL NEC, May 14, 1949, 8, ADL WB176; "Lest We Forget"; "Symbols of Democracy," *Defender*, July 5, [1951?], NC, ADL Chi-sub:12; A. L. Foster (Chicago UL) to Epstein, November 11, 1947, ADL Y1947:NRP; Louther Horne, "Human Relations Held Key Problem," *NYT*, No-

vember 4, 1949, AJCongress CLSA binder; *Conference on Research in the Field of A-S*, pamphlet, AJC, March 1945, 8–11, AJC VF:A-S; "Statement on the Purposes, Structure and CL Interests of AJC"; Mordecai Grossman, "Schools Fight Prejudice," *Commentary* 1, no. 6 (April 1946): 34–42; Weisman, "To NC"; Herbert List, ADL, to Jack Goldberg, Herald Pictures, Inc., September 17, 1947, ADL Y1947:NRP.

116. Chein, "Social Scientist," 5; "Tin Pan Alley 'Hits Spot' with Goodwill Jingles," *ADL Bulletin*, December 1947, 4; cow spot lyrics by Hy Zaret, quoted in " 'Spots' Sell Democracy," *ADL Bulletin* 4, no. 6 (June 1947): 4. See also Fineberg, "Insults Solicited," *HUC Monthly*, June 1945, 4, 20; Marjorie Cohen to Arthur Chiel, May 18, 1948, *Answers to Bigoted Questions You Hear*, manual, ADL Y1948:NRP.

117. "Jewish Behavior and A-S (Part One: Encountering the Bigot)," Series A-#1, September 1948, 16 (separate adjacent quotation marks *sic*); Harold Schiff to Trager, October 30, 1947, ADL Y1947:NRP. The idea for the ad campaign came from NUL's Ann Tanneyhill. See also Series A-#2: "Jewish Behavior and A-S (Part Two: Why Do We Worry about Jewish Behavior?)," January 1949. Both AJC VF:A-S:counter.

118. Haves to Jack Cuddy, UP, August 12, 1949; "Churchmen," 11; Philip Lerman to Cohen, memo re "Local Contacts: JACL," August 31, 1951 (quotation actually refers to old movies), ADL Y1949–52 Pro-org:JACL. Also see Granger to Gutstadt, March 7, 1947, 1; ADL NEC, June 24–25, 1955, 1, ADL WB178; "Nisei Make the Grade," 5; Women's Division, Chicago UL, "Because We Believe," leaflet, n.d. [1946], NUL SRO A78 regarding media stereotypes broadly; Melvin Ely, *The Adventures of Amos 'n' Andy* (New York, 1991), 228–36, regarding NAACP protest of the television show and AJC's positive but limited support.

119. AJC, "Purposes"; Theodor Adorno et al., *The Authoritarian Personality* (New York, 1950), AJC Social Studies series: Studies in Prejudice, #3; "Carefully Taught," from *South Pacific*, lyrics by Oscar Hammerstein, 1949. Similar topics from AJC materials: Oscar Handlin, "Prejudice and Capitalist Exploitation," *Commentary*, July 1948, 79–85; Richard Simpson, "Negro-Jewish Prejudice: Authoritarianism and Some Social Variables as Correlates," *Social Problems* (Fall 1959): 138–47; Robin Williams Jr., *Strangers Next Door* (Englewood Cliffs, N.J., 1964), esp. chap. 5.

120. David Robinson to Saks, "Case Report."

121. Rogers, "Integration," 80–81. Local NAACP head claimed her office, not the BBW, organized the petition (AJC, "Truth about Baltimore" 36). Perhaps both collaborated, but each took sole credit.

122. "History and Aims of the Joint Committee for Employment Opportunity," report, February 8, 1949, ADL Y1949–52:Pro-org. Both the strategy and success are reminiscent of Depression-era efforts in Harlem. Of the forty-four, at least twenty were women's organizations. Members: NUL, Jewish Council, CORE, NAACP, NCJW, YWCA, ACWC, nine church groups, several unions, and education groups.

123. Houser, "Education through Action," n.d. [Spring 1946?], ADL Y1946:NRP; Billie Ames, "CORE Fights Lunch Counter Discrimination," *CORE-lator*, October 1949, 2–3; "News You Don't Read in the Papers," *CORE-*

lator, October 1949, 4. CORE, pioneer of nonviolent direct action, conducted many such projects. Houser also describes CORE protests against University of Chicago's support of covenants, 2. See also August Meier and Elliot Rudwick, *CORE* (Urbana, Ill., 1973). CORE and its parent FOR also tackled A-S: see NVDA Committee Minutes, February 15, 1945, NUL SRO: A74.

124. Balkin to Trager, "Negro-White Relations—Miami Area," August 26, 1947; Balkin to Saks, memo, "Negro-White Relations—Miami Area"; Saks to Balkin, reply, July 24, 1947; Miller to Balkin, September 3, 1947, all ADL Y1947:NRP. Many similar examples can be found in ADL Y1949–52:NRP. ADL also monitored integrated southern baseball games: see Tom Freedman, memo re "Observations Observing a Segregated Audience Observing a Non-Segregated Athletic Contest," April 7, 1949 (Houston); Miller to "JHS," April 12, 1949 (Atlanta); ADL PR, December 3, 1950; Brant Coopersmith, ADL, to Cohen, February 28, 1951. All ADL Y1949–52:NRP. For northern efforts, see Max Flesicher [?] to [Colorado] Governor Thomas Mabry, June 17, 1948, ADL Y1948:NRP; ADL, "Memo," n.d. [cover letter, August 6, 1952], 1, ADL Y1949–52:NRP. It still monitored anti-Semites and racists: see NAACP, ROS, NAACP IIA145; Maslow, NCRAC Committee on CL, December 18, 1952, 6; ADL yearly Y:"Books—Undesirable," "MP," AJC VF:A-S:counter; AJCongress, "Catalog of . . . Materials Dealing with . . . Defamation"; *The Facts* 2, no. 4 (April 1947): 33–37; 2, no. 6 (June 1947): 19–21 (about worrisome publications). The files include Jewish protests against racism and black protests against A-S.

125. Max Heller, BB Lodge, Lebanon, Pa., to ADL, November 10, 1948; reply, Monroe Sheinberg to Heller, November 15, 1948, ADL Y1948:NRP; Granger to Gutstadt, March 7, 1947, 1. See also Elsie Elfenbein, ED, NCJW, to Epstein, June 14, 1950; reply, Braverman to Elfenbein, June 16, 1950; Miller to Elfenbein, June 27, 1950; Edward Zeisler to L. Zacks, President, Men's Club, Beth Israel, Vancouver, B.C., January 16, 1950; P. Allen Rickles to Leonard Krivencs, JCC, Stockton, Calif., October 20, 1949, all ADL Y1949–52:NRP. Dore Schary criticized Jewish bigotry: see 1948 ADL NC, transcript, 17–18, 21–24.

126. ADL, untitled manual "prepared as a guide for work in the field of social discrimination," n.d. [1947], 1, ADL Y1947:NRP; "Safeguarding," 19–20. They combined efforts to change laws and licensing requirements with direct intervention with discriminators. Jews also faced social discrimination, but blacks fared worse, Jewish studies stressed (e.g., Schwartz and Terman, "Study of Illinois," 12).

127. Hannah Arendt, e.g., argued in favor of free association. See Richard King, *CR and the Idea of Freedom* (New York, 1992); Polsgrove, *Divided Minds*. On persuasion as a CR strategy, see, e.g., Rabkin to Charles Evans, Watkins Glen, N.Y., November 7, 1949, ADL Y1949–52:NRP.

128. "CIO Sues N.J. Restaurant for Jim Crowism," *Defender*, July 27, 1946; Samuel Scheiner, Minnesota Jewish Council to Rabkin, Lukas (AJC), Maslow, Cohen (NCRAC), October 27, 1950, memo re "Negro bathing beach case," ADL Y1949–52:NRP; "Interracial Workshop," 2–3 (CORE); Rabkin to Trager, memo, February 25, 1949, ADL Y1948:NRP; "Far-Reaching Decision on Negro Rights," *CORE-lator*, October 1949, 1; "Non-Segregation Works at Palisades," 2. See also "Hudson [N.Y.] Bias Case Called," *Courier*, September 27, 1947; "AJC[ongress] Hails Court Ruling on Bob-Lo," *Detroit News*, February 13, 1948; "Baths in

Rockaway [N.Y.] Ordered to End Discrimination," *PM*, August 1947; "2nd Rockaway Beach Bathhouse Ordered to Cease Jim Crow," *New York Age*, September 13, 1947, all AJCongress CF.

129. Rabkin, Brooks to ADL RO and CRCs, AJC chapters, joint memo re "Decision of Ohio Court of Appeals Involving Racial Discrimination of Golf Courses," May 18, 1950, ADL Y1949–52:NRP.

130. Rabbi Benjamin Kahn, Director, Pennsylvania State College Hillel to Forster, March 10, 1948; Forster to Kahn, March 22, 1948; Kahn to Forster, April 5, 1948; Forster to Kahn, April 23, 1948; Rabkin to Kahn, November 22, 1948; Kahn to Rabkin, December 14, 1948; Rabkin to Kahn, December 20, 1948, all ADL Y1948:NRP. Also see Harold Zipser, chairman, Anti-Defamation Committee to Brauerman [Braverman], November 17, 1947; reply [unsigned], November 20, 1947, both ADL Y1947:NRP. The same strategy was used in the Rockaway campaign, and by 1930s communists challenging housing discrimination. The Pennsylvania law did not explicitly include barbers, a loophole an NAACP campaign finally closed. NAACP did launch a boycott and CORE opened an integrated shop.

131. "The Story of the CCREM March 1949–April 1951," April 20, 1953; Claire Selltiz, CCREM, "Procedures and Findings of Restaurant Audit, June 16–23, 1950," April 18, 1951; CCREM, "Instructions for Restaurant Audit," all NAACP IIA370. Discriminatory treatment included poor seating location and inferior service. CORE also tested discrimination by New York YMCA overnight residences ("Interracial Workshop," 4).

132. Milton Senn, Los Angeles CFPB, "ABC Drops Caucasian Rule," June 15, 1950; Rabkin, "Supplemental Fact Sheet on ABC," Report for NCRAC, May 13, 1950; Wilkins to N.Y. Attorney General Nathaniel Goldstein, December 6, 1949; Rabkin to ADL RO, May 15, 1950; untitled news item, *CORE-lator*, October 1949, 1; BB WSC, "Resolution: Women's International Bowling Congress," AM, March 1950, all ADL Y1949–52:NRP:Appendix. For similar action against the PGA (golf), see ADL, "Louis Scores TKO Over PGA," report, January 17, 1952, ADL Y1949–52:NRP.

133. Krapin to Haves (Connecticut ADL) memo re "National Duckpin Bowling Congress," February 28, 1952, ADL Y1949–52:NRP. See also Senn to Forster, July 12, 1950, memo re "Segregation in Theaters—Arizona"; Forster to Senn, September 6, 1950, both ADL Y1949–52:NRP.

134. Petegorsky, *Combatting Racism*, 10–11; "Struggle," 39. See also White to George [Mintzer], [draft], December 2, 1948, 3–4, NAACP IIA325.

135. Houser, "Education," 1–2; Granger to Gutstadt, March 7, 1947, 2.

136. For organizational philanthropy, see Steinbrink's fund-raising letter for NAACP; Granger to Gutstadt, March 7, 1947, 1 (black fund-raiser for United Jewish Appeal); Leo Shapiro to Bisgyer, memo re "UL Service Fund," December 5, 1947, both ADL Y1947:NRP; Trager to Sidman, April 27, 1949 (ADL contribution to NUL); Van Doren to Trager, June 10, 1948, ADL Y1948:NRP (ADL contribution to NAACP's legal work). For community support, see Murray Friedman, "The Jews," in *Through Different Eyes* ed. Peter Rose, Stanley Rothman, and William Wilson (London, 1973), 157. Clayborne Carson and others found Jews disproportionate among white supporters of the NAACP, SCLC, etc.: see

Carson, "Black-Jewish Universalism" in Salzman and West, *Struggles*; Clark, "Positive Transition," 6, 8; James Robinson, "Some Apprehension, Much Hope," *ADL Bulletin*, December 1957, 7. For earlier years, see Nancy Weiss, "Long Distance Runners." Progress was not absolute: bigotry, parochialism, and limited budgets remained. See, e.g., Schwartz and Terman, "Study of Illinois," 12; ACCR, "Portland, Oregon," Report, n.d. [1944], 4, NUL 3:2; CRC Minutes, May 25, 1950, 3–4.

137. Leo Shapiro to Mrs. Miriam [Renzler?], October 4, 1946, ADL Y1946. A New York study found 60 percent of Jews held negative views (Clark, "Positive Transition," 10). The same study found that 70 percent of African Americans held unfavorable Jewish stereotypes; see below. Other studies found Jewish students to be less racist than gentile whites (Clark, 11); "Jewish-Negro Relations in Post War Period," n.d. [1943?] found low but persistent Jewish racism, 4–5, AJC VF: NJR:AJC 38–49; Simpson, "Negro-Jewish Prejudice," 144 found that among Jews, the more highly educated, the less racist; J. X Cohen, *The Negro and A-S*, pamphlet (AJCongress, 1944), 7, found white gentiles to be more racist than white Jews; also see Schwartz and Terman, "Study of Illinois," 4–5. For white gentile views of blacks (and Jews), see G. Gilbert, "Stereotype Persistence and Change among College Students," *Journal of Abnormal and Social Psychology* 46 (1951): 245–54; NORC, "The Color Line in Industry," 8–11; Williams, *Strangers Next Door*, esp. chaps. 4, 7; poll data in *Fortune*, November 1942, 10, 14; November 1943, 10, 14; "Fortune Survey," *Fortune*, February 1946, 257–60; also October 1947, AJC IVF:Public Opinion Polls:Fortune Surveys; Elmo Roper, "What People Are Thinking," *New York Tribune*, February 2, 1945, and undated 1945 NCs, AJC IVF:Public Opinion Polls:Elmo Roper; Roper, "Study of Anti-Minority Sentiment in Colleges," report, October 1949, 14–15, 20–21, 26–27, 52–53, ADL WB42. For a caution regarding poll data, see Samuel Flowerman and Marie Jahoda, "Polls on A-S," *Commentary* 1, no. 6 (April 1946): 82–86. See also "Safeguarding," 59.

138. White to "Jewish leaders," memo, December 1, 1947 ["Cancel WW" written over it], NAACP IIA325. The memo was never sent (too explosive?). There was also elite black paternalism: see, e.g., Arthur Huff Fauset, "A-S Among Us"; Engel, "Report of Mrs . . . Engel."

139. White to Maslow, December 10, 1947, 2–4, NAACP IIA360. Emphasis his. The letter was in reply to Maslow's thanks regarding the UN.

140. Clark, "Positive Transition," 6; Jewish leaders quoted from Dinnerstein, *A-S in America*, 208. Emphasis in original. Some offered even harsher criticisms: see Clark, "Candor about NJR," *Commentary* 1, no. 4 (February 1946): 8–14; Keith, "Will Negro, Jewish Labor Leaders War over CR?" *Courier*, December 12, 1959, 3 (the explosive JLC article discussed above).

141. NCJW, Proceedings of 17th TC, November 10, 1943, vol. 2, 563, NCJW:43; "Struggle," 32–33; "Discussion Leader," 4. See also Petegorsky, *Combatting Racism*, 11.

142. See, e.g., Clark, "Candor," 10–13; Clark, "Positive," 6; "Our Guest Column," #7, APA, December 31, 1945, ADL Y1945; Randolph, "Our Guest Column, April 23, 1946, 2; Robert Carter (NAACP), at AJCongress, "Struggle," 19–20, 29–30; William Cummings, "The Jewish Problem from the Negro's Point of

View," *BB Messenger*, April 12, 1946, 21–22; Dan Gardner, "Jews and Negroes," *Louisville Defender*, May 5, 1945, both AJC IVF:NJR:Negro; Dinnerstein, *A-S in America*, chap. 10 (argues polls reveal higher black A-S than white); Simpson, "Negro-Jewish Prejudice," Robinson, "Apprehension," 4–5; Celia Heller and Alphonso Pinkney, "Attitudes of Negroes toward Jews," *Social Forces* 43, no. 3 (March 1965): 365. On A-S in general, see Dinnerstein, "Exposed"; Dinnerstein, *A-S in America*, chap. 8; "The [1946] Fortune Survey," 257; George Mintzer, "The Postwar Ebb," *New Leader*, August 21, 1948, 7; Rose, "Outlook for AS"; NORC, "CR in the US," March 1, 1948; Baldwin, "Harlem Ghetto," 168–70. The ADL surveyed A-S annually.

143. Mrs. A.B. [Stella] Counselbaum to Russell Babcock, CCHR, April 22, 1948, ADL Chisub:CRD; Jay Schultz et al., CCHR, to Counselbaum, June 25, 1948, ADL Y1948:NRP. See also Counselbaum to Gross, memo re "Chicago Defender Marva Louis Story of April 17," May 18, 1948. Other examples include Homer Jack to John Sengstacke, editor, *Defender*, April 22, 1948, both ADL Chisub:CRD; "What Can We Learn from Jews?" *Defender*, October 15, 1955, C, ADL Chisub:CRD policy; Arnold Rose to P. [Percival] L. Prattis, Executive editor, *Courier*, December 6, 1947, ADL Y1947.

144. *Crusader*, August 25, 1956), 1; AJC, "Baltimore," 38. See also "Jewish-Negro Relationships," 5; Baldwin, "Harlem Ghetto," 169; A. Abbot Rosen, memo, "Chicago Defender," September 8, 1952, ADL Chisub:CRD; Counselbaum to Rosen, memo: "Chicago Defender," July 16, 1952; Rosen to Sengstacke, July 21, 1952; reply, July 29; White to George, December 2, 1948. For invectives, see, e.g., Forster to Mary McLeod Bethune, May 1, 1952, ADL Y1949–52:NRP; "Josephine Baker Says," flyer, n.d.; Pinsley to Braverman, memo "re Josephine Baker," December 28, 1951; Braverman to Myron Schwartz, February 6, 1952, all ADL Chisub:CRD; "Southern Exposure," *Defender*, December 15, 1956; Berland to Will Alexander, ACRR, June 20, 1944, ADL Y1944:NRP; H. George Davenport, "Who's Crazy Now?" *Crusader*, n.d. [January 1945?], cited in Berland to Balm Leavell Jr., *Crusader* (who wrote "Are We A-S?" in same issue), February 13, 1945, ADL Y1945:NRP. Some A-S discourse was a byproduct of nationalist efforts to oust Jews and other whites from black neighborhoods, see, e.g., ADL regarding anti-Semitic orator Solomon Wright, ADL Y1948:NRP; Buy Black Committee, "Hit Now; Hit Hard: Oust the Jews from Harlem," handbill, n.d., AJC IVF:NJR:NYC.

145. Bibb, "Hating Jews," *Courier*, November 3[?], 1947; Foster to Epstein, November 10, 1947; Berland to Epstein, memo re "A.L. Foster's letter of 11/10," November 12, 1947, all ADL Y1947:NRP; White to Maslow, December 10, 1947, NAACP IIA360. Neither CCHR nor Counselbaum appeared greatly troubled. See also Lillian Friedberg to Forster, October 2, 1946, ADL Y1946:NRP; I. Joel Komarow to Epstein, memo re "'Pittsburgh Courier' March 27, 1948—Schuyler column," March 29, 1948; Counselbaum to Trager, Memo re "George Schuyler—Pittsburgh Courier," March 3, 1948; Counselbaum to Trager, April 19, 1948; Trager to Forster, memo re "Attached Folder of Clippings by Schuyler," May 3, 1948, all ADL Y1948:NRP.

146. "Do Unto Others as You Would Have Them . . ." *Call*, October 12, 1951, C, ADL Y1949–52:NRP. Even UNIA condemned A-S: "Is the UNIA Anti-Semitic?" *Centralist Bulletin* 2, no. 9 (September 1944), C, UNIA microfilm reel 2.

147. Sherman to Gutstadt et al. memo re "Conditions in the South," 4. For Jewish responses, see e.g., AJC, "Baltimore," 36–37; I. Joel Komarow to "Presidents and ADL Chairmen of Chapters," memo, September 18, 1950, ADL Y1949–52:NRP. On southern business tensions, see Harold Sheppard, "The Negro Merchant," *American Journal of Sociology* 53, no. 2 (September 1947): 96–99; Harry Golden, "Jew and Gentile in the New South," *Commentary*, November 1959, 409–10, 412.

148. Hollander to White, August 22, 1947, NAACP IIC78.

149. White to Arthur Spingarn, August 25, 1947; White to Wilkins, Marshall, and Current, August 25, 1947; Current to White, Wilkins, and Marshall, memo re "Baltimore Situation," August 28, 1947; Wilkins to White, August 28, 1947, all NAACP IIC78.

150. White to Current, September 2, 1947, memo. See also Walter Zand, Baltimore BB Council, to Herman Zand, September 5, 1947; Spingarn to White, September 11, 1947; White to Hollander, September 15, 1947; reply, September 18, 1947, all NAACP IIC78. Jewish shopper petitions were never mentioned.

151. Rabkin to Forster, June 27, 1947, memo re "Essex County NJ JCRC Action against Orbach's"; Rabkin to Forster, July 10, 1947, both ADL Y1947:NRP. For a similar effort, see Samuel Scheiner, Minnesota Jewish Council, to Eleanor Belack, ADL, November 2, 1948, regarding Katz Drugstore, Des Moines, Iowa, ADL Y1948:NRP.

152. George Schermer, "Report of Meeting . . . to more effectively organize East Side Merchants Association," April 18, 1947, Detroit Commission of Community Relations Collection Part 3, box 19, provided by Tom Sugrue. Owners complained that insurance companies, fearing another riot, refused to insure them; these Jews, seen as exploiters, were themselves vulnerable.

153. Richman to Trager, December 9, 1946; NCRAC to Actors Equity, "Re National Theater, Washington," n.d. [May 28, 1947], both ADL Y1947:NRP. See also Steinbrink to Epstein, May 28, 1947; Richman to Saks, memo re "National Theater, Washington, D.C.," May 7, 1947, both ADL Y1947:NRP. On the petition, see "Joins Tolerance Fight," *Chicago Times*, August 27, 1947; "Tallulah Raps D.C. Prejudice," *Defender*, September 6, 1947, both AJCongress Cs. The petition failed: see White to George, December 2, 1948, 1–2. For a similar effort see "Near Morningside Theater Drops Jim Crow Policy," *Indianapolis Recorder*, July 17, 1948; Indianapolis JCRC, "Report on Segregation in Neighborhood Theaters, Indianapolis, Indiana," n.d. [1948], both ADL Y1948:NRP.

154. Clark, "Positive," 5–6; Robinson, "Apprehension," 7. Brooklyn AJCongress Women agreed: see Newman, "Safeguarding," 59. For more on hostile suburban Jews, see chap. 6.

155. Ray Mohl, "South of the South?" *JAEH* 18, no. 2 (Winter 1999): 3–36; NCJW National Committee on Social Legislation, minutes, May 28, 1943, NCJW:141; John Harris, "Progress Report to members of [NUL] Interracial Committee," n.d. [1950?], 2, NUL 6:21. Other examples can be found in Harold Braverman to Arthur Levin, October 26, 1951, ADL Y1949–52:NRP; Henry Green,

Gesher Va'Kesher: Bridges and Bonds (Atlanta, 1995); Leonard Greenberg, memo "Re: Milton Kramer," n.d. [1946], ADL Y1946:NRP; Greene, *Temple Bombing*; Krause, "Rabbis and Negro Rights," 28–34, 38–42 (Reform rabbis). Pierce, *Polite Protest*, 33–37, 43–44, describes participation of local rabbis and AJCongress members in (failed) Indianapolis desegregation efforts in the late 1940s, although he stresses the limited, "polite" methods used. Also see Clive Webb, *Fight against Fear* (Athens, Ga., 2001). On Southern "lay" Jews, see Dollinger, " 'Hamans' and 'Torquenadas' "; Greenberg, "The Southern Jewish Community," Nathan Kaganoff and Melvin Urofsky, *Turn to the South* (Richmond, Va., 1979); Suzanne Nossel, "Weathering the Storm: The Jewish Community in Birmingham, Alabama during the CR Revolution" (bachelor's thesis, Harvard University, 1991), 59–64, Krause, "Rabbis and Negro Rights," 21–25; ADL NC, October 24–25, 1952, 303, ADL WB176; Miller to Nelson Jackson, NUL, February 21, 1951, NUL SRO: A124; Miller to Berland, and letter to *Lighthouse and Informer*, both July 12, 1946, ADL Y1946:NRP. For a more personal story, see Edward Cohen, *The Peddler's Grandson* (Jackson, Miss., 1999).

156. Forster to CRC and ADL RO, memo, January 26, 1951, ADL Y1949–52:NRP; Handwritten notes, n.d., NUL 6:22; Milton Ellerin to Gilbert Balkin, ADL, December 12, 1952, ADL Y1949–52:NRP. See also Fineberg to Slawson, memo re "Situation in Miami," January 21, 1952, 3, AJC VF:Communities: Miami FL; Miller to Novins, NJR; Golden, "Jews of the South," 9–11; Bernstein and Bernstein, "Washington," 401; Friedman, "Episode," 171. On black anger, see, e.g., "Southern Exposure," *Defender*, December 15, 1956. Others understood Jews' dilemma: see Robinson, "Apprehension," 6; Wilkins to Isaac Toubin, June 26, 1958, AJC VF NJR:AJCongress; Clark, "Positive," 5.

157. Lukas, "New Threats to Freedom of Voluntary Association," Speech to Detroit Public Schools Human Relations Institute, March 1, 1958, 19–20, NUL 1:4. For the Southerners' pressure to tone down, see Friedman, "Episode," 174–81; Albert Vorspan, "Dilemma of the Southern Jew," *Reconstructionist* 4 (January 1959): 24–26; James Lebeau, "Profile of a Southern Jewish Community," *AJHQ* 58 (June 1969): 429–44; Wilkins to Toubin, June 26, 1958; ADL NEC, January 7–8, 1956, 9, ADL WB178; Nossel, "Weathering the Storm," 54, 70–76; AJCongress, "Southern Jewish Community," resolution, BC, May 14–18, 1958 (in Maslow to Moon, May 21, 1958), NAACP IIIA196; "Controversy." "Controversy" praised ADL's southern CR work; Levine, "Southern Jewish Views," criticized the League's timidity, and that of JLC, AJC, BB (20–23, 33–34).

158. NCJW, 17th TC, November 1943, minutes, vol. 2, 393–94, NCJW:43. The resolution passed.

159. NCRAC meeting, September 9–11, 1949, 5, ADL Y1949–52:Pro-org:CRC. The minutes paraphrased Hexter.

160. David Rose, ADL NC, 1952, 94–104, 126; AJC DAC, October 8, 1952, 5; ADL NEC, January 15–16, 1955, 18, ADL WB178. See also Forster to National CR committee, memo re "ADL Brief Amicus in Public Elementary School Segregation Cases," July 21, 1952; memo, August 20, 1952; memo re "Briefs Amicus in Racial Segregation Cases," October 13, 1952, all ADL Chisub:12; ADL NC, October 20, 1951, addendum page regarding SRO Resolution, ADL WB176.

Beyond faith in gradualism, Jewish organizations also hesitated to act publicly for fear of being labeled communist. See chap. 5.

161. White to Epstein, June 2, 1949; reply, June 9, 1949, NAACP IIA363; Miller to Murray Friedman, December 31, 1958, ADL Y1953–58:Orgs: NAACP. See also White's eulogy at Stephen Wise's memorial service, May 25, 1949, 11–13, NAACP IIA362.

162. H. E. Trevvett, Secretary-Treasurer, Commercial Travelers, to Mr.__ (sic) February 18, 1942, NAACP IIA360; Maslow, "Struggle," 23; see also Bureau on Jewish Employment Problems, "Placement Experiences of Applicants to a Private Employment Agency," September 1955, AJC VF:CF; "For Drive On Discrimination" (on Columbia University applications).

163. Maslow, "Advancement," 6.

164. Maslow, "Advancement," 8. During World War II, e.g., firms might require photographs to accompany applications. "Attorneys-General" identified this difference between the more private A-S and the more structural and legal racism (589, 595). See also: Wilkins to Aronson, April 5, 1954, NAACP IIA386; Nathan Glazer, "Jews and Blacks," 105–12; Matthew Holden Jr., "Reflections on Two Isolated Peoples,"182–211, both in Washington, *Jews in Black Perspectives*.

165. Schwartz and Terman, "Study of Illinois," 4. Still, Jews were more committed to FEPC than other comparably well-off whites, although it would have little impact on Jewish employment (5). Few unions discriminated against Jews; many did against African Americans. See also: Emanuel Muravchik (JLC) to Max Weintraub, memo, "Discrimination within the Labor Movement," July 8, 1948, ADL Y1948:NRP.

166. Maslow, "Advancement," 6–8. On irrational prejudice, see, e.g., Gutstadt to W. E. MacKee, November 12, 1946, ADL Y1946:NRP. Some recognized other factors. McWilliams, *Mask for Privilege*, argued that economic forces created anti-Semitism. Handlin critiqued the roots of racism in formal systems of thought, personality formation, and economic determinism ("Prejudice," 80–85).

167. Clark, "Positive Transition," 6. See also Maslow, "Advancement," 8. On the Jews and middle class, see, e.g., Glazer, "American Jew and Attainment of Middle-Class Rank," 138–46.

168. Edelstein, "Jewish Relationship with the Emerging Negro Community in the North," address to NCRAC, June 23, 1960, 8–9, AJC VF:NJR:AJCongress; Wilkins to Aronson, April 5, 1954. See also Delany, "Integration," 76–78 (regarding weak black support for Israel).

CHAPTER FIVE
Red Menace

1. For overviews, see e.g., Anderson, *Eyes Off the Prize*; Thomas Borstelmann, *The Cold War and the Color Line* (Cambridge, Mass, 2001); Paul Puble and Robin D. G. Kelley, "Allies of a Different Sort," in Salzman and West, *Struggles in the Promised Land*, 197–229; Dudziak, *Cold War*. For local stories, see, e.g., Martha Biondi, *To Stand and Fight* (Cambridge, Mass., 2003) on New York;

Bill Mullen, *Popular Fronts* (Urbana, Ill., 1999), on Chicago. The prewar left is discussed in previous chapters.

2. For intellectuals and the left, see e.g., William Chafe, *Never Stop Running* (New York, 1993), on Allard Lowenstein; Martin Duberman, *Paul Robeson* (New York, 1989); Freedomways Editors, *Paul Robeson* (New York, 1998); Gerald Horne, *Black Liberation, Red Scare* (Newark, Del., 1993), on Ben Davis; Horne, *Black and Red*; Manning Marable, "Peace and Black Liberation," *Science and Society* 47, no. 4 (1984): 385–405, both on Du Bois; Ellen Schrecker, *No Ivory Tower* (New York, 1986); Wald, *New York Intellectuals*; see also chap. 4 and below.

3. BB 15th NC, Resolution #12, June 1938; Granger to Mr. Clagett, May 9, 1956, NUL I:49. See also AJC, "Confidential Background Memorandum on Communism," n.d. [1947?], AJC VF:CJ:AJC.

4. See, e.g., Minsky, "Jewry and Democracy," *Reconstructionist*, March 25, 1938, reprinted in "Jewish Communism' Is a Lie!" *Modern View*, February 15, 1940, AJC IVF:CJ.

5. AJC, "Confidential," 2.

6. Statement endorsed at AJCongress EC, October 5, 1949, 6 (inserted into every brief regarding loyalty), Cyrus Adler (AJC), Alfred Cohen (BB), B.C. Vladeck (JLC), "Public Statement on Communism and Jews," October 21, 1935, AJC IVF:CJ. See also AJCongress Statement; AJCongress Opening Plenary, transcript, BC, November 9, 1949, Justine Wise Polier, 49, AJCongress box C&C; Henry Schultz, "Are We a Nation of 'Againsts?'" ADL *Bulletin*, November 1953, quoted in Schultz to Werner Markus, January 29, 1954, ADL Y1953–58:I:McC.

7. Granger, "Statement Presented to and at the request of THE HOUSE COMMITTEE ON UNAMERICAN ACTIVITIES," Washington, D.C., July 14, 1949, 1, 8–9, NUL I:155; Wilkins to Charles Howard, November 3, 1949, NAACP IIA467. The other enemy, Granger noted, was the racist. More on the dual argument against right and left below.

8. Frank Crosswaith, "Communists and the Negro," address to Catholic Moderators' Labor School, n.d. [1938?], 5–7, Crosswaith additions box 1, Schomburg.

9. "Project Big Four!" leaflet, n.d. [1954?], NUL I:49.

10. Granger to Edwin Lukas (AJC), December 7, 1955 (Lukas to Granger, December 2, 1955, contained Big Four leaflet), both NUL I:49. Granger to Executive Staff, memo, December 15, 1955, describes the meeting; "AJC Raps Tenney in Answer to Charges," *Eastside Journal*, April 7, 1948, AJCongress CF. See also Granger to ESs of Affiliated Organizations, memo, October 15, 1954, regarding community chests; Theodore Leskes to Manheim Shapiro, AJC, memo re "Attack on UL," September 28, 1956, AJC VF:Names:NUL; "The Smear," ADL "Fact Sheet," August 23, 1954, ADL Y1953–58:Communism A-Ill.

11. Friedman to Forster, memo, "The Smear That Failed," February 11, 1952, ADL Y1949–52:NRP.

12. "Declaration of Constitutional Principles," March 12, 1956, in *Debating the CR Movement, 1945–1968*, ed. Steven Lawson and Charles Payne (Lanham, Md., 1998), 54–59. See also, e.g., *NAACP v. Alabama* (1958). For fuller discussions, see Mark Tushnet, *Making CR Law* (New York, 1994), chap. 20; Snyder

and Goodman, *Friend of the Court*, 34–35 (refers to ADL's amicus brief); Carl Rowan, *Dream Makers, Dream Breakers* (Boston, 1993), 254.

13. Ruth Raphael to White, July 24, 1930 (includes Wood testimony, July 16, 1930), NAACP IC219; Granger, "Statement," 3–7. See also Crosswaith, "Communists," 3, 4; Edward Turner, statement to HUAC, February 26, 1952, 2, ADL Y1949–52:NRP; Wilson Record, "The NEGRO and the COMMUNISTS," *New Leader* [1951?] reprinted by ADL, WB182. Groups also stressed their own anti-CP credentials.

14. Statement to State Department for Voice of America, in ROS for May, n.d. [May 1949], 2, NAACP IIA145; Alex Miller to Alvin Stokes, Committee on Un-American Activities, May 25, 1949, ADL Y1949–52 NRP (the concerned investigator was himself black). See also Commission on Interracial Cooperation, "Few Reds among Atlanta Negroes Says Committee," PR, November 27, 1934 (released December 1), NAACP IC311.

15. Marshall quoted in AJC, "Confidential," 11. See also AJC, BB, ADL, ZOA, AJCongress, Orthodox, Conservative, Reform movements, "The Protocols, Bolshevism and the Jews," December 1, 1920, reissued in "Jewish Communism."

16. AJC, B'nai B'rith, JLC, "Public Statement," October 21, 1935, AJC VF:CJ:AJC; Rabbi Edward Israel, interview with *Hebrew Advocate* and *Connecticut Hebrew Record*, March 24, 1939, cited in AJC, "Jewish Statements on Communism," n.d. [1939?], AJC IVF:CJ:AJC. See also ADL October 1950 NC, transcript, 351. On the smear linking Jews to the CP, see, e.g., "Close-Williams Pamphlet on the ADL," ADL, *Facts* 2, no. 12 (December 1947): 7–15.

17. ADL Fireside Discussion Group, *Hitler's Communism Unmasked*, pamphlet, 1938. See also Finder to Gutstadt, November 11, 1938; ADL NC, October 21–22, 1950, 19–20, ADL WB176.

18. On the AJC and news, see, e.g., AJC DAC, August 16, 1950; August 23, 1950; October 10, 1950 (Rose column, 3); November 2, 1950; January 9, 1951; May 18, 1954, 2–5, 7; June 22, 1954, 1–4; Slawson to Joseph Roos, ED, Los Angeles JCRC, January 14, 1954, ADL Y1953–58:CRC. Jewish agencies recognized communism's attraction for Jews, so they also directed propaganda internally: see Samuel Feller, AJC, "Current Trends in A-S," address before AJC EC, May 10, 1952, AJC VF:A-S:AJC; Slawson to AJC Domestic Program committee, memo re "Unwarranted Identification of Jews and Communists," January 16, 1948, AJC VF:CJ:AJC.

19. JWV, NC Resolution, January 8, 1939; "Jewish Communism." See also CCAR, "Social Justice Message,"1936, all AJC IVF:CJ:AJC. For other agency statements, see "Jewish Statements"; S. Andhil Fineberg, AJC, "Answering the Communist Charge," memo, April 1, 1947, AJC IVF:CJ:AJC; Fineberg, "Whom Do Communists Serve?" 1947, AJC IVF:CJ; Fineberg to Slawson, "Seventh Report of Staff Coordinator of Program on Communism," memo, February 1955, ADL Y1953–58:Communism A-Ill. On the Jewish press, see, e.g., *Forward*, editorials, January 18, 1935, September 14, 1935; "Defenders of Murder," *The Day*, January 2, 1935 and "The Third International and the United Front," July 27, 1935; "Democracy in Russia?" *Morning Journal*, January 3, 1935, and I. Fishman, untitled article, December 29, 1935; Rabbi Abba Hillel Silber, "Are American Jews Communists?" *American Hebrew*, July 2, 1937; Louis Rittenberg, "Ex-

ploding Another Myth," *American Hebrew and Jewish Tribune* 135, no. 14 (August 17, 1954): inside cover, 244, all in "'Jewish Communism'"; [AJC?], "Activities of the Jewish Press in America toward Soviet Russia before and after the Communist International Congress," 1935, AJC IVF:CJ:AJC. On individual rabbis, see, e.g., Rabbi Israel Goldstein, interview, *Newark Ledger*, May 8, 1939, in "Jewish Statements"; Rabbi Israel, interview. Jewish agencies also monitored CP policy regarding black or Jewish recruitment and investigated suspected front groups. See, e.g., *AJCW*, editorial, November 22, 1946; Frederick Woltman, "Reds Now Anti-Jewish, Wise's Group Warns," *N.Y. World Telegram*, November 22, 1946; George Field (Freedom House), letter to editor, *NYT*, December 11, 1946, all AJC VF:CP&J; AJC, "Confidential," 2–3, 9–10; Betty Kaye, JLC, to [J]CRC's, ADL RO, memo re "recent shifts in CP line," April 13, 1953, ADL Y1953–58: Communism:JLC; James Allen, "The Negro Question," *Political Affairs*, November 1946; "Defeat of the Comrades," *ADL Bulletin*, October 1950, 1, 7–8; Epstein to ADL RO, memo re "CP Policy Work in the Jewish Community," September 11, 1950, AJC IVF:CJ:CP propaganda. On the investigations, see Gutstadt to Finder, August 22, 1939; Epstein to Stanley Jacobs, October 27, 1939; Jacobs to Finder, October 12, 1939, ADL Y39:NCJC [National Council Jewish Communists]; Robert Greenfield to Gutstadt, October 7, 1939, and memo, re "NCJC," December 18, 1940; Maurice Fagan to Greenfield and Gutstadt, December 9, 1940, memo re "NCJC"; Greenfield to Fagan, December 9, 1940, memo re "NCJC"; NCJC to "Friend" accompanying "The Jewish People and the War"; NCJC, "Call to All Jews," n.d.; Greenfield to Miles Goldberg, April 27, 1940, memo re "NCJC"; Greenfield to Finder, December 23, 1940; Barbara Biegeleisen, "Report on NCJC," n.d.; Emanuel Muravchik, JLC, to [J]CRC's and ADL RO, memo re "N.Y. Jewish Conference," July 8, 1952, JLC:21–5.

20. SCA (Orthodox, Conservative, Reform rabbinic, and congregational bodies), PR, June 25, 1951, in ADL Y1949–52:Pro-org:NCRAC; Granger, Address to National Conference of Social Work, May 15, [1951], NUL I:169. See also AJCongress, "Statement on World Peace," AJCongress NEC, July 20, 1950, AJCongress box AEC 1946–50.

21. AJC, "Confidential," 3. Actually, polls revealed the public generally did not equate Jews and communism. See, e.g., AJC DAC, January 9, 1951, 1 and May 18, 1954, 3; "Brief Summary of Community Replies to NCRAC Request for Information on Local Experiences Re Combating Communism," marked "Confidential," n.d. [1950?], JLC:21–5; Fineberg to Slawson, 1, 6.

22. "Timely Topics," *AJCW* 17, no. 32 (December 4, 1950): 3–5; NAACP, MMBD, December 10, 1951, 7, NAACP IIA135; ADL, NC, October 1950, transcript, 361 (Novins). JWV also affiliated. See also Slawson to Roos, 2. NAACP declined to join. ADL, the Federal Council of Churches, and a few other liberal organizations also joined the Conference to press it to combat all totalitarian and fascist groups (see AJC DAC, February 28, 1950, 3).

23. "WHY A JEWISH LEAGUE AGAINST COMMUNISM?"*JAC* 1, no. 1 (July–August 1948): 2. On Cohn, see "Roy Cohn Promoted," *JAC* 5, no. 3 (Autumn 1952): 1. For praise for the AJLAC, see Gretta Palmer, "The Jews Fight the Reds," *Commentator* (1948): 8–13 (copied by AJC), AJC IVF:CJ. The AJLAC was founded in 1947.

24. Letter reprinted in "Reds Stir Race Hatred," *JAC* 1, no. 2 (High Holy Days 1948): 1–2. The critique of liberals is in the same issue "False Messiahs—Liberals, Beware!" AJC VF:AJLAC.

25. Granger to Officers and Directors of National Newspaper Publishers Association, October 13, 1955, NUL 1:49; ADL NEC, January 7–8, 1956, 9, ADL WB178; Lukas, "New Threats to Freedom of Voluntary Association," to Detroit Public Schools Human Relations Institute, March 1, 1958, 19–20, NUL 1:4; Mohl, "'South of the South?': Jews, Blacks, and the Civil Rights Movement in Miami, 1949–1960," *JAEH* 18, no. 2 (Winter 1999): 7–8.

26. Fineberg to "Members of the Association of Jewish Community Relations Workers," n.d. [1953], ADL Y1953–58 I:R; Granger to Claggett, May 9, 1956; "For a United Front Policy among the Jewish People," *Political Affairs* (1950): 4, 20–21, in AJC IVF:CP Propaganda. See also AJC DAC, "Statement of Policy toward Communist Affiliated and Communist Led Organizations," JLC:21–5; Steinbrink, ADL NC, October 24–25, 1952, transcript, 20, ADL WB176. United-front efforts included the New York Jewish Conference: see Muravchik to CRCs, ADL.

27. AJCong GC, August 6, 1935, 3–4, AJCongress box:GC April 1935– October 1938. See also "Communist Jews—Get Out!"; *Modern View*, September 28, 1939, AJCongress box:Publications 1915–41; "United Front," 4; Slawson to Roos.

28. Katherine Engel to Section President[s], December 31, 1952, NCJW:74. The text of the president's objection is below.

29. Muravchik to CRC, ADL, 1; AJC DAC, June 27, 1950, 2–4; Epstein to Roos, December 15, 1953; Cohen to Milton Senn, February 8, 1954, both ADL1953–58: Comm.:A-Ill. Actually, the JPFO was socialist, an offshoot of the Workmen's Circle. See also AJC "Policy"; DAC, June 22, 1954, 3; Slawson to Roos; Polier, "Safeguarding," 157; JWB, "Resolution on Use of Jewish Community Center Facilities, Public Forums and Controversial Speakers in Jewish Centers," adopted at NC, May 1952, ADL Chisub:12; David Robinson to Milton Ellerin, May 11, 1953 and May 25, 1953, ADL Y1953–58:Communists; Senn to Cohen, February 11, 1954, ADL Y1953–58:Comm.:A-Ill.

30. White to Murphy, memo, May 5, 1939. For similar cooperation, see Miss [Edith] Edmunds to White, Memo, May 31, 1939; Edmunds to Murphy, April 27, 1939, all NAACP IC207.

31. Murphy to White, May 12, 1939, NAACP IC207; Wilkins to Fred Gearing, February 21, 1950, NAACP IIA186. There were also controversies over methods of exclusion: e.g., draconian credentials committee for 1950 CR Mobilization (national coalitional lobbying effort): see Gearing, University of Chicago NAACP, to Wilkins, February 10, 1950; reply, February 21, 1950, NAACP IIA186.

32. Granger to Clagett, 1, 2.

33. Meier and Rudwick, *CORE*, 64.

34. White to Harry Davis, Cleveland NAACP, January 27, 1936; White to Randolph, February 3, 1936; reply, February 4, 1936; Houston [to White?], January 31, 1936, all NAACP IC383.

35. Wilkins, "Memorandum to the Board of Directors on NNC," March 9, 1936; Wilkins to Davis, March 11, 1936. Also see Davis to White, December 20, 1935, all NAACP IC383. NNC leaders included Randolph, Davis, Marion

Cuthbert (NAACP), Granger, Arthur Huff Fauset, Snow Grigsby, Rufus Atwood (President, Kentucky State College), Augustus Hawkins (Rep., California legislature), T. Arnold Hill, McKinney (Southern Tenant Farmers Union), James Ford (CP), Bernice Copland (Milwaukee YWCA).

36. Roy [Wilkins] to Charles [Houston], February 15, 1936, NAACP IC383. See also Wilkins, "Memorandum," 2, 5. Wilkins's enthusiasm cooled, more because of NNC's apparent resistance to interracial organizing: see Wilkins to Davis, March 3, 1936, NAACP IC383.

37. Davis to White, January 20, 1936; Wilkins to Davis, telegram, February 7, 1936; undated bulletins, 1937; White to Davis, April 9, 1937. Also see A. C. MacNeal, Chicago NAACP, to White, January 18, 1936. All NAACP IC383 (includes other examples of collaboration).

38. Davis to White, February 2, 1938; White to Davis, telegram, February 26; Davis to White, February 28; White to Davis, March 1; Davis to White, March 7, 1938, all NAACP IC383.

39. White to Wilkins and Houston, memo, March 8, 1938 (draft letter to Davis attached), NAACP IC383.

40. Final letter, White to Davis, March 9, 1938, NAACP IC383. Mostly Wilkins's revisions.

41. Davis to White, March 30, 1938; White to Davis, April 1, 1938; White to Houston, Marshall, and Wilkins, memo, April 1, 1938. All NAACP IC383. Davis's conference PR (March 24, 1938) is also there.

42. Wilkins to Pickens, April 19, 1938, NAACP IC383.

43. White to Edward Lovett and Gertrude Stone, March 14, 1938; Fauset to White, April 16, 1938 (reply to White's letter, March 30, 1938). All NAACP IC383. The files are filled with similar concerns.

44. "Church Leaders in Opposition to the Program of NNC," n.d., NAACP IC383. Actually, NNC had a Committee on Churches.

45. CRC PR, "Cicero Shows Attack on Negro People Similar to Nazi Violence against Jews, CRC Charges," July 17, 1951, NAACP IIA369. The CRC emerged from the NNC, International Labor Defense (ILD), and National Federation for Constitutional Liberties. For more on Cicero, see chap. 4.

46. Patterson to Daniel Byrd, Philadelphia NAACP, March 9, 1951. Byrd rejected claims: see Byrd to Patterson, March 12, 1951, both NAACP IIA369. Ultimately the charges against five of the men were dropped; the other defendant was paroled. See *State v. Cooper*, 10 N.J. 532 (1952) (Jack Greenberg, *Crusaders in the Courts* [New York, 1994], 537–38 n. 101). Also see 530 n. 45. For CRC actions post-withdrawal, see NAACP MMBD, March 12, 1951, 6, NAACP IIA135.

47. Marshall to Wilkins, memo, November 16, 1949, NAACP IIA369. For CRC offer see letter to NAACP, November 14, 1949.

48. Wilkins to Patterson, memo, November 23, 1949, "The Patterson-Wilkins Correspondence," NAACP IIA369 (response to CRC letter, November 14, 1949). Also see Wilkins to Charles Howard, November 3, 1949.

49. Patterson to Wilkins, June 7, 1950, NAACP IIA369.

50. Marshall to Patterson, June 9, 1950, NAACP IIA369.

51. Patterson to Marshall, June 15, 1950, NAACP IIA369. Emphasis his. No reply in files. N.B., the derogatory "hush-hush" parallels intra-Jewish arguments.

52. Patterson to Byrd; sharp reply, March 12, 1951, both NAACP IIA369.

53. White's words, quoted in Tushnet, *CR Law*, 44.

54. Du Bois, "An Appeal to the World," 1946, reprinted (abridged) in *Oxford W.E.B. Du Bois Reader*, ed. Eric Sundquist (New York, 1996), 454–61. For more on UN petitions, see Anderson, *Eyes Off the Prize*, chaps. 3–5.

55. Gerald Horne, "CRC," in *Encyclopedia of the American Left*, ed. Mari Jo Buhle, Paul Buhle, and Dan Georgakas (New York, 1990), 135.

56. See, e.g., AJC, "Confidential," 2–3; Fineberg to Slawson, 3; "Safeguarding," 126–27; Wilkins to Howard, November 3, 1949; Oscar Cohen to ADL RO, memo re "New Line on the CP, U.S.A.," May 12, 1954 , ADL Y1953–58:Communism:A-Ill.

57. NAACP ROS for December 1946, 8, NAACP IIA144; Wilkins to Howard, November 3, 1949, 1–2; Lewis to Granger, September 6, 1949, 1–2, NUL I:155.

58. White to NAACP Branches, September 29, 1950, memo "Re: Communist Infiltration," 1–3. NAACP IIA369.

59. The entire correspondence is reproduced in NAACP ROS, "Department of Branches," June 9, 1952, 4–7, NAACP IIA145.

60. Edelsberg to Forster, November 4, 1952; Ellerin to Edelsberg, November 6, 1952, ADL Y1949–52:I:R. There is no resolution in of this case in the files.

61. Granger to Clagett, May 9, 1956, 2.

62. Baldwin, "Safeguarding," 98 (for an elaboration of the ACLU's policy, see 98–103). On CORE, see Meier and Rudwick, *CORE*, 65. The Pittsburgh chapter disbanded in 1953.

63. Granger to ESs, 3; Lewis to Granger, September 6, 1949, 1.

64. Granger, statement, 1–3, 7, 10, 11, emphasis his; CIC, "Few Reds." For similar arguments, see Thomas Emerson, "Safeguarding," 147–48; ADL NC, transcript, October [22], 1950, 355 (Novins); 411, 413 (Zara); ADL WB176; Turner, statement to HUAC, 1; NCJW, "Planks Recommended for Inclusion in 1948 National Party Platforms," June 16, 1948, 2, NCJW:74.

65. NCRAC Committee on the Communist Issues, January 2, 1952, 3, ADL Y1949–52:Pro-org:NCRAC; Steinbrink to Hoover, January 5, 1951, ADL Y1949–52:Pro-org:FBI. On ADL and AJC contact with HUAC, AG, et al., see ADL PR, September 15, 1953; Edelsberg to Forster, July 3, 1953; Hoover to Henry Schultz, ADL chairman, February 20, 1957, all ADL Y1953–58:Communist:A-Ill; AJC DAC, May 18, 1954, 3, 7; Fineberg to Slawson, 3. Predictably, the AJLAC went further: see Benjamin Schultz, AJLAC, to Epstein, November 6, 1953, ADL Y1953–58 I:McC; "Nixon, Baruch, FBI Head, Hail AJLAC Director," *JAC* 6, no. 2 (Autumn 1953): 5. On information-gathering, see, e.g., Ellerin to Alan Belmont (FBI), October 8, 1951; Hoover to Steinbrink, April 5, 1952; Edelsberg to Nichols, September 1, 1950, all ADL Y1949–52 pro-org:FBI.

66. Steinbrink to Hoover, July 29, 1952, ADL Y1949–52:pro-org:FBI; Forster, interview with author, August 13, 1991.

67. Vorspan to Ad Hoc Committee on Communist Issue, memo re "Communist Party Line on Rosenberg Spy Trials," April 23, 1951, ADL Y1949–52:Pro-orgs; M. Danzis, *Jewish Day*, April 12, 1951. See also H. Laivik, *Day*, April 16,

1951, both cited in Joseph Brainin and David Alman, CSJRC, to Steinbrink, April 25, 1952, ADL Y1949–52 I:R.

68. Steinbrink, ADL NC transcript, October 1952, 20, 21. See also ADL PR, March 14, 1952, ADL Y1949–52 I:R; AJC DAC, May 18, 1954, 3. Hoover commended the ADL: see Hoover to Steinbrink, March 26, 1952 and May 5, 1952; Irving Kaufman to Steinbrink, March 19, 1952; Kaufman to Epstein, memo, March 31, 1952, all ADL Y1949–52 I:R.

69. Gross to Forster, memo re "Progressive Party," February 5, 1952, 1, 2, ADL Y1949–52:I:R. See also Nathan Belth to Iz Zack, April 3, 1952, ADL Y1949–52:I:R; Chicago CR, March 5, 1952, ADL Y1949–52:Pro-orgs; Forster to National CR, memo, May 12, 1952, ADL Chisub:12: CR 1948–52.

70. NCRAC, "NCRAC ORGANIZATIONS DENOUNCE 'NCSJRC' FOR RAISING FRAUDULENT ISSUE OF A-S," May 18, 1952, ADL Y1949–52:I:R (signed by AJC, AJCongress, ADL, JLC, JWV, UAHC, NCRAC); Rosen to Mrs. B.C. Bolotin and William Kaplan, November 19, 1952. See also Forster to Gross, November 11, 1952, memo re "Ethel and Julius Rosenberg case." Both ADL Y1949–52:I:R. The NCJW followed: see Mrs. Irving [Katherine] Engel to NCSJRC, December 31, 1952, NCJW:74. See also Fineberg, "The Communists Find a New Opening," n.d. (cover letter to AJC, May 21, 1952): 1, 2, 5, 7, 8, ADL Y49–52:I:R; AJCongress: "A False Issue," *AJCW* 19, no. 19 (May 26, 1952): 3.

71. Editorial, *Forward*, April 6, 1951. See also "Meaning of the Rosenberg Death Sentence," editorial, *Daily Worker*, April 9, 1951, ADL Y1949–52:Pro-orgs. On clemency appeals, see Chicago CSJRC, "The Truth Is Dear Above All," statement, n.d., ADL Chiind:R reel 47; [NCSJRC?],"Local Religious Groups Ask Clemency for Rosenbergs," December 31, 1952, ADL Y1949–52:I:R. ADL observers reported audience make-up at protest meetings: see, e.g., "Mass Meeting of CSJRC, November 6, 1952" [Washington, D.C.?], report, ADL Y1949–52:I:R; Chicago CSJRC meetings, May 28, 1953; October 10; November 21; November 23, all ADL Chiind:R.

72. Henry Schultz to Eisenhower, July 1, 1953, ADL Y1953–58:I:R. See also Herbert Levy, ACLU Staff Counsel, to "Whom it may concern," memo re "Rosenberg Atomic Espionage Case," May 2, 1952, ADLY1949–52:I:R.

73. Forster, interview, August 13, 1991. Also see Forster, *Square One*, 128–29; G. George Fox, "Columnist Writes Another 'J'Accuse'; Raps Jewish Spokesmen for Their Negative Stand on Rosenberg Case," *The Sentinel*, January 15[?], 1953 C, ADL Chiind:R, reel 47.

74. Bolin to Arthur Spingarn, March 9, 1950, Bolin, box 3.

75. NAACP, MMBD, March 12, 1951, 5–6; Du Bois, *Autobiography of W.E.B. Du Bois*, 395. The NAACP's relationship with Du Bois was stormy for years, largely because of his more radical leanings.

76. See, e.g., Marable, *Race, Reform and Rebellion* (Jackson, Miss., 1991), chap. 2; Horne, *Black Liberation*; Anderson, *Eyes Off the Prize*; see also note 1.

77. NAACP, MMBD, February 18, 1952, 3, NAACP IIA136.

78. Ellerin to Forster, memo "Re: Rose D. Bloom," October 18, 1950, ADL Y1949–52:NRP. On a similar situation in Columbus, Ohio, see Harold Braverman to Allan Tarshish [?], December 30, 1946, ADL Y1946:NRP.

79. JLC to "Bronx Organizations, Settlements, Y's, Unions et al.," memo re "Bronx-wide Committee for Integrated Housing," JLC:21–5; Mollison to White, December 17, 1935, 3, NAACP IC208. It was precisely the left's attraction that threatened liberal groups' dominance, and encouraged their opposition. A case study of the cross-tensions of CR and anticommunism, and differences among Jewish agencies and between leaders and community members, is an attempt to integrate a Brooklyn Junior High School in 1955: see Adina Back, "Blacks, Jews and the Struggle to Integrate Brooklyn's Junior High School 258," *JAEH* 20, no. 2 (Winter 2001): 38–69.

80. "United Front," 16, 18.

81. Bolin to Spingarn, March 9, 1950, 3; AJC DAC, August 16, 1950, 5; Harold Lachman, ADL NC, October 20, 1951, 2. For a similar complaint by Charles Howard (denied by Wilkins), see Wilkins to Howard, November 3, 1949, 1. See also ADL NC transcript, October 1950, 372 (Steinbrink), 409 (Zara).

82. Holmes to Finder, September 4, 1943; reply, September 8, 1943, ADL Y1943:NRP; Baldwin, *Notes of a Native Son*, 24. For a different perspective on anticommunism, see Richard Powers, *Not without Honor* (New York, 1995).

83. AJC DAC, March 16, 1948, 3–4. Irving Engel made similar comments at AJC DAC, August 16, 1950, 6.

84. White to Truman, November 18, 1948, ADL Y1949–52:Pro-org:NCRAC:A-S; NAACP, ROS for June 1948, n.d., 8.

85. ADL, "Smear," 2–3; Fineberg to Slawson, 1. Similar discussions can be found in Eisenberg, "Safeguarding," 134–35; AJC DAC, March 16, 1948, 3–4; ADL NC October 1950 transcript, 362, 404, 406. I found no comparable evidence on black community sentiment.

86. "Raps Tenney."

87. Emerson: "Safeguarding," 104; White, ROS for December 1946, 3. See also ADL, "Smear," 1, all NAACP IIA145.

88. Polier, "Internal Security Act of 1950," *AJCW* 18, no. 10 (March 12, 1951): I–II; For the NAACP listing; see ROS, March 10, 1952, 4. The army later claimed the listing was an error. Similar points were made by Zara, ADL NC October 1950, transcript, 405; Granger, statement, 7. For the AG list, see "List of Organizations Which Have Been Designated Totalitarian, Fascist, Communist or Subversive," 1950 (included CP, KKK), ADLY1949–52:pro-org:NCRAC.

89. Turner, statement to HUAC, 2; Dubinsky, *NYT*, April 24, 1936, in "'Jewish Communism'"; Granger, statement, 9. See also ADL NC, October 22, 1950, 20, ADL WB176; Record, 4; Wilkins to American Legion, VFW, Catholic War Veterans, August 29, 1949; Wilkins to Governor Dewey, August 29, 1949, both NAACP IIA369; CCAR, "Social Justice Report," 1934, in "'Jewish Communism'"; Polier, "Security," I-II; Feller, "Current Trends," 1; Schultz to Markus, 2.

90. AJCongress Statement adopted at EC, October 5, 1949, 6–7; NAACP; ROS for November 1948, 2. See also ADL PR, May 22, 1953, Chisub:13.

91. NCRAC, "Policy Statement on CR," December 17, 1947, signed by UAHC, JLC, JWV, AJC, ADL, AJCongress. N.B. NCJW was absent, despite holding the same views.

92. AJCongress, Final Plenary, BC, April 4, 1948, transcript, 419–73, AJCongress library; White to Truman, November 18, 1948. For broad opposition, see,

e.g., "Significant Roll Calls in the Senate, 82nd Congress," August 13, 1952, NCJW:74; "Resolutions,"*AJCW*, December 3, 1951, 14; CLSA, Joint Meeting, EC, AC, January 24, 1954, 2, AJCongress A&EC, 1953–56; White, ROS for March 10, 1952, 3, NAACP IIA145; NAACP, ROS for June 1948, 13; AJC DAC, February 28, 1950, 2–3. CRC was also opposed: see, e.g., Russell Meek, Harlem CRC to "Friend," September 7, 1950, NAACP IIA369. The National Women's League of the United Synagogue and the Conservative Rabbinical Assembly also opposed HUAC procedures; see Dollinger, *Quest for Inclusion*, 140–41.

93. Post Office, "Loyalty Case #748, In the Matter of the Loyalty of Raymond Lieberman, Highland Park, Michigan," ADL Y1949–52:Pro-org:NCRAC. ADL collected hundreds of such cases. See also "Brief Summary of Community Replies to NCRAC Request," 1–2; NAACP, MMBD November 8, 1948, NAACP IIA135; AJCongress, "CL," 14.

94. Monroe Sheinberg, ADL, to David Rose, NCRAC, March 9, 1949, ADL Y1949–52:Pro-org:NCRAC; Sheinberg, "Loyalty Program under Executive Order 9835," n.d [1949?], 1, 2; "Supplementary Memo on Loyalty Program," n.d. [1949?], ADL Chisub:CR 1948–52. See also ADL NEC, May 1953; NC, November 1953, 10–11; Forster to National CR, April 14, 1954; "Fact Sheet on Loyalty Oaths," attached, both ADL Chisub:13. On the NCRAC, see Sheinberg, "Report of the NCRAC Subcommittee on the Government's Loyalty Program" ["Confidential"], n.d., ADL Y1949–52:Pro-org:NCRAC. On actions, see, e.g., Detroit JCC, "Resolution," December 23, 1948, ADL Y1949–52:Pro-org:NCRAC; "JOINT STATEMENT OF AJC, AJCONGRESS AND ADL RE COMMUNISM AND CL," December 26, 1950, ADL WB182 and JLC:21–5. The Loyalty Board planned investigations in Detroit, Newark, Cleveland, Postal Employees Association, and Washington, D.C. (including the offices of the NAACP, AJC, ADL, AJCongress, and NAACP's Mitchell).

95. ADL,"Smear," 3.

96. Wilkins to NAACP branches, October 18, 1949. See also NAACP MMBD, November 14, 1950, 4, NAACP IIA135. On membership lists, see Tushnet, *CR Law*, chap. 20. For more on the Smith Act, see Samuel Markle to Forster, August 30, 1954, ADL Y1953–58:Communism, and below. The decisions to take part in these cases were neither easy nor unanimous; see, e.g., ADL NC October 1950, transcript, 373.

97. AJCongress EC, October 1, 1949; NCJW, "Statement on the Mundt Bill," May 18, 1948, NCJW:117; NAACP MMBD, May 10, 1948, 6, NAACP IIA135. The NAACP also protested Hollywood probes: see ROS for November 1948, 2. See also White to Walter Winchell, May 20, 1940, AJC VF:names:NAACP. For AJCongress staff activity, see, e.g., "Statement of the AJCongress to Subcommittee of Senate Judiciary Committee Holding Hearings on S. 2646," March 5, 1953, ADL Y1953–58:Communism:Jenner. The NAACP also opposed the McCarran Act: see MMBD, February 9, 1953, 9, NAACP IIA136. See also "Individual Freedom and National Security," *CCAR Journal* 1 (April 1953): 2–6.

98. The NAACP is quoted in Tushnet, 45–46; NCJW: "Report of the Civil and Political Rights Committee, April 3, 1947"; Mrs. Welt to President Truman, April 18, 1947; Mrs. Joe Willen to Chairs of Social Legislation, memo re "municipal anti-Communist ordinances," December 21, 1950, all NCJW:72. For others, see,

e.g., AJCongress, "Safeguarding" (includes interorganizational disagreements); "Statement of Policy Adopted . . . on November 19, 1950," *AJCW* 17, no. 32 (December 4, 1950): 5–6; "CL," in "Resolutions of Congress Convention," *AJCW* 18, no. 31 (December 3, 1951): 14; ADL NC, "Examination of Loyalty Program Procedure," May 13–15, 1949; ADL NC, "Dangers to Democracy," October 24, 1952, and similar, all ADL WB42; Jacob Grumet to National CR, memo re "Possible ADL Intervention in Harrison Loyalty Oath Situation," December 15, 1952, ADL Chisub:12; ADL NEC, September 10–11, 1955, 12, ADL WB178 (interagency fights); AJC DAC, December 6, 1949, 1–2; October 10, 1950, 4–6; November 2, 1950, 2. For a similar ambiguity, compare AJC, "Statement on the Purposes, Structure and CL Interests of AJC," September 17, 1953, NAACP IIA203, with AJC, "Statement on Internal Security," AM, January 28– 30, 1955, NAACP IIA360.

99. NAACP MMBD, June 26, 1953, 2, NAACP IIA136. Eisenhower received a Democratic Legacy Award at the ADL fortieth Anniversary dinner, November 23, 1953.

100. Schultz to Markus, January 29, 1954, Edelsberg to Forster, confidential memo, December 8, 1954, ADL Y1953–58:I:McC. Stephen Whitfield suggests Jews' opposition to McCarthy, despite his lack of anti-Semitism, demonstrates Jews' liberalism: see "Bourgeois," 162. For criticism of McCarthy, see, e.g., John Horwitz, PR to Oklahoma newspapers, July 20, 1953; Henry Schultz to Sen. Michael Monroney, July 20, 1953; ADL Special Committee on McCarthyism, report, adopted by ADL Regional Advisory Board, May 12, 1954, both ADL Chisub:13; ADL, "Interpretation of Prior Policy," NEC, May 2, 1954, ADL WB42; Meier and Rudwick, *CORE*, 66; Dorothy Kenyon, New York City Chapter ADA, J. George Fiedler, New York Region Chairman, AVC, Murray Meyerson, Manhattan Division AJCongress, Russell Crawford, New York Branch, NAACP, to Epstein, April 16, 1954; "Vet Leader Raps McCarthy Method," *San Francisco Chronicle* [C], April 5, 1954; both ADL Y1953–58:I:McC; AJCongress PR, "Fifth Amendment Cited as a Valuable Principle of American Justice at AJCongress CL Forum," May 5, 1954, AJC IVF:CL; Epstein to ADL RO, May 7, 1954, memo re "Use of 'McCarthyism,'" ADL Y1953–58:I:McC.

101. Quoted in "And Rabbis Who Are Not," *JAC*, Spring 1954, 2. The sermon was also covered in the New York *Herald Tribune*, May 25, 1952.

102. Biddle and Wilson, "THE NATIONAL CL CLEARING HOUSE: What It Is, and What It Does," draft, October 7, 1949, NCJW WO:15 (also other NCLCH materials). NCNW:7 has more on CL coalitions.

103. Polier to Regional, Divisional and Chapter Presidents, CLSA Chairmen, March 31, 1950, emphasis his. The unnamed coalition is probably the CLCH. See also "Joint Statement on Mundt-Ferguson-Johnston and Nixon Bills," March 30, 1950, seventeen signatories including AJCongress, ACLU, ADA, AJC, AVC, ADL, Friends Committee, JLC, JWV, NCJW, National WTUL, Social Action Committee of the Congregational Christian Churches, Amalgamated Clothing Workers, Textile Workers, in AJCongress EC, April 12, 1950; "Joint Statement on National Security Legislation Now Pending before Congress," August 25, 1950, in AJC IVF:Subversive activities (same signers, plus NCRAC, UAHC,

United Council of Church Women, and others); PR, Manhattan Citizens Committee to Defeat the Mundt Bill, April 11, 1950, ADL Y1949–52:Pro-org:MCDMB.

104. Lukas to Wilkins, January 4, 1954, NAACP IIA203.

105. Mary Alice Baldinger, notes on liaison group meeting, January 13, 1954, NAACP IIA203; Minutes, November 4, 1954, January 6, 1955 meetings of national women's organizations (included YWCA, NCNW, United Council Church Women, NCJW); NCJW, "Extending Intellectual Freedom," draft, December 8, 1954; *Extending the Frontiers of Freedom*, pamphlet, all NCJW:72; NCJW, "Outline for Discussion on Communism and CL," December 20, 1950, NCJW:74.

106. Record, "NEGRO and COMMUNISTS" 4; ADL NC transcript, October 1950, 411.

107. Schare, ADL NC transcript, May 5–8, 1948, 26–28.

CHAPTER SIX
Things Fall Apart

1. Nathan Edelstein, AJCongress, "Jewish Relationship with the Emerging Negro Community in the North," address to NCRAC, June 23, 1960, 6, AJC VF:NJR:AJCongress.

2. Carson, "Blacks and Jews in the CR Movement," in *Bridges and Boundaries*, ed. Jack Salzman, with Adina Back and Gretchen Sorin (New York, 1992), 36–49. See also Nathan Glazer, "Blacks, Jews, and the Intellectuals," *Commentary*, April, 1969, 37; James Yaffe, *The American Jews* (New York, 1968), chap. 16.

3. Inge Lederer Gibel, "The Negro-Jewish Scene: A Personal View," *Judaism*, Winter 1965, 19, 21. On Orthodox activity, see, e.g., "Rabbis Establish Rights 'Task Force,'" *NYT*, March 26, 1965, 23. On class, see below, and Friedman, "The Jews," esp. 157–58.

4. NCRAC Committee on Community Consultation, Subcommittee on Special Concerns of Southern CRCs, "How Southern Jewish Leadership Views the 'Sit-Ins,' " confidential report, February 25–26, 1961, 4; "Summary of Meeting," February 25–26, 1961, 8, both NCRAC:74.

5. NCRAC, "Southern," 3.

6. "Prinz Breaks Jews' Silence on 'Sit-Ins,'" *Courier*, April 9, 1960, AJC IVF:NJR. On the plenum, see NCRAC, "Summary," 9. On the JLC, see Emanuel Muravchik to JLC Field Staff and CRCs, April 22, 1960, "Pittsburgh Courier Memo #4." The number of Jews in the southern grassroots movement is unknown. Most agree Jews constituted a small but disproportionate number of white participants, especially in Freedom Summer and the Freedom Rides. See, e.g., Carson, "Black-Jewish Universalism," 177–96; Debra Schultz, *Going South* (New York, 2001); Friedman, *What Went Wrong?* 181; Jonathan Kaufman, "What's a Jewish Liberal to Do?" *Moment*, June 1994, 41–42; Paul Lauter, "Reflections of a Jewish Activist," *Conservative Judaism* 19 (Summer 1965).

7. NCRAC, "Southern," 5–7. See also NCRAC, "Summary," 3.

8. NCRAC, "Southern," 11, 15; NCRAC, "Summary," 2, 9, 11–12. Also see Webb, *Fight against Fear.* On southern rabbis, see Krause, "Rabbis and Negro Rights," 24–27.

9. Krause, "Rabbis and Negro Rights," 44. On Rothschild, see Krause, 38–39; Greene, *Temple Bombing.* On Mantinband, see Webb, "Big Struggle in a Small Town," in Bauman and Kalin, *Quiet Voices,* 213–29. MSC is now the University of Southern Mississippi. On Olan, see Cristol, *Light in the Prairie,* 185–86.

10. NCRAC, "Southern," 13–15; Krause, "Rabbis and Negro Rights," 46. See also NCRAC, "Summary," 4–7. Exceptions include Houston; Atlanta; Norfolk, Va.; and New Orleans (6–7).

11. NCRAC, "Summary," 7; NCRAC, "Southern," 14. Also see Krause, "Rabbis and Nego Rights," 23.

12. NCRAC, "Summary," 1–2; NCRAC, "Southern," 3.

13. Quoted in John Dittmer, *Local People* (Urbana, Ill., 1994), 302). On Freedom Summer, see Doug McAdam, *Freedom Summer* (New York, 1988); Nicolaus Mills, *Like a Holy Crusade* (Chicago, 1992). On this phase of the movement, see, e.g., Carson, *In Struggle* (Cambridge, Mass., 1981); Glenn Eskew, *But for Birmingham* (Chapel Hill, N.C., 1997); Mary King, *Freedom Song* (New York, 1987); John Lewis, *Walking with the Wind* (New York, 1998); Anne Moody, *Coming of Age in Mississippi* (New York, 1968); Taylor Branch, *Pillar of Fire* (New York, 1998).

14. NCRAC, "Summary," 1–2.

15. Jack Nelson, *Terror in the Night* (New York, 1993), 214, 218–19, 224. The ADL minimized the threat: see Irving Spiegel, "Jews in the South Told to Shed Fears of Fighting Bigots," *NYT,* September 26, 1959, 28.

16. Shuttlesworth and Henry quoted in Krause, "Rabbis and Negro Rights," 22–23. On Birmingham, see Andre Ungar, "To Birmingham and Back," *Conservative Judaism* 18 (Fall 1963): 10–11. See also Webb, "Struggle," 229; Nossel, "Weathering the Storm"; Webb, *Fight against Fear.*

17. On the debate, see NCRAC, "Summary," 11. Leonard Fein suggested dependence on law and order helped explain the Jewish fear of black insurgency: Fein, *The Negro Revolution and the Jewish Community,* pamphlet, Synagogue Council of America, 1969, 12, 34. On fears of the left, see Nelson, *Terror in the Night,* 214–15. The FBI also conducted surveillance and counterintelligence programs against black civil rights groups and leaders. See David Garrow, *The FBI and Martin Luther King, Jr.* (New York, 1983); Kenneth O'Reilly, *Racial Matters* (New York, 1989). See pp. 317–18 for a discussion of COINTELPRO tactics around anti-Semitism.

18. Henry Cohen, *Justice, Justice* (New York 1968) 18. See also, e.g., Albert Vorspan, "In St. Augustine," *Midstream,* September 1964; Marc Schneier, *Shared Dreams* (Woodstock, Vt., 1999); Albert Friedlander, "We Went to Selma," *Reconstructionist,* April 30, 1965.

19. Polier, "The Jew and the Racial Crisis," July 15, 1964, AJCongress PR, 4–5, Polier:14.

20. Quoted in Gibel, "Negro-Jewish Scene," 13. Still, it was a minuscule number. An excellent undergraduate thesis by Erik Gellman, "Black and Jewish Rela-

tions during the Civil Rights Movement" (Bates College, 1997), includes interviews with Jewish SNCC workers.

21. King, "What Happens to Them Happens to Me," reprinted in Salzman, *Bridges and Boundaries*, 88; Rustin, "The Negroes, the Cops, the Jews," *Dissent*, March–April 1967, 175. On Nasser see Edelstein, "Jewish Relationship," 9. See also NAACP, PR "NAACP Asks Clemency for Convicted Soviet Jews," April 9, 1962, AJC IVF:NJR:Negro. Whitney Young and others also protested. For a hagiographic discussion of King and Jews see Schneier, *Shared Dreams*. Rustin, who worked alongside A. Philip Randolph and King, helped organize FOR and CORE CR actions and the 1963 March on Washington, and had been engaged in CR trade union, socialist, and pacifist causes since 1937.

22. See Hamilton, *Adam Clayton Powell, Jr.*, esp. 129–30 and chaps. 16, 17. See also Forster to National CR Committee, memo re "Anti-Segregation Amendments to the Federal Aid to Education Bill," June 28, 1955, ADL chisub:12; NCRAC Special Committee on Reassessment, "Advancement of Community Relations Objectives through Law and Legislation . . . Conclusions and Recommendations," December 11, 1954, 9, NAACP IIA387; LCCR, Summary of EC, March 3, 1955, 3, ADL Y1953–58:LCCR.

23. Tom Brooks, "Negro Militants, Jewish Liberals, and the Unions," *Commentary*, September 1961, 215. For analysis of the links between labor, CR, and black-Jewish relations, see, e.g., Green, "Blacks, Jews, and the 'Natural Alliance,' " 79–104; Alan Draper, *Conflict of Interests* (Ithaca, N.Y., 1994).

24. Wilkins to JLC quoted in Harold Keith, "NAACP Official Paints Muravchik as 'Apologist,' " *Courier*, April 9, 1960 (retyped in JLC, "Pittsburgh Courier Memo #4"). Hill, "Black-Jewish Conflict in the Labor Context," 80–81.

25. Edelstein, "Jewish Relationship," 11; S. Andhil Fineberg to __, August 14, 1963, AJC VF:NJR:AJC 1938–39, 1.

26. "Wilkins on Powell's Attack," *New York Post*, March 29, 1963; Crosswaith, "We Need Them," letter to editor, *Amsterdam News*, April 6, 1963; Robinson, Secretary-Treasurer, Dist. 65, Retail, Wholesale and Dept. Store Union, "Symposium on Negro-Jewish Tensions," April 7, 1966, New York City, 4, Polier:14. See also "Powell and the Times," *Post*, April 4, 1963, C, Crosswaith, box 1; "Wilkins Says Jews Help Negro Escape 'Ghetto,' " *NYT*, April 5, 1963.

27. Rustin, " 'Black Power' and Coalition Politics," *Commentary*, September 1966, 37–38.

28. Carmichael and Charles Hamilton, *Black Power* (New York, 1967), 52.

29. Rustin, "Black Power," 36–38.

30. Ibid., 43–45.

31. Ibid., 42, 45, 46. See also David Danzig, AJC, "In Defense of 'Black Power,' " *Commentary*, September 1966, 41; Friedman, *What Went Wrong*, chap. 10.

32. Carmichael and Hamilton, *Black Power*, 37, 40–41. King made a similar point: see David Garrow, *Bearing the Cross* (New York, 1986) 582.

33. Farmer, *Freedom—When?* (New York, 1965), 87. See also Nathan Glazer, "Negroes and Jews: The New Challenge to Pluralism," *Commentary*, December 1964, 29–34. Carl Gershman made the same criticism of African Americans: see "The Andrew Young Affair," *Commentary*, November 1979, 28n.

34. See, e.g., ADL, "Fact Sheet II: The Negro Revolt," January 1, 1963, 1, ADL Chisub:12. On Hamer's resignation see *Local People*, Dittmer, 408. Carmichael opposed the expulsions: see Carson, "Blacks and Jews," 41–42.

35. See, e.g., ADL, "Fact Sheet II," 1; Fein, *Negro Revolution*, 11–12.

36. Diner, *Almost Promised Land*, introduction.

37. Samuel Lubell, "The Negro and the Democratic Coalition," *Commentary*, August 1964, 23; Rustin, "From Protest to Politics," *Commentary*, 39, no. 2 (February 1965): 25–31. Quotations from Rustin, "Black Power," 35–36. See also Danzig, "Defense," 41. On the Panthers' conservative and capitalist tendencies, see, e.g., Tom Milstein, "A Perspective on the Panthers," *Commentary*, September 1970, 36–38, 40; Paul Feldman, "The Pathos of Black Power," *Dissent* 14, no. 1 (January–February 1967): 69–79, esp. 70–72. The militants were not a majority: Feldman cites a *Newsweek* poll that found 90 percent of blacks saw King as a leader; three-fourths considered the NAACP the main CR organization (74–75).

38. Fein, *Negro Revolution*, 14. See also Oliver Cox, "Jewish Self-interest in 'Black Pluralism,'"*Sociological Quarterly* 15 (Spring 1974): 183–98, esp. 187–91.

39. Perlmutter, "Remarks," following Fein in SCA pamphlet, 21.

40. Edelstein, "Jewish Relationship," 2. The huge number of examinations of black A-S attest to the extent of this concern. Studies differed on whether black A-S was rising; all agreed that general A-S was declining. On black A-S rising, see "Negro Leader Sees A-S Rise," *NYT*, June 12, 1963, 19 (the leader was James Farmer); Friedman, "Black A-S on the Rise," *Commentary*, October 1979, 31–35; Lee Sigelman, "Blacks, Whites, and A-S," *Sociological Quarterly* 36, no. 4 (1995): 649–56. On black A-S not rising (or the data unclear), see Heller and Pinkney, "Attitudes of Negroes toward Jews," 364–69; Irving Spiegel, "No Rise Is Found in A-S," *NYT*, April 13, 1969, 35 (reports on a NCRAC study); Glazer, "Blacks, Jews," 33–39; Walter Karp and H. R. Shapiro, "Exploding the Myth of Black A-S," in *Black A-S and Jewish Racism*, ed. Nat Hentoff (New York, 1969), 129–41; "Negroes in Study are Not Anti-Jew," *NYT*, October 2, 1966, 66 (on an ADL study of the non-South); Gary Marx, "Negro A-S," *Nation*, January 1, 1968, 11–13; B. Z. Sobel and May Sobel, "Negroes and Jews," *Judaism* (Winter 1966): 3–22. Also see James Baldwin, "Negroes Are Anti-Semitic Because They're Anti-White," *NYT Magazine*, April 9, 1967, 26–27, 135–40; Robert Gordis, "Negroes Are Anti-Semitic Because They Want a Scapegoat," *NYT Magazine*, April 23, 1967, 29, 130–32; Stephen Whitfield, "An Anatomy of Black A-S," *Judaism* 43, no. 4 (Fall 1994): 341–59.

41. Baraka, "For Tom Postell, Dead Black Poet," in *Black Magic* (Indianapolis, 1969), 153; Baraka, "Black Art," in *Black Art* (Newark, N.J., 1969); Cruse, *Crisis of the Negro Intellectual*; Robert Weisbord and Arthur Stein, *Bittersweet Encounter* (Westport, Conn., 1970), 140. Despite Baraka's "Confessions of a Former Anti-Semite," *Village Voice*, December 17–23, 1980, 1, 19–23, he offered anti-Semitic canards following the September 11 attacks. Also see Whitfield, "Anatomy." On black good will toward Jews, see "Negro A-S Declining, Leaders Believe," *New York World Telegram and Sun*, August 10, 1964, C, Polier:14.

42. Polier, "Jew and Racial Crisis," 1, 2. See also Edelstein, "Jewish Relationship," 4; Rustin, "Cops," 173–75. Jews owned 40% of Harlem businesses in 1968

(white businesses constituted 47% of total Harlem businesses); Jewish economic presence in black neighborhoods remained strong (reported in Louis Harap, *Dramatic Encounters* [New York, 1987], 14).

43. Fineberg to __, 1; King, March 25, 1968, quoted in Schneier, *Shared Dreams*, 176. See also Polier: "Symposium," 4; Joe Wood, "The Problem Negro and Other Tales," in Berman, *Blacks and Jews*, esp. 111–15.

44. Gibel, "Negro-Jewish Scene," 20. See also Wilkins, "Jewish-Negro Relations," *Crisis*, June–July 1977, 258; Cox, "Jewish Self-Interest," 195. On the New York poll, see Louis Harris and Bert Swanson, *Black-Jewish Relations in NYC* (New York, 1970), chap. 4.

45. Jules Cohen, JCRC of Greater Philadelphia, "Build or Burn?" n.d. [December 1966?], 28, 33, NCRC:74[?].

46. These and other examples described in Gellman, "Black and Jewish Relations," 45.

47. NCRAC, "Impact of Riots and Other Disorders on Jewish Attitudes toward CR Issues," September 1967 (updated December 5, 1967), 2–4, NCRAC: 67; Nathan Agran, JCRC of Greater Philadelphia, "Our Philadelphia Jews—Their Problems—And What Is Being Done about Them," report, 1971, 3, 5, NCRAC:74. There are similar findings in a 1968 AJCongress report: see Friedman, "Jews," 163.

48. On non-Jewish entrepreneurial tensions, see, e.g., Claire Kim, *Bitter Fruit* (New Haven, Conn., 2000); Edward Chang, "Jewish and Korean Merchants in African American Neighborhoods," *Amerasian Journal* 192 (1993): 5–21; Anna Deveare Smith, *Twilight: Los Angeles 1992* (New York, 1994). On continued black-Jewish economic tensions, see Paul Berman, "Medieval New York," *New Yorker*, January 15, 1996, 5–6.

49. Edelstein, "Jewish Relationship," 5; Silberman, "A Jewish View of the Racial Conflict," *Conservative Judaism* 19 (Summer 1965): 7. See also Polier, "Symposium," 2; Fein, *Negro Revolution*, 12–13.

50. Kramer, *Children of the Gilded Ghetto* (New Haven, Conn., 1961). See also, e.g., Agran, "Our Philadelphia Jews," 1; Glazer, "Negroes and Jews," 31.

51. Fein, *Negro Revolution*, 12; Sobel and Sobel, "Negroes and Jews," 15–22. See also Arnold Wolf, "Remarks," following Fein and Perlmutter, *Negro Revolution*, 24. On Jewish racial views, see Kenneth Berg, "Ethnic Attitudes and Agreement with a Negro Person," *Journal of Personality and Social Psychology* 4, no. 2 (1966): 215–20; Andrew Greeley, "Ethnicity and Racial Attitudes," *American Journal of Sociology* 80, no. 4 (January 1975): 909–33.

52. Edelstein, "Jewish Relationship," 5; unnamed leader quoted in Charles Silberman, "Jesse and the Jews," *New Republic*, December 29, 1979, 13. Organized Jewry did support integrated housing: see Snyder and Goodman, *Friend of the Court*, 16–17. For local studies of changing neighborhoods, see Debra Kaufman, Alan Snitow, and Bari Scott, *Blacks and Jews*, California Newsreel, 1996; Pritchett, *Brownsville, Brooklyn*; Louis Rosen, *The South Side* (Chicago 1998); Sanchez, "Boyle Heights," 633–61.

53. Agran, "Our Philadelphia Jews," 1–2. See also "Symposium," 1–2; Polier, "Jew and Racial Crisis," 2–3. George Sanchez finds the same in Boyle Heights, Los Angeles ("Boyle Heights," 654–55).

54. Ellison et al. quoted in Polsgrove, *Divided Minds* 162–63; Robinson, 4; NCRAC, "Impact," 3; Reider, *Canarsie*; study of Brooklyn Jews quoted in Friedman, "Jews," 158; Perlmutter, "Remarks," 20. Also see Bernard Rosenberg and Irving Howe, "Are American Jews Turning to the Right?" *Dissent* (Winter 1974): 36–37. For similar examinations of Jewish attitudes in Boston, see Hillel Levine and Lawrence Harmon, *Death of an American Jewish Community* (New York, 1992); J. Anthony Lukas, "Troubled Ground," *Partisan Review* 59, no. 3 (1992): 428–34. On New York, see Harris and Swanson, *Black-Jewish Relations in NYC.* See also Friedman, "Jews," 159–61. On general white northern resistance, see, e.g., James Ralph Jr., *Northern Protest* (Cambridge, Mass., 1993). On the "new right," see, e.g., Lisa McGirr, *Suburban Warriors* (Princeton, N.J., 2001). On Jews and emerging whiteness, see Goldstein, *Price of Whiteness*, epilogue.

55. Podhoretz, "My Negro Problem—And Ours," *Commentary* 35, no. 2 (February 1963): 93–101. On the 1950s, see Wald, *New York Intellectuals*; Polsgrove, *Divided Minds.*

56. Robert Mills (Baldwin's agent) to Samuel Caplan, AJCongress, March 6, 1963. Justine Wise Polier and Shad Polier, "Witch's Brew: Fear Turned to Hatred," draft, n.d., [1963], 1, 8. Young to Shad Polier and Justine Polier, March 19, 1963, all Polier 14. For more on black, white, and Jewish liberal responses see Polsgrove, *Divided Minds*, 167–70.

57. See A. J. Bacvich, "What Have You Done for Us Lately?" *First Things*, May 1996, 49; Mark Gerson, *The Neoconservative Vision* (Lanham, Md., 1996); Rosenberg and Howe, "American Jews Turning?" 41.

58. George Breitman, ed., *Malcolm X Speaks* (New York, 1990), 106–7. Also see James Meriwether, "African Americans and the Mau Mau Rebellion," *JAEH* 17, no. 4 (Summer 1998): 63–86.

59. The CRC had made similar point about Korea: see CRC, "54 NEGRO SOLDIERS AT FORT DEVENS ASK: WHY KOREA? WHY A JIM CROW ARMY?" PR, July 1, 1951, NAACP IIA369.

60. June–July newsletter quoted in Carson, "Blacks and Jews," 43–44; ("ferment" quotation from fall 1967 SNCC *Newsletter*, quoted p. 45; Newfield quoted in "Pride, Prejudice, and Politics" *Response* (Autumn 1982): 5. King quoted in John Lewis, "King's Special Bond with Israel," *San Francisco Chronicle*, January 21, 2002; Jackson, in Johnson administration, quoted in Schneier, *Shared Dreams*, 167. See also Rosenberg and Howe, "American Jews Turning," 37–39. For more on Panther A-S, see Milstein, "Perspective," 43; *A Black American Looks at Israel, the "Arab Revolution," Racism, Palestinians and Peace* (on Young), pamphlet, AJC, October 1970.

61. Polier, "Jews and Racial Crisis," 2. See also Edelstein, "Jewish Relationship," 3, 7; Friedman, "Jews," 162 (on New Politics); Silberman, "Jesse," 13–14; Wilkins, *Standing Fast*, 268; Rosenberg and Howe, "American Jews Turning," 36; I. F. Stone, "The Mason-Dixon Line Moves to New York," in *Polemics and Prophesies* (Boston, 1970), 108.

62. "Golden Criticizes S.N.C.C. and Quits," *NYT*, August 22, 1967, 24; Saperstein cited in Gellman, "Black and Jewish Relations," 206. Also see Kathleen Teltsch, "S.N.C.C. Criticized for Israel Stand," *NYT*, August 16, 1967, 28. On the decline in SNCC contributions (also decline to CORE), see Edward Burks,

"Militant Rights Groups Feel Pinch as Gifts Drop," *NYT*, July 25, 1966, 1. For earlier evidence of limited A-S, see "Negro A-S."

63. There are many conflicting accounts; see, e.g., Jerald Podair, *The Strike That Changed New York* (New Haven, Conn., 2002); Jonathan Kaufman, *Broken Alliance* (New York, 1988), chap. 4; Friedman, *What Went Wrong?* chap. 12; Julius Lester, *Lovesong* (New York, 1988), chap. 6. See Back, "Blacks, Jews and the Struggle," 38–69 for a very different story from the previous decade.

64. See Podair, *Strike*, chaps. 4–5; Kaufman, *Broken Alliance*, chap. 4. On Mayor Lindsay see Vincent Cannato, *The Ungovernable City* (New York, 2001).

65. See Podair, *Strike*, chaps. 5–6. The JDL organized in response to the Ocean Hill–Brownsville controversy: see Friedman, "Jews," 160. ADL's "crisis" claim, made in February 1969, is cited in "Jew and Black," *National Review*, February 11, 1969, 106. There were also related incidents, e.g., the introduction to a Metropolitan Museum of Art photographic exhibit catalogue, *Harlem on My Mind*, described black-Jewish tensions in terms some found anti-Semitic: see Glazer, "Blacks, Jews," 38.

66. For Lester, see "A Response," in Hentoff, *Black A-S*, 237. See also Hentoff, "Blacks and Jews: An Interview with Julius Lester," *Evergreen Review* 13, no. 65 (April 1969): 21–22, 25, 71–76. Lester later converted to Judaism. Glasser quoted in John Kifner, "Echoes of a New York Waterloo," *NYT*, December 22, 1996, D5. See also Karp and Shapiro, "Exploding the Myth." On the AATA see Podair, "'White' Values, 'Black' Values: The Ocean Hill–Brownsville Controversy and New York City Culture, 1965–1975," *Radical History Review* 59 (1994): 51.

67. Kifner, "Echoes." Conflicts between (often Jewish) civil servants, and (often black) grassroots welfare activists also fueled tensions.

68. Forman, "Total Control as the Only Solution to the Economic Problems of Black People," Conference presentation, April 26, 1969, 3; "The 'Black Manifesto' of the Black Economic Development Conference: A Policy Statement Issued by the Synagogue Council of America and the N[J]CRAC," May 12, 1969, 1–3. See also Aronson to [NCRAC] "Member Agencies," memo re "Black Manifesto of the National Black Economic Development Conference," May 28, 1969; SCA (coordinating agency for three main branches of Judaism), "Guidelines for Dealing with James Forman or Other Representatives of the Black Economic Development Conference," n.d.; NCRAC, "Suggested Guidelines for Communities for Dealing with James Forman, his Representatives, or Attempts by other Extremists to Disrupt Synagogues or other Jewish Communal Agencies," n.d., all NCRAC:67. The NALC became the Randolph Institute.

69. Ben Wattenberg and Richard Scammon, "Black Progress and Liberal Rhetoric," *Commentary*, April 1973, esp. 43–44. See also Feingold, "From Equality to Liberty" 97–118; "The Anomalous Liberalism of American Jews," 133–43; Jerold Auerbach, "Liberalism, Judaism and American Jews," 144–48, all in Seltzer and Cohen, *Americanization of the Jews*; Jim Sleeper, *Liberal Racism* (New York, 1997).

70. Rosenberg and Howe, "American Jews Turning," 31; Wolf, "Remarks," 22. Karp and Shapiro, "Exploding the Myth," 134–38.

71. See also Himmelfarb, "Is American Jewry in Crisis?" *Commentary*, March 1969.

72. Friedman, "Jews," 149. For some evidence in support, regarding New York City, see Harris and Swanson, *Black-Jewish Relations in NYC*.

73. Council of Jewish Federations and Welfare Funds, "Jewish Community Activities in the Urban Crisis," report, May 16, 1968; NCRAC EC, "Resolution on the Urban Crisis," April 7, 1968, both NCRAC I:17; "Jews Urged to Help Struggle of Negro," *NYT*, November 5, 1966, 20; Polier, "Symposium," 1. Polier had earlier commented, "A Jew, therefore, a liberal."

74. "'3rd Society' Held Forgotten in Racial Tension," *NYT*, November 18, 1968, 26; "UJA Aide Sees Jews Committed to Civil Rights," *NYT*, November 17, 1968, 85; Israel Shenker, "50 Rabbis and Negro Clergymen Searching for Racial Peace," *NYT*, January 31, 1969, 77; "Unit Formed to Aid Jewish-Negro Ties," *NYT* , August 10, 1970, 37; Poussaint, "Blacks and Jews: An Appeal for Unity," *Ebony*, July 1974, 120–26. Also see Sobel and Sobel, "Negroes and Jews," 13–14; "More Jewish Aid to Negroes Urged," *NYT*, February 27, 1968, 28; Irving Spiegel, "Jews Told of Gain in Ties to Blacks," *NYT*, March 30, 1971, 18.

75. There was a flurry of writing about black-Jewish tensions, not seen since the early 1940s, from the late 1960s through the early 1970s: see, e.g., "The Black and the Jew: A Falling Out of Allies," *Time*, January 31, 1969, 55–57; "Jew and Black," 106; Donald Kaufmann, "Soul Pass Over," *Midstream*, May 1970, 30–37; Gershman, "Blacks and Jews," *Midstream*, February 1976, 8–17; Eli Ginzberg, "The Black Revolution and the Jew," *Conservative Judaism*, Fall 1969, 3–19; Harry Halpern, "Reply to Eli Ginzberg," same issue, 20–23; Fein, *Negro Revolution*, 8; Earl Raab, "The Black Revolution and the Jewish Question," *Commentary*, January 1969, 23–33; Himmelfarb; "American Jewry in Crisis"; Glazer, "Blacks, Jews." (The *Commentary* pieces were a dialogue on the tensions.) There was also much on Jewish politics and CR; see below.

76. Robinson cited in Gary Younge, "Different Class," *Guardian* (London), November 23, 2002. In 1972, McGovern received 38% of the overall vote, but 65% of the Jewish vote; blacks and Jews were his two largest groups of supporters. In 1968 81% of Jews voted for Humphrey; 27% for Nixon; only African Americans voted Democratic more heavily. Jews supported Kennedy in 1960 in higher numbers than Catholics did. Thanks to Kathleen Frankovic, Director of Polling, CBS News, for election figures, and Perlmutter, "Remarks," 21; Sowell, *Ethnic America* (New York, 1981), 99. Data more limited for 1940s and 1950s, but polls suggest even larger proportions of Jews supported Democrats. (Himmelfarb, "American Jews: Diehard Conservatives," *Commentary*, April 1989, 44–49). Later figures are below.

77. Gershman, "Blacks and Jews," 10, 11, 14, 15; Paul Montgomery, "Blacks and Jews Viewed as Drawing Closer Again," *NYT*, April 14, 1975, 1, 60. See also "Jewish-Black Ties Urged to Improve Lot of Minorities," *NYT*, January 15, 1974, 39; "Jews and Blacks: A Relationship Re-examined," *Midstream*, January 1974, 7.

78. Bronstein, "Eldridge Cleaver—Reborn," *Midstream*, January 1977, 57–58.

79. Wilkins, *Standing Fast*, 269. Thomas Johnson, "Urban League's President Appeals to Blacks and Jews to Seek Unity," *NYT*, January 23, 1980, B6; BASIC quoted in Gershman, "Blacks and Jews," 9. full-page "APPEAL BY BLACK AMERICANS FOR UNITED STATES SUPPORT FOR ISRAEL," appeared in national and black newspapers (e.g., *NYT*, June 28, 1970, E5), signed by sixty-four black liberal lead-

ers, e.g., Dorothy Height, Vernon Jordan, Martin Luther King Sr., John Lewis, Randolph, Rustin, Wilkins, Whitney Young. Black leaders helped other Jewish causes, e.g., Soviet Jewry; see Montgomery, "Blacks and Jews," 60, and above.

80. *DeFunis v. Odegaard* 416 U.S. 312 (1974); *University of California Regents v. Bakke* 438 U.S. 265 (1978); Young quoted in Martin Plax, "Jews and Blacks in Dialogue," *Midstream*, January 1982, 10. In *Grutter v. Bollinger* and *Gratz v. Bollinger*, 2003, the ADL filed "in support of neither party," arguing that although it was possible to consider race, the university's affirmative action policies did so unconstitutionally. The AJC, CCAR, Hadassah, NCJW, UAHC, Progressive Jewish Alliance, National Conference for Community and Justice, and Federation of Temple Sisterhoods filed in support of the university.

81. Rosenberg and Howe, "American Jews Turning," 42–43; Fein, *Negro Revolution*, esp. 10–13, and Fein, "Thinking about Quotas," *Midstream* 19, no. 3 (March 1973): 13–17.

82. Gold quoted in Poussaint, "Appeal for Unity," 126; HEW letter quoted in Gershman, "Blacks and Jews," 9; mentioned in Montgomery, "Blacks and Jews," 60.

83. Brief cited in Snyder and Goodman, *Friend of the Court*, 81 (*Bakke* discussed, 83–84). Rustin similarly opposed quotas: see *Midstream* interview, 5.

84. See Halpern, "Reply to Eli Ginzberg," 20–21. (Halpern chaired Joint Commission on Social Action, [Conservative] United Synagogue of America.) Also see Snyder and Goodman, *Friend of the Court*, 84–87.

85. Statistics from Sidney Goldstein, "American Jewry 1970: A Demographic Profile," *AJYB*, 1971, 3–88; Rosenberg and Howe, "American Jews Turning," 35; Wolf, "Remarks," 24. See also Glazer, "American Jew and the Attainment of Middle-Class Rank," 138–46; Whitfield, "Bourgeois," 154–55; Thomas Sowell, ed., *Essays and Data on American Groups* (Washington, D.C., 1978), 364–65; Sowell, *Ethnic America*, 5, 98.

86. Omi and Winant, *Racial Formation*, 20, emphasis in original. Also see Lewis Killian, "Black Power and White Reactions," *Annals* 454 (March 1981): 42, 46–9; Milton Gordon, "Models of Pluralism," same issue, 178–88. Nathaniel Jones, "The Future of Black-Jewish Relations," *Crisis*, January 1975, 24–27, discusses implications of differences over affirmative action.

87. On multiculturalism and Jews, see, e.g., *Multiculturalism: A Critical Reader*, ed. David Theo Goldberg (Oxford, 1994), esp. Peter McLaren, "White Terror and Oppositional Agency," 45–74; David Biale, Michael Galchinsky, and Susannah Heschel, eds., *Insider/Outsider* (Berkeley, Calif., 1998); Michael Galchinsky, "Glimpsing *Golus* in the Golden Land," *Judaism* 43, no. 4 (Fall 1994): 361–68; Arnold Eisen, "Limits and Virtues of Dialogue," and Edward Alexander, "Multiculturalists and A-S," both in *Transaction* 31, no. 6 (September–October 1994): 18–22 and 56–64; Goldstein, *Price of Whiteness*, epilogue; Marla Brettschneider, ed., *The Narrow Bridge* (New Brunswick, N.J., 1996). Afrocentrism fared similarly: Jews, alongside conservatives have been its greatest critics: see, e.g., Mary Lefkowitz, *Not Out of Africa* (New York, 1996).

88. "Falling Out," 55; Ginzberg, "The Black Revolution and the Jew," *Conservative Judaism*, Fall 1969, 4–6. See also Rustin, "Cops," 178–79. On white blindness to structural racism, see Micaela di Leonardo, "White Lies, Black Myths: Rape, Race, and the Black 'Underclass,'" *Village Voice*, September 22, 1992, 29–

36. Jews felt insecure: see Rosenberg and Howe, "American Jews Turning," 36. Glazer was also critical: see "Blacks, Jews," 36–37.

89. On neoconservatism and race, see, e.g., James Nuechterlein, "A Farewell to CR," *Commentary*, August 1987, 25–36; Nuechterlein, "The End of Neoconservatism," *First Things* 63 (May 1996): 14–15; Norman Podhoretz, "Neoconservatism: A Eulogy," *Commentary* 101, no. 3 (March 1996): 19–27; Irving Kristol, *Neoconservatism* (New York, 1995); Leon Wieseltier, "Taking Yes for an Answer," *Time*, February 28, 1994), 28; Joshua Muravchik, "Social Problems and Conservatism," *Commentary* 100, no. 5 (November 95): 86–87. Not all neoconservatives are Jewish; see, e.g., Sowell, "Affirmative Action: A Worldwide Disaster," *Commentary*, December 1989, 21–41. Also see J. J. Goldberg, "Portrait of American Jews."

90. Identity politics, too, strays toward essentialism. Several articles in Berman, *Blacks and Jews*, address these issues.

91. Fein, *Negro Revolution*, 13. See also Rosenberg and Howe, "American Jews Turning," 33, 36, 43–44.

92. Hill, "Black-Jewish Conflict in the Labor Context," 89, Agran, "Our Philadelphia Jews," 5. On Jews becoming white, see, e.g., Brodkin, *How Jews Became White Folks*; Goldstein, *Price of Whiteness*; Jacobson, *Whiteness of a Different Color*.

93. Watts quoted in "Falling Out," 57. See also Cox, "Jewish Self-Interest," 195. On the neoconservative argument, see, e.g., Podhoretz, "Is It Good for the Jews?" *Commentary*, February 1972, 7–13; Jacob Neusner, "Dissent from the Right," *Transaction* 31, no. 6 (September–October 1994): 28–32; Gary Dorrien, *The Neoconservative Mind* (Philadelphia, 1993), 191–92; Kristol, "Why Religion Is Good for the Jews," *Commentary*, August 1994, 19; Kristol, "The Political Dilemma of American Jews," *Commentary*, July 1984, 23–29; Muravchik, "Facing Up to Black A-S," *Commentary*, December 1995, 26–30; Seth Forman, *Blacks in the Jewish Mind* (New York, 2001). For a broader examination of diversity and conservatism, see Angela Dillard, *Guess Who's Coming to Dinner Now?* (New York, 2001). On Jews and liberalism, see Michael Staub, *Torn at the Roots* (New York, 2002); Dollinger, *Quest for Inclusion*.

94. Perlmutter, "Black-Jewish Relations," *Judaism* (Summer 1981): 290, 291. See also Friedman, "Black A-S," 31–35; Lee Sigelman, "Blacks, Whites, and A-S," *Sociological Quarterly* 36, no. 4 (1995): 649–56; Whitfield, "Anatomy," 352; Milton Morris and Gary Rubin, "The Turbulent Friendship," *Annals*, November 1993: 47–49; Cornel West, "Black A-S and the Rhetoric of Resentment," *Tikkun* 7, no. 1 (January–February 1992): 15–16; Michael Lerner, "Black A-S," editorial, *Tikkun* 6, no. 6 (November–December 1991): 11–12; Michael Kramer, "Blacks and Jews: How Wide the Rift?" *New York*, February 4, 1985, 26–32. On the question of whether black and white A-S are different, see Adolph Reed Jr., "What Color Is A-S?" *Village Voice*, December 26, 1995), 26; Doris Wilkinson, "A-S and African Americans," *Transaction* 31, no. 6 (September–October 1994): 47–50; ADL, *Highlights from an ADL Survey on A-S and Prejudice in America*, pamphlet (New York, November 16, 1992), 32–33. On Jewish attitudes, see Morris and Rubin, "Turbulent Friendship," 50–51. Harris and Swanson found in New

York, Jewish racism and black A-S varied by income, borough, and (for Jews) level of religious commitment.

95. Gershman, "Young," 25–33; Wilkins, "Black Leaders' Meeting," *NYT*, August 24, 1979, 11; "11 Jewish Groups Reject Criticism from Blacks, but Urge Cooperation," *NYT*, August 24, 1979, A11. There was extensive press coverage of Young's resignation. See also Thomas Johnson, "Black Leaders Air Grievances," *NYT*, August 23, 1979, 12. The leaders included Clark, Rustin, Julian Bond, Vernon Jordan, Dorothy Height, Benjamin Hooks, and representatives from the SCLC and Congressional Black Caucus. See also John Herbers, "Aftermath of Andrew Young Affair," *NYT*, September 6, 1976; Silberman, "Jesse," 12–13; "How—and What—to Overcome," editorial, *NYT*, October 16, 1979, 20; "Black Leaders Assert Some Jews are Pressuring Them on Mideast," *NYT*, October 26, 1979, 10; Roger Wilkins, "For Earl, for Roy, for X," *Washington Post*, November 6, 1979, A21 (reprinted from *Village Voice*).

96. See, e.g., Rustin, op-ed, *NYT*, August 30, 1979, 21; Current to the Editor, *NYT*, September 8, 1979, 20. Polls suggest black support of Israel decreased over the 1970s: see Robert Newby, "Afro-Americans and Arabs: An Alliance in the Making?" *Journal of Palestine Studies* 10, no. 2 (Winter 1981): 50. Meanwhile, Jewish commitment intensified after the Six Day War. See also Taylor Branch, "The Uncivil War," *Esquire*, May 1989, 96, 105; Ira Chernus, "Are American Jews an Obstacle to Peace?" *History News Service* (online journal, History News Network), June 4, 2002, http://hnn.us/articles/770.html.

97. See, e.g., Adam Clymer, "Disputes between Blacks and Jews Divide Democrats in Several States," *NYT*, March 30, 1981, 16; "How Not to Overcome," editorial, *New Republic*, January 21, 1985: 7–9. On Louisiana and California, see James Zogby and Helen Samhan, "The Politics of Exclusion," report, 1987, Arab American Institute, 9–14, provided by Derek Musgrove.

98. See Himmelfarb, "Diehard," 47–48; Himmelfarb, "Jackson, the Jews, and the Democrats," *National Review*, November 7, 1988, 42–44, 78; Adolph Reed Jr., "The Rise of Louis Farrakhan," *Nation*, January 21, 1991, 55–56; "Stirring Up New Storms," *Time*, July 9, 1984, 8–9; "Blacks and Jews Come Apart," *Economist*, August 27, 1988, 15–16; Victor Gold, "From Hymie's Son," *National Review*, May 18, 1984, 28–29; Arch Puddington, "Jesse Jackson, the Blacks and American Foreign Policy," *Commentary*, April 1984, 19–27; Kitty Cohen, "Black-Jewish Relations in 1984: Survey of Black US Congressmen," *Patterns of Prejudice* 19, no. 2 (April 1985): 3–18; "Jews for Jesse and Other Callings," leaflet distributed by Marilyn Lowen to fellow SNCC veterans, April 15, 1988.

99. These events were covered by local, national, and campus newspapers across the country. For analysis, see Nat Hentoff, "Blacks and Jews: Those Were the Days," *Village Voice* 36, no. 33 (August 13, 1991); Joseph Epstein, "Racial Perversity in Chicago," *Commentary*, December 1988, 27–35; "Black Extremists Join with White Hatemongers to Attack Jews," ADL *Frontline*, January 1995, 6. The NAACP protested such statements: see "Black Muslim Leaders Attack on Judaism and Israel Condemned by NAACP," *Crisis* 91, no. 7 (August–September 1984), 45.

100. The Crown Heights events were extensively covered by mainstream, black, and Jewish newspapers. See, e.g., "Justice in Crown Heights," editorial,

NYT, September 7, 1991, 22; David Evanier, "Invisible Man," *New Republic*, October 14, 1991, 21–26; Jonathan Rieder, "Crown of Thorns," *New Republic*, October 14, 1991, 26–31; Philip Gourevitch, "The Crown Heights Riot and Its Aftermath," *Commentary*, January 1993, 29–34 (includes descriptions of actions by Dinkins and the police). Also see Anna Deveare Smith, *Fires in the Mirror* (New York, 1997). There was also cross-ethnic heroism, mostly black people aiding Jewish victims and in at least one case, averting a mob beating. For a retrospective, see John Kifner and Felicia Lee, "After a Decade, Scars Linger in a Healing Crown Heights," *NYT*, August 19, 2001, 1, 34.

101. See, e.g., Craig Horowitz, "The New A-S," *New York*, January 11, 1993, 21–27; Arthur Hertzberg, "Ghosts of Crown Heights," *NYT*, December 23, 1992, 19. For an interesting parallel, see Susan Rubin, "The Jewish Response to the Los Angeles Riots," *Western States Jewish History 25*, no. 3 (1993): 195–210.

102. "Divided by a Diatribe," *NYT*, December 29, 1993, B1, 6. The ADL ad appeared in the *NYT*, January 16, 1994, 27. The speech was given on November 29, 1993. It provoked a Jewish neoconservative/liberal battle: see "The Black-Jewish Alliance: Who Needs It?" *Moment*, June 1994, 31–42, 68–74. See also Arch Puddington, "Black A-S and How It Grows," *Commentary*, April 1994, 19–24. For Jewish articles on 1990s black A-S, see above. On Farrakhan, see Arthur Magida, *Prophet of Rage* (New York, 1996); Mattias Gardell, *In the Name of Elijah Muhammad* (Chapel Hill, N.C., 1996). For Jewish concerns about NOI, see Edelstein, "Jewish Relationship," 2; Wilkins, "Jewish-Negro," 268; Irving Spiegel, "Report Terms Black Muslims a Source of Anti-Semitic Views,"*NYT*, January 31, 1972, 14; Reed, "Farrakhan," front cover, 51–56; Reed, "All for One and None for All," *Nation*, January 28, 1991), 86–92. Several articles in *Transaction* 31, no. 6, collectively "Jews, Blacks, and Others," discuss Farrakhan and black/Jewish tensions.

103. Steven Holmes, "Farrakhan Repudiates Speech for Tone, Not A-S," *NYT*, February 3, 1994, A1; Reed, "One," 86; Clarence Page, "The Rift between Blacks and Jews," *Hartford Courant*, August 5, 1992, D13. On protests against a "litmus test," see, e.g., Reed, "Color" 26. On local tensions, see, e.g., Ellen Bernstein, "Mayor, Jewish Leaders Meet," and "Mayor Kelly's proclamation," both *Washington (D.C.) Jewish Week*, July 30, 1992. Black leaders *had* repudiated A-S: see, e.g., "Black Muslim Leader's Attack." Ten years later, the NAACP ED, Benjamin Chavis Jr., moved closer to the NOI. Jack Greenberg (former NAACP counsel), "Identity Crisis," op-ed, *NYT*, May 23, 1994, 15, protested.

104. Jeremy Milk, "Inspiration or Hate Monger?" *Chronicle of Higher Education*, January 19, 1994, A33–34. On Jewish student absence, see, e.g., Peter Wallsten, "Why Black Students Reject Us," *Moment*, June 1994, 43.

105. *Nommo* 1991; Historical Research Dept, NOI, *The Secret Relationship between Blacks and Jews* (Boston, 1991). See also, e.g., Jeffrey Alexander and Chaim Seidler-Feller, "False Distinctions and Double Standards," *Tikkun* 7, no. 1 (January–February 1992): 12–14. The Howard incident occurred February 23, 1994. There was a flurry of responses: see, e.g., Thomas Sowell, "Scapegoating," *Forbes*, April 11, 1994, 52. Also see Boston NOI newsletter, "Blacks and Jews News." On similar campus tensions, see, e.g., Bob Blauner, "That Black-Jewish Thing," *Tikkun* 9, no. 5 (September–October 1994): 27–32, 103.

106. Each "side" interprets this complex tale differently. See *Black Scholar* 19, no. 6 (November–December 1988); Lester, *Lovesong*; Cheryl Greenberg, "Once More with Feeling," *Jewish Currents*, February 1989; W.E.B. Du Bois Department of Afro-American Studies, *James Baldwin on Blacks and Jews*, pamphlet (transcript of talk, February 28, 1988), University of Massachusetts, 1988.

107. Gates, "Black Demagogues and Pseudo-Scholars," *NYT*, July 20, 1992, 15. Also see Hentoff, "Skip Gates: Speaking Truth to Bigotry," *Village Voice* 37, no. 40 (October 6, 1992); Gates, "Memoirs of an Anti-Anti-Semite," *Village Voice* 37, no. 42 (October 20, 1992); bell hooks, "Keeping a Legacy of Shared Struggle," *Z Magazine*, September 1992, 23–25; Debra Nussbaum Cohen, "Black Academics Decry A-S but Jews Wonder Who Is Listening," *Hartford Jewish Ledger*, December 4, 1992, 6. *Emerge*, March 1993, discussed black intellectuals' responsibilities in black-Jewish debates, excerpted in *NYT*: Gates, "A Weaving of Identities"; Cornel West, "How to End the Impasse," both April 14, 1993, 21. Martin, *The Jewish Onslaught* (Dover, Mass., 1993). On these and related issues, see "Blacks, Jews and Henry Louis Gates," *Black Books Bulletin* 16, no. 1–2 (Winter 1993–1994): 3–31. Wieseltier, "All or Nothing at All: The Unreal World of Cornel West," *New Republic*, March 6, 1995, 31–36. Also see Gourevitch, "The Jeffries Affair," *Commentary*, March 1992, 34–38; Derrick Bell, "Great Expectations," lecture, Baruch College, New York, 1994. Even historical associations' annual meetings offered panels on black-Jewish relations. See, e.g., Karen Winkler, "Debating the History of Blacks and Jews," *Chronicle of Higher Education*, January 19, 1994, A11.

108. Barbara Smith, "Between a Rock and a Hard Place," in Elly Bulkin, Minnie Bruce Pratt, and Barbara Smith, *Yours in Struggle* (New York, 1984); Kaufman, "Jewish Liberal," 40–42, 73–74; Kaufman, *Broken Alliance*; David Theo Goldberg, *Multiculturalism*; Adam Newton, *Facing Black and Jew* (New York, 1999); Salzman, *Bridges and Boundaries*; Rogin, *Blackface, White Noise*; Melnick, *Right to Sing the Blues*; Washington, *Jews in Black Perspectives*; Berman, "Other and the Almost the Same"; Weisbord and Stein, *Bittersweet Encounter*; Lewis, "Parallels and Divergences," 543–64; Diner, *Almost Promised Land*, Cheryl Greenberg, "Ambivalent Allies," in *Black Resistance Movements in the U.S. and Africa*, ed. Felton Best (New York, 1995), 159–94; William Phillips Jr., *Unillustrious Alliance* (New York, 1991); Bracey and Adams, *Strangers and Neighbors*; Friedman, *What Went Wrong*. For Black/Jewish discussions also in broader books, see, e.g., Cornel West, *Race Matters* (Boston 1993); Dollinger, *Quest for Inclusion*; Letty Cottin Pogrebin, *Deborah, Golda, and Me* (New York, 1991); Biale, Galchinsky, Heschel, *Insider/Outsider*. For more critical views, see Friedman, *What Went Wrong*. For literary perspectives, see Newton, *Facing Black and Jew*; Harap, *Dramatic Encounters*. Lerner in particular has sought to build bridges among the many parts of the liberal and progressive black and Jewish communities.

109. Glazer, *We Are All Multiculturalists Now* (Cambridge, Mass., 1997). For articles, see, e.g., Jon Katz, "Blacks and Jews in Black and White," *New York*, May 2, 1994, 22–23; "Jews, Blacks, and Others"; Kaufman, "Public Discourse," *The Center Magazine*, November–December 1987, 54–57; Manning Marable, "Black America in Search of Itself," *The Progressive*, November 1991, 18–23;

"Blacks and Jews," editorial, *Dissent*, Summer 1995, 371–72; "Panel Delves into Issues of Israel, Images, Quotas," *Jewish Exponent*, June 2, 1989, 41–43; Leonard Quart, "Jews and Blacks in Hollywood," *Dissent*, Fall 1992, 528–31; Martin Kilson, "Paradoxes of Black American Leadership," *Dissent*, Summer 1995, esp. 371–72; *Tikkun* has been a particularly active forum for such discussions. See also Howard Freidman (AJC), "Black-Jewish Relations: Healthier than Perceived," *USA Today*, November 1984, 14–15; "When Blacks and Jews Fall Out," *Economist*, July 7, 1984, 19–20; "Come Apart"; Branch, "Uncivil," 89–96, 105–116; David Brion Davis, "Jews and Blacks in America," *New York Review of Books* 46, no. 19 (December 2, 1999): 57–63. The Washington University conference preceedings were later published: see Franklin et al., *African Americans and Jews in the twentieth Century*. On scholarly panels, see Winkler, "Debating the History." For a more critical view, see, Reed, "What are the Drums Saying, Booker?" *Village Voice*, April 11, 1995, 31–36.

110. Lynn Landsberg and David Sapterstein, eds., *Common Road to Justice* (Washington, D.C., 1991). See also AJC, *E Pluribus Unum?* pamphlet (New York, February 1997); "Who Needs It?"; Irving Howe, Michael Walzer, Leonard Fein, and Mitchell Cohen, *American Jews and Liberalism*, pamphlet, Foundation for the Study of Independent Social Ideas (New York, 1986); Elaine Jones, "It's Time to Revitalize the Black-Jewish Alliance," speech excerpted in ADL *Frontline*, September 1994, 5, 9. The Marjory Kovler Institute for Black-Jewish Relations, the Martin Luther King Jr. Center for Nonviolent Social Change, and the Carter Presidential Center sponsored "The Black-Jewish Alliance: Reunion and Renewal" conference in 1989: see Rachel Flick, "Blacks and Jews," *National Review* 41, no. 1 (January 27, 1989): 14.

111. Arthur Hertzberg, "What Future for American Jews?" *New York Review of Books* 36, no. 18 (November 23, 1989): 29; Ruth Bader Ginsburg, "Justice, Justice Shalt Thou Pursue," in *The Women's Seder Sourcebook*, ed. Sharon Anisfeld, Tara Mohr, and Catherine Spector (Woodstock, Vt., 2003), 182. On Jews' social liberalism, see Goldberg, "Portrait." On gender issues in particular, Jews' liberalism has never waivered.

112. Himmelfarb, "Diehard," 44–46. He points out that Orthodox Jews had become Republican (45). For the situation in 2000, see Goldberg, "Portrait." In the presidential voting in 1992 78% of Jews, and 43% of the total U.S. population voted Democratic. In 1988, 69% of Jews supported Dukakis; 30% supported Bush (polls varied slightly. African Americans gave Dukakis 88%); of all voters, 53% supported Bush. In 1984, 67% of Jews supported Mondale compared to 40% of the total U.S. voting population. In 1980 30% of Jews, and 51% of all voters, supported Reagan. In 1976 Jews preferred Carter to Ford by two to one. See CBS/*NYT* polls; Morris and Rubin, "Turbulent Friendship," 53–54; Himmelfarb, "Diehard," 44–49. For earlier data, see above. Still, there has been a decline in Jewish Democratic voting on state and local levels: see Rosenberg and Howe, "American Jews Turning," 32, 39–41. For congressional elections, see "A Look at Voting Patterns of 115 Demographic Groups in House Races," *NYT*, November 9, 1998, A20. The trend has been fairly consistent at least since 1980. See Goldberg, "Portrait," for more.

113. Friedman, "Jews, Blacks, and the CR REVOLUTION," *New Perspectives*, Fall 1985, 7; Sanders: Remarks to the W.E.B. Du Bois Working Group on Black-

Jewish Relations, Washington, D.C., January 5, 1996. Also see Gershman, "Blacks and Jews," 9. On the arrests, see Gerald Boyd, "Jews Back Blacks in Racism Protest," *NYT*, December 11, 1984, A5. On the UFT, see Friedman, "The Jews," 164. Also see Jewish Council for Public Affairs (formerly NCRAC), "Building One Nation: Race, Ethnicity and Public Policy," report, 2000.

114. Local groups include the African-American/Jewish Coalition for Justice: Seattle; Black-Jewish Economic RoundTable: Boston; African American/Jewish Coalition: Tidewater. See also Lynda Richardson, "Off the Bench, Judges Unite to Fight Bias," *NYT*, July 22, 1996, B1, 3, on dialogue between judges; Colbert King, "Past Politeness and into Honesty," *Washington Post*, December 2, 1995, A21 on D.C.'s Operation Understanding; Robert Leiter, "Rekindling a Flame," *Jewish Exponent*, July 7, 1989, 28–30 on Philadelphia, Pennsylvania's "Philadelphia [Pa.] to Philadelphia [Miss.]" program; "Blacks and Jews on the Relationship," *NYT*, December 20, 1992, 40, on Project CURE in Crown Heights. Electoral examples and UFT cited in Friedman, "The Jews," 164. On Los Angeles, see Raphael Sonenshein, "Dynamics of Biracial Coalitions," *Western Political Quarterly* 42, no. 2 (June, 1989): 333–53; Sonenshein, *Politics in Black and White* (Princeton, N.J., 1993). Jewish Angelenos supported a Mexican-American candidate (progressive) for City Council over a Jewish one: see Sanchez, "Boyle Heights," 26–27. On the situation elsewhere, see Morris and Rubin, "Turbulent Friendship," 54–58; Gourevitch, "Crown Heights," 34.

115. See Goldberg, "Portrait"; Biale, Galchinsky, and Heschel, *Insider/Outsider*.

116. Jackson, "Mission from the Moral Center," *Washington Post*, August 10, 2000, A29. Lieberman's selection also sparked some black A-S: see Lynne Duke, "Some Blacks' Harsh Comments about Lieberman Stir Old Tensions," *Washington Post*, August 20, 2000), A2.

117. Laurie Goodstein, "He's Just Red, White and Blue," *NYT*, August 13, 2000, sec. 4, pp. 1, 4. Other surveys indicate lessening bigotry against both African Americans and Jews; see, e.g., Leonard Gordon, "College Student Stereotypes of Blacks and Jews on Two Campuses," *Social Science Research* 70, no. 3 (April 1986): 200–201; recent ADL surveys on white racism and A-S.

118. Lynette Holloway, "Democrats Now Back Jackson's Role in Voting Concerns," *NYT*, November 13, 2000, 26. See also Dana Canedy, "Vote Spices Up Bubbling Ethnic Stew," *NYT*, November 11, 2000, 13.

POLITICS AND SOCIETY IN TWENTIETH-CENTURY AMERICA

Pocketbook Politics: Economic Citizenship in Twentieth-Century America by MEG JACOBS

Taken Hostage: The Iran Hostage Crisis and America's First Encounter with Radical Islam by DAVID FARBER

Morning in America: How Ronald Reagan Invented the 1980s by GIL TROY

Phyllis Schlafly and Grassroots Conservatism: A Woman's Crusade by DONALD T. CRICHTLOW

White Flight: Atlanta and the Making of Modern Conservatism by KEVIN M. KRUSE

The Silent Majority: Suburban Politics in the Sunbelt South by MATTHEW F. LASSITER

Troubling the Waters: Black-Jewish Relations in the American Century by CHERYL LYNN GREENBERG